Elixir

Also by Kapka Kassabova

To the Lake: A Balkan Journey of War and Peace
Border: A Journey to the Edge of Europe
Twelve Minutes of Love: A Tango Story
Street without a Name

Elixir

In the Valley at the End of Time

KAPKA KASSABOVA

Graywolf Press

This publication is made possible, in part, by the voters of Minnesota through
a Minnesota State Arts Board Operating Support grant, thanks to a legislative
appropriation from the arts and cultural heritage fund. Significant support has
also been provided by the National Endowment for the Arts, the McKnight
Foundation, the Lannan Foundation, the Amazon Literary Partnership, and
other generous contributions from foundations, corporations, and individuals.
To these organizations and individuals we offer our heartfelt thanks.

Published by Graywolf Press
212 Third Avenue North, Suite 485
Minneapolis, Minnesota 55401

www.graywolfpress.org

Published in the United States of America

ISBN 978-1-64445-233-2 (paperback)
ISBN 978-1-64445-234-9 (ebook)

2 4 6 8 9 7 5 3 1
First Graywolf Printing, 2023

Library of Congress Control Number: 2022946504

Cover design and art: Kimberly Glyder

Dedicated to healers, living and dead.

And in memory of my grandmother, the forager, and my great-aunt, the gardener, who first showed me the green way.

The planet does not need more successful people. But it does desperately need more peacemakers, healers, restorers, storytellers, and lovers of every kind. It needs people who live well in their places, people of moral courage willing to join the fight to make the world habitable and humane. And this has little to do with success as we have defined it.

David Orr, ecologist

We need a revolution. It begins with falling in love with the Earth again. There is no difference between healing the Earth and healing ourselves.

Thich Nhat Hanh, *Love Letter to the Earth*

Contents

elixir: from the Arabic 'al-iksir', miraculous substance

eco : from the Greek 'oikos', dwelling place

Some people appear with pseudonyms. Some circumstantial details have been merged. No mind-altering plants were used in the making of this book, only a sense of wonder.

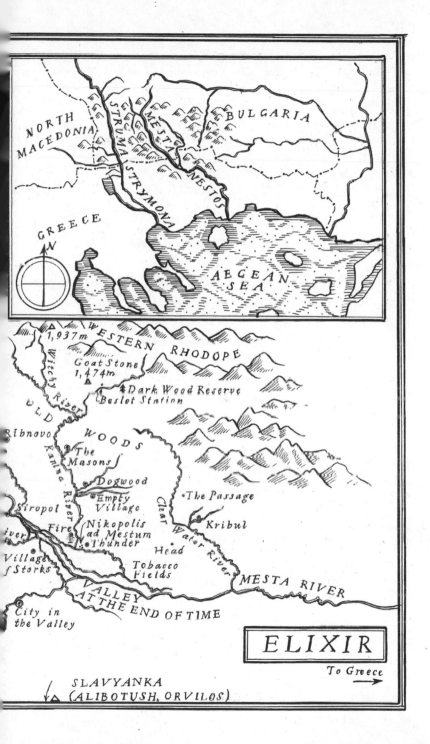

VALLEY AT THE END OF TIME

The sun was setting on the valley, giving everything a gilded edge. The great mountains to the west and east, the scorched fields studded with human-sized thistle where a mare and her foal lifted their heads from grazing as if hearing a distant sound, even the potholed road shimmered with golden heat. The silence was that of humanity gone for a long nap. Crickets tuned their scrapers for the evening concert.

In the river plains a Roman city lay in ruins. Invaders, plagues, recyclers, nature and neglect had left their mark. The interpretative boards in three languages and with the EU flag were so bleached by the sun that no interpretation remained. Cherry trees thrived in the tepidarium, snakes mated in the banquet hall and the girl in the reception kiosk was asleep with her head on the desk where the ceremonial entrance had been, and where the children of grandees had walked their lion-cub pets on chains.

The villages of Thunder and Fire were deserted with heat, as after an exodus. The road was nibbled by high grasses. Then – an unharvested field of sunflowers black with seeds, all heads turned to the sun. I abandoned the car and entered the sunflowers.

Blue-faced ranges on all sides. And on all sides – out of view and out of earshot – the rivers that made up the big Mesta River. I sensed their smiling gallop downhill. Men had spent their best years waist-high in these rivers, moving logs downstream. Women had beaten their laundry and anger into the waters, children spent endless summers catching fish with their hands, vast herds of buffalo and horses drank, bird colonies nested. The land is fat and the mountains bathed by Mediterranean currents, an ideal climate that blends seasons like nectar in the cup of the valley. Once, the valley held one of the largest fairs on the continent – merchants and craftsmen, weavers and matchmakers, cattle and horse breeders, fortune-tellers and shepherds, speaking a Babel of languages and wearing all manner of fur hats and turbans, capes and aprons in linen and wool. Houses were built in stone above the valley, with grey schist-slated roofs, orchards planted. Many seasons passed. Then, in the last century of the last millennium, people began to leave and with them the animals too. The river flats where golden apples ripened were dug up.

It was August. I'd been in the mountains and news reached me that Siberia's forests were on fire and Arctic peat smouldered. A virus whose biological form already seethed was still in the future, but it was also in the past. I was inside some interregnum of sunflowers. Calendar time released its grip and I was free to roam Earth's broad valley.

I plucked a seed from a sunflower head and cracked it open with my teeth. It was warm. Drunk on sunset, I pushed through the sunflowers. Beyond the plantation – a scorched pasture. Goats and sheep were scattered on it, and a skinny boy in a white singlet with sun-bleached hair and a shepherd's crook. Shafts of light poured through cloud, making him look like a golden child with his unearthly flock. Inside that funnel of light, the boy rested on his crook.

Until a hundred years ago, travel was slow in the valley – cartslow, chariotslow, horseback and muleslow, buffalo and footslow. At the end of the day, the boy walked the animals past the recent ruins, the older ruins and the ancient ones – though to him unfinished new builds, communist, post-communist, Ottoman, Roman and Thracian ruins meant the same thing. Across the floor of the valley, past the village of Fire so named because of the year-long sunshine and the hot springs where humans have sat throughout the centuries, sat with psoriasis and ulcers, cramps and battle wounds, melancholia and gout. Back to his village of Thunder so named because of the thunderstorms that roll in like an army from the north.

Like the boy, I would rejoin the road. Past the spring vapours. Past the hotels shaped like turreted faux-castles in gangster-baroque style, where the new rich arrive in cars like armoured vehicles, their listless children playing games on tablets. Past the Roma slum where laundry hangs over open dumps and a man leads a horse on a rope with small children bestride, no saddle. Garbage lines the riverbank. Past the 600-year-old sycamores, past the mansions built with public funds and pretending to be guesthouses, past a drinking fountain with a broken spout, the cement still bearing a hammer and sickle and 'BUILT BY A STAR BRIGADE OF THE NATIONAL FRONT'.

What is this strange place? This is Europe in the new millennium.

Above the slum I'd follow a steep road that fills you with awe at how people built dwellings so high up, but you got why they did it – to avoid the fate of low-lying districts in the hands of brigands, floods and pandemics. I'd pass a single soul – a handsome man in rags with copper skin and ash hair, with a cloth sack full of something, who for a moment looked like an extra in a film of the ancient world, like *Spartacus*. I'd offer him a lift and he would smile shyly, revealing an old man's mouth with rotten teeth, saying he'd been picking mushrooms and preferred to walk. His smile touched a nerve. It was like the valley. I'd reach a village where only one house is inhabited full-time, and in this empty village I'd rent a house. The next year, I'd do it again. I would fall under the spell of the valley.

For the past ten years, I have lived by a river called Beauly in the Highlands of Scotland. Until this move to the rural north of Scotland, I had defined myself as an urbanite, yet I never missed city life. Every day, I felt joy for no reason. Before, I'd needed a reason. Daily contact with the river and the woods changed my life, as if a door opened and I stepped into a place where everything was clearer.

That place was not new – it was remembered from my Bulgarian childhood. That place was in the wild strawberry woods of the mountains and in the foraging expeditions with my paternal grandmother in the pre-Danubian countryside. Her family were prominent vintners in that wine-growing region who lost everything during collectivisation. But even if she was dispossessed, grape juice ran in her blood. We would leave the house in the morning with shoulder bags and spend the day foraging for nettles which she rubbed into her fingers for arthritic relief, then made into fritters, eating mulberries and sour cherries off the trees that stained our clothes, collecting lime blossoms and elderflower which made me sneeze, and she would sit knitting shapeless doilies in a pine forest while I picked last season's acorns to glue together into shapeless figurines. There was a bed in her house where herbs dried on newspaper and she was always chewing something just-pulled from the ground.

My great-aunt nearby had an edible garden under the grapevine that shaded the courtyard, and chickens and goats in the barn. The morning thrill of finding eggs in hidden places, the smell of barn and roses! There was a room in her house where food was stored and processed. Yogurt jars fermented overnight, wrapped in newspapers, fresh cheese dripped in cloths, crates of apples rested for winter, bottles of elder cordial fizzed and honeycombs dripped into trays. She was always next to a bubbling pot or work bench where she rolled out pastry, beat up mayonnaise with warm eggs and peeled still-muddy vegetables for an oven roast. We watched transfixed at how she turned the unshapely stuff pulled from the ground into something else, like a scientist in her lab. Things had to be constantly sampled, of course. And then there was the Making of the Jars in early autumn, a seasonal rite, when she sat regally on a creaky chair by a cauldron, boiling jars of goodies to seal them. She was an accountant during the week, mistress of the land on weekends. Nourishment was her talent and although she didn't have children of her own, she was everybody's favourite mother.

This is how I became enchanted by the edible Earth. Thirty years later, in a northern country, I drove away from my urban life and put on my wellies with glee as if I had seen off the last day of school. I was finally deinstitutionalised. Now, the river textured the days with its soundtrack. Its wooded paths became an extension of my feet. I dreamt of the river rising and falling. When I visited towns heaving with people, I felt in transit. Then I'd stand still with my feet planted on the ground and water would flow through me. I stood in the river. The river was there even when it was out of view. At sad times, I'd sit where the flow is fast and watch the water rush to the sea until I was smoothed, pebble-like. All is change. In happy times, I'd sit by the same bend and relish the rush of water. All is joy. Before the hydro-electric era, there had been a waterfall and I see the ghost of the cascades inside the dam wall.

The river is flanked by a mixed forest but next to the river, a gravel quarry had taken root and next to the quarry, Scotland's largest power substation, and one day, a column of new mega-pylons appeared, trampling forests and overstepping river and hills. Wires buzzed in the moist air. The quarry and the substation were separately owned but moved in the same direction – expansion. Another day, a large new swathe of forest was cut down. The stumps still bled resin when I went for a walk and discovered that the walk was no more. The quarry men finished off the smaller trees with chainsaws. The sight nearly cut me off at the knees. The quarry had cut so close to the nearest mega-pylon that the pylon stood on the edge of the quarry now. Like a man sawing off his own legs.

Pictish cairns with cysts and carved stones had been dug up. This had been a sacred place for the last two thousand years. Within a week there was a new thundering hole with barbed wire. Within two years, the forest floor was exhausted. Murky water sat at the bottom. Next to the quarry was the logging station. It used to be small, but like the quarry it grew, and its sawing became constant. An angry man operated the logging truck – once a small-scale woodcutter, now his van said 'Contracting services'. His expansion was bolstered by the quarry for which he used to work. He was riding the wave of earth-flattening. In the first spring of the pandemic, while birds nested and the world was in lockdown, the multi-million pound quarry company felled another large chunk of forest and sold it as pulp. The nightmare was recurring. Gone again were the trees, the paths, the blueberries, the mushrooms, the birds' nests, the beds of animals. Deer ran across the narrow rural roads and were hit by lorries that had also grown too big for the place. I wandered the battlefield in shock. Metal was replacing wood wholesale.

When you live with it, this mass assault on the land produces a sensation in your own body, a sensation of pain caused by a blow with a metallic object. It is truly psychosomatic: *psyche* is soul, *soma* is body. I could not work for the crashing noise of the quarry. In my dreams, I visited a wasteland with furrows like open graves. The ground literally shifted under my feet. The people and animals of the woods were running out of dwelling places but there would be a lot of gravel to build wider, longer roads, ultimately going nowhere.

The local has become inseparable from the global and our shared condition travels across borders freely, even when people don't. How does illness begin? I stood on the edge of the quarry abyss. It was a war trench. A pointless health-and-safety sign was stuck next to it. The river glinted through the remaining trees.

How does health begin? For years, I'd received treatment from a medical herbalist in Scotland. I became curious about the plants that went into the potent tinctures that changed my life for the better. At the same time, I discovered the benefits of Traditional Chinese Medicine (TCM) and its companion practice QiGong. It gave me relief and new tools to understand the energy that flows through all living things. I now understood why I felt unstoppable every spring: because energy rises in the human body when it rises in plants.

In the Daoist view, each person's constitutional personality is a microcosm of the Earth's ecosystems. Each individual has a blend of five elements: wood, fire, earth, metal and water. So there are wood people, earth people, metal people, though most of us have two to three dominant elements. Spring is the season of wood – the creation season. My trees whispered of other woods even as they were felled by metal and I had to follow the trail. Then summer – the season of generative fire, which adds fuel to the wood. Come May – June, the open road surged through me like a dragon awakening. I couldn't sit at my desk. I'd roam the forests, pick raspberries and startle the deer. My blood sloshed like a river jumping its banks. The hunter-gatherer in me was awake and yearned to meet new faces and places. I'd leave home with a pack, braced for the unknown, trying not to look back to the one I loved because then I'd stay. He was a gardener, I was a forager. He would see the two sunflowers he planted in spring grow human-sized with heads like lions, then fall to the ground when I came home in autumn, as if shot.

And here I am in this unknown valley. From the north-westernmost to the south-easternmost highlands of Europe, from one river to another, I've come to seek connections across borders and seas, human and vegetal, physical and metaphysical. I lie on the floor of the veranda, cracking sunflower seeds with my teeth and the thunderstorm crashes into the valley like cannon firing. Warm rain pounds the slate roofs built without nails in a masonic tradition meant to last forever and bunches of staggering light pierce the cloud like a prophecy. But there's no telling how this prophecy works – forwards or backwards – and whether this is the key moment or a rehearsal. One afternoon, a lightning bolt struck the elder tree by the veranda where I stood. I staggered back but an aftershock ran through me and in this *coup de foudre*, I saw why I had come here on nothing but a hunch.

This valley was suspended in an exquisite web of earth, water, fire and air, and inside the web was some trail I had to find. Something was forgotten that I had to remember. It had called me and I had come. Apart from the language, I was a stranger. I didn't know a soul. And I didn't bring personal pain this time, I brought the pain of my Scottish river and woods.

People in the Mesta basin knew suffering, but they had something precious – the forest. Everything was still connected – peaks, people, plants. This place still had something of the old, wild kind – medicine, meaning, magic. Bulgaria, I discovered, is a leading exporter of medicinal and culinary plants. Many of them are still gathered in the wild and the Mesta basin is a hub because of its ecological wealth: three mountains, layered climate zones, virtually untouched by industry and, until the 1950s, unspoiled by mechanisation or modernity altogether. The communist state exploited the valley to the full – here were plantations of the world's most aromatic tobacco, the Basma Oriental leaf and millions of tonnes of fruit were harvested each year in the valley. Those mega crops were gone, but something else survived: a cultural ecosystem.

There are few places in Europe where Christians and Muslims have lived enmeshed for hundreds of years, all of them are in the Balkans, and the Mesta basin is a vital scene in this moving mosaic. Women still wear shalvars and headscarves painted with flowers because this is the ancestral home of the Pomaks – the Muslims of the southern Balkans who are not ethnic Turks. The Pomaks intrigued me. Their culture was like nothing else I knew and they had weathered calamity for over a hundred years. How was it that these people have been a permanent part of the landscape yet remained invisible, the last unknown Europeans? I wanted to meet the people of the Mesta basin, discover what was left of them and their knowledge of the earth, what I could learn about ailing and healing.

The boy with the herd saw me across the thistles and there was no reaction, as if he had seen me before; me and everybody else. There was nothing to say, there was nothing new. At first glance, he was a boy from the valley and I was a visitor in a rented car, but we both stood neck-deep in ruins and warm milk thistle looking for the way through. Our world was beautiful and broken, this was our inheritance. If we were the last people in the valley, we'd have to join forces. I could hear distant thunder. It was coming. The mare had known it for an hour.

The boy took the potholed road, crook in hand. The woolly sheepdog with human eyes rounded off the herd and together yet separate, we continued across the valley, fragrant with imminent storm.

OLD WOODS

FIRE

There was once a town [. . .] where all life seemed to
live in harmony with its surroundings.

Rachel Carson, *Silent Spring*

Bone of dandelion

It was dusk when I arrived at my rented house. In the kitchen were dusty bottles of wine and rose cordial. Because nobody lived here, the garden was a jungle of edible weeds. My first supper was a bowl of dandelion leaf, bramble and hazel leaf, chickweed and nettle tips. There was a cherry tree for dessert. It was the taste of a summer's white night by the Beauly River, but without the venison steaks.

Jars with candles were placed around the house. I lit a few and sat by the cold hearth in the kitchen. I picked up a book from the shelves, opened it at random and read:

> When I die
> I'll be the dandelion that listens
> to the world's pain with its stem.
> I hear it grow already,
> the bone of dandelion that I will be.

EMPTY VILLAGE, FULL VILLAGE

The Mesta River runs north to south. Its journey starts in Musala Peak – one of Europe's coldest and remotest places, smack in the geographical heart of the southern Balkans, halfway between the Adriatic and Black seas. It travels 230 kilometres to reach the Aegean and its basin is at its widest in the valley. By now, it has gathered myriad rivers in a web so logical a spider could have woven it and it is only halfway through its course.

Two ranges flank it here – Pirin to the west and Rhodope to the east. Their characters are strikingly different. Pirin glints with its hundred glacial lakes, Rhodope sprawls with its dark woods. Alpine Pirin is 80 kilometres long, north to south, and 40 kilometres across. Rhodope's length runs 240 kilometres west to east, the size of a small country. Called Rhodope, Rhodopi, Rhodopa, even the plural Rhodopes, and always invoked in the feminine, she is worlds within worlds. Inside the mountain range are fifteen protected natural reserves, Thracian cult towns and oracular sites, cave labyrinths like cities, the oldest coniferous forests on the continent, Orpheus's mooted birthplace and even the abysmal waterfall cave whence he was said to enter the underworld. Rhodope can't be contained in a book or known in a single lifetime, not because of her breadth but because of her depth. Some say there are canyons untrodden by human feet, despite the fact that humans have trodden here for a long time.

The valley was where a western corner of Rhodope touched the floor of the earth and provided an entry point to humans. This corner was called Old Woods, with a surface of 900 square kilometres. From the spine of this range three main ridges ran into the valley and each formed its own domain with its own rivers feeding into the Mesta. Only the lower levels of this stone palace were accessible and humans attached themselves to whatever floor they managed. I attached myself to the empty village above the valley. From here, I hoped to get my bearings in this place which struck you dumb with its cascading majesty. The valley was the floor of this cauldron and it sat at 600 metres above sea level. Once, this had been the bottom of an ocean.

The ruins on the river plain were Nikopolis ad Mestum. The City of Victory on the Mesta was built by the Roman emperor Trajan at the turn of the second century to mark the end of his war against the Dacians to the north. The city was large, with a forum and amphitheatre, walls 4 metres high and was important enough to be mentioned by the geographer Ptolemy. Later, a writer in the fifth century described its opulence as an episcopalian regional centre. It flourished for a few hundred years. Traffic and trade galloped along this corridor between the western and eastern Roman Empire – because the north–south antique Dervenya (Pass) road met with the Via Egnatia in the Aegean Plains. When Justinian's plague struck, and killed up to a quarter of the Roman world in a couple of decades, Slav and Avar tribes erupted into the valley. They pillaged Nikopolis to build their own dwellings. In the Middle Ages another city, Nikopol, emerged on top of the ruins and thrived from the ninth to the thirteenth centuries when it was devastated by passing Crusaders. When the Ottoman Turks invaded, the township moved to the other side of the river. Town and Valley became known as Nevrokop. Nikopolis – Nikopol – Nevrokop: a case of Latinity gently Balkanised. The name stuck. The city is still here, still a hotchpotch of dialects and styles of dress. Its market, though a beggar's shadow of its former exuberance, is alive. There is even a bit of the animal market left, where horse sellers turn up every Monday by the town's cemetery, Christian graves on one side, Muslim graves on the other. 'The cemetery was small and now it's big and the city was big and now it's small,' said a Gypsy horse seller with gold teeth. 'Lots of young people, cos the system kills folks.'

At the level of Nikopolis was a row of villages with mineral waters. The main ones were Fire and Thunder. Fragments of tombstones and antique columns lay discarded in their courtyards. Locals had been digging up their own heritage for a long time. Fire and Thunder were not as sleepy as they'd first appeared to me. Visitors flocked to hotels with mineral pools all year round.

In the wooded hill above was the 'hood – the Roma settlement set up by the communist state in the 1960s with the aim to settle and control Travellers. It had remained a slum. In the early morning, kids in hoods snuck through the woods and scouted the village streets looking for things to sell, recycle or steal.

My empty village above the 'hood was the first on the next floor up Old Woods. The other two were Dogwood and the Masons, like a ribbon wrapped around the rocky flank, and the ribbon ran out at the Masons. The defining feature was the steep gully of the River Kanina which fought its way through creeks to join the Mesta. Three origin myths competed for the euphonic name Kanina, two of them with tales of bloodshed, but the most musical was the Latin 'canto' for sing, chant, thunder – because it was a river that cantoed its way through crazy terrain.

At the entrance of the Empty Village sat a new luxury hotel built in traditional style. Guests of the hotel drove past the 'hood, taking the new road that circumvented it, windows up in case of a beggar child on the road. Once here, they didn't leave the complex. They sat in the pool and were served by the remaining young people of the valley. Almost every house in the village was for rent. A demand for romantic getaways had driven this fad for posh ethnic-style houses, and some weekends the gully cantoed with loud party music. You felt bullied by the high decibels, and that was the effect that the big business who lorded it over the empty village, like triumphant colonists in a subjugated province, desired.

My rented place was owned by an architect who had ingeniously rebuilt it and was full of salvaged agricultural tools and hand-woven rugs. She had returned from France to the country of her birth and turned a ruin into her dream home (and mine) – whitewashed and schist-slated in the local masonic tradition, rustic kitchen with a sweeping view and upstairs – cool bedrooms with shuttered windows and the pièce de résistance – the veranda. Made from massive old beams, the covered veranda jutted above the lush gully. It was the size of a small apartment and had a futon bed. Here, I worked and ate at a big table. When the outlines of Pirin darkened, I lit candles in jars. The city in the valley turned on its lights too. Mornings and evenings on the veranda, the resonance between peaks and valley was so precise, I could hear it like a perfect note.

In summer the village buzzed with visitors but in winter it was just one family. They lived next to me. They were a poet and a painter with their teenaged son. The poet turned out to be a famous recluse whose work featured in school books. The dandelion poem was his.

Between gallery, shop, garden and creative work, their life was still on the surface and active within, a state I recognised. They were private people. They had moved here thirty years ago in the first wave of alternative-leaning urbanites renovating old houses and their only regret was not doing it earlier. Even if the others had since drifted back to their city lives, or abroad, like the owner of my house who, disappointed with the way mass tourism had bulldozed its way in, had moved to the Greek coast and managed her property remotely. Among the weeds I found a flat stone inscribed MASON IBRAHIM ZELENKOV, meant to be built into the house. This was the man who rebuilt the house, the last of the old masons.

In the main and only street, a rustic taverna that had once been a school served organic food. It was run by a middle-aged couple from Dogwood. He'd been a goatherd before tourism replaced animal husbandry. He wore a leather waistcoat and I never knew what mood I'd catch him in, effusive or sullen, as he scribbled in his pad. When I asked questions, his face twitched, he looked over the valley and walked off, overcome with meaning.

Danera, the voluble cook, made crispy fried potatoes, burgers, finely chopped salads, stuffed peppers, chutneys and pancakes with blueberry jam. My favourite was the sheep's yogurt in a clay pot, topped with honey and crushed walnuts. Danera had arrived with her parents from the interior of the Rhodope on a buffalo-pulled cart piled high with seven kids, one wardrobe and two iron beds.

'My mother tipped us from the cart like chicks, sat down by the spring and wept.'

They became the only Muslims in the Empty Village, which was not empty at the time, though the emptying had begun. In less than a century, it would go from five hundred people to three – my neighbours. Its actual name was Leshten, meaning hazel. Once, there had been hazel woods.

Dogwood had grown while the other two villages had emptied. From a bunch of barns and animal sheds it had become a hub where new homes were built into the terraced crags facing the valley. There was a school, a mosque, a library and a hotel. Dogwood was an all-Muslim village and women wore the floral shalvars and patterned aprons of the Pomaks. Older married women wore the trademark Pomak mantles in blue or brown. They wore them buttoned up or undone like mountain capes. Girls wore Western clothes, especially if they studied or worked away. Men were indistinguishable from the rest of the population, except for a small woollen skull cap worn by elders.

All the labour in the gully came from Dogwood, whose young men were builders following in the footsteps of their predecessors. In summer, they flew to Western Europe to work on farms or build houses. The older men and women tilled their allotments and tried to make a buck from Empty Village guesthouses by buying, selling and managing. The young women went abroad to do menial jobs in the summer, or worked here at minimum-wage jobs like hotel staff, teachers and seamstresses.

Two kinds of people breezed in and out of the Empty Village taverna – lunching visitors and gossiping locals. Men who worked on building sites, layabouts, couriers. The monthly issue of a Christian magazine came here but the church was often locked, so it was perused by Muslim locals and tourists. The taverna, not the church, was the heart of the Empty Village. You could sit here all day and watch the remaining world go by, with Danera's running commentary.

'We might be peasants but we've seen all sorts in our time', she said. 'One time, these lost Germans came by and saw us making winter jars. Peppers, aubergines, the usual. They looked worried and asked if we expected a war!'

There was laughter. Communities like these, who lived embedded in the woods, who knew privation in their bones and who were marginalised by the mainstream had never stopped being self-reliant. They were prepared for pandemics.

Most of Dogwood's young people were away picking fruit and later in autumn, 'pulling asparagus' in Western Europe. A few hung around, idle, resting from their months of farm work abroad. Battered vans and horse-driven carts lumbered uphill at the pace of centuries. And the faces of the Roma looked centuries old – mahogany brown and stamped with a hardship that wouldn't go away. These families from the 'hood headed to the highlands of upper Kanina where they gathered plants. Some came back at the end of the day to sell them to a plant dealer called Rocky the Enchanter, others sold them to a dealer from Thunder.

'We all used to do it,' Dancra said. 'The villages emptied, only the old folk were left. We'd jump on trucks and buffalo carts with our parents and head up to Beslet for the summer.'

Beslet was a highland area near a Thracian sanctuary. The young guys and girls sitting with coffees nodded in remembrance.

'And we'd still do it, if the money was half-decent,' said a young builder. 'Cos mushrooms and berries are like an itch. Once you do it, you've gotta do it.'

'Not anymore,' said another one. 'The system killed my itch.'

But some still went picking blueberries. This year they went all the way across to Pirin because the blueberry bushes in the Rhodope were hit by unseasonal hail storms. Professional foragers used a special metal-and-wood comb which they ran through the plant for large scoops of berries. I bought myself such a tool from the Dogwood general store, but never used it and gave it away.

Outside the taverna, a young woman in folkloric national dress sold local goods – herbal teas, jams, honeys. She was from Dogwood, but deliberately didn't wear the Pomak shalvars and floral headscarf of her mother and grandmother. Looking at her in these borrowed clothes worn for the benefit of tourists who might be displeased by the sight of Muslim shalvars, I sensed layers of backstory.

'So many layers,' the poet said over the low stone wall separating the two gardens, while puffing on his pipe under the cherry tree, 'that it takes decades before you give up trying to reach the bottom.'

He had spent decades roaming the hills, collecting stories, recording songs, collating memories and dialects. Under his garden was a library. He went down a hatch and handed me rare books. I asked if I could use his dandelion poem.

'Use whatever you need,' he waved it away. 'We're all writing the one book, in the end.'

You will not hear this from many authors.

He had collated a little guide to the Empty Village for visitors. The houses had names: the Captain's House; the Lawyer's; the Brothers-in-Law; the Upper one; the Priest's; the Disputed one and there were houses with people's names – a united nations of names: Bulgarian; Greek; Armenian; English; French.

After a prolific oeuvre of poetry, prose, music and film, in his seventies he had become a poet of stone. He photographed moss, gazed at its patterns and wrote what he called syntheses. The human world had shrunk and the more-than-human world expanded.

'The more I sit with this mountain, the more everything else pales into insignificance. Even literature, to which I've dedicated my life. Even that.'

The Chinese poet Li Bo would have agreed:

'We never tire of looking at each other/the mountain and I.'

Once a week his wife, the painter, went down to the city. People who lived in the mountains called it just this – the city. When I asked her whether it was the people or the geography that kept them here, she said:

'People are ephemeral. And people here know this because they've gone through horror.' She meant the Pomaks. 'The landscape is the main event. Living here, you can't deny it. I cling to my son but I know that he too will go and I will be left with the valley.'

She was a stargazer and had an ethereal quality. Her paintings moved steadily towards abstraction. Fingers of light pushed through doorways. The valley was ever-present.

★

The couple told me why these houses had slated roofs – because the Kanina shores are metamorphic and the layered schist and gneiss make good slates. The village cultures were layered too. Visitors stopped in the Empty Village to admire the slated houses, then drove through Dogwood, not knowing what it was because it was not on tourist itineraries. It was the invisible village with a mosque that fed and serviced the rest. Dogwood was not a place where people came to buy a dream house, it was a place where people were born.

The top village was the feted architectural reserve of The Masons, known for the period dramas filmed here. In the closing scene of a 1970s film called *The End of the Song*, the lead actor sings a song called 'Rufinka Lay Dying' before he rides off into the hills to meet his own death. Before filming, the director made him chop wood for a week without food, to wipe the smugness from his face and give him a highlander look. That look was still on the faces of Dogwooders, even the young ones – a hungry, haunted look. The look of people who did hard physical labour and to whom nothing had come easily.

The Masons was settled in the late Middle Ages by masons from Macedonia. The Macedonians brought a style of construction that was popular and from here they travelled in guilds to the Aegean Coast. The village became wealthy from this and from its herds. In its day, there were 50,000 grazing animals to just 1,500 people. In winter, the cattle were taken down the Mesta corridor to the Aegean Plains and in summer to highlands like Beslet. A supershepherd from the turn of the nineteenth century had for instance looked after tens of thousands of sheep with the help of ninety dogs and nine shepherds on horseback.

The Masons had thirty residents left, no children. It was an open-air museum. Visitors came for lunch and a wander down the cobbled memory lanes of how mountain village life had been – until the wrecking ball of forced collectivisation smashed it. The dispossessed Masoners took their craft and even their wood on cattle carts and emigrated to other parts of the country; like their ancestors had done. Incomers who started buying houses in the 1980s and 1990s found exactly ten per cent of the inhabitants left. When Communism fell, gangster enterprise finished things off. Houses fell down or were sold for a pittance. Mansions were built in the Masons style by the successful gangsters, but in the original village houses had been touching so that if you were on the run from something, you could walk over the entire village from roof to roof and disappear into the woods. In contrast, the new houses had high walls and didn't talk to each other.

The Masons' little library had been the best in the valley. The library was still open but hadn't acquired books since the last century. It was all souvenirs and lunches. The capture of the village by absentee owners and hapless tourists was complete. Dogwooders were poorly educated and practically skilled and their ranks had swelled, while in the Masons and the Empty Village, education had given people a ticket out – and killed the village.

A couple from the 'hood came in a van like an Aladdin's cave full of the valley's textile heritage: shagpile rugs; woollen kilims made on looms; long knitted socks; embroidered cotton cloths and thick stripy aprons. Knitted socks here are knee-high and the women snipped the final thread that normally hangs from the top to avoid being followed 'by snakes and lizards'. Yet they attached long cords to the backs of their tweed waistcoats which swayed 'like snakes' as they walked and drew the male gaze. The snake was a trope of secret power here.

These discarded heirlooms and expired dowries came from households either defunct or ashamed of their peasant roots, something I saw a lot in Muslim homes where synthetic rugs were displayed as totems of aspirational urban modernity. But they were late with modernity because the synthetics would disintegrate in a few years and then their children would have to buy back their own heirloom from the Roma, who everyone despised. The Roma were in fact the last custodians of this textile wealth; they bought stuff wholesale and flogged it. In this way, they salvaged precious handcrafts from the rubbish tip and kept up the trading tradition between lowlands and highlands.

Until the mid-twentieth century, the people of Thunder and Fire came up in carts to sell vegetables to the cattle-rich Masons. The

Masons and the Empty Village had started as a refuge. Here, you could start afresh, back to back with the mountain. To come here was to opt out of the system because the system in all its guises, from empire to dictatorship, had failed to conquer the mountain. Each house had a stash of weapons and if a house caught fire, you didn't rush to help in case of an explosion.

I witnessed a house catch fire one day, although it didn't explode. I'd come to the Masons for lunch. A fire engine made it up the steep road but couldn't enter the cobbled lane and locals helped take the hose to the house. But the locals were not Masoners because the Masoners were too old. They were Dogwooders who drove up to help their neighbours. Generations before, when the Masons was about to be torched by Turkish irregulars, it was a Dogwooder who galloped to the city like the wind to plead with the Ottoman governor Rifat Bey to spare their Christian neighbours.

'That's being a Pomak for you', a young guy I knew said in passing. 'You help and get no thanks.'

He was covered in sweat after helping put out the flames while guys from local families sat in the café not lifting a finger.

'But we're used to it,' he added.

It was a play on words and a truth. The word Pomak had started as an informal mark of difference and ended up as an ethnonym. One etymology traces it to *pomachen* or tormented one, another to *pomagach* or helper. Both had negative overtones. Pomaks were either the tormented ones (forced to convert to Islam) or the helpers (of Islam).

They have been both, but in a different sense. Helpers needed for their expert knowledge of the land, and yet tormented by cruel policies, mean revisionism, subtle snubs and the ignorance of those in the majority. The majority were fed a malignant historical narrative in which all Muslims, living and dead, were conflated with the crimes of the Ottoman Empire during its tyrannous decay. By this token, if you were a Muslim, you were guilty until proven innocent. This narrative was to reality what the quarry was to the forest: a continuous desecration of truth. Single-minded metal replacing the rich web of wood.

The truth was that the Pomaks were autochthonous people deeply woven into the land. 'We are Bulgarians with Turkish-Arabic names who go to mosque instead of church,' said many younger Pomaks. Most of the young were secular by belief and Muslim by identity. But many in the older generations didn't identify with this definition. Pomak identity was complicated by compounded trauma. In a typically low-key gesture of self-reclamation, the Pomaks informally referred to themselves simply as 'Our Folk'. *Nashentsi.* Such and such married a *nashenka*, one of ours.

The Pomaks were incredibly hard grafters. It seemed almost constitutional, but it was inherited. Hard work is what it took to survive and thrive in this mountain. Above the Masons, I stopped to chat to an elderly couple from Dogwood who were pottering in their orchard. They'd built a holiday house here, just a mile from where they lived, for something to do.

'I don't know why we work, all our lives we've done nothing but work,' said the man.

'Because,' said his wife who had thick-lensed glasses and a white head-shawl, 'if we don't work, all we have left is death and the telly. And it's a fine day for weeding.'

'One moment you're young and handsome,' her husband said, 'and the next moment you're old and crippled.'

They were not into small talk. His wife cut a red rose and gave it to me. 'Life is an illusion,' she said and smiled, not wistfully, but the way you smile when you really know that life is an illusion.

The Masons was an odd place, folded into its past because it didn't have a present. You couldn't see anything except the plunge of Kanina and it was easy to forget about the valley. You were pressed hard against Old Woods. The houses were gorgeous but there was a lurking shadow, a malaise I couldn't explain, and that made me relieved to leave the Masons and head down the road back to Dogwood where people went about their business, and the Empty Village where they didn't, but where the bigger picture opened up and I could breathe again.

One rainy afternoon in my rented house, I slept and heard the house speak with a voice. The house showed me people inside it. I saw them.

They slept on wide wooden bunks covered with shagpile blankets, sheepskins nailed to the walls, sheep and cows downstairs, chewing, the family on rugs around a low round *sofra* table, also chewing. I saw how the village had been, houses packed with families, fields down the slopes. Now the slopes have gone wild and the houses have multiplied, but there are no people or animals.

But it's all still here, the house whispered, this is not the end. They wanted me to know this. What you think is here is only the surface view of something deeper that runs through us like electricity through the air, the house wanted me to know. Beams that in a flash illuminate the valley and its breathing creatures. Then darkness again.

The rain storm travelled south, down the Mesta corridor, I could hear it like a galloping army fading away. I rose from my slumber. A massive rainbow straddled the valley. The mountain across it was the outline of a perfect world. I went to see Danera in the tavern.

Danera had seen the heyday, decline, rise from the ashes and commercial takeover of the Empty Village. My dream was accurate. The houses in the three villages had been the same. The first floor for the animals, the second for storing winter foods like corn, and the third for humans to sleep, cook, keep milk, make cheese and churn butter. A back room was reserved for chests of dowry, extra rugs and dried goods like couscous. Threshing was done with up to three horses. Danera remembered the last of the old people, like the gentle wood carver who was buried with his chisel and transistor radio. It was the custom in the valley to bury Christians with their favourite things, once the dead person had lain at home for a while with a candle burning and a bowl of wheat before them, their hands and feet tied with a handkerchief against vampirism and a coin in their mouth to settle debts in the otherworld. The dead were carried to the graveyard, the procession led by a child who mustn't turn back – turning back augured more death. The coffin was wrapped in white linen, on which the priest wrote with coal 'Jesus Christ', and a cross. Before going inside the coffin, the dead had their hands and feet untied. Family visited the grave for forty days and smudged it with frankincense. Seven years later, the body was disinterred, the bones washed, placed in a cloth bag and reburied with ceremony.

When new houses were built on old sites, human remains popped up that had to be re-interred in the cemetery above the village, where a path took you into a pine wood so dark, I was afraid to go far inside it even in the daytime. This was bear territory and the occasional gunshot you heard was meant to scare off bears who got too close to Dogwood orchards. My neighbour the painter carried a 'bear spray' on walks and we laughed about it because we knew it would be useless in the face of an actual bear.

The Empty Village enjoyed an eccentric revival in the 1990s. Its main protagonist was a man called Marin. He now lived in Greece but still owned houses and the taverna, and his name floated like a rural legend. One day, I heard that Marin was here and staying in one of his houses.

We sat with a bottle of wine on the taverna terrace. He was a heavy man with eyes that watered and the look of someone who had lived fully, too fully. By the time he ended up here, he'd been a successful entrepreneur for a decade. But he was jaded.

'I came by accident,' he said. 'We'd come for a spot of fishing. My friends and I were looking for the Kanina. But we couldn't find access to it and ended up here.'

They stood by the old sycamore and took in the valley. The village was in decline – no modern sewage or electricity, not even cobbles in the streets. Just crumbling houses and old people and chickens.

'It was love at first sight. I bought all the houses for sale. Dogwooders were buying them up just for the roof slates! Then I went down to the Nevrokop animal market and fell in love with a cow. She lived for eighteen years and gave the most aromatic milk. In that overgrown building you see, which is where we kept the animals.'

Danera's brother looked after the cow. Marin moved here with his young family and in the following years invested a fortune in turning the dying village into a self-sufficient rural community for the modern age. He created the infrastructure that is here now with labour from Dogwood and the surrounding area. They piped water from the Kanina at a 400 metre gradient and when that proved too difficult, piped it from a spring above the village. They laid down cobble stones, installed indoor toilets and began to renovate the old houses.

Marin and other home owners, like my absentee hostess, introduced organic restoration architecture. She too had fallen in love with the valley on a chance visit. Marin employed shepherds from Dogwood to look after the goats, cows, sheep and pigs that he bought. Workers from further afield rode here on horseback across the Rhodope, like in some western. He paid willow weavers to make baskets and fences, bought sheep's wool from the women of Dogwood for loom-woven carpets and everybody who moved here got into homemade cheeses, churning butter, making sausages and living what Marin called 'authentic village life'. He drove a busload of Roma from the 'hood to a region known as the Valley of Roses in another part of the country to pick roses and make syrups and cordials, and give them a livelihood. Those were the dusty bottles of rose syrup in my house, which I opened and sipped; the syrup was strong and thick and made you smile with relish. 'Rose syrup is good for an upset gut,' Danera said. 'Rose syrup is good for heart comfort,' an Irish friend said. 'Rose syrup is good for emotional stress,' my herbalist said. In TCM, the heart and the stomach are paired organ systems. The state of your gut and the state of your heart are inseparable. It is difficult to be in a good mood when you have indigestion. Ulcers make you dyspeptic in temperament. And whenever I meet someone miserable, I wonder if they suffer from constipation.

The old taverna had been right beside the church.

'And everybody there had a glass that sat where they left it,' Marin said. 'I got the tail end of the old life and held on to it for as long as I could.'

Then the old taverna was struck by lightning and burned down. Danera's brother, who looked after the prized cow, was poisoned by his wife and died. Racketeers came looking for Marin and he went into hiding in upper Kanina like an outlaw.

'I didn't mind,' he said. 'When you lie on a meadow, everything changes. When I first came from the city, I was numb. Here I learned to feel again.'

He'd gone from being a hunter with a rifle, to hunting with a bow and arrows, to photographing, to nothing. Now it was enough to look at an animal.

The success of his project had delivered it into the hands of developers. The social, cultural and ecological revival of the Empty Village drew the sharks of profit who started building it up. When Marin arrived, a house sold for 150 euros. Now it sold for 150,000 euros. From a thriving modern village, it had turned into a resort. Nothing was produced anymore, only consumed.

My neighbour the poet had a poem called 'The Ants are Singing', an elegy for his village where 'everyone diverts the water to his own mill' until there is no water left and then no people, only an ant heap slowly demolishing the wall of the last house. Once it was the people who sang as they harvested the fields, their hair down to their knees, and now it is the ants. The ants are singing.

Marin had run away, unable to stop the building frenzy or convince this second wave of incomers who were after profit, not after community, that there is enough water in the hill above, but only through a shared reservoir and that by building hotels, they were destroying the very thing that people came for: village life.

Now he had found an unspoiled coastal patch in Greece, but he was also tempted by a ruined mountain village on the other side of Old Woods. It wouldn't take much to get it up and running, do up the houses, a couple of families, living off-grid with some animals. . . . Seeing a ruin and turning it into its best self was his life's mission. He hadn't given up his dream of organically recycling the ruins of yesterday, and yes, it was a rich man's dream, but if more of the rich followed his example instead of owning shares in quarries that rip the guts out of forests, the bountiful empty villages of this world would be repeopled.

'It used to make me mad, but I'm resigned now. It's just that, by the time people see where the answer lies, it'll be too late,' he said. The answer, for him, was in making human beehives, sharing resources.

We took in the human-like contours of Pirin and the reptilian back of another massif at the far end of the valley.

'Even now, with this monster of a hotel, with everything that's been spoiled, all I see is this mountain. This is still the purest place in Europe, for me.'

Marin showed me the old beams of the terrace. They were the work of the last of the old masons, Ibrahim Zelenko 'Greenie'.

'Greenie told me that every piece of wood has a heartbeat. And I can feel it,' he said, his hand on the warm oak beam. He left the next day and I didn't see him again.

I could feel it too, a deep pulse. I drank from the spring that Marin had unblocked and that watered the weeping willow and the shady sycamore, where the women of the Empty Village had gathered of an evening to sing and knit knee-long socks for the winter. The fatal flaw in Marin's project had been the people. Not just the profit chasers who'd taken over, but also those involved in the project in the first place. The insular Dogwooders had not supported the venture enough, suspicious of anything new, even if it benefited them. And the cosmopolitan urbanites who came to repeople the Empty Village had the choice of leaving when things got tough. Only my neighbours had stayed, with the disappointment, the crass hotel, the water shortages.

'You have to let things decay in their own time,' said the poet, handing me a bunch of fresh oregano. 'Without blame.

'And hold space for joy, no matter what's going on around you,' he said. 'With your work, you'll get to a stage where you lose yourself. To disappear into that which you love, that's the destination. That's Nirvana.'

We ate cherries from the tree. They left wine-like stains on the flagstones. The couple had found their destination. I drifted into fantasies of buying a little house in the Empty Village, but all the houses were big. And what becomes of a dream house if you have no running water and the river is out of reach? You are left with the view and the dream.

On Sunday mornings someone tolled the church bell but there were no churchgoers. Swallows murmured in the crystalline air. The church had been restored and its central piece was a large fresco of the patron saint of rain, thunder and lightning, Saint Elijah, flying in a chariot pulled by four fire-red horses. The village of Thunder had a ruined hilltop monastery dedicated to St Elijah and there's a long history of humans, animals and trees struck by lightning in the valley or nearly struck, like me.

Saint Elijah was everywhere in the thunderous valley, this avatar of the old shamanic deity of lightning, fire and fertility, Perun, brought into the valley by early Asian settlers. In Greek mythology, Perun's equivalent is Zeus, and in Norse mythology, it's Thor. Perun is a many-faced god, a shape-shifter represented with scales of precious metals on his body, like a forger burning in the fire of his own metallurgy or a dragon of creation. The dragon-snake known as the *zmey* is an expression of this creative fire. The zmey travels across realms like a ball of fire and when it hits the ground, it may turn into a human. Though if you are unlucky enough to see this, you'll waste away and die, unless a healer is at hand to make you a strong herbal brew. The zmey is a custodian of harvests, weather and desire.

Every morning the valley opened for the new day like a lotus, the green abyss below ran with sun-quickened juices, the blue outline of Pirin lay ahead like a substance to be tasted, but for now, a spoonful at a time was enough because too much would knock you out. The enchantment was such that part of me lifted off the creaky floor of the veranda and carried on past the Kanina clefts, over the valley, from where I saw a further mountain to the south and another one in the north. The southern mountain was a separate entity, a ring of volcanoes, quivering like a mirage in the bodiless air. That was the oldest massif in the Balkans, Ali Botush, renamed Slavyanka, though it looked neither like Ali's boot nor like a Slavonian woman. It looked like the spine of a curled-up reptile. The distant blue mountain to the north was Rila (Reela), where Mesta originates below Musala Peak, 2,925 metres high and meaning 'close to God'.

My projected self hung over the valley like a swallow separated from the flock, disoriented by so many delicious prospects and for a moment was tempted to fly down the corridor, through the open gate of the mountains towards the Aegean light and the delta, or perhaps the other way, north and head to the source. But it returned to the veranda instead, to have breakfast.

I spent entire days in the house, sipping oregano tea and moving piles of books from veranda to garden, pretending to do work. All I wanted was to drink in this place. Juicy nettles grew in the plunging undergrowth and I faced bramble and snakes to make nettle risotto. A small scorpion lived in the kitchen sink. Some hefty animal made itself known in the roof every evening, but I only caught a glimpse of it once when it slithered onto the elder tree, looking like an alarmingly large lizard. Big red ants crossed the courtyard. What they were doing, I couldn't tell. Perhaps you don't always have to know what you are doing or why, just that you *have* to. At night, when they went into their hole, I sat on a stump and listened. Poets are always right: the ants were singing.

The setting sun lit the wall of Pirin. The air was still and transparent, so mild I could drink it like a potion. One afternoon, the air became turbid and sepia-coloured, the mountain more distant and the atmosphere turned poignant as if we'd been sent into the past without warning.

'Desert dust from Africa,' said my neighbours. It happened sometimes. Saharan currents travelled across the Aegean and up the Mesta corridor.

Clouds of midge-like flies moved over the green abyss, making and unmaking dark shapes and the moment the sun slid behind Pirin, they were gone.

Another evening, a sunny rain came down, except I couldn't see it or even feel it, only hear its drumming on the leaves of the elder.

One night, I slept on the veranda futon. When I lay down, I was boxed in and all I could see was the sky. The moon was halfway between new and full. I felt halfway too. I dreamt of stars, millions of stars. If you aren't used to sleeping roofless, it throws you. Because there is no boundary between sleep and awareness under the stars, I dreamt that I opened my eyes and saw millions of stars. I had never seen so many stars, except one winter night on the Hebridean island of Uist. I lay floating above the valley, stupefied by how little I know about stars, about anything. I can't comprehend where and what I am in relation to the stars. They call me with their star voices and I get up and lean against the wooden railing. The elder strokes my arm in recognition. Down in the valley, the city lights twinkle like glowworms in a cave. Nikopolis is lit by firetorches. I see horsemen on the

floor of the valley, galloping, loaded up with goods. When Nikopolis
was attacked, a few of the besieged loaded up the city's gold on horseback, put the horseshoes backwards on the animals and fled the city
through an underground tunnel that led to a cave along the Mesta,
nobody knows where. The tunnel hasn't been found either, but the
people of the valley have seen the guardian of the ruined city. Its
shadow keeps watch over the remains, it has seen the stone thieves (all
of them locals) and one of these days, the guardian shadow will
emerge into the light and tell all.

Then a gunshot wakes me up. It is still night-time. Out in the cosmos it is always night-time. I have no idea why someone is out in the
forest with a gun at this time. I can't go back to sleep. The stars are
under my closed eyelids and I lie there until dawn, as if shot. I see the
Milky Way and maybe Venus and Orion. The people of the valley
named stars and constellations their own way: The Shepherdess; The
Nomads (the Pleiadeans); The Priest's Hay (Orion) because once
there was a priest so thieving that he stole hay from the poor and as
he walked, the hay dropped behind him as a reminder of his crime.
The children of the valley had been treated with herb poultices and
incantations for 'moon seizure', a malaise thought to be caused by the
moon.

The birds awaken before dawn. I get up and make oregano tea.

'One night this summer, I woke up and looked at the sky,' said my
neighbour the painter in the morning. 'And I saw the constellation of
Orion the wrong way up. It's always horizontal and now it was vertical! My God, I thought, the earth has turned upside down, the
magnetic field has dropped. I had to wake them up.'

The three of them stood on the veranda and looked at the night
sky. Orion 'The Hunter' was in its place, running across the galaxy
with big strides, but a colony of new satellites had been launched by
Elon Musk's company and that is what she had seen.

In *Aion: Researches into the Phenomenology of the Self*, Carl Jung cites
an early writer who describes the Christ as the one who could 'join
the Pleiades and loosen the bands of Orion'. A cryptic meeting of
cosmos and poetry in the archetype of the Christ, who in the context
of human consciousness embodies the psyche healed. The whole self.

For some reason, I think of this when I think of the three residents of the Empty Village. As the aeon of patriarchal Abrahamic religions wanes, we still have Orion, the Pleiades, Mars, the moon and especially the earth to awaken to. For we seem to have been dozing among the stars.

I see the three residents – perched on the eastern balcony of the valley, the only humans awake at that hour of the night – the woman wrapped in a shawl, the white-bearded man with bare feet, the Afro haired boy next to them who would soon leave home, looking for the right constellation. And I know that, like the cosmos, the Empty Village is not empty, not empty at all.

Brightness of the mountain

Its heads of purple and white mini-cups make me think not of some Mediterranean place, but of my garden in Scotland. Oregano comes from the Greek *oros* for mountain and *ganos* for bright. Its use goes back to remote antiquity. Mythical Olympus was fragrant with its flowers and for millennia oregano has been known to give feelings of well-being. Bright feelings. A cup of oregano lifts you up, as if it knows what you need to feel good and provides it. If you have congestion in your airways, muscles, endocrine glands and if you are overrun with a bad kind of bacteria, which you probably are, oregano will help. Our predecessors used it against convulsions and poisoning. A type of oregano called Amaracus is mentioned by Homer and other ancient writers as an aid for stomach ulcers and to induce uterine contractions. In her twentieth-century plant bible, *A Modern Herbal*, Maud Grieve mentions that to protect dairy milk from 'turning' when thunder struck, peasants placed bunches of oregano and thyme next to it. Here in the valley of Thunder and Fire, it makes sense.

Looking for a way to the Kanina River and not finding it, I found oregano instead. I waded through the wild growth, where women had spent their lives bent down between spring equinox and the end of harvest with their hands in the earth and their long hair tied up in headscarves, singing and cursing, vibrating with the brightness of the mountain, their men gone down the Aegean corridor, their destiny cast against this flank of the valley for better or worse. And I had no idea whether things were better or worse now, here where the river can't be reached, only its canto heard and wild oregano still grows.

BLUEBERRY BLOOD

Dogwood was a patchwork of houses that clung to the steep terraces of Old Woods. You entered and exited it through a long street that began and ended with barns, and along that street were two wholesale buyers of plants: Rocky the Enchanter and the Ayrolevs. Ayrolev Senior was the region's plant guru, but I had missed him by a few weeks. I found his widow, his daughter Djemilé and his son-in-law who ran the business now.

Entering their warehouse was like stepping into a temple. The first thing was the smell. A busy smell of wormy soil and whispering roots, of shrivelled buds that resurrected in water, of dried petals that turned your head with their pheromones and glossy berry leaves that looked ordinary underfoot in the forest, but could poison you or save your life, depending on the dose. A smell of vegetal beings, ancient and immutable. A smell that said 'Stop and take off your shoes' and also, 'Come in, come in, come in'.

The warehouse, once used as a barn and then a saw-mill, was stuffed with jumbo sacks. Djemilé took me a on a quick tour while her husband and their son itemised stock. The couple were teachers in the village school, and the business was done on weekends and late evenings. He looked tired if dapper, with a paisley cravat, and she was a relaxed-faced woman in floral shalvars and a blue overcoat that she wore undone. I saw what an ingenious piece of clothing the Pomak mantle was, with its pockets and back cover. Underneath it, you could carry any amount of stuff on your person, dress as you pleased and shelter from sun and wind. You looked like a cross between a factory worker and a bee keeper.

'Thyme, an all-time favourite. Take a pinch.' The half-wood, half-flower fragrance that always delights. 'People drink it for everything.'

We moved to the next bag.

'Calendula?' I tried to show off. I had only recently started recognising common herbs. Or almost recognising them.

'Marigold,' Djemilé buried her fingers in the dried yellow heads. 'They're related.'

'Bearberry!' I couldn't help myself. She smiled at my enthusiasm.

'Mountain cranberry, stems and leaves. *Uva ursi*, or bearberry, is banned at the moment. Ruthless picking. People pulled it up by the roots. Careless government policy contributed. But we do have bearberry over here. From Spain.'

I kept quiet about the fact that the previous day I'd gone up to the Thracian sanctuary of Goat Stone by Beslet and picked some. My guide had shown me how to tell uva ursi – 'bear berry' because bears eat the fruit – apart from cranberry, whose leaves and fruit are similar. Both have made a huge contribution to the health of humans' urinary tracts, and presumably bears'. They were so abundant that he encouraged me to carefully cut a handful of leaves from both with my pocket knife. 'You can nip bladder infections in the bud with a strong brew and avoid antibiotics,' he said, and it's a fact.

'Bearberry is our most sought-after plant,' said Djemilé in the warehouse.

The bearberry they sourced from Spain was sold to pharmacies and herbalists here. People don't discuss their urinary tracts much, but these infections are more common than you'd imagine, in people of all ages and genders.

Other medicinal herbs on the red list were yellow gentian, and blue gentian was on the brink of being endangered. Also on the list was golden root or *rhodiola*, a highly prized herb.

'Golden root is a powerful immune booster and mood regulator. Known as Bulgarian ginseng but we haven't dealt in it for some time. It was exhausted by incorrect picking.'

'The biggest problem is there's no gatherers left,' her husband came over, covered in fine vegetal dust after moving sacks. They were both slender people with an alert intelligence about them. Their son hovered in the background with a notepad.

'The shortage of qualified pickers, plus lack of regulation on the ground, led to poor picking and general shambles,' said the husband.

'The irony is, everybody goes to pick berries and mushrooms in Western Europe instead of here. We fall back on the Roma. Without them, we're lost,' said Djemilé.

The roots of this trade are deep. Plant gathering and dealing is passed down through the millennia by people like Djemilé who live in wild-ish places, and that means high places. Only high places survive plagues, floods, invasions and industrialisation. Because industrialisation came very late, wild plant harvesting and dealership survived. I sensed the stakes of this trade were as high as its roots were deep – but just how high and how deep, I didn't yet grasp.

We stopped by a bag full of the yellow-green tips of mursala. Known locally as Pirin tea, this rarefied plant looks the way it tastes – of the higher realms. It is endangered in the wild, but cultivated in Pirin, Rhodope, Slavyanka and Shar Mountain in Macedonia, and this batch came from there. Perhaps it was cheaper, or perhaps the large quantities they needed could not be supplied by local growers alone.

The Ayrolevs bought herbs from Macedonia, Albania, Spain and here, and sold them to big producers in Bulgaria and Greece. From Greece, they often travelled repackaged to America and Western Europe, renamed and with a much higher pricetag.

The mursala grown and picked in Bulgaria and Macedonia was sold internationally as Greek mountain tea.

'I can't drink mursala,' Djemilé said. 'It's too stimulating. I get jittery.'

Months later, when I found myself feeling a little too invulnerable, I reviewed which herb I'd been drinking the most. It was my favourite: mursala. I went off it but then found myself throwing a tip or two in my daily brew again. When you ingest the emanation of a plant, your body becomes coupled with its essential body. Mursala gave me a sense of how Balkan warriors from Alexander the Great onwards must have felt before going into battle, fortified by this velvety plant. It was the Balkan equivalent of whatever the Vikings took to make them berserk. Its official name, *Sideritis sciardica*, means the iron one for a good reason – it makes you powerful because it strengthens the blood, the immune system, the waterways and the respiratory tract.

Could I buy some mursala off them? No, they were wholesalers. 'We deal in large quantities only,' Djemilé said.

Commercial clients drove here and filled their vans. Or the Ayrolevs filled up their van and delivered.

'This is a competitive business. Everything must be freshly dried.' If a plant was over a year old, you couldn't sell it.

'This is St John's wort. It was almost extinct. It fetched a high price in America, so people went crazy picking it. Fortunately, it restored itself.'

Everywhere in the mountains here, I saw its distinctive yellow florets with faint red spots perched along long stems, but they were not distinctive to me straight away. It took a while to tell it apart from other yellow-flowered plants of the same height. The clue was in the leaves, which gave the plant its Latin name, *Hypericum perforatum*, because the minute sweat glands along the leaves' edges look like perforations. In Scotland, I found it a few metres from my door. It had been there all along, delighting the bees. Drunk as a tea, it has an almost instant uplifting effect, like sunshine. I don't imagine there is depression among the bees that hang around it. In Britain, people found it was most potent when picked on summer solstice. That's why it was later called St John's, because that saint's day is around solstice. Wort just means plant or herb in old English and many things are called 'wort'. A simple salve of this noble wort helps with burns and cold sores.

'Once there was a red variety, but it's rare now,' Djemilé said.

That's European centaury. It was revered as a panacea in antiquity and it's still known to be an exceptional plant, especially for the gut and for fever, hence its folk name, feverwort. I've taken it in a tincture for a sluggish liver. Its taxonomic name *Centaurium erythraea* literally means 'red centaur' (though its flowers are pink). Its cure-all reputation is in its name, after Chiron – the wounded healer, wise centaur and teacher horse-man. Chiron is the original healer of the forest who passed on his knowledge to his human students, including the healer Asclepius. He was of the mountainous Thessalian tribe of half-humans, half-horses and it seems apt that he died after being accidentally poisoned by one of his own students: Heracles.

Centaury is of the gentian family and has nothing in common with St John's wort which is of the Hypericum family. But their leaves and flowers are similar shapes and perhaps that is why here they are called red centaury and yellow centaury. In the Bach Flower Remedies, centaury essence is given to those 'willing servants who find it hard to say no'. The Bach Flower Remedies is a system for emotional balance where a plant essence is matched to an emotional problem. It was devised by the pioneering English phytotherapist Edward Bach. Most people know of the trademark Bach Rescue Remedy.

'Yarrow,' Djemilé walked on past the mounds. 'Oregano.'

The bags were dense and heavy.

'Restharrow. The roots are dug up.'

Restharrow? I'd never heard of it.

'It has a long history. Mostly used for urinary problems. It has diuretic and antiseptic properties. I remember learning from my father how to dig it up. It's easier after rain. The whole plant comes to you without force.'

Restharrow was the bane of farmers during ploughing season. Its roots are deep and get tangled in the teeth of the harrows, and it was named thunder thistle in Bulgarian and Spanish because its spikes crackle when it is crushed.

'Wild cumin. It fetches a high price because it's sought after in the culinary industry and people overpick it.'

Fifty euro per kilo was a lot for here, but to get a kilo of cumin seeds took a long time. When I travelled up the Kanina, my guide stopped at a riverside meadow of wild cumin, St John's wort, mint, yarrow and blue oregano, and we became lost in it for a time, each on different sides of the river. He was keen to find cumin and I was suddenly taken with the mint. It's common enough but on that meadow, it was flowering like crazy and full of bees and butterflies, a buzzing world of silence and colour. I stepped into the knee-high mint and disappeared from myself.

'Lavender,' Djemilé continued with the tour.

The zing of it, like a sigh of relief. You can't mistake lavender for another.

'Here's juniper. We sell it to a firm that makes essential oils.'

But juniper was being depleted by savage practices; some pickers sawed off entire branches, and then boiled them whole for the essential oil. It killed the plant, which has a long cycle of growth. Juniper berries, which are in fact cones, take two years to ripen.

What was it like to grow up with mounds of plants like this all around you? I was overwhelmed by the signals sent out by the sacks of herbs, as if they all spoke at the same time, each in their own language. And I was unable to answer back.

'It takes practice,' Djemilé said. 'Early on I learned to walk into a room, sniff the air and work out what mushrooms and herbs are in the room without seeing them. It's like blueberry blood runs in my veins. My parents dealt in plants for sixty years and I was around for forty-five of those. I don't know how else to put it.'

She smiled her sober smile. Lavish language and overstatement had no place in Dogwood. This place was about survival.

Waves of institutionalised terror had afflicted the Pomaks, who were a small but symbolic minority, in the 1960s, 1970s and 1980s. These experiences were not mentioned to outsiders. Where do you begin? And they were rarely discussed within the community. It was too painful. People carried it inside themselves. There had been no process of truth and reconciliation on a national level, only on a local one, privately. You could pass through the Mesta Valley without realising you were treading on trauma. In 1972, the state mounted a campaign to change the Turkish-Arabic-Persian names of all Pomaks. The campaign started with bureaucracy and ended with murder. Shop signs went up in the Mesta region: 'Persons in traditional dress will not be served' and 'Speakers of foreign languages are banned'. They meant women in shalvars and men in skull caps. And it meant Turkish speakers but in a region where Turkish is not spoken, it was staggeringly stupid, like the whole campaign. It showed how little the state knew about those whose lives it wrecked with casual brutality.

Danera the cook's mother had been at the spring in the Empty Village when a political commissar arrived with a pair of scissors, pressed her against the sycamore and cut her shalvars up to the crotch. Danera the child witnessed this. 'She cried with humiliation,' Danera said, 'and shock. Because he was from Dogwood and they'd known each other since children.' The cutting up of shalvars and yanking off of headscarves was government policy and dividing communities by pitting the handmaidens of the regime against the rest was part of the Machiavellian plot against this vulnerable minority. Every family in the Pomak community carried memories like these.

Djemilé and I left the warehouse and walked to a bench outside her house, where her mother sat with a friend in the morning sun. At their feet were bags of plums, apples, peppers, onions and leeks gathered earlier that morning in their gardens. People's extensive allotments were away from their houses, up or down the hill. You needed strong legs here.

Weather-bronzed and blue-eyed under the white headscarf draped around her neck and shoulders, Djemilé's mother had the expression of one who had seen, felt, understood, forgiven and had no need to add anything further, but she did it out of kindness. She sat, relaxed in her ample shalvars, her face resting in sadness, hands in her lap, though these were not hands used to resting. This latest loss too, of the man with whom for sixty years she'd picked, carried, packed, dried, re-packed, marinated, eaten and talked plants, would have to be accepted because life is an illusion. She smiled at me with ease as if she recognised me. I felt that I should take off my shoes before sitting next to her.

Her friend was a small-boned woman of seventy with a welcoming pixie-like face. She had a *sadilka* with her – a back harness with long cords cross-tied at the front and round the waist like I've seen in the Andes – made from spun wool in vivid stripy colours and used for anything you like, a baby, a newborn lamb, herbs, hay. These were once used by all country women, but only the more traditional Pomak women of Mesta used them today.

Pixieface was known for her bread-and-vinegar recipe that cured plantar warts and I'd heard that, while tilling the land, her husband had found an intact Thracian iron helmet, now in history books.

Both women's hands were large and thick like men's.

'She's interested in learning about plants,' Djemilé said.

'Which ones?' smiled Pixieface. 'There's a lot of them.'

Djemilé's mother handed me an apple from a bag.

Djemilé's father had 'contracted' a passion for herbs as a boy. He'd disappear for days in the woods and return with a distant look and a bagful. His talent was spotted. He and his young wife became a star couple in the vast, well-structured plant industry where the workers were many and the buyer was one: the state.

'Ask us specific questions because plants are us,' said Djemilé. 'It's like talking about ourselves. We're not used to it.'

I asked about quantities because the quantities impressed me.

'Things have shrunk, big time,' Djemilé said. 'Not the plants, they're still there. And those that are over-picked do recover. And there's more and more interest in natural products. People are returning to something they've forgotten. But the way of life has shrunk.'

A horse-driven cart trudged by and everybody waved.

'The Gypsies are the last ones,' she went on, 'but until twenty years ago, the whole of Mesta decamped to Beslet for the summer. Folk from upstream and downstream met at the top of Old Woods.'

The communist state had successfully streamlined nature's production chain in the Mesta region, giving communities employment and filling its own pockets many times over. Beslet had been one gigantic bivouac from June to September, a beehive of tents, government-regulated hotels, bungalows and *kolibi,* the Balkan shepherd huts. The logistical centre of this organism was the state forestry base. Thousands of families worked for them. Horses, flocks of sheep, goats, cows, all farmed in industrial-sized barns. There were farriers, foresters, canteens, warehouses for drying and processing plants, workrooms where tonnes of pine branches were boiled in cauldrons and pine oil was extracted. And crucially, a sapling-growing station with greenhouses that employed hundreds of expert agriculturists and planting hands whose task was reforestation. People sang by the evening fires, children rode horses, there were summer romances and quick sex among the berries. Overseen by the all-seeing, all-providing, all-grabbing commissars of the state who ran the whole show.

I saw the remains of that vegetal-human web. The day before, my ex-agronomist guide and I walked around the gutted buildings of Beslet and climbed higher up to a place where he'd been manager at a cooperative, managing one hundred shepherds and several thousand sheep. The derelict animal barns were on the path to the Thracian sanctuary, Goat Stone.

Goat Stone was a 30-metre-high labyrinth made from monumental stone slabs that appeared to be piled by an intelligent force. Over 300 cup marks were carved by a human hand in patterns that have not been deciphered yet, but archaeo-astronomers speculate that they represent constellations and were calculated to coincide with celestial movements at equinoxes and solstices. The cup marks were used to place objects and lights.

We sat and ate lunch with a view to die for – literally, if you placed a foot wrong here, because the plunge was final. Please don't fall, my guide said, and we munched our shop-bought cheese that tasted like plastic, not like the sheep's cheese we made up here back in the day, he said.

'And could make once again, in the right conditions,' he added.

I placed my water bottle inside a cup mark chiselled by unknown hands and we gazed at the black-green patch of Dark Wood Reserve, 30 square kilometres protected by the state since 1948, and where a mature mixed forest was untrodden by human feet. Beech, fir, spruce and oak. It was the last surviving patch of the original biosphere.

'Dark wood once covered the whole of Old Woods.'

Old Woods sprawled on all sides. Its bristly spine ran from south-west to northeast with an average height of 1,600 metres. We were just below the spine, on one of the ribs. It was alive, mysterious, breathing.

'This is Dabrash. Old Woods,' said my guide. 'It could twitch and throw you off, if it felt like it.'

It was only now I saw the multiple meaning of Old Woods. Dabrash is an ancient word that means three things in one: oak wood, dark wood and old wood. To the people who named it, oak was life

itself. And there was a long-standing cult of the oak, just like in Scotland. The Gaelic name for oak grove (*diure*) shares a root with druid
because oak trees were seen as magical portals. Oak was believed to
attract lightning and Celtic festivals like Beltane at midsummer burn
an oak log. Fire, passion, power. In the natural mind, the oak is a con-
duit of the sun.

'A single old oak tree supports up to a thousand species of plant
and insect, did you know this?' my guide said.

Of course I didn't. I am trained to think of species separately. The
tree, the mushroom, the person. My Beauly River is lined with individual oaks hundreds of years old. They are what's left of the giant
oak forests of Scotland. There is a timber spell once spoken by wood
carvers, who incidentally knew not to cut a tree during a waning
moon because at that time the sap goes to feed the roots and makes
the body weak:

> Choose the willow of the streams,
> Choose the hazel of the rocks,
> Choose the alder of the marshes,
> Choose the birch of the waterfalls.
>
> Choose the ash of the shade,
> Choose the yew of resilience,
> Choose the elm of the brae,
> Choose the oak of the sun.

We descended Goat Stone. Even after seventy years of depredation,
this realm of pine and sycamore felt awesomely remote. We saw
where the Kanina was fattened by a tributary, Witchy River, with
thrilling meanders and secret meadows. The place where they forked
was marked by the cement and iron remains of a collapsed communist-
era bridge. Upstream, the Witchy River was a demilitarised site from
communist times called the Army Barracks. Here too, the forest had
quickly swallowed up the politics.

At the Beslet station, Gypsy tents were scattered on the meadows. Some of the Roma pickers squatted in the gutted buildings
of communist-era hostels and festooned the rusted railings with

laundry washed in the river. Horses grazed. Children ran around bare-bottomed with T-shirts on and women had long Gypsy skirts and tresses. It was a tatty, timeless tableau. There were a few tourist tents too.

'Yes,' my guide said. 'Life was lived up here like this. This region is the richest in wood in the country, if not in the Balkans. Or was. There were many more hawks and eagles too, now you barely see them. There was more of everything.'

Communist-era signs hung on broken nails.

'IN THE FIGHT AGAINST NATURE, WE SHALL BE VICTORIOUS!'

My guide smiled sadly. 'They failed, but didn't fail enough.'

The destruction of native forests began during Communism and with it, the cycle of erosion and micro-climate change. One day in 1985 my guide was riding his motorbike along Bear's Creek, returning from a visit to the shepherds on Beslet, when a tornado hit the mountain, one of those that go down in history. Old Woods was famous for its once-a-century cyclones.

'I felt it approach like a beast, something was sucked from the air, then the whole forest leaned on the ground and everything went black.'

He ran under a bridge that we passed, an old little bridge you wouldn't notice even as you crossed it because it's part of the landscape. That bridge had saved his life. In the deafening crash he saw his motorbike fly through the air. When the storm passed he walked down to Dogwood, across a battlefield of uprooted pines. It took brigades of forestry workers years to clear Old Woods.

'But at least there used to be strict reforestation,' said Djemilé on the bench.

Whole villages were roped into replanting campaigns. The men made holes in the soil with iron spikes and the women planted saplings.

'Now there's no replanting,' said her mother.

I remembered those childhood brigades. How we collected recycled paper at home and sold it in bundles for small change at school (the children of intellectuals always had the largest bundles because of our parents' old academic manuals for which there was no space in small flats!). How we had rubbish-collecting Saturdays in the neighbourhood and I liked it because we were outside on the grass among the concrete buildings. True, these were compulsory activities, but we relished the results. You also knew that if you threw a wrapper on the street, it would be you that picked it up later.

'When I smell pine, it takes me back to those summers,' said Djemilé. 'You asked about quantities. We picked tonnes of blueberries every summer. Literally tonnes. Our fingers were permanently blue. Blueberry is sticky. Cranberry and bearberry are easier. A skilled gatherer could collect 50 kilos of berries a day.'

Fifty kilos!

'Wild strawberries are the hardest to pick because they bruise,' said her mother. 'You pick them in a vessel, in small quantities.'

Strawberry leaves were picked for tea too, like raspberry leaves.

'There was a hierarchy, so only a few pickers dealt in soft fruit,' said Djemilé.

The Ayrolevs were top of the crop and could pick twelve whisky-sized barrels of raspberries in a single day and have them clean by the small hours. They'd stay up at night processing berries or mushrooms because they couldn't wait.

'At dusk, you'd see stags cross the river,' her mother smiled at the memory. 'Slowly, slowly. Kings of the forest with a crown of horns. Now the hunters shoot them all.'

During Communism, environmental and human crime had strictly been the domain of the state and its servants. Now, crime was not just endemic, it was ubiquitous. 'Because of their productivity, my parents had certain privileges,' Djemilé said. 'They were paid in hard currency and given bonuses like the odd holiday abroad.'

They'd been under the patronage of cooperative directors who made the fattest cut without having to lift a finger.

The pixie-faced woman had worked with her husband at the hydroelectric stations in upper Kanina and the Witchy River. They'd lived there all year round in basic accommodation. In winter, she'd break a hole in the snow, put a cauldron inside, light a fire underneath and wash her children's nappies.

'Life was tough and I was tough, and the children were tough,' she said fondly. 'Even the bears didn't faze us.'

Djemilé's mother nodded. But in the 1980s, a double blight struck the family. Ayrolev Senior had elderly grandparents and one night their house caught fire. Another grandson who lived next door dived into the flames and found them hacked to death with an axe. He carried them out of the flames and laid them out on the street. Private murders were unheard of during the dictatorship, precisely because crime and power converged and in this community, everyone was disempowered except those who went around cutting up women's trousers and being promoted for it. The murder remained unsolved, but the backstory tells of a hoard of gold belonging to the matriarch's clan and that the thief-murderer allegedly wanted. But much more likely, and darkly, the secret police had orchestrated events. Their agents were everywhere and the Pomaks were marked for extra harsh treatment. The grandson who found the couple and who'd been a notorious gambler and entrepreneur, and overplayed his luck with the authorities was instantly framed and spent a year in jail under torture. He was made to stand in freezing water and deprived of sleep. The secret police could do anything to you if you were awkward. The hoard of gold was never found.

Djemilé's father had insisted on burying his slaughtered grandparents the traditional Muslim way, without a coffin, wrapped in canvas. But the state had outlawed all Pomak customs: funerals; weddings; dress; names, so he was sacked from his job. But Djemilé's parents bounced back and found jobs in the plant cooperative in Thunder, which harvested up to 1 million tonnes of Golden Delicious apples per season. No doubt the Ayrolevs contributed to that Stakhanovite output.

'Then democracy came and they set up the family business,' said Djemilé. 'Going for thirty years now.'

Her mother gave me a plum. Other women came and went to our bench for a spot of gossip, all in shalvars with bags of garlic, tomatoes, oregano and mursala tea which was cultivated here. These latest harvestings were discussed, munched and recipes were shared. I couldn't buy anything here, but I ended up with a bag of edible gifts, given to me with hands that were as brown, veined and great as the earth.

I asked Djemilé where her favourite place was.

'Pine,' she said. 'When I step into a pine forest, it's like going home.'

'Many used to go up to the stone. That was their special place,' said her mother.

The stone was a cult site in the hills with a submerged cave containing 'treasure'.

'A snake guards that rock,' said the pixie-faced friend matter-of-factly. 'A girl was snatched from the village dance by a nymph who lived at the stone. She was the snake in human guise.'

'Aye, my great-grandmother worshipped that stone, the murdered one,' said Djemilé. 'Even if the *hodja* told her off.'

Hodjas are clerics, teachers or just wise men and women who serve the community in some way. The church and the mosque, and especially the Communist Party, had officially frowned on nature veneration, but unofficially made use of it themselves. The way people worshipped, or not, remained deeply syncretic. Ritual and habit were blended in the chalice of time and marriage. Like with place names and people's names, echoes of things past were heard clearly in things present. The historian Noel Malcolm calls this shape-shifting quality of the Balkan peoples 'religious amphibianism'. Like a creature of the woods too wondrous to behold by the mundane gaze, this quality was reduced by those whose aim was centralised power. The byproduct *and* the result of tyranny is homogenisation in humans, plants, all ways of life. Shapeshifting is a threat to tyranny.

But you could still see it in action. The worship of stones and springs has never gone away here, because wild nature itself has not gone away – it was too great to destroy. And another thing, there has never been organised persecution of folk practices in Bulgaria.

This is why the stone above the village was visited by countless generations of women. They went to perform rituals for healing and fertility, for the ruination of their rivals, perhaps to bawl their eyes out or make love with the wrong men, anything they couldn't do in the village. It was a place where human taboo was normalised by nature.

I asked Djemilé's mother if she used herbs.

'We do, in cooking. But, I've been in herbs all my life,' she spoke for the first time. 'And may they rest in peace, those cured by herbs. Sip your thyme tea daily, don't be a stress bunny and try not to get sick is all I can say.'

Pixieface had buried her husband, sister and brother. Her husband had worked in a uranium mine upstream and died young from cancer. Her sister had unbraided her hair one evening, turned to her and said: 'It has come for me,' and fallen down dead there and then.

'The most medicinal plant in this region is elder,' said Djemilé.

'Every part is used,' said Pixieface. 'Leaves, flowers, fruit. Every plant has its uses. Broom. We used to make sweeping broom and broom chutney. You boil it.'

The most elusive wild plant was called the enchanter.

'Believed to act even at a distance,' said Djemilé. 'But I've never tried it.'

'Let me tell you about the enchanter,' said the mother. 'A couple came to us, he was looking for something to make her want him again. We gave them the enchanter. Like a joke, but a year later, he came back to thank me. She turned, he says!'

She rubbed my hip, pretending to hold an enchanter flower, suggesting how a woman turns and laughed for the first time. Enchanter is the charming avens, a small red flower with a yellow centre. It could no longer be found in Old Woods.

'Come,' said Pixieface and took my hand, 'I'll show you my special place.'

She strapped on her *sadilka* full of herbs and we said goodbye to the Ayrolevs, whose legacy might be continued by Dejmilé's son who had grown up in a house of plants, just like his mother.

'Because plants and us go a long way back,' Djemilé said in parting. 'And have a long way more to go.'

Pixieface took me on a goat path along the cliffs to another tributary. Here were idyllic water features, huts and shelters, and a flower garden, where she came to contemplate things. This was her holiday spot.

'I get up at five and by nine I'm done in the garden,' she said. We sat on stumps by a chattering weir and picked plums from a tree. 'Then I come here to be alone.'

It was about the water. She'd spent her life measuring the levels of the Kanina and doing maintenance at the stations upstream. She cleaned detritus in the stream with a hook, monitored the shifts of the river bed and shored it up with stones and sand.

'I worked like a man, but one day I see that my pay is less. So I walk up to the boss and go, "What's up with the pay, after all the rocks I've moved?" He raised my pay on the spot and now I get a nice big pension.'

It was dangerous work, like all forest work. Some traced the name of Kanina to the Arabic for 'blood'. It ran with blood during a forced Islamisation campaign in the seventeenth century, one story went. It ran red with the blood of men transporting logs, another story told. In the impassable forests, rivers had served as transportation channels. Loggers manoeuvred tree trunks downstream from the shallows with chained hooks and were often swept away and crushed to death. Well into the mid-twentieth century! I learned this up at Beslet and my ex-agronomist guide smiled at my surprise. Yes, he said, rivers went out of use only in the late 1940s when the Communists began a shock mass-scale industrialisation of our agricultural communities, and the first roads were built in the Valley. Until twenty-five years ago, logs were dragged on chains by yoked buffalo pairs, through the forest where no trucks could pass. When they were no longer needed, the buffalo were slaughtered.

Pixieface often dreamt of the rivers where she had spent her life. The Witchy one moved like a snake through the forest of her dreams. The Kanina was no longer bloody, but it still cantoed.

'Dreams are true, you know,' she said. 'Sometimes truer than the rest.'

That's why she came to sit here, to be close to the sound of water. Everything here was spiralling, without straight lines, the way it needed to be. It was impossible to follow the rivers all the way upstream because of plunging metamorphic shores. The level had fallen over the decades because of deforestation and the hydroelectric diverting the flow excessively, often to feed into lucrative hydro schemes. Astonishingly, this river was untouched until 1969 when its major tributaries were captured for the first time in its millennial life.

My guide, the ex-agronomist, showed me where the Kanina was diverted. And he showed me some of the unexpected silver lining of the last thirty years. Self-seeded reforestation was taking place, thanks to the perfect climate, and some harmful practices had stopped. We saw a forest of scarred white (Scots) pines, where the lower bark had been cut and bled through horizontal incisions for resin. This stripped the bark and stunted the tree further up. The resin has medicinal and industrial uses and was harvested in this brutal manner, but no longer. It occurred to me that the prized balsamic oils of myrrh and benzoin were harvested in the same surgical way. The benzoin tree is bled and disabled at the age of seven to make it secrete its resin.

I saw that meadows, pastures and all forest clearings are man-made, and how the disappearance of large-scale animal husbandry led to slow but natural rewilding. The man-made holes were closing up. Among the monoculture pine plantations other species took root. They travelled on the wind from Pirin across the valley. The forest was healing itself by recovering some of its original variety.

'And we need the same to happen with people,' said my guide, and handed me a small bunch of wild cumin, on that river meadow where we lost track of time. 'Those of us who stayed behind have been damaged by the mafia state. If those who left decades ago returned, you'd help rebalance things.'

I had left the country of my birth thirty years ago. Could I live here again without having my heart broken by all that has gone wrong?

We walked to the car with our bunches of herbs. His eyes welled up. It was the cumin, the meadow, all that had happened here to animals, humans, plants and that he had witnessed, colluded with, fought against and accepted. Everything vibrated at the merest touch and made me want to save it forever.

Rewilding and re-peopling. It was about restoring a network of people and plants that understand each other. My guide used to hunt. 'I'll tell you how I stopped. One day I shot a roe deer. When I approached, she looked me in the eye and she was crying. I saw what a stupid and perverse animal man is, the only animal that kills for pleasure. And I was ashamed.'

He'd thrown his rifle on the forest floor and sat by the dying deer.

Back home on the veranda, I drew the network of rivers and the peaks of the Kanina and Witchy rivers. I wanted to capture their shape with my own hand and stay close to them that way.

That night I had a dream in which a man appeared at the Kanina hydrostation where Pixieface had worked. He wore the overalls of hydroworkers, and a safety helmet. He was telling me something. The thunder of the waterfall was deafening. Somehow, here was the original waterfall as it had been before the hydrostation. I understood him because he could convey things telepathically. He was a custodian and wanted me to know that the river is not what it was, that it's been *reduced*, because the forest was reduced.

Reduced, his mouth kept saying.

But he also wanted me to know that the river is still great. That's why he'd brought me here, to show me that *the river is still itself. Look, it is still a great river* and he shone a torch of white light at the waterfall. He wanted me not to give up on it. I was filled with tenderness for him and his river, because it was my river too and the Kanina waterfalls dammed up were also the Beauly waterfalls dammed up.

The following summer, I came to see Pixieface again. She was making pastry with a friend for a grandson's wedding. They invited me to learn how to roll pastry.

'No, we're not afraid of death,' they said when I mentioned the pandemic, by then in its first season. 'We get together and enjoy our little selves.'

Pandemics come and go, but the main event is to have no fear and enjoy your little self, they said. 'Well done, you folded that bit nicely,' they praised my pastry-making efforts. Did they mind that the young women of Dogwood no longer wore traditional shalvars, the same shalvars they'd suffered so much for the right to wear?

'Ach, no,' they said. 'That was then and this is now. The young must do what's best for them.'

These women had seen through the veil of nostalgia and rejected it for something more nourishing: the present.

Until the late 1950s the people, like the river, were untouched by industry.

'We had no jars, no tins, no plastic,' said Djemilé. 'And no pesticides.'

'Everything was sundried,' said her friend. And completely organic.

The communist state introduced mechanisation for a few decades. Once the Soviet system fell apart and the economy went into freefall, the mountain and its people were left to survive any way they could. Things drifted back to their default condition, then globalisation and digital technology opened the door to the wider world.

This generation of women, born in the mid-twentieth century, had weathered historic eras, political regimes and environmental change. In addition to the terror campaigns, there had been two shocks. First, in the 1950s, the forced nationalisation of land and animals to create the totalitarian economy. And second, the collapse of that way of life forty years later. The planned economy eventually ground to a halt. It meant living with a chronic deficit of everything, except propaganda. In the 1980s we lived with empty shops and shortages of everything, from cars and furniture, to food and clothes. There was no choice to speak of. People were grateful to have one type of everything, as opposed to none. It was permanently pandemic-like conditions for all, except the governing kleptocracy. Bulgaria was reknowned as the garden of Eastern Europe but the bulk of crops, forestry and other natural products was exported. The food you couldn't find in the shops, you found in the allotment of your country relatives.

In 1932, a correspondent for *National Geographic* magazine travelled through the country and titled his essay 'Bulgaria, Farm Land without a Farmhouse'. The absence of American-style farmhouses puzzled him, then he realised that the farmhouse was the entire village and its countryside. Here, the village was always a place of production and self-sufficiency. To be a peasant or villager meant working the land and often, that was your own land. To be a villager was by no means to be a serf. The merchant class in turn linked producers and consumers. My Danubian grandmother's father came from a clan wealthy enough to send him to study viticulture at Heidelberg University for a few years, after which he co-founded the hugely successful Gamza wine cooperative with his fellow villagers. It was thriving at the time our American correspondent visited. And less thriving once it was nationalised twenty years later and experts like my great-grandfather were banished. The family was stripped of their houses in the village and he was even stripped of a pension and lived out his days in the capital, sharing a one-bedroom flat with his other daughter.

A man said to our American correspondent: 'Our poverty is our wealth' and this holds true once again nearly a century later. Back then, it was about a non-industrial nation weathering the Great Depression through self-sufficiency and the source of resilience was the working village. Between national independence in the late nineteenth century and the arrival of the Soviets, this was a prospering agricultural economy. The vast majority of people owned land and cultivated it. The shock industrialisation and urbanisation imposed by the Soviet system wrenched people from their ancestral lands. The Soviet machine ploughed into living flesh. To own land became 'bourgeois' which made you an 'enemy of the state'. The state then took your land. This is how a new 'working class' of dispossessed people was beaten out of the agricultural and merchant class: with theft and murder. And this was the beginning of the shaming of the village. Something similar had taken place generations before in Western Europe during Industrialisation, when villagers were conscripted into the ghettoes of new mining towns to fill the pockets of Empire.

Today, the large-scale manufacturing of Communism is gone, agriculture is ten per cent of what it had been and it is back to self-reliance in these almost-working villages. Women like Djemilé's mother and Pixieface were at the heart of it. It was women and men of their generation that had the skills to pass on. And in a depleted

natural world, there was the added value of rewilding through neglect. The problem was that the next generations who were meant to
receive these skills were working in foreign countries, or not interested. They had inherited the shame of the violated. Every family
owned land but the young didn't want to be landowners. The trans-
mission chain was hanging by a thread. Djemilé and her son were the
exception.

When a village loses its earth experts, it becomes an empty village.
The nature culture link is uncoupled. It turns into a resort, or becomes
a satellite suburb, or goes feral; a place neither cultivated nor wild,
with ruined houses, heartbroken old people and illiterate youths
from the nearest 'hood looking for something to sell, recycle or steal.

When I visit my grandmother's ancestral village and see the handsome houses that were once full of people and plants, I find derelict
courtyards where wild vines grow, and the silence of a graveyard.
Homeless dogs howl at night. History is a feral creature.

This is how the land that was once a giant farm without a farmhouse became a land of empty villages. Something tells me that the
collapse of our consumer civilisation will fill them again. Where else
would we go but back to grandma's patch where things still grow
among the ruins?

When you wander the haunted hills of the Scottish Highlands you
feel this too; there are no highlanders left. The working crofts are
gone. The crofters became Lowlanders and immigrants during the
Highland Clearances that began in the mid-eighteenth century and
whose official name was 'the improvements' and 'the enclosure
movement'. The people were replaced with sheep. The ecosystems
were replaced with nibbled pastures and stayed that way. The Highlands were *reduced*. Today, the hills are for hikers and hunters. The
hills are orphaned.

Pixieface saw me admiring some orange-red flowers that turned
out to be nasturtiums. I like eating them. She took a handful of
nasturtium pods from the pocket of her blue mantle and gave them
to me.

'I'll sow some marigold instead. Now, when I take a plant from the ground,' she said, 'I put something in its place. It keeps every-body happy.'

She had tended to her losses by replanting them with healing daily routines. That's how she had accommodated death and the loss of her life savings to a scam, a personal calamity she didn't mention but I knew it from others. I also knew that every week she put tomatoes, peppers and stuffed pastry in her sadilka and went to visit the poor and lonely of Dogwood. To put something in places where it was lacking.

We walked back along the goat path with the late sun on our faces.

I saw myself planting the pearl-like pods in my garden in Scotland to the noise of a gravel-crusher where the forest used to be and how the following season when they open up, I'd see her pixie face again, and enjoy my little self.

Botani

'I take you, *botani,* whose name is [say the herb's name]. I take you with my *pentadaktilo,* I whose name is [say your name]. I take you with me, so you will help in my hour of need. I swear in God's name that if you don't hear me, may the soil that birthed you never give you moisture again.'

Botani means plant in Greek. Pentadaktilo means five-fingered hand.

So went a prayer for collecting herbs with magical properties before dawn. This, and the following ritual, come from the Greek Magical Papyri, scrolls found in Egypt that date from the second to the fourth centuries. These are among the oldest written records of ritual plant picking.

'The gatherer first of all smudges herself and the plant with pine resin, by walking around the plant three times. She then pours milk and pulls out the plant by the roots, while saying: "You were planted by Cronos, conceived by Hera . . ." ' The prayer lists a dozen deities of the Graeco-Roman world and ends with "Be purified through my prayer, and give me strength [. . .] I take you in good fate, with a good spirit, at a good hour, on a good day, to make all good." After that, the gatherer wraps the plant in a piece of linen, and drops in the hole seven grains of wheat and seven grains of rye pre-soaked in honey, then covers up the hole with soil. And leaves the scene.'

Here is an extinct Scottish ritual for collecting juniper or 'mountain yew'. You collected juniper by dividing the branches into four bunches between your five fingers and pulled it by the root, saying:

> I will pull the bounteous yew
> Through the five bent ribs of Christ

In the name of the Father, the Son and Holy Ghost
Against drowning, danger and confusion.

Botani is still around, I'm drinking it in a cup. Pentadaktilo is still around, I'm typing with it. But something is missing. What is it? I did not pick the tea that I am drinking and I don't know who did, where, when, and what kind of road this herb has travelled to get to my mug.

ROCKY THE ENCHANTER

Candles burn across the field. Wind can't blow them out. Sun can't melt them down. What is it?

'Yellow primrose, of course! Are you writing it down?'

Rocky's milky blue eyes scanned me in an unfocused way. He trudged with swollen feet past stacked crates, a fridge, touching things with his short fingers. A humousy smell permeated his person and the whole house.

'Primrose is one of the first spring plants. It comes up earlier each year cos winters are warmer. If you remember, I told you yesterday that there are spring herbs, summer herbs, autumn herbs and winter herbs.'

Rocky the Enchanter was catching his breath after a fresh delivery, while Nafié lined the street with shallow crates of chanterelles and ceps. Her rotund figure was commanding in her blue mantle with loose ends.

You couldn't miss their house at the corner. It was a tower of crates: crates laid out on the pavement outside, crates loaded and unloaded from a van, weighed on large standing scales. The balcony was so covered with crates that it looked turreted. The inside and the outside of the house was one.

The couple were knobbly people with fleshy faces who waddled in and out of their darkened ground-floor stockrooms from mid-afternoon to midnight every day because the gatherers arrived from the Kanina highlands between 3 p.m. and 6 p.m. Rocky and Nafié moved in a cloud of vegetal dust and spores, fungi just emerged from the earth in a dishevelled state. At first they were cagey but on my second visit, seeing I was not spying for the competition, they took me in as a helping hand.

'If you wanna learn, you gotta work, that's the rules here,' said Rocky.

I threw myself into the stacking and weighing of crates, then I saw that I was getting in the way. They were pretending to make use of me because they wanted to indulge me and because: 'I like people who want to learn about plants,' Rocky said.

'So like I was saying, there are two types of herbs: dead herbs and live herbs,' Rocky went on.

What's a dead herb?

'A dead herb is a winter herb. In winter, you dig up its roots. Dandelion, burdock, restharrow. We've processed half a tonne of restharrow already this year.'

'Half a tonne! Aren't roots light?'

'Roots can be very heavy,' countered Rocky. 'The root of bryony can weigh 2 kilos.'

To me, a plant was something that showed overground but that was just half the story. Later, I bought some dried restharrow roots from a herbal pharmacy in the city of the valley and infused them. They smelled and tasted astringent and tobaccoey like yerba maté, the stimulating tea drunk in South America.

'Of course there's *no* dead herb,' Rocky said. 'It's just to say that the herb rests in winter and comes out in summer. Like burdock.'

Burdock was included by my herbalist in a tincture during a recovery period.

'Burdock is for when you're depleted. People use it for the urinary tract, diabetes, anaemia and to detox. Here.'

He found a pouch of burdock on a dusty shelf and opened it. The small woody roots smelled of chocolate. He gave me a few pieces and when I boiled them in a pot later, the aroma was like tobacco. You sipped it and the bitterness was gone from the taste, only a sweet astringency remained. The boiled root tasted sweet and mild with a yielding bite. Chewing them on my veranda, I grasped at once why my herbalist in Scotland always told me to eat more root vegetables, because my constitution and temperament lacked the element of earth and the supplementary earth I needed to 'ground me' was contained in edible roots. It took chewing burdock root for this to sink in. I began to feel like burdock. Calm, in my place.

There is a secrecy about roots. Roots are hidden from view. Roots are different from the above-ground part of the plant in shape, behaviour and properties. The taste is a concentrate of the whole plant and the effects of the root are stronger: but only in some plants.

'I don't know if you know it, but you've stumbled into the cleanest place around. We have many problems, but there's no industrial pollution of soil, ground water or air,' Rocky said.

What was his favourite herb, I wondered.

'How do you mean, favourite?' He bumped into the doorframe. There was something wrong with his eyes. Under the three-quarter shorts, his swollen calves were bruised.

'There are 742 medicinal herbs on our national territory. Twenty species of migrating birds propagate them. And there are the pollinators.'

He received the crates of mushrooms handed to him by Nafić, who was less chatty, though she looked on approvingly at our conversation and I joined in with the weighing of the crates, even if I was in the way.

'They're all my favourites,' said Rocky.

He and Nafié were ones for eating plants, not making dainty cups of tea with them. It was about taste, texture and immediate contact. It was more intimate that way. And eating plants has been the way for humans. Taking them as watery infusions is more recent.

The mother of European phytotherapy, Hildegard of Bingen, recommended eating the warming types of plants, like sage and rue, fresh. Or making 'cakes' with them, like wild thyme and wheat flour cakes for when 'the brain is ill, as if it is empty'. Many of her medicines are herbs cooked in 'good red wine'. Hildegard of Bingen was an influential German Benedictine nun in the twelfth century. A polymath, a mystic, a complex genius, her work is once again remembered, republished and it speaks to our time. She is best known for her devotional music and alchemical paintings created in deep states of meditation but she was also a pioneer of nature medicine.

Rocky found dandelion root too bitter as a tea, but the leaf was good in salad.

'With olive oil, lemon and crushed garlic,' he said. 'On the other hand, if you take dandelion as a strong extraction, it cleans you inside out.'

Dandelion. When I see its yellow heads, I am taken to childhood's mountain meadows and city parks. We wove dandelion and daisy wreaths and crowned ourselves like fairy queens. But until I started taking it in tinctures, I had no idea it was medicinal. When you search the internet for 'dandelion' in English, the top question is 'How do I permanently get rid of dandelions?'

We kill it before we know it. Yet, did you know that Theseus ate dandelion for thirty days before slaying the Minotaur? And if you run out of coffee, dig up dandelion roots, roast them and grind yourself some Gypsy coffee; it's so-called because Romani travellers made a tonic drink with them. Dandelion has been used in Ayurveda and TCM for five thousand years as a blood-cleanser, diuretic, laxative and general detoxicant, and for brightening the eyes because the eyes and liver are seen to work together in organic medicine, just like the skin and lungs. The Scots used to eat dandelion sandwiches for stomach ulcers. Leaving no doubt about its function, people called it 'piss-a-bed'; *pis-à-lit* in French. My herbalist said: 'Dandelion rinses the renal filter and squeezes the hepatic sponge.'

The seventeenth-century English polymath Nicholas Culpeper had this to say:

'It is of an opening and cleansing quality, and therefore very effectual for the obstructions of the liver, gall, and spleen and the diseases that arise from them, as the jaundice, and hypochondriacal passion.'

Hypochondriacal passion! That was me not long ago. My interest in cures is recent, but my interest in the origins and symptoms of suffering is lifelong. At university, my most-thumbed book was an encyclopaedia of psychopathology. I studied psychology but drifted back to literature, because literature seemed to contain all of psychology, especially the pathological parts. Since childhood I was tuned into the intangible, curious about how the invisible becomes visible and then invisible again. Children sense that every event has a foreshadow and an aftermath. This turned me to poetry, and later, hypochondria. The poet and the hypochondriac want to know themselves. They want to know the miraculous and the terrible within and how they are connected. I stayed up late at nights, looking up symptoms with dread. This is what separates hypochondria from a healthy impulse to know: dread.

The Greek word hypochondria is constitutional; it literally means 'underperforming organs below the ribs', which are the liver and spleen, and once this was associated with 'melancholia', literally black bile. Melancholia is a form of existential dread. In TCM, every organ system has a ruling emotion and the lungs are associated with grief, the liver with anger, the heart with joy, the spleen with pondering and the kidneys with dread.

A Chinese doctor and QiGong master once told me that my spleen was sluggish, which caused a domino effect of stagnation in the body–mind.

'Don't worry,' she reassured me: 'All writers have sluggish spleens. Because they sit and think a lot. And worry.'

My regular Chinese acupuncturist confirmed this.

'Read less, eat less, move more,' she told me. 'If you want to be well.'

Did I want to be well? This took me aback. Like most people, I didn't actually know how to be well. I didn't even know if I wanted to be well.

'When I put my dandelion leaves and my wild garlic on a plate and eat it with a squeeze of lemon, I am myself again,' said Rocky. 'And dandelion is a sundial.'

Because its flower opens on cue when the sun comes out and closes when the sun declines. On a cloudy summer's day it may not open at all.

In Gaelic lore, dandelion is the power plant of the goddess Bride, or Brigid, mistress of fire and thunder. It was woven into a wreath with milkwort, butterwort and marigold, bound with thread named for 'the Father, the Son and the Spirit', and placed under vessels to protect the milk from having its essence stolen by elemental spirits like thunder.

Culpeper concludes his entry on the dandelion in *Culpeper's Complete Herbal*, a book that has been in print since the seventeenth century, with: 'You see here what virtues this common herb has, and that is the reason the French and Dutch so often eat them in the spring.'

Nicholas Culpeper lived 350 years ago and was a pioneer of astro-botanical medicine, an ardent advocate of nature intelligence and an early socialist who challenged the closed-shop practices of doctors, priests and other salaried gatekeepers of knowledge. Marked by tragedy all his life: his father died days before his birth, his beloved was struck and killed by lightning and later, six of his seven children died in infancy, he dedicated his short and interesting life to serving others. His mission was to study and disseminate knowledge of the healing powers of plants, and to empower people to know their bodies and their earth. His famous preface to *Culpeper's Complete Herbal* runs:

'I consulted with my two brothers, Dr. Reason and Dr. Experience, and took a voyage to visit my mother Nature, by whose advice, together with the help of Dr. Diligence, I at last obtained my desire; and, being warned by Mr. Honesty, a stranger in our days, to publish it to the world, I have done it.'

His democratic approach to healing and self-healing is still radical in the eyes of old-school Western medicine, which is only now barely waking up to the need to educate us about our own bodies and environments before we become forever-patients in an environment filled with forever-chemicals. In Britain, where medicine was already uncoupling itself from nature, Culpeper sounded the alarm and gave people tools to set themselves free. He had many enemies and was dismissed by the medical establishment, ostensibly because astrology was integral to his work, but in reality because he dared to publish phyto-medical information in witty prose, which was one in the eye of the establishment, and because he treated patients for free in a poor part of London – sometimes up to forty a day – which undermined the medical business.

This subversive genius was slowly killed at thirty-eight by a bullet in the shoulder during the English Civil War, during which he was a battlefield medic; he survived the wound but tuberculosis set in.

'Three kinds of people mainly disease the people,' he wrote. 'Priests, physicians and lawyers – priests disease matters belonging to their souls, physicians disease matters belonging to their bodies and lawyers disease matters belonging to their estate.'

After him, botany and medicine divorced in much of Western Europe. For the first time since Theophrastus and the other early naturalists, botany forgot the medicinal properties of plants and medicine forgot plants. The written 'herbal' became extinct for over three hundred years until the British herbalist Maud Grieve picked up where he left off. Her opus *A Modern Herbal* profiles over 800 medicinal plants. During the First World War, the British experienced shortages in medicinal plants due to the breakdown of international trade and she trained a new generation of herbalists in how to grow and process herbs and sell them to chemists.

'Are you paying attention?' Rocky goggled at me, close-up. 'To become a herbalist, you have to meet plants in the flesh. That's where the power is. It's not enough to read about it and study botanical drawings. There's no power in that. Now, another sought-after herb is *echinacea purpurea*. Do you know it?'

Nafié had cultivated it, but no longer. My only contact with echinacea had been as drops in brown bottles from the pharmacy. Now I saw whole dried echinacea flowers.

'When I look at a plant dried in a heap,' I said to Rocky, 'it looks dead. Then you get to know its history, you see it open up in water and it's like a miracle.'

Nafié stopped and smiled at me in a motherly way.

'You have a way with words,' she said. She was too busy for words herself.

'You got it. The world of herbs is full of mysterious things,' Rocky beamed. 'And it's endless. Because nature is endless. Now, like I was saying, are you focusing? There are spring herbs. Early herbs, like our friend the primrose. And the iris, the lovers' herb, collected in early spring or autumn. Spring is a busy time.'

'Nature comes back from the dead,' I nodded wisely. He grinned with patchy teeth.

'Nature comes back from playing dead,' he said.

Autumn was busy too. Milk thistle, rosehips, juniper.

'Juniper berries are very sought-after,' he said. 'You know what's best for sweet dreams?'

'Lavender,' I said, showing off.

'Lavender is excellent,' he approved. 'But better yet is a small pouch of juniper berries under your pillow. Juniper is a wonder plant.'

Did he have a little pouch to sell me?

'A little pouch? No. But I have 500 kilos of juniper in my warehouse. I don't like to run out.'

In Scotland, juniper was once collected in large quantities and come August, it was exported through the ports of Aberdeen and Inverness into Holland, where it took part in gin making. It was a favourite of highland and island households, where it was taken in hot whisky for almost everything, from epilepsy to snake bites and general disinfection. The original 'hot toddy'! Rocky approved of this Scottish use but he couldn't understand why it wasn't used anymore, why we didn't pick juniper in Scotland when we still had it.

'Juniper is good when you've overdosed on a stimulating plant,' said Rocky.

'Like mursala?' I said.

'Ah, mursala! The purest of all. The highest. The noblest. Once taken by the elites only, priests and the like. How much mursala do you drink? That's too much. Don't drink it for more than two weeks cos it's too potent. Great for the heart and pretty much everything. But take a break and sip yourself some lavender and juniper in between.'

I think I was addicted to invincible-making mursala. I think I still am. Who doesn't like to be invincible?

'Now, milk thistle. If you're a guy and you drink tincture of milk thistle mixed with baba's teeth, you better have spare trousers,' he said.

Baba's teeth is caltrop, a spiky creeping plant with yellow flowers that grows in warm climates and is prized in Ayurveda. But if you do a quick English-language search for it online, it'll come up as an 'agricultural pest' with advice on how to destroy it.

'A strong aphrodisiac. Boil 200 grams and let it sit overnight. Give it to him and you won't be rid of him. And for women, iris. Iris sets women on fire.'

Gorgeous iris has petals resembling female genitals but it's the sweet roots that are used in traditional medicine and that are dug up in autumn or spring when it's not flowering, Rocky said. It's mostly used for decongesting. Maybe that's what an aphrodisiac does, it decongests desire.

'You are quite the expert on aphrodisiacs,' I teased him. He waved it away.

'It's the plants. I just spend my time talking to plants. And trust me, they have more to say than people. What else do you want to know? Ask me specific questions.'

'Tell me about belladonna,' I said.

'That's not specific,' he said. 'She is a world in herself.'

Until the twentieth century, belladonna was used by Romanian women for wish-granting. The plant is addressed with the polite 'you' out of reverence and called 'mother'. Two mature women walk to the plant before dawn in silence. The plant must be found away from humans, 'where no cock crows neither cat mews'. Before approaching the plant, the two women strip naked, turn east and bow three times. As they dig it out with a spade, they must state their intent – for love or for hate – then act it out. For love, they embrace each other and direct tender words to the belladonna. For hate, they scratch each other's backs and turn their faces away from the plant, facing west. East for constructive results, west for destructive. They leave an offering: a coin, bread and salt. Then they cover up the hole and bow three times.

'What do you want to know about the *atropa belladonna*?' said Rocky.

Atropa sounded familiar. Three Fates sit at the loom of your life. The first spins the thread, the second weaves it and the third snips it. The one who snips it is Atropa.

'Also known as crazy herb and old herb,' Rocky added.

'Do you have it?'

'We have it. Also known as wild tobacco. It has a relaxing effect, helps with insomnia. They exported huge amounts of it during Communism and just about killed it. It recovered but it's on the red list again.'

I could buy a dried leaf of belladonna from him and roll it up like a joint before bedtime.

'Go to where she grows and meet her in person. I'll explain to you where she grows. You lie down under her, smell her, feel her and drift into slumber like a newborn lamb.'

That was the best way to know plants, he said: in a state of relaxation.

'She likes shady beech forests. That's why she only grows in one place on Pirin now. Eagle Reserve. Just don't eat the fruit.'

I didn't go. It was remote and I had no guide to take me. Rocky promised to take me there another time, but there was no other time.

Belladonna is of course deadly nightshade. Culpeper reports: 'It is of a cold nature; in some it causes sleep; in others madness, and shortly after, death.'

Shakespeare's Juliet successfully faked her death with belladonna. My herbalist told me that it is grown in Scotland and that she uses it for people with severe anxiety and attention deficit hyperactivity disorder (ADHD). I began to see that the line between poison and cure is fine; as fine as the line between life and death.

Over time, allopathic Western medicine distanced itself from plant medicine, even as it relied on plants to create its drugs. Biophilia – the human instinct to be one with the rest of nature – was suppressed. The body-as-garden was replaced by the body-as-machine. This reflected the dominant Western view of the earth as a machine, rather than as a living organism. It is this split between the organic and the inorganic world that has made human health go into decline. We became subsumed by the inorganic; metal replaced wood and we lost our way.

The crushing wheel that eventually ground down organic living was set in motion by Western Christendom. Emperor Constantine I was the first to institutionalise the persecution of healer-herbalists and of the nature-magicians called *magi* at the time. His punitive laws were implemented in the early fourth century and laid the foundations for the Inquisition. Never mind that the emperor himself had sought the counsel of astrologers and magi to attain the throne, but it was not about belief or practice, it was about power and profit. By the fifth century, Europe's male clergy had officially monopolised people's minds and bodies. Freelance healers were punished and even killed, and anyone who wanted to practise healing had to be part of the system and accountable to the clergy. Ironically, senior monks and nuns throughout the Christian world were often herbalists and healers and Hildegard of Bingen systematised this in her writings on herbal, plant, animal and mineral medicine. Meanwhile, lay healers retreated underground.

Yet, like the roots of plants they only played dead during a very long winter. A crucial part of that winter was industrialisation and urbanisation, and its frozen nadir came in the twentieth century with the rise of a new behemoth: the pharmaceutical industry. In North America and Europe, pharma economy pushed out plant economy completely as manufactured mass drugs became the norm, while plant medicine was marginalised and shamed; humiliated and discarded like the working village. The argument was that phamaceuticals are controlled by man and homogenised in factories, while plant medicine is variable like the weather, but the plain truth is that mass-produced pharmaceuticals are infinitely more profitable for large corporations than plants.

The communists were not the first with their Pyrrhic shout: 'IN THE FIGHT AGAINST NATURE, WE SHALL BE VICTORIOUS!' Corporate capitalism got there first and is still at it. Yet aspirin, the world's most consumed pill, is extracted from the plant *spirea*, in body and in name. Spirea is meadowsweet, used for its painkilling and anti-inflammatory salicylic acid for thousands of years, and to repel pests in summer when it flowers in fragrant white bunches.

In Britain, wild plants are *still* associated with 'witches' because in the phytophobic collective mind, plant use is conflated with the horrific fate of witches at the hands of the church. I go for river walks with a Scottish friend and the first time she saw me collecting St John's wort she said, only half-joking: 'In the past, you would've been burned for this.'

And we half-laughed. Because we only half-know how damaged we are.

'It's crazy,' she said, the second time I picked it. She was recovering from a mental breakdown. 'The mood stabilisers have side effects as bad as the illness. And I could've taken this when my symptoms were mild. But there is a stigma around plant medicine, so I didn't.'

And yet, until the Second World War, foraging for plants and algae was part of everyday life in coastal Scotland.

Another time, I was picking blueberries in the woods, the ones that are now a quarry pit. A woman with a child passed me.

'Aren't these poisonous?' she asked, and inside that question was trauma that led back to the torture chambers of the church where salaried torturers called 'prickers' punctured, with long needles, women (and men) who were accused of witchcraft or in possession of nice land that, once the owner was disabled or killed, could be confiscated.

In late sixteenth-century Scotland, a woman was tried for witchcraft for healing 'sundry women' with honeysuckle. Another woman was tried for treating heart symptoms with *plantago* leaves. Both medicinal plants are still in use today and in the Bach Flower Remedies, honeysuckle is administered to those who 'live in the past'. Those women were just two of tens of thousands in Christian Europe who helped people with plants and suffered for it. It is significant that the persecution of women-as-witches was at its worst in parts of Europe that were monocultural and religiously homogenous. Cultures that were religiously mixed, like the entire Balkans, did not endure witch hunts. Part of the reason was Ottoman laxity towards local custom. Balkan Islam is syncretic itself, like Balkan Christianity.

The woman let her child pick a single blueberry and eat it before moving on.

In *Women Who Run with the Wolves*, the psychologist Clarissa Pinkola Estés speaks of 'the injured instinct'. Once your instinct is injured, you make poor choices. You cannot distinguish between poison and food because these choices cannot be made through the mental faculty alone. This injury happens when our wild, creative nature – every child's nature – is suppressed for too long.

Most people in the post-industrial world suffer from injured instinct.

'Tell me about the immortal flower,' I said to Rocky.

'It's a mysterious plant. Rare and expensive. Forty euros per kilo.'

The roots had the properties that earned this elusive plant its name, although Rocky couldn't explain what these properties were. Or wouldn't.

'Once you taste the root, you can't forget it. It's sweet, peculiar. It does something to you,' he said. 'You see, there's always a lot going on with herbs,' he went on. 'And if this was a normal country, we'd be able to give our people a living from it.'

The valley and its mountains still looked like a palace of plants to me, but the masterplan was clearly gone.

'Gutting the forests is the biggest problem,' Rocky said. 'Because each tree you cut changes the microclimate. What grows in place of a felled tree? Bramble and juniper. Nothing else.'

The gravel pits of my river in Scotland will be planted with pine at best, or left to the broom at worst. Monocultures.

'As above, so below,' goes the old Platonic principle, reiterated in the twentieth century by Carl Jung: 'The only equivalent of the universe within is the universe without.'

Monoculture on the ground produces monotony in the mind. In *The Lost Language of Plants*, the naturalist writer Stephen Harrod Buhner calls this the 'two wounds'. The external wound and the interior wound, caused by 'no longer sharing soul essence with the world around us'. The external wound has been discussed and surveyed for a long time; 'the destruction of the rain forest, the pollution and destruction of rivers . . . all the desecration of our exterior world'.

And the internal wound, the invisible one, is experienced by living beings as pain. All kinds of pain.

Plants become extinct from our planet at the rate of one or more per day. That means that the 742 medicinal plants that grow in this corner of the world can disappear in just two years.

'Take berries,' Rocky said. 'All berries like to grow in clean, well-aired places without invasive species. When you cut the forest, invasive species arrive and the air changes, the soil changes, and the berry goes off somewhere else.'

'You should've come twenty, thirty years ago, when things were looking hopeful,' Rocky went on.

'When we could have been Europe's top exporter of wild plants and organic tomatoes, peppers, you name it, it grows here. Growing, picking, exporting and taking care of ourselves too. It was possible. What you see now is what's left of us. We're still here, but we're much reduced.'

Us humans and plants.

Bulgaria is still one of Europe's biggest exporters of edible and medicinal plants. Every year, between 60,000 and 80,000 tonnes of the 300 most popular species in the wild are collected, though organic herb plantations are on the rise: for calendula, lemon balm and mint. Bulgaria is Europe's largest exporter of lavender and paprika, for instance. Eighty per cent of those harvests leave the country wholesale and are processed and sold elsewhere, mostly in Germany, Austria, Spain, Britain and Greece.

'Our plants owe their quality to the rich soil and the climate,' said Rocky.

To the complex ecosystems which are their home. There are still fertile swathes of land here that have been untouched by agriculture for half a century. In an ecosystem, you have to know which plant to pick when, how, why and where. Every plant taken has consequences. Herb gathering, processing and use in healing practices was secret knowledge for much of human history, yet it was needed by everyone. That's why every community had its own practitioner or five, usually women but sometimes men.

For hundreds of years itinerant herbalists were a feature of everyday life. They called themselves *bileri*. The bileri were herb-gatherers, root-diggers and plant-dealers and the word *bileri* came from *bilé*, herb. If you had a pain, they had a bilé. They walked everywhere. They'd arrive in town with their dirty bags and dusty feet, exotic in their long black felt coats and black turban-like head-wraps that were solid with the grime of the road.

'*Bilerin bilki sells!*' they called in a drawn-out melancholy voice and children and women gathered around them. What made these travellers special was that they brought plants and recipes from other places. Plant knowledge was jealously guarded by people in the know, but with time it became more accessible, and the wandering bileri contributed to the spread of plant power among ordinary people.

Even so, there was something about the plant realm that remained perennially hidden from the mundane eye. As late as nineteenth-century France, the spells spoken by women when they picked verbena, for example, were secret knowledge.

'Vervaine is one of very few things that help periodontitis,' said Rocky. 'Mixed with mugwort.'

Rocky and Nafié were herbalists in the sedentary tradition. In the old days, your local plant gatherer-prescriber was the same person because she who digs up the belladonna root, she who picks the lady's mantle before dawn to gather its special dewdrops, is also she who makes an infusion and says the words.

'Lady's mantle is prohibited,' Rocky said. 'It's picked in autumn.'

'In Scotland, I pick it in summer,' I said.

'That's the leaves and flowers. I'm talking about the roots. Plus you're in another climate zone. What's the name in English?'

He chuckled, delighted. 'Yes, it looks exactly like a lady's mantle!'

Among its many names here are queenly because it's a queen of herbs for women and shapiché, from *shap* (foot-and-mouth disease) which it treats. For Culpeper, lady's mantle will not 'suffer any corruption to remain behind' in the body. Lady's mantle was named *Alchemilla* in the Middle Ages – and it stuck – because alchemists believed its dewdrops had special qualities. If you drink the round dewdrops inside its leaves, you'll taste a subtle fragrance.

'Every herb has ten different names in just one language. Regional names, folk names, old names and that's before you even get to the taxonomy.'

Rocky had been bitten by the plant bug young. He rose to be the top supplier for the country's largest herbal business. Then, in the 1990s, something happened. Or rather a number of things happened. One was Rocky's discovery of the Icelandic moss in high altitude places here. It was a big deal.

'It's a lichen by the way, not a moss,' he said. 'A highly prized, pure plant. I made money from it. But I was followed. They shadowed me and took it from me. It's not a pretty story. And we've work to do now.'

Icelandic moss, sorry, lichen, is expensive. It's used for lung disease, bowel upsets and Maud Grieve reports that it relieved the symptoms of advanced tuberculosis. In Britain, it is apparently still found in the Grampians of Scotland, in Wales and Yorkshire. Until Rocky found it here, it was unheard of growing in the southern Balkans.

'There's another nice lichen, old man's beard,' Rocky said. 'It grows on pine and oak and most others. It's not choosy. You chew it for a headache and it's a natural antibiotic. You'll spot it by the white thread inside.'

'Now,' he went on, 'there's a plant that makes you laugh for three days, and on the fourth day sends you off to the graveyard. Still laughing in your coffin.'

'What is it?' I wanted to know.

'Ah. I'm under strict prohibition. Can't disclose its name.'

'Bryony?'

'No, but you have promise!', he said. 'You see, there are herbs I can't name because they are classified. People aren't supposed to know them.'

'Why not?'

'Because they can harm you. Only pharma companies handle them.'

Really? That sounded interesting. But he would not say more. I wondered to whom he was beholden, who held him in a grip. If he fell out with his nameless boss, he could be destroyed overnight.

'I've tried my hand at all sorts of things,' Rocky went on. 'In the '90s, we got into salt-curing sheep and goat skins and we made potato crisps, and sold them to the big chains, me and my nephew.' His nephew had been trained as Rocky number two.

'But he went to Finland and didn't come back,' Rocky said. 'Have you tried our potatoes?'

I knew from Danera's potato salads that they were packed with flavour.

'Cos they're organic. In Greece they put chemicals in the potatoes to boost crops and it makes them watery.'

Rocky was quite the phyto-patriot. In the 'murky years' of the 1990s Transition, Greek dealers came to buy plants from Rocky at rock-bottom prices, then repackaged them as Greek or EU gourmet foods for the international market. A bit like today. Lots of locals had gone to Greece to work in agriculture with poor living conditions and wages.

'It pained me to see our boys and girls working their butts off in the potato fields of Greece for 25 euros a day. Now they go to the West for better money and it still pains me.'

But 25 euros was still the rate for manual labour here, from logging to painting and decorating.

A stack of crates were filled with a pink-flowered plant whose leaves looked and smelled minty. Rocky brought a leaf to his face and sniffed it.

'Wild basil.'

I grasped the extent of his eye problem then. He was more blind than not. That's why he stood so close, because he couldn't make out my face. The plant's popular name was cat's paw, because the florets were like soft paws.

'Good for ladies' problems, indigestion, kidneys, prostate, skin. A regenerative plant,' he spoke as he pottered about the room.

'But it's more potent than people realise. Such a strong antioxidant, one of these days they'll start treating cancer with it. Mark my words.'

He handed me a small pack of ground red chillies.

'Our chillies, organic and sweet.'

Later in Scotland, I looked at a packet of organic chillies in my cupboard. It said: 'Country of origin: packed in the UK'. I went through my whole cupboard: the same story, time after time. I was eating foods picked by people in places not mentioned. The 'Authentic Italian sundried tomatoes, produced in Italy' admitted in tiny letters that these were 'non-EU sundried tomatoes'. Even the oil in which they were marinated came from somewhere not mentioned. They looked like they were authentically Albanian.

But there are exceptions, showing that honouring the origin of a plant doesn't take away from the authenticity of your food

experience, it adds to it. One seller I use lists the country of origin on
the labels of its herbs. It seems important to know that the passion
flower is from France, the slippery elm from the USA, the marigold
from Egypt and the rose petals from Pakistan. It makes me curious
about the hands and faces, and lives of the people who picked the
plants through which I run my own hand.

'Go on, ask me specific questions,' Rocky reminded me.

'Tell me about mandrake,' I said.

'We don't have it,' he said at once. 'But we have white bryony.'

Like the mandrake, white bryony is a 'man-plant' with humanoid-
shaped roots.

'Also known as wild hop or false mandrake.'

Since antiquity, people have believed that you can't pull out mandrake with your hands or it will make a screaming noise and strike
you dead; so you had to tie a dog to the plant and make it run. In
Arabic, it was called *beid-el-djinn*, eggs of the djinn.

But white bryony is even more striking. It looks like a wild vine
with small poisonous fruits, like the deadly nightshade.

'Also called wild pumpkin and crazy pumpkin because of its
pumpkin-like leaves,' he added. 'And crazy because it is psychotropic.'

Rocky sliced the root and dried it. He used to sell a lot to Greece.
Last year, a German grower bought 300 kilos of fresh bryony root
from him to plant in his greenhouses.

'You make a salve from the slices. When you apply it to a sore back
or slipped disc, it raises a terrific fever. It draws the inflammation
from your body.'

'Three hundred kilos seems a lot!' I said.

'That's what I'm saying to you,' Rocky said. 'A lot of wild plants
have disappeared already in Germany and other countries. And more
will disappear. Humanity has got off the train, my friend. In a hundred years' time we won't be around to tell people about these
mysterious things. Because a lot has been lost. Yet there is still elixir.'

He handed me a small pack of dried ceps for my dinner.

'But you've got to work for me!'

I busied myself. A beaten-up pick-up truck arrived and a Roma
family spilled out with bags and crates. I recognised the tall man in

tatty clothes, with the sack and the old mouth, who hadn't wanted a lift. Nafié sat at the desk inside, receiving the produce with a stern face, handing out cash from a drawer and writing amounts in a ledger.

Chanterelles fetched 4 lev (2 euros) per kilo. Ceps fetched 8 lev (4 euros) for 'first quality' and 3 lev for 'second quality' which meant older ones, you could tell from their browner underside. The younger ones were lighter, perkier. A young woman brought a huge cep – 2 kilos. She had dark circles under her eyes and a tired smile. An old man came in, his Indian face etched with hardship.

'Is that soggy cep?' Rocky picked one up from the man's crate. Some sprinkled their mushrooms with water to make them weigh more. 'Don't try to fool me, I have a university degree.' But he didn't say it harshly.

The man started explaining but Rocky figured it out, it was fine. The ceps had 'sweated'. They would dry later.

'The old eyes let me down, mate,' Rocky apologised. 'And sometimes the hands let me down too.'

The man was forgiving.

'We've grown old, mate,' he smiled with a wrecked mouth and I recognised him from a few days before. He'd arrived on a horse and cart with his wife when I was at Beslet with my guide. There, we witnessed a brutal scene.

The Roma, who bivouacked without coming down, sold their harvest to a dealer from Thunder. The dealer arrived at four o'clock in a van full of empty crates and filled them with chanterelles and ceps brought to him by the sackful. He paid the same rate as Rocky. While my guide and I chatted to the dealer, two women got into a fight over a sack of chanterelles each said was hers and grabbed each other by the clothes and hair. One picked up a stake. The other picked an axe – her eyes were bloodshot, maybe she was drunk – and they both screamed and raised their weapons. I nearly screamed too.

That sack of chanterelles fetched them 10 euros at most. The dealer from Thunder sold the produce to Italian dealers in the valley and these fungi would be either packed here and despatched, or sent off wholesale to Italy. I would next see them in my local deli in Scotland as 'porcini', priced at 10 pounds for 100 grams. The label would say 'produce of EU' or 'made in Italy' or 'packed in the UK', so that the consumer paid 100 pounds per kilo, while the pickers of that kilo received 4 pounds if they were lucky. True, for 1 kilo of dried mushrooms you need between 7 and 10 kilos of fresh ones, so the consumer pays not for one, but for up to 10 kilos.

Either way, the consumer would be excused for not knowing that two women from the Mesta Valley nearly died for your porcini risotto tonight. The Indian-looking man stepped in and pulled the women apart, risking an axe in the head.

'We sure have aged, mate,' Rocky agreed with him. 'It's the system.'

This Roma man had spent his youth picking berries, snails, primrose, whatever was going. Here were the world's most skilled foragers, making a pittance for their tonnage, losing their teeth at forty and dying at fifty. The oldest person in the 'hood was a sixty-year-old woman. Men didn't make it to sixty.

A small boy stepped in with a single cep and Nafié weighed it.

'Eighty grams, first quality.' She gave him some change and the boy remonstrated coarsely. She spoke to him gently and he left, his head hung.

Nafié sighed a veteran's sigh.

'It's hard with the young Roma. They can't count, they can't read, they want money and they can get aggressive. You need a special understanding.'

'Yet we rely on them,' said Rocky. 'They're the only ones left.'

There were a few other pickers; local women who came with a bucket of mushrooms, but ninety per cent of the foragers were Roma. A van arrived: three young Roma guys with sackfuls of leaf. It was dark on top and white on the underside.

'Coltsfoot,' said Rocky.

In Bulgarian, it was called *podbel*, underwhite. And the shape of the leaves were just like the hooves of young horses, hence its English name, and the French folk name was *pas d'âne*, ass's foot.

'Good for coughs and stomach problems,' said Rocky.

I took some and started drinking it for a chesty congestion I'd had for a few weeks. The Latin name *Tussilago*, from '*tussis*' for cough, adds to this plant's description. One of its English folk names is cough wort. It was taken as tea by miners with damaged lungs and for centuries was smoked as a herbal tobacco by northern Europeans to relieve chest ailments like asthma. For persistent coughs, the Roman naturalist Pliny the Elder recommended this: burn coltsfoot leaves and inhale deeply through a reed straw, pausing in between each inhalation to sip warm red wine. Definitely something to try at home!

It dawned on me that taken together, all the different names of a herb completed a pharmacopoeia. They described all the principal uses of the plant and its appearance.

'I like people who can learn,' said Rocky. 'Come back next spring and I'll take you places that'll make your jaw drop.'

Rocky and Nafié had children but no apprentices. Their plant lineage would end with them. That's why they were delighted by my interest. It was a quiet tragedy.

Meanwhile, the three guys brought staggering quantities of coltsfoot from their van. They had picked 69 kilos of this leaf in an afternoon, for which they received 35 lev (18 euros). That was 6 euros each.

'Do you enjoy it?' I asked one of them and flinched at my own question.

He looked at me wildly. He was a red headed guy, skinny and covered in tattoos, his face lined from working outdoors, his teeth already bad. Then he smiled, seeing my notebook. They were all skinny and prematurely aged, and regarded me curiously, not used to the attention. One had LOVE tattooed on his forearm.

'We've grown up in the forest picking stuff,' he said. 'That's all.'

It took them an hour to drive the broken road to Beslet, then an hour back to the 'hood. For 6 euros each, not counting the fuel, but they used old frying oil.

'We're used to it,' another guy smiled and they climbed into the van. I felt the prickle of tears.

Coltsfoot leaf and tincture are not cheap. For a kilo of dried coltsfoot at my favourite Napiers Herbalists in Edinburgh, you pay 54 pounds. And I saw how little Rocky and Nafié made on this rung of the distribution ladder. They were the key link in the chain: between forest picker and town buyer. They had to have plant knowledge and people knowledge because they operated at that point of contact between the two. From the next rung onwards, it was all human business. The pickers vanished into their slum, Rocky's name was never mentioned again, the plant became a commodity and the trail back to the forest was lost. This coltsfoot would next appear in a pretty bag with a ribbon, in a smart boutique near you. Between forest floor and consumer, big bucks were made. But not by the Roma guys and not by Rocky.

Coltsfoot likes disturbed soil where other plants have been removed, so there is plenty of it by my Beauly River. But nobody picks it. When I looked at the label of a coltsfoot bag from a wholesaler in Glasgow, the country of origin was Poland. To gather it, you have to crouch low and stay close to the ground and you would demand more than 6 euros for half a day of 'unskilled work'.

Unskilled workers: that's how the British press describes the people who plant, harvest, process, package and bring food to our doorsteps.

We stacked the crates of coltsfoot, making sure they were even at the top and not too densely packed so as not to crush or sweat the leaves. It was the last delivery of the day. Nafié would spend the evening tidying up. Tomorrow, the coltsfoot would be despatched to the next dealer who had it de-dusted, dried and shredded. Then a firm here or abroad bought the leaf, packaged it, stamped it with their logo and sold it to the final buyer, who would sell it to the consumer.

'It's the going rate,' Rocky said, smelling my revulsion at the three pickers' pay. 'The big cut goes to the sharks. The ones with their fingers in the plant pies that take the subsidies and keep them for themselves. We've been sat on by the mafia for thirty years. But we are tough. We endure.'

'Aye,' said Nasko. 'We endure.'

Nasko the driver had just arrived, ready for the long drive. He was from Dogwood. Nasko's generation were children of the Transition. That was the period after the fall of the regime in 1989. It was meant to be short but it has lasted thirty years. The first ten years were marked by mass emigration and armed *grupirovki,* racket gangs that called themselves businesses. Some of today's big business owners in the region were part of that early mafia. Nasko's peers had grown up in this slow-burn war zone, receiving brutal lessons in toxic masculinity.

'And now I must earn an honest living. Impossible in this country. So I've got to pull asparagus in Germany.'

We loaded up the crates. I sat with Rocky and Nasko in the driver's cabin and we were off. Down the Kanina, up the Mesta through Maiden Gorge, to a town where the next dealer couple lived. They weighed the mushrooms again and their children loaded the crates into their own van. They were a gruff lot and regarded me with mistrust. Outsiders are an uncommon sight in this industry. As Rocky's assistant, I wrote down the weight and price on a pad in large print. The mushrooms would be cleaned, cut and dried the following morning, then sold to dealers in nearby Bansko; of skiing fame.

On the way out, I saw a patch of fresh nettles and Nasko insisted on picking me a bag, even without gloves. From him, I learned that you can avoid the sting of nettles by avoiding contact with the top of the leaves and only touching underneath the leaves. He worked fast and I could see how he made extra money for his overtime hours 'pulling asparagus' in Germany.

We drove down a rocky flank with no people, just an eagle above.

'Do you know that in Bansko dialect they address each other with "herb"?' said Rocky. 'You're a strange herb.'

Bilé. The same as wort in English or *herbe* in French. You're a strange fruit. *Mon petit choux.*

Rocky sniffed the air. 'Can you smell it? The coal mine.'

I couldn't. The mine still worked, but at minimal capacity. Coal mining required large amounts of water and this resulted in water shortages in households when Mesta was exhausted.

'Rocky's special power is his sense of smell,' said Nasko. 'Smell doesn't lie.'

'You know how you get to know a plant once you pick it?' Rocky said. 'You put it on the table and leave the room. Then you enter the room again. And there it is. It fills the room.'

We talked about food. Rocky liked everything as long as it had mushrooms in it.

'How do you cook your green beans?' Rocky turned to me in the dark cabin of the van. His face was a blur and that's how the world was to him: a blur, smells, textures.

'Put some ceps in and you won't go wrong,' he said.

Mushrooms had been Rocky's fortune and his misfortune. Rocky's business was really taking off in the 1990s, then something happened.

'I had mushroom for 7,000 euros in the house. Due to be loaded up in the van and delivered in the morning. They arrived at four in the morning and took it.'

The armed racketeers. In the murky years, plant dealers were all visited by them and businesses were taken at gunpoint. They were that valuable. I heard about a local man who'd been put on a wood-sawing machine by racketeers and threatened to be chopped like a log unless he signed away his business to them: which he did and they prospered. There was just one village in Old Woods that kept its herbal business from the tentacles of the mafia back then. The villagers got together, organised and armed by a retired local general, and intimidated the racketeers by pushing their Jeeps into a precipice. The rest, like Rocky, had suffered the consequences of violent assault. And now they survived, but didn't quite thrive in the post-gangster kleptocracy that had taken hold like a poisonous weed.

After the shock of that loss, Rocky developed diabetes overnight, then eye damage that led to progressive blindness.

'The guys who took his stock are now bigwigs,' said Nasko.

A mafia state is no less unjust than a dictatorship. For Rocky, it was worse, because there were no safety nets, no rules.

'But cheer up! You've still come to the right place,' Rocky nudged me. 'You've found the loveliest spot around. It's not a coincidence that I am a plant maniac. Watch out cos plant passion can consume you. You think you're consuming the plant, but it's the plant that consumes you.'

When we got back, Nafié was tidying up. She was small under a tower of stacked crates. Tomorrow they would do the same: receive and sort deliveries from afternoon to midnight.

They waved to me from the illuminated doorway of their tower of crates. I drove down the road to my dream house in the Empty Village. I wondered if they would ever retire. They couldn't afford to, and anyway, would they want to draw the curtains and watch the telly? Perhaps they would. But I couldn't imagine them without spring, summer, autumn and winter herbs, dead and living herbs, weighed and dried herbs, herbs felt and brought close to your face to inhale and munch because appearances are an illusion and the ungainly root contains untold beauty.

I lay on my veranda. I couldn't sleep. All I saw was ceps and colts-foot. Their yellow-green shapes crowded me from the inside, as if I generated them myself.

The second-century physician, Galen, mentions an earlier botanist's account of a man who actually turns into a plant. Rocky was that person: half plant, half man. If I spent long enough with Rocky and Nafié, I'd go into a biophilic merger too. I already felt the first stirrings. It's when you sense that being human is only half the story.

Rocky suited his enchanter nickname. He had been mauled by the system but never lost his capacity for enchantment. Alchemists called this creative impulse *imaginatio*. Rocky had it and it was this that kept him going. 'The *imaginatio* is the star in man, the celestial or super-celestial body,' said the European alchemists, *Astrum in homine coeleste sive supracoeleste corpus.*

There is nothing more tangible than 742 herbs, with 10 names each. Yet when I snaked down the road that imitated the river, the thought of anything growing in the darkness was enchanting. You had to imagine it to make it real, the way the earth had imagined it. Then in the morning, you saw that it was real and you were enchanted all over again.

At night, everybody went underground. While the overground slept, the underground stretched, yawned, fed, hissed and conversed with 742 voices, and it's easy to see how, pulled roughly from the ground without warning, the mandrake screams with a human voice.

Elixir

There is still elixir, Rocky said. El-iks-ir. A word like a forgotten mantra. The word is the thing. Even if you can't spell it, you can taste it. It is an alchemical term that first appeared in the seventh century, and like alchemy, it goes as far back as the human search for meaning.

But what is alchemy? We think of alchemy as the pseudo-science of turning base metals into gold. That kind of alchemy might never have existed in the first place. The true meaning of alchemy is transmutation and this is why alchemy has never gone away. The universe does it by itself, and humans at their best imitate, from primal matter into consciousness, from chaos to higher order. In a sense, alchemy is the very principle of becoming, a conscious process of unfoldment, with no beginning and no end.

Alchemy is ancient. Its earliest recorded practitioners were in China and India. The Islamic Golden Age (from the ninth to the fourteenth century) was an apogee of medicine, alchemical philosophy and all the arts. The most influential of those early Eurasian renaissance men was the Persian Avicenna (or Ibn Sina, 'son of Sina') whose *Book of Healing* and *Canon of Medicine* shaped Western medicine in the centuries to come.

The early alchemists of Eurasia grasped that there was no clear boundary between the visible and invisible dimensions. In the *Alchemy of Happiness* (*Kimia yi-Sa'adat*), the twelfth-century Persian Sufi philosopher al-Ghazali explores the nature of the contemplative life as if it is a sacred experiment conducted in a cosmic laboratory. Eastern mystics like him and Western mystics like his contemporary

Hildegard of Bingen had a lot in common and it is no surprise that spiritual teachings moved from East to West.

In the twentieth century, the pioneering Swiss psychologist Carl Jung brought the forgotten world of alchemy into the modern age, polished it symbol by symbol and made it shine again. 'The fact is that the alchemists had little or nothing to divulge in the way of chemistry, least of all the secret of goldmaking,' he writes. The alchemical *opus* deals with psychological and spiritual matters dressed in 'pseudochemical language'. Jung decoded the alchemical dreams of the Graeco-Egyptian philosopher Zosimos of Panopolis who described elemental creation, the death and rebirth cycle and the Earth's relationship with the cosmos in metaphors. 'It is a stone that is not a stone,' Zosimos concluded about the philosopher's stone.

If you become an apprentice in an alchemical workshop, the first thing you learn is the philosophical principles of alchemy. They will strike students of Western philosophy as Platonic or Gnostic, students of Eastern philosophies as self-evident and students of quantum physics as familiar. All things are as one; everything is alive; consciousness precedes matter; transform yourself before you try to transform anything else; creation is 'divine' or ineffable and contained within each being; a new flower, stone, substance, being, or state of being can be produced by human-divine intervention, but the laws of nature must be respected. This is transmutation, made possible through the raising of vibrations. This is one of the definitions of alchemy: the raising of vibrations. It starts at the mental level and ends at the material.

You – the apprentice – would learn the physical and metaphysical properties of the four elements: fire, earth, water and air (in the Chinese tradition there are five elements: water, earth, fire, metal and wood). Each element is expressed on Earth and in the human body in myriad ways, and each has a guardian spirit. Modern alchemical psychologists named seven transformative stages of the psyche and four of them correspond to the four elements: *calcination, coagulation, solution, sublimation*. The order of the stages varies and the process is messy, full of false starts, relapses and failed experiments – like life itself – but the activator is always fire. Fire was taken from the gods by Prometheus, and for empowering mortals 'the system' punished him. But fire stayed. Without fire, there is no creation, no evolution and the hearth is cold. I almost wrote the heart is cold, which is also true. Fire cooks, impassions, electrifies and turns the experiment to ashes. The spirit creature of fire is the salamander.

You, the student of alchemy, would learn that the holy grail of ancient and medieval alchemy was to distil a substance that contains the essence of life and heals all disease. From plants, rocks, metals: a drop of immortality. Hundreds of names have been given to this elusive substance: Amrita, elixir of life, lapis, the philosopher's stone. The search for elixir was at times linked with gold because gold doesn't tarnish, hence the idea of transforming 'base metals' into pure ones. Precious stones were treated as pure beings of high resonance. Hildegard of Bingen, who was an alchemist in the broadest sense, recommended placing a diamond in your mouth 'against your own meanness'. The search for elixir is thrilling but risky. Over centuries of experimentation, medicine women and men, and at least one emperor from the Ming Dynasty, died by drinking what was supposed to be an elixir of immortality but turned out to be poison. This is radical curiosity: to be prepared to die in the name of immortality. That is, of ultimate knowledge, *gnosis*. Avicenna said it: 'I prefer a short life with depth to a narrow one with length.'

But the search for elixir is not really about a liquid or an object because it is a search for completeness. In Old English, heal means whole; to heal is to make whole again. This is the root of 'holistic'. This is why the apprentice would train in all the arts: mathematics, astronomy, physiology, art, poetry, music and natural sciences. You would learn how to have a relationship with liquids, stones, plants, animals, the luminaries and your innermost self, which is a microcosm of all that there is. You would be in pursuit of a two-fold enlightenment: through direct experience and through lifelong study.

You the student of alchemy know that humanity's longing for elixir has never gone away. But we have forgotten its true meaning because somewhere along the way we gave up the search for it. We settled for a long, narrow life instead of a short one with depth. We forgot how to heal. We gave our power away and debased elixir to an anti-ageing cream. We settled for less than the whole. Your task is to remember how to make whole again.

THE PASSAGE

Each evening in Arif's guesthouse, I'd sit on my high balcony like a watchtower over Clear Water. I'd eat slabs of fresh goat's cheese as pure as snowdrift and track the cars crawling up the road. They were all coming from faraway places to here, the little village of Kribul with its one main street that climbed until the tarmac ended and a forest road began.

The visitors drove past Arif's guesthouse, past the ramshackle house of the goatherds who boiled 200 litres of milk every night, past the houses of the last tobacco growers with their golden leaf strung up on wooden frames, past the outdoor table where the village drunks sat without moving as if made of glass, past the Kebab café, past the older village women collectively known as *babi*, who sat on benches in floral headscarves and shalvars munching pumpkin seeds, past the village shop that did brisk business in lead bullets – not for hunting, but for diagnostic rituals performed by the babi – and that's where they gave up. They got out of their cars and asked after baba Ava.

'Baba Ava? Keep going,' the villagers said. 'It's the pink house at the top.'

Kribul sat on the dry flanks of the western Rhodope above Clear Water. It was one of those hewn-into-the-hillside villages not suitable for people fearful of heights and drops: which some of the visitors were. Some were fearful of everything. The pilgrims ascending the road in the early morning or late evening were in possession of a wide spectrum of conditions, diseases and every kind of affliction under the currently waxing moon. They were riddled with anxiety and depression, mute, autistic, heartbroken, struggling to conceive or just having a bad time. Some were simply curious, they said, while nursing a secret hope.

They came because of a remote megalith known as The Passage to locals and The Stone of the Black Snake to tourists. The place was ascribed curative value and became popular after a television feature about it.

After hearing about The Passage at The Empty Village taverna, I packed up my dream house, said goodbye to my neighbours and Danera, swapped phone numbers with Rocky the Enchanter and moved here. Kribul was at the southern tip of Old Woods. To get here, you left the valley behind.

You left behind Fire, Nikopolis ad Mestum, the 'hood, Thunder and drove past a long stretch of cultivated fields where people were bent in their furrows from early morning to avoid the heat. Here were the last tobacco fields of the valley, leafy and tall. The 'mixed' villages like Fire continued; mixed meant Muslim and Christian together. One of them sported an oversized Wahabi-style mosque that smacked of laundered money in this small village that already had a medieval mosque. Some young women wore the raised hijab imported from Turkey; ostensibly a statement of Islamic conservatism. But fashion was key, not dogma. Others wore nothing on their heads and looked Western, while the older women stuck with the traditional, relaxed floral headscarf. The Western look said: 'I'm emancipated and urban', the traditional look said: 'I'm a Pomak villager and know my place' and the high hijab said: 'I'm a Muslim and a citizen of a global world.'

The road climbed into the interior of the mountain. Clear Water was the next big tributary south of Kanina and dozens of waterways flowed into it.

Geographic vitality and human diversity went together. The Mesta basin had sprouted an ethno-cultural web known as the Chech and historically, the mountain villages of the Chech were home to Our Folk, that is Pomaks, with large Christian and Gypsy minorities. The Chech began at the latitude of the valley and followed Mesta into the Aegean Plains. Its people spoke Bulgarian. Then the Ottoman Empire collapsed. Waves of terror, exodus and crude homogenising nationalism on both sides of the new border began. The new border tore up an old web of waterways and pastoralist routes. The Chech no longer exists as a geocultural entity. But some of its villages are still here – like Kribul – and its territory is still here because its territory is the mountain.

The road passed glades full of rock stacks that looked like gatherings for some long-ago occasion. The Rhodope was like this – mimetolithic: a chameleon of a mountain. Millennia of cults had shaped the land. But the land was the original cult. It's as if the mountain anticipated the human psyche by self-sculpting. The mountain thought herself into being in sympathy with rocks, plants, animals and finally, humans. Each had their own timescale but the mountain contained them all.

One stone ensemble was scattered in a forest just before Kribul. The zoomorphic and anthropomorphic shapes had been named Dragon-snake, Priestess and Space Ship, but the most striking was a giant head. These figures were fancied as man-made thousands of years ago, though they were likely natural or mostly natural. Oddly, the complex had only been 'discovered' in the 1980s by a Polish archaeologist and only recently turned into a tourist attraction. Fragments of looms, ceramic pots and roof tiles had popped up in excavations, and there were stone thrones with carved steps.

The head reclined on a green canopy, gazing through semi-open lids, Buddha-like. At dusk, the valley of Clear Water was infused with all the colours of the spectrum. The stone town took an hour to see and on a summer's day it was a scorched place with a sheer drop. Archaeologists had measured the electromagnetic field and established that, because of the structure of granite, the area accumulated a high voltage. I have no idea what that means, but if you wanted serenity to be your superpower, you'd come and camp by the head until you glimpsed a moment in time without your little self, without humans at all. You glimpsed that the mountain had welcomed us, fed us, watered us, healed us, kept us going even when we hacked into it, dammed it and drained it, and it might just see us off too. The head would remain to imitate our long-ago presence.

The Rhodope bristled with cult sites like this, big and small, on hilltops with strategic positions. The head complex, Goat Stone in

Old Woods and The Passage above Kribul were survivors of an ancient network, just as the villages were survivors of the Chech.

The overnight television fame achieved by The Passage had startled sleepy Kribul awake. On busy days, visitors outnumbered locals.

'It's the energy,' a voice came from the garden below, where guests gathered every evening for dinner, drinks and therapeutic chat, over-seen by our host Arif.

'It's a triangle,' said another voice. 'Kribul, The Monastery of H. and Goat Stone.'

The once harmonious nearby monastery of H. had been wrecked by over-restoration in a gaudy neo-Orthodox style. It was the equivalent of the new mosques with their cold neo-Islamism.

Kribul had a little old mosque whose minaret had been broken with a crane by the communists. You could see where it had been reattached.

'Have you been to the nymphs' spring in K.?' another voice said.

'No, but did you know that if you wash yourself in the St Athanasios spring near the Golden Meadows, you cleanse your family of karmic debt?'

This was the woman who was here with her emaciated adult daughter. Her daughter stared into space with her skull-like face.

'Have you been to the Black Madonna for orphans in H.?'

A couple from Belgrade. The woman wore outlandish make-up.

'And The Passage in K.,' said her husband. 'We're touring the Balkans.'

'Until we find relief,' his wife rejoined.

'We already feel better,' he said.

Something about them was so damaged it walked everywhere with them.

Arif's voice was rarely heard. He let his guests get things off their chests. He drank the homemade spirits brought by them, although he wasn't a drinker and he chuckled politely at the men's poor jokes, while the women tried to ignore the men and gazed at the moon, unhappy with their lives but happy to be here.

Arif was a slender man in his fifties with beady eyes that betrayed

nothing except impatience with the more unbearable guests. His
wife worked in the city in the valley. His daughters travelled to England to pick fruit and work in cafés. The women were worked off
their feet and he'd built the guesthouse. Otherwise, the livelihood for
men was quarrying and cutting the slate stone of the Rhodope.
Unregulated quarries proliferated in the area, causing deforestation,
erosion, drought and water shortages.

'Come on, Arifie, open the other bottle. The night is young.'

The international lorry driver who addressed everyone in the
diminutive. He was a large, loud man whose doctor wife made her
excuses early and sat on her balcony next to mine. They lived in
Spain. Twenty-five years ago, he'd been drawn into some shady business and she had refused to be a gangster's widow, she said, so they
emigrated. On our high balconies, we talked late under the stars. Her
daughter had become ill with diabetes after suffering a shock and this
had changed her approach to health.

'We know little about human health,' she said. 'The biochemistry
of emotions. The effect of the environment on the endocrine system.
Immunity. The key to health.'

She was studying Eastern health traditions and found the chakra
system useful.

'Because everything is connected but not always in an obvious
way. Yet Western medicine still has a mechanical approach to the
human being. It teaches us to take patients apart, but not to put them
back together in a meaningful way.'

Her daughter had chosen not to take medication for her diabetes
but changed her diet and lifestyle, supervised by her mother, and her
blood sugar had normalised within a year.

'You know what these conversations always come down to?' Arif
asked us one night in the garden.

'Illness,' I said.

'No, belief,' he said. 'What people believe and how that impacts
their health.'

'Correct. The patient's mental-emotional state is ignored by medicine, because it can't be quantified,' said the GP from Spain. 'Yet it's
a powerful factor. I see it again and again.'

Under the stars, among the honeysuckle, knowing they might never meet again, Arif's guests opened up. The vast majority were not Muslims and this was their first contact with a Muslim community. Many of them returned, they liked it here.

'I look at a person when they arrive and I see what they need, even when they don't know what they need. Then I try to provide it,' Arif told me privately.

Like a good doctor.

'And like you, I take notes, but mentally,' he added. 'For the book I'll never write.'

Arif's generation were raised to be tough and obedient. They'd walk to the nearest secondary school, through dark glades, across the river which swelled in spring. They'd spend the week in dorms. In winter, parents accompanied them to make a trail in the snow, but they had to find their way back: two hours each way. After finishing high school with top grades in the city of the valley, then two years of compulsory army service, Arif wanted to study further but was recalled home to help with the tobacco harvest. He was bitterly disappointed because he wanted a life of the mind, but bowed before the double judgement of state and clan.

Arif seemed tense and in the morning I discovered why Krihul had fallen prey to Passage politics. I had come looking for baba Ava, but her house was full for the night and it didn't take long to find out that she was one of five women who operated at the stone.

'You don't need baba Ava,' a woman told me. 'You can go with another baba. They all have drivers.'

The babi's role wasn't very clear to me but that was about to change. Early in the morning, we piled into Arif's Jeep: me, the couple from Spain and a young Roma couple. The mother and daughter took their 'karmic debt' elsewhere and I was glad.

Squeezed in the back hatch with her walking stick made from cherry was our baba, a woman named Acivé. Arif was her friend, driver and champion.

'She is the only genuine baba,' Arif said.

Acivé was self-contained and rarely spoke uninvited.

'I've known her all my life. Her mother was one of only two

women who frequented the stone during Communism. In winter too,' said Arif.

As with the stone above Dogwood, visiting The Passage had been banned and the relationship between people and stone had all but vanished.

I liked Acivé straight away. For all that her life had never extended beyond this side of the mountain and her formal education was basic, she had a bright intelligence. Being in her presence was like enjoying fine weather. She was small and had a limp; a granary door had fallen on her hip and crushed it in her youth, and it hadn't been fixed. 'But I'm fine, I have my cane,' she said, and she did move with surprising speed.

'I used to stutter too,' she said. 'My mother took me to the stone and it stopped.'

The Jeep bumped roughly over the dirt road. We entered a sparse glade.

'The old road used to wind over the mountain,' Acivé said. 'But then they made this new road that takes you straight there.'

Straight there was pretty crooked and we were trailed by a cloud of sand. Before the village became wealthy enough for Jeeps, there were Soviet UAZ vehicles and before that: mules.

Inside Arif's car, the Roma woman kept pulling away from me on the back seat. 'Don't touch me,' she kept saying. The couple from Spain had come without previous knowledge of the stone, just for the mountain air.

'All sorts come,' baba Acivé said.

'Stop touching me!' the Roma woman recoiled again.

'I'm not touching you,' I said, 'you're paranoid.'

'Don't mind her,' said her uxorious husband.

'Some that can't walk,' Acivé went on. 'Some that can't talk. Some that can't see and some that can't hear. Some with tumours and fright. Some come for babies. Some with sick children.'

To her, there was no hierarchy of ailments, or people.

'We try to help them all,' she said, 'but it's not us that helps. It's the stone. The stone is God. We are nobody.'

'A Spanish woman came,' said Acivé, 'with six miscarriages. After passing through the stone, she gave birth to a living child. A government minister came to have his bad energy cleared.'

'And?'

'And we helped him. It took a while,' she said, deadpan but not mocking. She didn't mock anyone, even corrupt ministers.

The road ended in a small clearing where two army stretchers rested against trees. We walked to The Passage through an eerie forest. Every tree had clothing tied to it. The forest teemed with ragged spirits, the sick parts of themselves that people had left behind.

This was syncretism fully cooked: place-specific pilgrimage blended with nature worship, stirred by gestures from a remote past, leavened by imagination and sugar-dusted with Abrahamic religion. I'd seen such dressed-up woods before, usually near a spring. In the Balkans, they have a faint Christian or Muslim flavour depending on who lives there at the time, but the template is the same. On the Black Isle in Scotland, near my river, is a spring called the Clootie Well of Munlochy. It is one of the last active sites of water-and-wood veneration in Scotland. There is no human custodian and people have forgotten why they tie a piece of clothing on a tree. They do it instinctively, from a body-earth memory, even when meaning has been erased from the mind.

Human culture begins in nature. That is the memory. When you live without nature, you forget. When you come to a place like this, you remember.

Hairbands, socks, bras, strips of fabric, trousers, T-shirts, shawls.

Acivé showed me a special place for children; a small rock with 'children's footprints' in it. The children made her sad, Acivé said, because often their illness came from their ancestors and could not be cured in this life.

Acivé limped along with her walking stick at great speed.

'This is the old path, the animal path. But when The Passage became famous, they made the new one.'

The old path was only visible to her. Although it was early, we were not the first visitors. Another woman with a headscarf and a stick was returning from the stone. A few people walked behind her. We greeted them.

'See,' Acivé said, 'she's not even from Kribul. But she comes and brings her own people and that's good. Cos the stone belongs to all. And before her is the dawn shift with baba Nishidé. Later in the afternoon comes baba Nailé.'

There was a roster! We reached the stone. She threw a couple of pebbles she'd picked from the path at it, to alert it to our presence.

'Salaam Aleikum, Aleikamu Salaam', she said the traditional Muslim greeting, and tapped the stone with her stick as if knocking on someone's door.

'We have come a long way, give us healing,' she said to the stone and climbed the wooden ladder. You had to climb it to reach the stony plateau on the other side.

'Bismillah Rahmani Rahim,' she muttered as she climbed. In the name of God, the merciful, the beneficent.

The sun was rising from the east, the moon declined to the west. The birds were singing at full throttle. The area around The Passage was festooned with piles of red woollen threads left behind by people.

To get a good view of the proceedings, I climbed onto the plateau from the other side where the babi didn't go. Below was a sheer drop into the gully.

A small tree growing through the rock was hung with little outfits; an offering from childless couples.

People had inserted coins and bits of folded-up paper with their wishes into the rock cracks, even small photographs.

'We tell them not to and they still do it,' Arif said. 'This is not a monastery, it's a stone.'

'The stone doesn't need no money and no paper,' said Acivé.

The plateau was covered with white flour.

'To feed the keeper,' Acivé said.

She put down her shepherd's shoulder bag and swept the flour into the gully. There was a little resident broom for this. 'Tsk tsk,' she tutted. 'They don't clean up after themselves.'

Meaning the other babi. Watching her sweep, I could see why the broom is one of the witch's sacral objects. Another object is the sieve. For flour, herbs and to catch the shadows of things.

This is how it went for the supplicant. You were to bring red thread, the same length as your height and which you placed on the railing by the ladder. You were leaving your measure for the stone. You then climbed the ladder starting with your right foot. You enter the mosque and your house with your right foot, you only go into the latrine with your left foot, baba Acivé explained. In the unwritten book of archaic rules, right was day, left was night. Right was male, left was female. Right was Cosmos, left was Chaos. Right was the sun, left was the moon. Right was conscious, left was unconscious. Likewise, in TCM, the right side of the body is yang, the left yin.

You were supposed to bring flour and salt. But you didn't, so the babi provided it.

'Salt is the most precious thing on Earth after water,' said Arif.

'For the keeper,' said baba Acivé. 'To feed him.'

'Him? I thought it was a black snake,' the lorry driver from Spain winked at us and lowered himself heavily onto the flat stone next to me.

'It ain't a black snake,' Acivé said calmly, sweeping. 'It's a person. A young youth.'

The village was torn by feuds but agreed on one thing: there was a keeper of the stone. In the days before ready bought flour, her grandmother brought grains of rye and threw them at the stone. 'Here,' she'd call to the keeper, 'make yourself a necklace with this.'

The first time Acivé saw The Passage was at the age of seven, when she ran away from school one day and snuck up here. She saw her grandmother talking to the invisible keeper and doing a ritual for a woman with a sick child.

Acivé's mother was a young woman when she came through the woods on her mule to ask The Passage for a favour and this smiling man-boy appeared. Very tall and made of light, in a long white gown. A giant hologram. Her mother talked to him and all he did was laugh and disappear. Her grandmother had seen him too, a generation before.

'A young youth. She asked him three times "Who are you?" and three times he said nothing.'

But the keeper, being a shapeshifter, could manifest as an animal or reptile. Some spoke of seeing a black snake over the years. A small lizard darted past us and a yellow butterfly alighted.

'A sign!' baba Acivé and Arif said in chorus. 'A welcoming. See, the butterfly is looking for the Koran. Because this place is all about the Koran.'

She meant relief. For women of her generation, the 'Koran' stood for compassion, right action, divine law, healing and holy scripture all in one. Later, when I spent time with her, Acivé said things like:

'When judgement day comes, the Bible where the Koran is written with all its pages will turn blank.'

To her, the holy book was everywhere, it was nature itself. Our Folk the Pomaks had a habit of saying 'Allah-God' when talking to non-Pomaks, to make it clear that Allah was just like everybody else's god.

'And just as Allah-God is one, so people's little soul is one,' she said. 'They think they're separate, but they're not.'

I saw how she treated cynical people who mocked her and the stone: with firm openness. Because she had no need to prove anything, she also had no argument with anyone.

'You come here to stand before Allah. If you don't think so, don't come. This place is about your maker.'

'This place is about symbols,' said Arif, and lay down on the sun-warmed stone. 'This is my spot. I feel the energy here. Every time my girls are about to go abroad, we come here and they lie on the stone to charge them up and give them strength in England.'

They didn't bring a baba and they never came in the dark, no, you never hang around after dark, Arif said. You wouldn't want to, and the keeper didn't like it either. There were tales of campers on a nearby meadow who'd heard eerie music in the night: flutes and drums, and laughing voices. The stone itself wouldn't let you sleep, Acivé said, and I never spent the night here because I know my limits.

'I don't even know whether I'll reach here when I set out each time,' she added.

That's why she said a prayer to *Hazreti* (Prophet) Elijah before and after each visit, because you never knew when you might be struck by lightning and stopped in your tracks. May as well say a little *duva* to the prophet and there's a duva for every occasion. Duva is a prayer from the Koran. From here, we could see St Elijah Peak on the other side of Clear Water, and next to it, Islamov Peak. It was a perfect twinning in a landscape animated by a force so old, it had no name.

Acivé crouched at the opening of The Passage like a midwife and burned some hemp on a portable stove to smudge the air of unhealth, then scattered flour at her feet.

'Come up,' she called to the Roma couple.

The couple wound their red thread around the nearest tree, climbed the ladder and stood before Acivé in their socks. Acivé turned to the gully with raised hands, palms up and began a prayer for fertility. The couple, who were Christian, were supposed to pray too, but they looked lost.

Acivé produced an apple from her apron, cut it in two, and gave them each half to eat, with the seeds. They ate it without joy. In a mixture of Bulgarian, Turkish and Arabic, Acivé prayed. She really stood before some nameless force, a mediator between the seen and the unseen, the great unmoving mountain and the small human in socks. In her blue mantle, perched over the abyss with the awakening forest around her, she was completely at home.

To see this scene – the eternal crone and her two charges with their apple like a gormless Adam and Eve – was so striking that even the lorry driver from Spain was silenced: briefly.

'This place is really something,' he said.

'People need places like this,' his wife said. 'It's therapy.'

I saw that the battle of the babi was not just about money. It was about the title of chief priestess. It was a cultural contest. These women understood that they were custodians of unity in a fractured world. The wheel of time had turned and their once-spurned customs had become valuable again. Being a priestess of The Passage gave them a livelihood, but also purpose and worth.

The Great Goddess has been worshipped in the eastern Mediterranean for about 8,000 years. The last two thousand have been difficult, yet here she was.

There were two holes at the stone: you climbed through the first, the baba received you and you slid down the second. When the driver's turn came, the first hole proved too small. His wife pushed him from below and baba Acivé pulled from above. The rest of us were in stitches, but baba Acivé smiled sympathetically.

'You're full of sin, that's what it is!' his wife quipped.

'You must eat less,' Acivé said. 'When the moon wanes, it's a good time to fast.'

The driver had no such intention. Acivé did fast.

'When the moon is thin you feel less pain,' Acivé said. 'And you lose weight faster.'

The truck driver grazed his knee on the way down and declined a second go.

'This is known in traditional medicine,' said the GP. 'Lunar waning is a good time for surgery, tissue healing and generally shedding.'

'The best time to come is full moon, Wednesdays and Saturdays,' said Acivé.

These were propitious days in everyday Balkan Islam where numerology, seasonal cycles and folk rites play a big role.

'Women understand the moon better than men,' Arif said. 'Women understand most things better than men.'

We were all lying next to him on the stone, our faces in the sun.

'And sacred places like this were always overseen by a woman who is a maiden or whose periods have stopped,' he said.

Acivé had never married. In these conservative communities, this was unusual.

'Have you noticed something about the names of peaks here?' said Arif.

They were named after people, sometimes saints.

'Female saints,' he said.

I looked at the map of Old Woods, then the whole of western Rhodope and the Pirin side of the valley too. There they were, in the hills: St Petka-Paraskeva, St Varvara, St Nedelya, St Marina, St Tekla (an early Roman martyr), many St Marys Mother of God, and Mitrovitsa, a feminised echo of the Zoroastrian Mitraic cult where Mithras of the mind vanquishes the bull of matter. Place-names like 'Holy name' or 'God's name' signalled a nature cult that became taboo under the Church but continued to be worshipped.

Amazingly, an annual Kurban feast was still held at Mitrovitsa Peak, at which only female animals were slaughtered in offering; a clue to the remote female divinity behind the name. And then there were the female names without a saint attached to them. They had been people of the mountain: shepherdesses, mystics, healers, cobblers, foresters, musicians, wives of local chieftans and people who had died on the hills or performed feats on them. It was impossible to know whether they had been women or men because the men's names had acquired a feminine suffix: Boyanitsa, Milushitsa, Stankovitsa, Vassilyovitsa, Orlovitsa, Vishteritsa (Witchy River) and Ablanitsa. Many of the villages had feminine names too.

Like the hills, the babi incarnated these avatars of the Mother Goddess.

Then it was my turn. I climbed through the first hole and emerged on the plateau. It was awkward and slippery and that was the idea, to squeeze through a threshold of discomfort and emerge anew. The early people of the mountain had venerated womb-like caves where sunlight enters like a seminal liquid and rebirth is mimed. Baba Ava prayed for my health:

'Bismillah Rahmani Rahim, make her healthy today, healthy tomorrow, chase away the djinns, the sheitans, bring her kismet, selemet, bereket. Amen!'

It was actually a much longer prayer, but this is all I could remember. Then I slid down the opening. The stone was polished from thousands of behinds. I scraped my knee like the driver and didn't repeat the experience.

At this point, baba Ava's party appeared in a single file among the ragged trees led by baba Ava herself, who was small and square and carrying her walking stick. With her flowing mantle and followed by fifteen people and her two drivers, she looked like Moses leading her people across the desert. She also looked in a foul mood. It was time for us to clear off.

I decided to stay on for the next shift, though. Baba Ava's two drivers gave Arif a dirty look as they passed each other on the path. Baba Acivé vanished up her goat path.

Baba Ava was a buxom woman with a large nose and the traditional braid down her back. Her face said: 'this is work, don't piss me off.' She nimbly climbed the ladder and assumed the position. She lit the small camping stove for the hemp-burning and said a prayer to 'open up the stone'.

'Tsk tsk tsk, this place is a dump,' she muttered. 'They don't clean up.'

It was true that baba Ava's team were the only ones who did clean-up operations, collecting hundreds of kilos of fabric and red thread several times a year in jumbo bags that lined the edge of the ragged glade and were eventually taken away by trucks. They used to burn them in the glade above, where night campers had heard eerie music and laughter, until it was prohibited because of the risk of fire.

Meanwhile, people queued up for the ladder in an orderly manner, instructed by the two drivers. One of them was baba Ava's nephew, a man in a tracksuit who liked to show people the 'hand print' and other marks in the rock; all of which looked recent. The commercial value of The Passage had obviously unlocked dormant entrepreneurial talent.

The other driver had a slow expression and served as bodyguard and intimidator for the baba Ava ring.

'Just for the record, there are no other babi,' he said, giving me a look, knowing I was here with the previous party. 'There's only one. The others are fake babi.'

But baba simply means old woman or crone. This was a place where women competed to be authentically old, or failing that, authentically crone-like.

Ava's knitted shoulder bag began to fill up with banknotes. People were generous. And desperate. Because of the sheer numbers, who kept coming down the path from additional vehicles driven by other men in her entourage until there were thirty people in the glade, she could not do individual rituals. She just muttered under her breath continuously, only breaking off to help the stuck, encourage the fearful and give hope to those weakened by despair and decay. Which was everyone.

'Come on now, you can make it!'

Like Acivé, she had a kind word for everyone and made people feel like she saw their pain and that it was okay to have this pain, but they also had to let go of it and she would help them. Women like her and Acivé have served as midwives, wish-granters, spell-lifters, spell-casters, medicine dispensers and physio- and psychotherapists for most of human history. They had held things together when things were falling apart. As political experiments came and went, as the patriarchy issued its decrees, ran its murderous bureaucracies, changed people's names and clothes and robbed until there was nothing left to rob, the babi of the mountain kept at it. That's why a folk festival, called Babinden, Baba's Day, dedicated to the midwife, crone and all-round healer of women's problems is still celebrated in January.

'This is a nightmare,' said a woman who hugged the stone wall without moving, as if the stone had literally petrified her. She had climbed the ladder and received baba Ava's prayer without hope. Her face said: All of life is a nightmare.

The faces in the queue agreed with her. They all wore wilted expressions, not seeing the sunshine, not hearing the birds, too busy taking morose selfies. They were like souls at the gates of hell. I don't know what each person's illness was; some didn't have illnesses, or not physical ones, but the group emanated something like a dark gas.

Baba Ava had allegedly cured herself of inoperable bowel cancer by coming to the rock. She'd then taken a vow to help people for as long as she could without asking for money. But the money came anyway and her entourage swelled. Now she needed the extra minders to orchestrate the crowd.

Unlike Acivé who lived an ascetic life, Ava was a standard baba. She had a large family, animals and a couple of big houses at the top of the village where visitors stayed and where she melted the bullet for them. But the numbers were overwhelming for one baba and it was handy to have several who were natural hostesses. Most of them did the bullet procedure as part of the package.

If you could ignore the politics which bred a malignant atmosphere not aligned with the benign purpose of the place, you saw that when she did her work, like the other women, Baba Ava embodied the qualities that visitors sought out like parched pilgrims. They were the qualities of this mountain. Having a baba to guide your passage through an imaginary threshold was to be cared for in a careless world.

And some expressed their gratitude in large sums of money. A man whose daughter had been cured had wanted to give Baba Ava 10,000 euros. She asked him to fix the road instead which made transport to The Passage easier. Another man had built a drinking fountain along the road, dedicated to Ava.

'She's a holy woman,' someone muttered.

Most of these people had exhausted all medical avenues. This was their last resort. They were prepared to try anything.

The glade darkened with fresh arrivals. A disturbed boy was put through the hole by his parents, screaming. Couples wanting children, couples with sick children, old obese people, young obese people, a mathematician with glasses whose education didn't allow him to believe in some stone, he said, but he didn't mind if his hypertension and diabetes spontaneously healed.

'This is my second time,' said the woman sitting next to me on the stone. She was a GP and she'd brought her sick friend. 'I feel different here. And it's nice to have somewhere to go,' she said.

The last pilgrim that day was a man of sixty, an ethnic Turk from the Danube, covered in faded army tattoos, who'd lost the use of his legs after a stroke and was puppet-walked, step by step, by his girlfriend and nephew. It took them an hour from the car to the stone. A couple of men stayed behind and helped him through The Passage. Baba Ava encouraged him from the top. Afterwards, the exhausted trio sat on the stone.

'See, you made it!' a kind helper said, and shook the man's limp hand while another slapped his back.

Tears rolled down the man's cheeks and he smiled his thanks. He had also lost his speech. I came to The Passage three days in a row and so did this trio. Before my unbelieving eyes, this man improved to a staggering degree. On the third morning, he was walking alone with the help of a cane. He was also smiling with a newfound confidence and his girlfriend and nephew beamed. A genuine transformation had taken place. As if the fire of life had been breathed back into him. I have no idea what caused it.

Baba Acivé was unsurprised.

'It cures all,' she said, 'If you believe in it, the stone will cure you. It was planted there by God.'

She needed no further analysis. A guy with progressive blindness had come here and restored his vision. I had difficulty accepting this, but it didn't matter whether I accepted it. Miracles don't need approval.

The following day, I came up again in the Jeep with Acivé, Arif, the couple from Spain who made the three trips after all but minus going through The Passage, and some new visitors. When we were done, I decided to stay on and wait for baba Ava's party alone. Arif was happy to leave me: because there's a keeper, the place is protected, he said.

For a blissful hour, I sat on the plateau facing the valley. An eagle hung motionless above. Being here on your own was a completely different experience. The sun rose from the east, illuminating this flank of the mountain, and the moon faded to the west. At once I grasped why some herbs, like verbena, were collected only when both moon and sun were visible. The stone emanated a friendly pulse. I melted into it.

It is because people are not in the habit of peace that The Passage made them well up with gratitude and stuff wads of cash into a baba's bag. Why did spontaneous healing occur here? I don't know, but I don't believe it was because of the geomorphology of the stone. More likely, it was a psychological phenomenon. The place was culturally designated as a passage and here, people had permission to experience miracles. We can have an encounter with the miraculous anywhere, but because of our injured instincts, we need designated passages. In a place like this, the psyche performs its own alchemy and healing can occur.

The smell was acrid; flour combined with burned hemp. Processed flour had replaced the cereal grains that the supplicant offers to the plant she digs out or to the *locus dei* of the stone. Cereals come from the goddess of harvest and fertility: Demeter-Ceres, avatar of the mother goddess, a direct link to the earth. The salt was a usual suspect too. Salt has purity and fixity and is one of the alchemical ingredients.

Then my reverie was broken by voices. The baba Ava party had arrived.

'Hello,' said the first arrival, a boy with dark circles under his eyes. 'Are you sad?'

'No,' I said. 'I'm resting.' He sat next to me.

'My dad is sad,' he said. 'I think it's because of me. Yes.'

The glade buzzed with arrivals. Baba Ava climbed the ladder with her knitted shoulder bag, muttering prayers or curses. The atmosphere changed. People brought their damned misery with them. The ritual began, a queue formed, the stench of burned hemp and flower wafted. Worried faces, slumped bodies, eyes avoiding contact, men holding their distended stomachs as if about to give birth, women clutching their handbags as if surrounded by thieves. Poor suffering humanity was here.

Baba Ava was quick to see what people had come for.

'Today one of you, next time three of you!' she called out to the young guy who had come asking for a baby.

Another formula of intention setting which I saw enacted by women in the valley was that the intention could be directed at the illness itself:

'Today I see you, tomorrow I don't see you.'

'Here now, gone tomorrow.'

The driver-nephew promised to show me a photograph of baba Ava on the stone with the spectre of a giant snake behind her. He never did and I was sure the photo was a dud. But it no longer mattered. The place had a life of its own. In a millennial pattern of dormancy and activity, it was simply doing its job. Baba Ava, baba Acivé, baba Nishidé, baba Nailé and baba Aishé were doing their job too. At a time when humans needed a stone for reasons of their own, the babi came out of obscurity with their sticks and their prayers, and donned the priestess mantle.

Some, who had seen the keeper, said that he could appear with two children at his sides. Some said he was so gentle-faced, he could be a woman. An androgynous, fluid quality permeated these impressions and this ambiguity was what 'the system' had always feared and tried to erase from the face of the land.

'How old are you?' the boy with the dark circles asked. He was fifteen but seemed younger and I feared he may stay a child forever. 'Guess,' I said.

'Twenty,' he said. 'Twenty-five.' He tried again, 'Sixty?'

'Not bad,' I said.

'I want to grow old,' he said. 'But first, I want to have a girlfriend. Yes.'

His sad-looking dad didn't make him go through The Passage. They just came for the ride once a year.

That day, a woman collapsed after going through the hole and had to be revived with water.

'We've seen it all,' the driver-nephew said to me. 'One time, a woman started wailing when she touched the stone and fell to the ground.' The following year, she'd returned to report that she was cured.

A couple popped out of the forest; he sweaty in a singlet with an unhinged look, she pallid in white clothes. They'd walked from Kribul. They looked like they'd escaped from the same asylum. He began to shake hands with people in a messianic way, like a politician.

There are two types of people: those who know they are unwell and those who don't. The second type are dangerous. They project their sickness onto the rest.

People in the queue shuffled their feet, trapped between the stone where Ava waited for them, and the messiah and the nymph who removed her shawl and tied it to a tree. When I heard they were walking back – they had energy – I cut my losses and caught a ride in one of baba Ava's Jeeps, where we were crammed, but at least everyone knew they were unwell.

There was a routine: morning trips to the stone with your baba and her driver, afternoon melt-the-bullet sessions at your baba's house and evening meals with the food you'd brought. Though some people ate at the Kebab café.

Baba Acivé often sat at the Kebab café with a couple of other babi and I joined them. They approved of my blue slacks, because blue repels the evil eye and there were people here with the evil eye.

Men with the evil eye were less common, but worse than women, they agreed.

'Never mind the evil eye,' said the Kebab owner, a pleasant woman in jeans and a T-shirt. 'Greed is the problem.'

'It's wrong,' said an alcoholic called Ahmet who hogged the space with his rants. The skull showed under his face. 'This idolatry of a stone. If you want God, here's the mosque. Or the church. It's gotta be man made. And if someone wants a baby, they need a cock, not a baba.'

'We opened this Kebab café for visitors,' said the café owner.

'But we don't know how long this craze will go on,' said her husband, another lorry driver.

'It has stuck a wedge in our community,' said another baba. 'The village is divided into camps. It all happened after they showed us on the telly.'

'It unlocked the greed in people,' said Ahmet. He ironed clothes in a sewing workshop for ASOS. The money was decent but the work humiliated him because it was "women's work". Still, it was a job and it meant that he didn't have to go picking fruit abroad.

'Sewing has replaced tobacco,' said the Kebab owner. 'Every family used to grow tobacco. Now it's down to a few.'

'They still punish themselves,' said Ahmet. 'Why?'

'Cos it's in our blood,' said one baba. She still grew tobacco. 'We can't give it up.'

'Our Basma is the sweetest. One kilo equals twenty kilos of any other tobacco, for taste,' said the lorry driver.

Tobacco connoisseurs know this to be true. The legendary Basma, an Oriental tobacco grown along the Mesta, is considered the finest aromatic tobacco in the world. It's also called Nevrokop tobacco, after the valley. It's the alkaline, sandy soil and the dry mountainous climate that make this crop possible only here. The story of Oriental tobacco is epic. Fortunes were made from it for a century and a half. In the 1960s, Bulgaria was the world's largest exporter of cigarettes in the world via the state holding company Bulgartabac, which was privatised during the 'murky years' of the 1990s. The new tobacco barons came down harshly on growers and undercut them to the point where they were losing money. These growers, who for generations had carried the state's economy on their backs in times of capitalism and Communism, were finally betrayed by the oligarchy. Hearts and lives were broken as the industry all but folded. The mass exodus of persecuted ethnic Turks in 1989 had been the beginning of the end; they had been the key workers of tobacco. Ten years after their traumatic exodus, the remaining tobacco growers and pickers were forced to work in Greece where climate conditions were similar, because the Nestos River and the Rhodope continued into Greece.

But some stayed. Today, in the valley, for a kilo of your dried Basma, you got 3 to 4 euros. Downstream in Greece, you got 18 euros. One kilo of dried Basma, after being mixed with broad-leaf varieties like Virginia, produces about sixty cigarette packs. Tobacco is still a lucrative business and the growers are poorer than ever. Tobacco is a tough crop to grow and it was a miracle that anyone still did it on either side of the border.

'You grow it from seed. You keep it from frost, you water it. Then you pick it, string it, dry it, pray over it,' said the baba who still did it.

I saw her wooden frames with strings of tobacco leaves, suncuring under a plastic roof. She and her daughter sat on a blanket and did it in the shade. It was the easiest part of the work. If your crop wasn't blighted and you didn't mind a chronic bad back, walking to your field in the darkness, and if you didn't mind yellow fingers and the smell of it, you could at a push make 250 euros a year.

'Today is Wednesday, a good day for work and healing,' said Acivé brightly.

'Wednesday and Saturday are good days,' agreed the Kebab owner.

'Every day is a good day when you know your days are numbered,' said Ahmet.

'All the days on Earth belong to the One above,' agreed the lorry driver and we watched a man covered in dust puff up the street. He had walked from the valley.

'Greetings, good people,' he smiled. His teeth were black in a medieval way.

'Are you lost?' Ahmet mocked him.

'Not at all, I'm glad to be here among the good people of this mountain,' said the man with such sincerity that the sneer went from Ahmet's face.

'He comes every year,' said the Kebab owner. 'And always has a kind word. When I see people like him, I remember that I'm the grandchild of refugees. They too walked over the mountains with just the clothes on their backs.'

In the wake of the First World War, border territories were redistributed.

'My grandfather's family walked here. Their village in Greece is down to four houses now,' she added. The family never went back.

'My grandfather got lost in that war,' said baba Acivé. 'Fighting somewhere in Greece. And my other grandfather too. The both of them. But my father survived the next war and lived to a hundred. He was the best. Took me with him everywhere, to country fairs and markets on horseback.'

'All the lads of the village wanted her,' said another baba about Acivé. 'Cos she was the prettiest.'

Acivé smiled with equanimity. It was hard to flatter or offend her.

'And in the end, she remained a maid,' said the other baba.

'I thought everyone had to marry,' I said.

'Aye, we do,' said Ahmet. He was married twice.

'Not everyone,' said Acivé firmly. 'Only those who want to.'

She hadn't wanted to. She had been devoted to her parents. There was something devotional about her. While others were concerned with houses, ostentatious weddings, more grandchildren, she focused on staying tuned to some inner rhythm. Most people have an active outer life, Acivé had an active inner life. That's why she was interesting. Her idea of success was to maintain harmony with all around her, every moment of every day, and to help, but only those who wanted it. She did not force her help on you.

She told me how, twenty years ago, walking to the nearest town, two hours over the hills, she had seen a woman on a rock, bent over. But when the woman lifted her face, Acivé was stunned to see that it was made of light, immaterial. Acivé ran away. When she looked back, the woman was gone.

'She was a holy woman, an *evliya*,' Acivé said. 'Someone killed her for a piece of land and she was showing herself to ask a favour, but I was so scared, I told people about it and she never appeared in my dream.'

Evliyas deliver their messages in dreams but sometimes they appear in the waking world too. It is an unwritten law of the Otherworld that you mustn't blab about its visitations. The numinous requires discretion.

'How did you know about the stolen piece of land?'

Acivé smiled. 'People think you can only know things if you're told or if you read it in the newspaper. But you can know in other ways.'

After buying a shiny new lead bullet from the shop, I followed Acivé to a dark house next to the mosque. Here, she melted-the-bullet. It is the most popular ritual in folk diagnostics. It uses three substances in a way that can be described as basic alchemy: fire, lead and water.

'Everything has imitators,' she said, 'except lead. Lead doesn't lie.'

It was sympathetic logic: lead couldn't be falsified, therefore lead didn't falsify. She asked me to hold my bullet while she lit a small camping gas stove on the carpeted floor. It was a gift from a man whose wife had recovered after Acivé poured her a bullet.

She placed the bullet in a big ladle and held the ladle over the gas fire until it began to melt, saying a duva under her breath. When the lead turned liquid, she brought the ladle head to my feet and 'scanned' them. Then she poured the liquid lead into a dish of water and it solidified again. She studied its shape. It was a regular shape.

'Your feet are fine,' she pronounced, and held the ladle over the fire again, to re-melt the lead and repeat the procedure for my knees, abdomen, heart, back, neck and head. It took a while and was strangely relaxing. She looked like a magician-forger, pouring and decanting the liquid state of her charges and I wished I was her apprentice.

'Oh, there's a problem with the belly!' she said when the lead crackled and spat. I did have abdominal pain that worried me a bit. The lead hardened in a prickly shape which indicated disturbed energy. She repeated it until the lead came out round.

'It's cleared. Nothing serious,' she concluded, satisfied.

I had no understanding of the chemistry of lead or sympathetic magic, but I was still relieved. With some people, she had to re-melt the bullet so many times that it fell into crumbs and several bullets were needed.

The babi here used lead, but in other regions they used coal: one or three hot coals named for the patient were placed in water, just like the melted lead. Fire is the activator, the named object is the mediator and water is the environment. These were very ancient 'reading' practices – lead, coal, coffee grounds, tea leaves, smoke, sea conches, animal bones, broken egg, wine, blood.

'There was a mute child,' Acivé said. 'But the problem showed up not in his head, but in his heart and arms.'

'A woman came with her breast removed. Cancer. She was unhappy all her life, an orphan. Never felt loved. The cancer was gone, but the bullet still picked up a lot of trouble with the heart.'

She had complete faith in the lead because she had complete faith in the invisible laws of the universe. That gave her the serenity of the wise crone that is so rare. Most people don't become wise, they just become old. At the end of the session, she dropped the lead in a small jar of water, dabbed my forehead, lips and chest with the water and asked me to sip from it, then threw the water into the sink.

'We flush illness away,' she said.

This is what the anthropologist James Frazer termed 'sympathetic magic'. He found two main forms of it worldwide – homeopathic and contagious – and the babi of Kribul used both. The first is based on the 'law of similarity', like the red rope and the clothes people left on the stone to stand in for them. And the second is based on the 'law of contact', like the bullet. Distance made no difference in the world of energy healing. I saw Acivé perform a bullet ritual for a woman who was not there and who had requested it by phone; the lead was intended to be in contact with her imaginal self.

It was a kind of performance art, too. Its lowest aim was lucre. Its highest aim was spontaneous healing; a phenomenon dismissed by mainstream Western medicine, but well known in Eastern traditions. Spontaneous healing is contact with the philosopher's stone. And the philosopher's stone can only be produced through 'art' – nature alone does not produce it in the way that it produces crystals and salt. Art can be many things but for the babi, it was this. The Passage was their studio, the mountain their canvas. Ancient mysteries were their palette, their walking sticks were brushes, prayer and poetry their language, and people their spectators and collaborators. Healing was their holy grail.

I kept the lead which had cooled into a pleasing shape in whose magma swirls Acivé showed me an 'angel'. Some wore their bullet as an amulet. I keep mine on my desk and I used to put it in my mouth occasionally and taste the metallic coolness, like those soldiers during the First World War who sucked lead bullets to rehydrate when they had no water; until I remembered that lead is toxic.

'You are well, may Allah look after you,' Acivé concluded and asked where I was going next.

'Ah, The Birches,' she smiled. 'That's Pirin. It's different.'

How is it different?

'Pirin is a crystal,' she said.

Yet I didn't know anyone there. Here I had friends. The people, the houses where I slept and visited, the plants, the paths, the trees under which I lay too briefly. The Old Woods had welcomed me as one of them.

Acivé was poor, uneducated and had slept alone for seventy years, yet she had a better relationship with life than most people I knew.

Not because she was simple, but because she was wise. She was surrounded by coarse people but knew to tune into the non-human world for guidance.

Acivé was off to evening prayer and invited me to the mosque, but I had a date with the goatherds.

'Come again,' she smiled before she limped off. 'You know where to find me.'

It made me happy that I knew where to find her.

The Passage ritual was place-specific. I wanted to see a local ritual that was not attached to a place, so Arif took me to a healer hodja in a village upstream from Kribul.

The hodja received me in his kitchen after finishing work in the local sewing factory. He was a man of the people and did his hodja duties on the side. There was a loaf of bread on the table.

'Are you hungry? I can get tomatoes from the garden.'

He filled a piece of paper with his small writing and gave it to me. It was a Koranic prayer for exorcising unclean forces. I was to place the paper in a pot of water and sugar, and sip the water for seven days. He instructed me to cross a running stream seven times, throw a pebble in it and state what I wished to cleanse from my life.

'Water heals because water has intelligence,' he said. 'But it must be clean.'

I asked him how he became a healer. That's why I had come, pretending to bring a problem. His response made me feel the weight of my own small lie.

'I had a dream,' he said. 'I was by the river and I saw Archangel Michael next to Mohammed, together with Isa. That's Jesus in Islam. And I saw Mary the mother of Isa in white, like a Greek statue. I had that dream three times. Then I knew this was a calling. I had to help people for the rest of my life. I'll get you some tomatoes from the garden.'

Another hodja nearby operated from a small mosque. He was a professional cleric. Every Friday after the prayer called *djumaya*, the mosque turned into a consultation room and the tiny courtyard filled with people: Muslims, Christians, atheists, people with doctorates and illiterate Roma.

The hodja was an urbane middle-aged man with a taste in good shirts.

'I have two types of visitors. Clients and patients. The patients have health problems. The clients have other problems.'

The mosque was cosy, with an iron stove that boomed cheerfully in winter. In one corner sat the hodja on the floor, cross-legged behind a low table covered by a towel, to protect it from dripping liquids and burns during incineration rituals. I half expected him to levitate on his rug. On the table were sheets of paper for jotting prayers, numerological sequences and astrological charts, a small vial of an aromatic liquid, and the Koran. There were people with sick children, troubled families, siblings fighting over houses. The most difficult cases were those of possession. But what is possession?

'Possession is when an entity enters your auric field. It happens when your auric field is weak. You can strengthen it with prayer.'

This time I brought a real problem. He gave me a piece of paper he'd finely inscribed with a prayer in Arabic and dabbed with the pink aromatic liquid: amber, rose and saffron. Again, the instruction was to place it in a jar of water and sip the water.

'Water has a memory. The water becomes energetically encoded with the prayer and drinking it, you drink the intention.'

I asked him how he became a hodja.

'In the 1990s, I was a lost soul. There was no work and I got into treasure hunting. These hills are full of it. I climbed peaks and vales. But I was looking for myself. Then one night, I had a dream. I walked down into the river gully and a traveller came my way. A giant. "Merhaba," I said. "Merhaba," he said and we shook hands. His thumb was soft, without a joint. I still get shivers in my back. "Make a wish," he said, "but you must pick: it's either for this world, or for the other world." I said: "make it for the other world." The traveller smiled and vanished. I woke up and enrolled in the Institute for Islamic Studies in the capital.'

To deepen his studies he became an apprentice to a cleric in the village of Ribnovo, who had a large esoteric library. The young hodja climbed peaks and vales to visit his mentor. He crossed and re-crossed the river of his dream. He was still looking for himself, but this time as a different kind of treasure hunter.

And the thumb?

'That's why I get shivers. Prophet Hadar was charged with a mission: to appear on Earth momentarily when someone is at a crossroads. He has a jointless thumb. If you shake hands with Hazreti Hadar, you know it's him.'

Momentary manifestations, instant travel, telepathic communication, shape-shifting and dreams as gateways to expanded perception: these are trademarks of mystical Islam and of all the mystical traditions from the East. This organic blend of metaphor and dogma is typical of home-grown Balkan Islam. It can be traced back to the medieval Sufis who came from Central and western Asia to Spain and the Balkans. They were the first Neoplatonists and the first alchemists of post-antiquity.

The hodja took a sip from a small bottle.

'Nigella seed oil,' he said. 'Avicenna wrote about it. It is written in the Koran: there is a remedy for every ailment except death and that remedy is Nigella seed.'

I went to a grocer's in the city in the valley and bought myself a small bottle that came from Egypt. It is bitter, spicy and makes me dream of the black soil of the Nile.

'How did you learn about us?' Arif asked me when we walked the hills above the village.

'By following the Mesta River,' I said. 'One thing leads to another. It has so many branches that you always end up somewhere new.'

'And after Kribul, you'll continue to follow the river,' Arif smiled. 'How fortunate you are. I'd like to do that too.'

'You know,' he went on, 'there are passages like this all over the Rhodope. Passages, cliff niches and other strange things. But the rest is down to interpretation,' he said.

Unbelievable belief, hopeless hope, magical miracles, youthful youths. The conversation between humans and the mountain had never stopped.

We visited two overgrown fields, sites of an early Christian grave-yard that had fallen into disuse when people converted to Islam, and the old Muslim cemetery. Both were completely destroyed, first the Christian, then the Muslim one. The only remnants were oblong turbaned gravestones inscribed in Arabic and uprooted like teeth and the base of the medieval church. Wild fruit trees covered the hills and beyond them, anaemiac pines were planted in the wake of the old wood.

'We are a people without a history,' Arif said. 'Because we have no storytellers in Kribul. Yet a lot has happened here. Sometimes I want to write it all down, but it's not my forte. Still, we have the mountain with its mysteries. And we still have water.'

'Over there,' he pointed above the last houses, 'is the mother.'

'The mother?'

'The mother spring. The main water spring.'

On our way down, we passed a woman with matted hair who was digging small grooves in the forest and damming them with stones. It was a lot of work and she was absorbed in it. She had heavy bags full of stones that she moved around. Her hands were covered in cuts.

'She was fine,' said Arif. 'Then she went to the city to study, and when she returned, she lost her mind. Something happened to her there.'

Something that couldn't be named. The sky turned pink. We passed Arif's empty family house where he had grown up. Last year, his elderly father wandered into the hills, in the direction of The Passage. He had been hearing voices, music. There had been a search but his body was never found. I wondered what he had experienced out there, in his last hours.

The people of the Rhodope have been seeing spectral merry-makers for ages. It is always the same. A party appears; music and laughter, a weird procession. Usually in the darkness of the early morning when people went to the fields. Liminal places and times; on the edge of the forest, outside the village. Then the party passes right through the stunned witness as if through air, vanishing altogether and the witness knows that this is another reality. People put this down to the many necropoli and ruined dwellings. The past surfaced and made contact with the present. Or something altogether out of time, a parallel dimension.

'Some things we can't explain, yet,' Arif said. 'The question is: can we accept that they are there, independently of us?'

We stopped at the goatherds' house to buy fresh cheese. He was a man with a tired face and she was large and cheerful, sat on a low tree stump like a dairy queen. They were poor and overworked. A kilo of fresh, organic goat cheese cost just a few euros. The work of the earth's carers has been debased by the corporate mafia that eviscerates the mountain without putting anything back. In the morning, he took the 200 goats into the hills and in the evening they milked them and processed the milk, which was sold for small change. But she was a believer in the health benefits of goat milk, and proud that her children had never been sick.

Every time I bought a litre of warm milk from them, or a half-kilo of curd, they gave me half a litre *halal*. They had too much milk, not enough appreciators and big hearts.

Halal among Balkan Muslims is an offering, a gesture of generosity that brings back abundance. It comes from Koranic law and means permitted, as opposed to *haram*: forbidden, taboo, closed. Halal is yes, haram is no. In all my time among Our Folk, I didn't hear haram once but often enjoyed halal.

'What is she doing with those stones?', I'd asked Arif when we'd passed the 'mad' woman.

'Digging channels,' he said. 'To connect to the river. To bring the river to the village and cure it. She thinks that the whole village is sick.'

The river was a long way down and the mother spring was a long way up. She was here all year round, building and demolishing her waterless channels.

Before we greeted her, I'd seen her talking to someone who was visible only to her, perhaps a tree spirit and she seemed happy with her project, happier than those who arrived in Kribul with their everyday madness looking for a quick fix.

We had greeted her and she had smiled. It was the smile of one who had crawled through The Passage but hadn't returned because it was safer on the other side. The whole global village was sick, she was right about that. She knew how far the river was and that there were many more stones to be moved: but she would keep trying.

It is the only thing left, her smile said: to keep trying.

THE BIRCHES
EARTH

Place and mind may interpenetrate till the nature of both is altered.
I cannot tell what this movement is except by recounting it.

Nan Shepherd, *The Living Mountain*

BIRCH, BIRCHES

To reach The Birches you climbed from the floor of the valley up Stormy River.

Tucked out of view, Lazhnitsa, Kornitsa and Breznitsa were three rhyming villages united by a river and a fate. Fate and a river are alike. They flow in one direction only and there's no avoiding them.

Breznitsa meant The Birches and it was the highest village of Stormy River. Above it were glacial lakes.

During the 1972–1973 terror campaign against the Pomaks, two places rebelled en masse: Kornitsa and Breznitsa. It was the beginning of a bitter winter when the people of Kornitsa came out on the square to protest the changing of their names. To wait, in their own words, for someone to come and explain why they had to change their names and the names of their dead.

For three months, the people of Kornitsa camped on the square with fires in the snow. This was protest and safety in one; to prevent militias bursting into their homes. Their resistance – they were unarmed, isolated from the rest of the country due to an information blackout and surrounded by soldiers – represents a civic achievement in the history of Communist Europe.

The People's Army took up position in the hills. Until midnight every day, the army blasted out Soviet songs through megaphones, to break people through noise. But they didn't budge. At the end of the winter, the Birchers heard that their neighbours in Kornitsa were under attack and set out to help; not down the road blocked by tanks, but over the hills. They crossed streams and waded through snow. But when they came to the boundary river between grazing lands, the army opened fire on them. A schoolboy fell dead. After the peaceful protest was broken up by the army – with the help of a fire engine that sprinkled people with boiling water – the beatings and arrests began in the two rhyming villages.

A woman with a child strapped to her back was shot in the front but lived. Three more men were killed point blank and hundreds of men and women were savagely battered with stakes and batons, and the border army dogs were set on them. Some died later or were left crippled. A pile of twenty or thirty men lay broken by the mosque after a beating, their blood running in the gutter. Others were sent to labour camps, including the two leaders of the Kornitsa revolt, where they endured ten years of forced labour. 'It was hard,' said one of them in modest understatement in a short documentary, 'I gave the best years of my life to prison. But I don't regret it. We did the right thing, we showed the world that we didn't agree with their policies.'

Their charge had been 'conspiracy against the state'. These men and women, labourers of the land, had faced the guns with nothing but their bodies. In the aftermath of the pogrom, a curfew was introduced in the three rhyming villages. Women had their trousers and headscarves cut up with scissors and men wearing the small knitted skull cap were refused entry to shops. Silk kaftans, the padded striped overcoats worn by women on special occasions and reminiscent of Mongolia, were burned. The state even banned the sale of silk because it was a staple of Pomak identity. And instead of the customary black overcoat called *feredjé* and worn on top of other clothes by women when working (cotton) or feasting (velvet), the state issued synthentic worker's mantles for them; Soviet-*kolhoz* style with buttons at the front. If you wanted to go outside covered, you had to wear this. But they were so ugly that women barricaded themselves in at home or wore traditional clothes and walked long distances between work and home because rural buses were under orders not to take 'persons in traditional dress'. Schoolgirls had to swap colourful shalvars for tracksuit pants. Colour was banned in favour of greyness, in clothes, names and behaviour. This is why Pomak women in the region still wear the blue mantle reminiscent of Soviet-era factories. It's a remnant of that time.

When the border opened in 1990, forty per cent of the people of Kornitsa emigrated to Turkey: two thousand people. Even with the

regime gone and people's names and freedoms recovered, the hurt
ran too deep. The exiles, who spoke no Turkish, were given social
support by the Turkish government and settled in émigré colonies
near the Aegean coast.

Even if you didn't know this, there was something bold about Stormy
River's sharp twists and crumbly crags. It was rebel country. The soil
turned sandy. New peaks appeared that were not visible from the valley. The atmosphere changed, as if a veil lifted.

I arrived in The Birches at dusk. Women in floral shalvars sat on
benches placed against the walls of their houses, facing the street in
the time-honoured way. They scanned my registration plate and
became busy with speculation. Tourists were rare and you were
assumed to be visiting relatives. It was the start of preserve-making
season. Older women sat around bubbling cauldrons in their courtyards, bent forwards on low stools, elbows propped on knees and I
was ten years old again, elated by arrival in my great-aunt's village.
They were making *lyutenitsa*, pesto from tomatoes and peppers.

Younger women walked home from one of the sewing workshops. The Birches and the rest of the Mesta basin was a major
tailoring hub in Europe. The clothes, stitched from rag to label by
women and men here will next turn up in your nearest highstreet
shop with a label that says 'made in the EU'.

In the main square, where a small memorial listed the five killed
during the winter of terror, preparations were afoot. It was day one
of Kurban Bairam, the second-largest festival here after Ramadan.
Bairam simply means festival and is also a male name. Stalls sold
doughnuts and a DJ was setting up.

The Birches was a village the size of a town. But out of its four
thousand people, those not bent over sewing machines worked
abroad as builders, fruit pickers, tree planters, poultry farm workers,
drivers and warehouse managers, which is why it felt quiet. Across
from the mosque was a church. The Muslims helped build it when
the Christians arrived one hundred years ago and the Christians
helped rebuild the mosque after it was torched in the Balkan Wars
around the same time.

The evening swallows favoured the minaret. They murmured in the pink sky, making shapes. The air was cooler than in the valley.

Metko Fettahov was waiting for me at the outdoor village café. He rose slowly and we shook hands. It was warm and his hand was damp, or perhaps that was my hand.

'Welcome,' he said. 'Can I offer you an ice cream? I'm happy you're here. I hope you're not disappointed. You've come a long way.'

Metko Fettahov was the person behind the photographic archive which had made me come to The Birches. He was a tall, stooped man with gentle blue eyes. He turned his head slowly and looked at you with knowingness. He was the chronicler-scribe of The Birches and had compiled a visual and written history of his community. On my veranda in the Empty Village, I'd scrolled through a hundred years of life in The Birches. Men with generous faces and women with impish eyes smiling behind white veils that didn't quite cover their mouths, children and animals everywhere in the mud, weddings, stilted public events and visits from officials where people's eyes were full of all that was happening to them but could not be articulated, courting couples, secret Kurban Bairam outings on the glacial lakes in the opulent Pomak dress that was forbidden in the lower world of state control, seasonal carnival village processions with men dressed as characters, one of them a 'baba', another on stilts and a band with skin drums and trumpets. And youths in too-tight 1980s trousers and polo necks with transistor radios and the bad haircuts we all had then. At twenty, Metko had already had a knowing look that set him apart.

Who were these people, so familiar yet unknown? Their faces talked to me. I had the odd feeling of having been among them. Metko and his wife Asiné were captured over thirty years. Clean-faced and shy, courting, in hiking leggings and jackets at the glacial lakes, then married, then with two skinny sons, then Asiné with her moody smile going about her chores, gathering herbs, in a stripy silk kaftan with ornamental belt buckles, a striped apron and headdress like a mountain queen, Asiné carrying a festive loaf of bread, then with long flowing hair and a distant look in Istanbul, Asiné in the last stages of illness, smiling without eyebrows, aged forty-six.

Metko was a builder by profession and an intellectual by vocation.

He shuffled around casually in rubber slippers and old trousers, collecting and telling stories with a measured passion. Like a Diogenes of his community, he went about with a metaphorical lantern, looking for a human being.

'We are not what we are,' he was fond of saying about the Pomaks. And by extension, everybody else.

It sounded cryptic but later, I grasped its meaning.

'Where is she from?' someone called out with a shy chuckle from one of the wooden tables where men sat hunched, their faces full of hardship. The older ones especially. One man had no arm. Another had no eye. There was a quiet old man who had been in a labour camp and was keen to tell me 'a book's worth of stories', but I didn't make time for him and the following summer he died.

'From Scotland,' Metko shouted back, though we stood a few steps away. The men nodded, unconvinced, trying not to stare.

'People shout here,' Metko said. 'Don't mind them. And they have verbal diarrhoea. You ask them a question and two hours later you're still here. It's because they carry a hundred years' worth of stuff.'

Metko had worked in Scotland where he'd broken his arm in a construction accident and had come home before the end of his contract. He was determined not to go abroad again, picking their berries and building their houses, when we have everything here, he said. Now he was fitting out a neighbour's new house – marble, tiles, shiny surfaces. Shine was favoured as a mark of success.

'It's ironic,' he said. 'While my wife *rahmetliykata* was alive, I was always away trying to earn a crust. And now I have no need to go anywhere but she is gone.'

Rahmetlia is 'the late one, mercy upon his soul', from the Arabic *rahmet* for mercy.

'Anyway,' he rose to leave, 'you'll want to get settled in the hotel. I'm sorry that I can't invite you round. I'm a widower, my house is not fit for guests. But please know that our hospitality is still alive.'

And he shuffled with his invisible lantern across the still-empty square to his house full of ashtrays.

At the café where men gathered, shaking hands with 'Happy Bairam', I saw a familiar face. Two faces: the father and son were copies of each other. I'd briefly visited The Birches before and had coffee here.

' 'Welcome back,' the son shook my hand.

'Excellent, you're back!' the father whispered with damaged vocal chords. 'Let me get you a coffee.'

I'd sat down that first time, noticing there were only men, and got talking to a younger guy. Piled up behind him were bags of mushrooms just arrived from the forest. I'd asked what he did.

'Mushrooms,' an emphysema voice whispered. 'Mushrooms and women.'

His father had materialised and was answering on his behalf, although he was clearly talking about himself. I bought some ceps. I'm off for mushroom today, the locals said, or I'm off for blueberry, singular. The only difference from Old Woods was that many more locals foraged here. There was no Roma 'hood to rely on. The son sold them to an Italian dealer in the city and everyone made a cut.

'If not quite a killing,' the father whispered. He'd been operated on for laryngeal cancer and lost his ability to outshout others. Father and son had specked eyes that were on the lookout for all sorts of opportunities. Dealership ran in the family.

People poured into the square from the steep streets.

'Happy Bairam, happy Bairam,' he shook hands with men and women.

'I can't stand these family festivals,' he muttered to me. Children played hide and seek among the adults. Street lights were lit.

I'd heard that there were a dozen ruins above The Birches. 'Yes,' he said, 'but beware the sheepdogs. Shepherds are forced to take their flocks higher. Climate change. And the sheepdogs attack so don't hike alone.'

Where were the birches that the village was named after? I'd expected lots of birches.

'There was once an old birch in the heart of the village,' he whispered. 'Nobody remembers when it was cut down.'

Without memory, there is no story to tell. Without story, there is no memory.

'Do you like our women's dress?' another man asked shyly. He had battered hands. 'Back in the day, gold coins were sewn into them.'

So they could ride away quickly in case of attack with their fortune on their bodies and inside their horses' saddles. Some of the women arriving in the square wore the opulent shalvars and kaftans with bright shawls around their necks, as if they'd just stepped off a Silk Road caravan. The DJ put the first track on. The melody coiled like opium smoke with a disco beat to ground it. It invited you to step into the East and enjoy yourself.

The man talking to me was a builder who picked Scottish strawberries in summer. Did I think Scotland would break away from England? He could understand if they did. They had whisky, hills, people, water. 'A bit like here,' I said.

'Ach, we're poor,' he said. 'But we have the best nature.'

He told me to look out for a drinking fountain en route to the hotel.

'I built it,' he smiled and I glimpsed the confidence of belonging that had been chipped by harsh living in foreign lands. 'For *sevap*.'

Sevap: merit in the Muslim moral codex. It was the only drinking fountain between the village and the guesthouse. The Birches was the end of the road but the road didn't end with The Birches. It climbed upstream past fields, glades and a waterfall, to where locals had second houses. To build a second house was a mark of success.

The Birches Hotel was one such house, but built with EU funds. It overlooked a clearing inside a pine forest. Parked cars and the three-storey guesthouse was lit up like a wedding cake with pop-folk music blasting from speakers. The outside patio was full of demure dining families that didn't match with the music and its sexually explicit lyrics. Typically three generations marked Bairam together.

'Ah, we thought the bears got you!' A guy balanced plates with fragrant lamb, potatoes and salads on his forearms. That was the co-owner of the hotel. They were brother and sister. She was an elegant woman in jeans, a school teacher who ran the reception while her husband, a social worker, ran the kitchen. Their father Shefket drew up crafty business schemes for his family and looked after the grounds.

'And special guests,' said Shefket and invited me to his table where he was eating a potato salad. He was from an old clan who'd owned a lot of land.

'Tomorrow, I'll bring you my superfood,' Shefket lit up at my food questions. 'Since you like yogurt.'

He often slept in a back room with jars of creamy sheep's yogurt that became my staple diet. Each morning, I'd eat a pot of plain yogurt on the patio bathed by the sunrise while Shefket watered his marigold bed.

When the music beats ceased the cars disappeared, including Shefket's communist-era relic, and the restaurant was closed by the departing family. I stood on my balcony.

This was my first night in Pirin Mountain. I didn't really know where I was. There was no mobile signal and there was just one other occupied room, a city couple who seemed to have eloped. Pines closed in on all sides like a living wall and although the hotel was at the top of the road, it was also at the bottom of something. The boundary between the hotel grounds and the forest was a dragon-snake carved from dwarf mountain pine.

The moon hung big and buttery above the sharp outline of the pines. The day's heat had vanished and the air was cold on the skin. The forest silence was like a well with nothing in it, except the sound – clear and perfect, rising to touch your face – of spring water.

Shepherd's food

Sheep's milk, raw.

Simmer until it thickens, stir constantly. Drink warm or cold. It is dense with creamy lumps. It tastes of woods, wild grasses and wool, of seasons and sunrises unfolding out of sight, of something that you can't name anymore.

If you drink it in the morning, you don't get hungry all day, that's how nutritious it is, said Shefket. Pure protein and fat. Your consumption drops, but you are fully nourished. This is how shepherds kept their strength up all day in the milking season. Can you taste the thirty-six herbs that the sheep graze on? Some of them unique to Pirin. And Pirin is, how can I say it? Infinite. Not at all like a human life.

BY FATMÉ'S FOUNTAIN

'A human life is so short,' Shefket said. 'We forget what's important until it's gone.'

It was my second day. The grounds had such a pure atmosphere that I lost all desire to go anywhere, even down to the village where Metko expected me. I sipped Mursala tea by a marble fountain in the wood. Its cold water couldn't be turned off. It came through four spouts with the full force of the spring. I heard the water all night from my room, a conversation without words. The name Fatmé was inscribed inside a heart: this was a memorial fountain and after watering his marigolds, Shefket joined me with a jar of his superfood.

'Do you have sheep's yogurt in Scotland?' he enquired.

It's actually impossible to find sheep's milk in Scotland. Shefket was puzzled.

'But Scotland is the land of sheep! Isn't it wasteful to rear them just for meat?'

At some point not long ago, the Western world stopped drinking ewe and goat milk and turned to industrially produced cow's milk, to whose sugary lactose many are intolerant. Recipes with sheep's milk feature in *A Modern Herbal* and ten medicinal plants start with the word 'shepherd's', including the sea plantago so beloved of sheep, that in Wales they called it sheep's herb. Is there more than one reason for the decline of other animal milks in favour of cow, or is it as simple as this: industrial-scale farming? These were the things I pondered by Fatmé's fountain.

The next morning, Shefket brought me 'smoky milk'. It was freshly fermented ewe's milk cooked over slow heat, so the taste was slightly burned and bracing. It had lactobacilli that replenished your gut flora. Shefket had developed health problems after his wife's death. Fatmé had been the first university-educated woman of her generation in The Birches. After her death, he threw himself into building her fountain, the mosaic-inlaid pond and the picnic area. He'd kept sheep in the pen by the hotel, once a communist cooperative, but it was hard work and by the time you paid a shepherd to take them out to pasture and back each day, then milk them and process the milk, you might as well buy the milk from one of the small-scale farmers in the village. The resident sheepdog, Lucky, lived alone in the sheep pen. Until a few weeks ago, Lucky was chained outside. But a bear came to the compound and he lashed out. He got off with minor wounds but now Lucky was kept inside.

We walked to the mosaic-inlaid pond beyond the fountain. Shefket had built this too. The pond had its own microclimate. Cold, with a crystalline note. Whenever I lay by the pond with the dark pines above, I drifted and the forest whispered.

'Exactly as I intended it,' he beamed.

Out of the woods appeared a mare with a colt. Their eyes, their whole bodies, shone with a wild intelligence. But they were not wild.

'Gone are the days of wild horses,' said Shefket. 'And this is not the original forest.'

The beeches were thin and the pines were not native; the forest floor was pretty dead. Shefket had seen the ancient forest with beech this big – he opened his arms – giants, centuries old. They were all cut down by the communists, sold to the Soviet Union and hurriedly replaced with conifers.

'If you want to see what Pirin was like, go to Eagle Reserve.'

Where belladonna grows.

'The only true resident of the original forest was the Netikin,' said Shefket.

The word struck me at once.

'The mythical giant of Pirin,' said Shefket. 'The Netikin travels across the mountain fast. He communicates with all living things.'

'Was the Netikin benevolent?'

'I don't know. He's wild, like the mountain. But he is a person, with a body.'

Just not a human person.

Pirin was a masculine massif; from its name to its ascending energy. Although as soon as you called it 'the mountain' it became feminine, because a mountain and a forest are feminine in Slavic languages. So are rivers and valleys.

And the horses?

'These are domesticated, but there is a guy with semi-wild horses. They go to The Meadow and that's where he sleeps.'

In autumn, he brought them down and Shefket let him sleep inside the disused sheep pen, on a sheepskin, with the horses next to him.

'This spring we treated two of his foals in the pen. Their necks bitten by wolves. But the horseman's not easy to catch.'

The Meadow was a highland area, gateway to a trail that took in several glacial cirques. It was a steep three hour climb from here to The Meadow. Horseman walked it in an hour, Shefket said, and should be making a living with his skills.

'He can catch a wild horse with a rope. He talks to them. But in this country the hard-working honey bee gets nothing and the drone gobbles the honey.'

I noticed that people here didn't talk about conquering peaks.

'We have a different mentality from Westerners,' Shefket agreed. 'But living here, you just know that you can't conquer the mountain. It's bigger than you. And why conquer it? You want to be in harmony with it.'

Here, it had been about eking out a living from the mountain: the sandy soil; the edible forest; the seasonal harvests; the ebb and flow of Stormy River.

How do you cope with a failed crop? You replant for next year and go foraging because the forest doesn't fail.

There was an expression, *bayr budala,* from hill and fool, to describe a person seized by a senseless need to climb a peak.

'Instead of relaxing by a fountain like this,' said Shefket.

In the last generation, heavy toil had given way to a sedentary existence and very few Birchers hiked. They drove their 4x4s and picnicked by the nearest water source; a reaction against the back-breaking toil of their parents. The only people who walked the forests were mushroomers and the last of the shepherds.

'Take a walk,' he said, 'to feel the spirit of the forest. Take Lucky with you.'

If I got lost, the river would bring me back.

The river was lively. I'd spend the following winter in the valley and after torrential rains, I saw why it was called Stormy; it rose vertically like a dragon, formed new waterfalls and cut off the three rhyming villages from the valley.

Shefket resumed his groundskeeping. He'd been a physical education teacher and I was surprised to hear from a former student how once, a boy masturbated in class and Shefket lined all the boys up and beat the palms of their hands with a willow branch in a rage. But like plants, people have different faces through the seasons of their lives.

Sleep was so nourishing, I woke at sunrise. Mornings were cool. I ventured up the dug-out forest road. The odd mushroomer on a motorbike purred past and nodded good morning. The blue-flowered chicory brightened as I climbed. I stopped at a drinking spout dedicated to a man with a short life.

A retired shepherd from The Birches slept in a shelter here, because it felt good to sleep outside with a blanket and he repaired the shelter for something to do. His greetings were like the morning itself. He'd come down the road, barefoot and skinny, open his arms and call out:

'This is Piriiin! Good morning my friends!'

There was just me, but he was greeting all living things. I'd sit with him by the spout and have a dram from his homemade brew.

'Have you heard of the giant of The Birches?' he said one morning. 'The Netikin?'

'I'm his nephew,' he went on and I realised who he meant.

I'd seen photos of this man in Metko's archive, from the Kadiev clan. He had been a log transporter, eight-foot tall. He'd pick up a log and chuck it onto the horse saddle. When crossing flooded rivers with his mule, he'd pick it up like a goat and carry it across. The valley remembered him: for his size and for his kindness.

'Places round here are named after him and our clan,' said the retired shepherd. 'Kadiev Peak, Kadiev Meadows.'

Courted by the Nazis in their racist projects when they camped

here en route to Greece, the giant Kadiev fled to the giant forest
where no one could follow him. His father had been tortured to
death before his boyish eyes by armed bands in 1912; Kadiev wanted
no part in any kind of politics. There is a photo of him with his arms
around two dwarf-like German officers in The Birches, all smiles.
Later, he did time in a labour camp for being a 'collaborator'. You
could not escape history here, even when you were an eight-foot
giant in a remote forest.

After the war came forced nationalisation. The Birchers lost their
thousands of heads of grazing animals and were pauperised overnight. It was a double blight: forced collectivisation and crippling
reparation duties to Greece for the role Bulgaria played as a Nazi ally.
The prime herds of the valley were packed onto cargo trains and sent
south; the border is only a few kilometres away and although it was
closed to civilians during the Cold War, other transactions went on.
Sheep and goats travelled on a free deathticket on the railway line to
Drama. This railway had carried the tobacco fortunes of the Balkans
south and then the Jews of Macedonia north. Families marked for
extermination were packed into tobacco warehouses en route.
People, plants and animals were swapped, but the destination
remained the same: the death camp, the processing plant. The
extraction-extinction project of the twentieth century.

The people of the valley paid a high price. Cultivation of private
fields was banned, while bread was rationed in the shop. The giant
Kadiev gave his extra rations to his family and went grazing in the
forest.

There was something going on in Pirin with giants. Giant trees,
giant spirits, giant people, giant suffering and giant endurance.

The retired shepherd's identity had been changed four times. In
his first passport from the 1950s he was 'Macedonian'. The Pirin
region is part of the vast geographical region of Macedonia and the
hopscotch politics between Bulgaria and Yugoslavia resulted in
people periodically being told that they are not what they are.

In his next passport in the 1960s, he was 'Bulgarian Mohammedan',
although the Pomaks never called themselves Mohammedans.

In the third from the 1970s he had a 'Christian' name chosen by the state, though there was nothing Christian about the name other than not being Arabic.

And in the fourth, he had his birth name again: Ismail.

'I am a Pomak,' he summarised. 'Hahahaha!' he laughed, a hard-earned laugh.

'But do you know who I really am?' he said. 'I'm one who was born here and will die here. In Pirin. That's who I am.'

I took off my sandals and felt the sandy earth on my soles, and walked back to the hotel. He was happy to see me and happy to say goodbye.

A hermit is in relationship with the true self. Perhaps that is why I was so happy in the valley and happy by my Scottish river. I didn't have to be anyone except the one who was born and who would die here. Or there.

'Are monks and hippies and poets relevant? No, we are deliberately irrelevant,' said the philosopher and Trappist monk Thomas Merton at a gathering in Calcutta in the 1960s. 'We live with an ingrained irrelevance which is proper to every human being. The marginal man accepts the basic irrelevance of the human condition, an irrelevance which is manifested above all by the fact of death.'

My walk with Lucky was delayed by lunch with a picnicking family from The Birches who stoked the fire by Fatmé's fountain to heat a tray of yesterday's lamb stuffed with rice and handed me a spoon before they even asked my name. The lamb was one of their own, slaughtered for Kurban Bairam in the pagan custom of *kurban*: sacrifice.

'Eat up, don't be polite, I can see you're hungry,' the matriarch urged me. 'Let it be halal to you.' She was a small woman of sixty, a bride artist.

'What is a bride artist?'

'We get the bride ready, luv,' she said. 'The bride is called *gelina*. We decorate her face. Her face is like a painting. Everything means something. And it's got to be summetrical.'

'Symmetrical, mum!' her daughter laughed. She was better educated.

The mother wore a floral headscarf, shalvars, a chain-knitted sleeveless cardigan and the glittery round apron that was not for cooking but for beauty. The daughter wore jeans and nothing on her head. The bride artist's generation had missed out on education.

There had been a dreaded dormitory in the city of the valley for schoolgirls from out of town, dubbed by locals 'Communist Party Quarters' because its main purpose was indoctrination. Few Pomak families were prepared to send their girls there. In the chaotic 1910s, armed bands and assorted revolutionaries roamed the valley; murdering men and raping women in Pomak communities. Forty, fifty years later these communities were scared to let their girls out of their sight. The memory of kidnappings by bearded men was fresh.

The forced changing of the names during Communism confirmed that the outside world was a hostile place and the siege mentality became more entrenched. The state decreed that headscarves be taken off, and the long braids that were a staple of Pomak beauty had to go. Caught between tradition and assimilation, clan loyalty and a desire to advance, the brighter girls coped by having nervous breakdowns. Either immediately, or decades later when their children left home.

Dessert was a watermelon chilled in Fatmé's fountain.

'Anyway, luv,' said the bride artist. 'What about you. What brings you here?'

'I'd like to see a Ribnovo wedding,' I said.

'Come in winter. The wedding season. Or you can come to one of our performances and see how we do the whole shebang. If the boss invites you.'

The boss was a folk singer called Kadrié. It turned out that the bride artist plied her trade not at real weddings, but at dramatised folk concerts re-enacting for an audience what had once been real. Pomak weddings had been banned too.

Once held in the Pomak world all over the southern Balkans, the elaborate *gelina* wedding has been wiped out. There was just one bastion left: Ribnovo across the valley. The people of Ribnovo had revived the tradition in the 1990s when they restored their names and rights. *Gelina* meant decorated bride and it had developed into an elaborate rite of passage over the centuries. The wedding lasted three days, though it used to last a week. Once made up in layers of silk, wool, velvet, glitter and a painted face mask behind which all emotion was hidden, the bride went into a kind of mourning and fasting meditation. She didn't eat, drink or speak for two days — the idea being that she was going through a passage. The hapless bridegroom just got drunk with his mates. And anyway, the husband was likely to spend most of their married life working abroad. She would need to be man and woman in one. Ribnovo was one of those places where you saw women of all ages chopping wood with axes.

The trail of this rite is lost. Its survival across the mists of time is a mystery, a triumph of creative folk genius. Some trace it back to the Graeco-Thracian-Egyptians and even the Mycenaeans. Others see the hand of syncretic Sufism with all the aesthetic and ritual currents it hoovered up between Persia and the Balkans. When you see the mask that the team of bride artists create out of a woman's head, it is straight out of a shaman's rite or some other ancient ritual, half-performance, half-incantation, with the high crown of flowers a totem of fertility. Persephone goes down into the underworld of sexual maturity.

For three days, the bride holds a large mirror and gazes at herself and her village through her mask. She literally holds up a mirror to her community. And like Orpheus, she must not look back.

When I returned in winter, the pandemic restrictions were still in force and for the first time in twenty-five years, the Ribnovo weddings were cancelled. It produced an effect akin to collective mourning. The weddings were a highlight of the year. Demeter needs to ritually mourn for her Persephone once a year.

Otherwise, you don't know when to start mourning. Or when to stop.

I said goodbye to the bride artist and unchained an excited Lucky. He pulled me up on his rope, up the forest road so dug-out by spring torrents that you sank into its grooves knee-deep and scrambled out with effort, and we climbed into the forest that wasn't the original one.

Still, within ten minutes we were in another world. I stopped hearing the river below and the glade engulfed me with its forking

paths that you had to know to trust, its wild flowers and limpid clearings that looked set up for a gathering of nymphs. After an hour in
that dense silence of the forest that is so full of sound, which makes
space for you and closes behind you at the same time, that fills you
with enchantment and primordial fear, I felt closer to Lucky than to
many people in my life. Lucky was constantly checking that I was
okay and I broke Shefket's instructions and let him off the rope tied
to a chain that rubbed through his neck – they kept him as a guard
dog, not a pet.

Crouching to pick wild mint, I heard crackling in the woods.
Lucky growled. I froze, ready to bolt, sure it was a bear. The dogs in
my life will accompany me to the grave, an invisible pack that walks
with me – not only the two dogs I have lived with, but those like
Lucky, whom I met for an afternoon in places where I didn't know
my way. They showed the way, made me belong and asked for nothing in return.

The forest proper only just began here. The intense aliveness of
the mountain could be drunk like a potion. Moving through a
wooded mountain where you can only see as far as the path ahead of
you is very different from a bare landscape where all is knowable to
the eye. Any moving creature or weather can be spotted across the
land. The path ahead, and back, is laid out like a carpet.

In the forest, different forces operate. An arboreal hum surrounds
you, eyes everywhere, shapes that look like other shapes, movements
that might be sunshine dancing on moss or might not be. Then suddenly a deer appears and looks at you like the eye of God.

We scrambled down a churned-up path and made it to the river
where a pair of shiny horses grazed, different ones, and back to Fatmé's fountain. I put my face under the spout. The sun had moved, the
hotel grounds were in shade again and though the embers of the picnic fire were warm, the feeling of being inside a well had returned.
The first two horses had vanished.

The following year, Lucky would be kidnapped by unknown villains
and sold for meat. This happened to unlucky dogs and horses left
unsupervised. It was cruelty born of misery.

The moon looked full of churned butter. I felt the sap rise in the pines as the blood rises to the skin. At full lunations, all that is here is doubly here. In the moon's surface was a faint topographic contour that reminded me of an old Chinese poem: 'The rabbit in the moon pounds the medicine in vain'. Our distant ancestors perceived an alchemical 'moon hare' with a pestle and mortar in that contour, pounding some elixir of eternity, pounding, just out of human reach.

Morning tonic

St John's wort
Fig leaf, dried or fresh
Walnut, whole, cracked
Honey

Infuse and sip first thing in the morning. St John's wort is to lift your night blues. Fig leaf is to regulate blood sugar. Walnut for magnesium, to relax. And honey is for sweetness, the bride-artist had told me, even if you have diabetes, because diabetes is not the worst. The worst is when you have a heavy heart.

There really was something of the 'hare in the moon' about this high-pitched place so like a tonic that Shefket and his family wanted to share it with people, but from which they couldn't drink themselves. They were busy, worried, overworked.

In Chinese lore, the moon goddess had an alchemical rabbit companion who ground medicinal herbs, presumably to extract a drop of immortality. That's why another name for the moon was Golden Hare. Gold of every kind endures; literal gold and metaphorical gold. Treasure hunters want the gold of lucre, alchemists want the gold of truth. Both require digging.

The 10,000 things spawn from the one and return to the one, says the Dao. Like the morning tonic in my cup with its golden hue. Elixir has 10,000 names, 10,000 roads lead to it. To the zing of fig leaf, the brain shape of walnut, the completeness of honey, the way St John's wort is yellow but stains red, the shine of a horse's back in the pines.

US AND THE ANCIENT DARKNESS

It was late morning and I sat in Metko's courtyard in The Birches. Metko Fettahov, the local chronicler. We watched a cauldron bubble on an open fire. Inside it were sealed jars stuffed with lamb from the neighbour's kurban. The meat from the lamb was divided into three: one part for friends; one part for the needy; and one part for oneself. In winter, Metko put a jar of pre-cooked meat in a tray and baked it with vegetables. The sterilisation took hours and the smoke made our eyes stream.

Metko had a large following and was often contacted by researchers, but he was a lone chronicler. Storytelling and story-collecting was cathartic here, where people carried a hundred years of the untold. They had nowhere to put it except bury it under the weeping willow, the birch, the pear, the walnut. If they didn't cut the tree down in a fit of madness and then forgot, as with the original birch of The Birches. In folk stories when your voice is denied, you dig a hole and shout your truth into it. It becomes buried treasure. Metko held all of that on behalf of his people.

One of Metko's fingers was missing.

'A horse bit it off,' he said. 'My late wife and I worked on a horse farm near the capital one year. Lots of Our Folk did this in the communist days and later. To make a buck.'

The people of Mesta were renowned for their skill with animals and crops. I could see Metko shovelling manure and quoting Kafka to the horses: man's idea of freedom is a way of deceiving himself.

Metko was a universal kind of person. He could do any work and remain himself, but he'd polished this golden quality with the grit of adversity. In the last year of high school, his life hit a turning point. His school had a bully for a director and a bully for a headteacher.

The state appointed fanatics in the Pomak villages, like imperial missionaries sent among the natives.

'Psychos unfit to work with young people,' he said. 'The idea was to keep you in the system and brainwash you against yourself.'

The headteacher had it in for him because he challenged her. He underperformed as an act of revolt, but loved literature and consumed the school library. When he borrowed a book that might be seen as suspicious, he'd wrap it in newspaper and write on it: 'Geography'.

We all wrapped our books in paper. Because books were precious.

'There were no books in our house. I educated myself in the library,' Metko said.

'Books were our only entertainment,' I said.

'And our only travel,' Metko said.

Then came the turning point, when the results were announced. When Metko submitted his crowning essay on the pastoral roots of national literature, he knew it was good. 'A superior piece of writing is before you,' the teacher confirmed to the class. 'It's worthy of the top grade and shows a writer with a bright future.' She then read it to the class. Metko sat there beaming, picturing his university life in the capital. 'But,' the teacher countered at the end, 'there is a catch. The alleged author is citizen Fettahov, a well-known reprobate with no respect for authority. Do you think he could produce work of this calibre? I think not. We must conclude that Fettahov has copied it from another.' For 'plagiarism and uncitizenly behaviour', she gave his essay a low grade and blocked his chance of being a candidate for university. Metko's world collapsed.

'If you wanted to excel, it wasn't enough to have talent. You had to dance to their tune, swap your identity for a career,' he said.

Like the famous folk singer whose interpretation of a Rhodopean song was sent into space on the 'Voyager disc' in 1977. She had been recruited from her village, given a new identity so that nobody knew she was from a Muslim background and propelled into stardom under the state's tutelage.

'She became a manufactured product. The only authentic thing about her is her voice,' Metko said. A pact with the devil, yet the alternative was painful in a different way, and Metko lived it out.

One of the nation's best-loved folk songs was written by a Pomak community in the Rhodope. 'Rufinka Lay Dying' (*Rufinka bolna leg-nala*) was dedicated to a real girl called Roufié:

Rufinka lay dying
High in the mountain
No one was there
But her old mother

She gave her a sip of water
Rufinka, girl of mine
Do you love your dowry?
Do you cherish it?

I don't love it, mother, I don't cherish it
I am hurt and I am sad
That all things come up from the earth
But I am going down it.

'It's about the transience of human life,' Metko said. 'Like in many of our songs and literature. It's the pastoralist view.'

In the end, only the mountain remains.

Woman and the mountain. Man and the mountain. Woman, her mother and the mountain that keeps them together even in death. Man, woman and the mountain that separates them. The mountain songs are the most haunting too. They literally rise above the songs of the plains. They are also slower. You can't rush the mountain.

'The last lines hint that it's spring time, which an English poet called the cruellest season.'

A rare flower still grows on Rufié's grave; the Aquilegia white star.

Songs carried memory better than anything. Silks were burned, forests were cut, but songs travelled through time.

'Anyway,' Metko returned to his school story. 'I knew, and everybody knew, that I had the moral high ground. But the teacher had the power. I could bring it before the authorities, dispute it, but something in me was revolted. And I swore that I'd have nothing to do with any institution again. Even if that meant becoming a builder.'

That is what he did. He learned the painting and decorating trade and made a living refurbishing the apartments of the urban intelligentsia, and got intellectual food in this way. When the regime fell, The Birchers walked down to the city – no cars – to join civil gatherings in the exciting first years of the Transition. They fought hard to have their own high school and keep their young close to them. Twenty years after that fateful essay, Metko walked into the city council and saw his former teacher. She'd become a high-powered bureaucrat.

'"Do you remember me? I'm the author of that fake essay on the pastoral story." She remembered me. But to apologise means owning up. Still, it was a small triumph for me. Just to see her twitch.'

The handmaidens of terror had clung to power. Power is sticky like congealed blood and once the crimes were laundered by time, their children moved in with a clean, contemporary façade: a European façade.

Some of the worst oligarchs however rose in the 1990s and were Muslims. Vote buying and other forms of political bullying in the Pomak communities was now endemic. The fault line here had never been between Muslims and Christians but between power and justice. Power and justice had parted ways and existed in parallel realities; a sure way to perpetuate inequality and its myriad sufferings.

'The mafia is not new. It has been with us for the last two millennia,' Metko coughed. 'The mafia is the patriarchy. Its face changes, its name changes, but the principle remains. You have an elder, a man. He holds the ring of power like a warlock. He polices resources, decides who will have sex with whom and who will be punished and rewarded.'

Inside the house was a framed photograph of a girl in a ballgown. But it was not Asiné.

'The daughter of the previous owners,' Metko said. 'We bought this house from them when they emigrated to Turkey, in 1989. When they were changing names. Again.'

The campaign that had stricken the Pomaks in the 1960s and 1970s was visited upon the ethnic Turks in the 1980s by the same government and with greater violence. Three hundred and fifty thousand people fled to Turkey, including Pomaks.

'The house is still full of their stuff. I should get rid of it.'

The girl's photograph had been hanging for thirty years. Metko and Asiné wanted to keep her memory alive when they heard she'd died of leukaemia just after her wedding in Turkey.

It was the third and final day of Kurban Bairam and everybody had the week off work. One of Metko's sons came in and offered to keep watch over the cauldron. Both sons worked in the local sewing outfits when they weren't decorating houses with their dad.

'The sewing outfits are why this place still has people,' Metko said.

There were twenty-five sewing workshops in The Birches. Every second woman worked in the sewing industry. Master seamstresses could stitch a hemline in five seconds and tailors designed clothes for all the big high-street labels. Millions of rags were stitched here every day, then labelled and shipped to Greece, Italy, Germany, Britain and the USA.

They worked six days a week – and their monthly wage was less than the price of a Hugo Boss jacket. At dusk, the makers of our clothes walked home. You recognised them because the older ones wore glasses and had back problems.

'A lifetime of sewing,' Metko said. His late wife had been a seamstress too.

His son's detail was to iron sleeves.

'Sleeves for Hugo Boss till kingdom come,' he chuckled. 'I'd leave tomorrow. Not because of the money. No, it's this place.'

Metko went inside to splash his eyes.

'This place is full of eyes and ears,' his son went on. 'Even at night. Rumour doesn't sleep. Everything that happens reaches the grapevine in the sewing sweatshops and spreads like a virus. Sometimes they get drift of it even before it happens!'

We climbed round the back to the garden where tomatoes, red peppers and aubergines hung unharvested. He filled a bag for me.

'Can you feel it?' We surveyed the roofs and the square with the minaret and the church bell-tower.

A sleepy afternoon pall, like a brain fog. The heat was unmoving.

'But you must fight it. Darkness can't win. When I turn on National Geographic, I leave this place and I'm happy again.'

He took a swig from his beer bottle.

'After my mother's death, this house was like a tomb. That's when I started feeling cold. We've livened up but I'm still cold. I can't warm up.'

I liked his honesty. There was no small talk in this house. Metko and I set off across the oven-hot streets.

The village was defined by Stormy River and steep neighbourhoods. Our destination was a hilltop ruin but we took a detour to the Ranger district where village petered into mountain. I passed here every day en route to the hotel. There was a fulling mill in the last house, run by an old widow who tended her forest of green beans. When women brought their rugs she put them in the wooden vat with washing powder, turned on the water in the channel linked to a brook and the propellers bashed them. The widow then dragged them out with a strength unnatural for her tiny frame and put them on the drying line. Metko and I stood at street level and watched the heavy rugs churn in the vat below. It was therapeutic.

I got to know the widow the following autumn. We visited the cemetery in the city where her 'two boys' lay. Her husband and only son had died at the same age: fifty.

'I want to die but can't,' she said. 'I'm too healthy.'

She was one of the few remaining Christians in The Birches. Most had moved to the city for education and to get ahead. Their houses were locked and sold to their Pomak neighbours who earned money abroad and spent it here. Come the evening, the widow turned on the television and enjoyed an episode of some Turkish soap opera. And her Pomak neighbours in the Ranger did the same: The woman who lived alone because her husband worked in England, and who was rumoured to be a magician. The widow with beautiful cheekbones and patched-up shalvars who was bent at ninety degrees because heavy toil had broken her back but not her cheer; she lived with her three sons of whom one was blind and another was the wild horseman nowhere to be seen. The woman whose first husband had pushed a man into a gorge in a jealous rage and whose second husband was building a house extension but had run out of money so their laundry hung in a room without a wall.

These women observed the Turkish soap opera timetable as religiously as the Making of the Jars in autumn. Never mind that their own lives had just as much drama.

Ranger was named after the long line of hired rangers who kept an eye on the pastures against trespassing herds. There were rangers even after collectivisation.

'To keep an eye on pastures and people,' Metko said. 'The hills had eyes. And from the 1970s on, machine guns. In the 1950s, an incident happened here with my grandmother.'

The early communist state introduced something called 'pig tax', deliberately offensive to Muslims of course. A large piggery was started in the Ranger and Birchers were obliged to give three horse-loads of their already rationed crops to the pigs each season, which left the pigs better fed than the humans. It was a ritual humiliation. The pigs were then exported to the USSR, like everything else.

'My grandmother and my mother were returning from our fields with the mule loaded with potatoes. The mayor and the armed rangers were parked here, waiting for returning folk to confiscate their harvest.'

But his grandmother didn't want to give the potatoes to the pigs and watch her family go hungry. She even remonstrated with the mayor who hit her. She hit him back.

'She was a strong woman,' Metko said, 'and pushed him into the river.'

Right here, behind the widow's green beans. Then, mother and daughter ran home with the mule and hid the potatoes in the basement. The armed rangers turned up soon enough and arrested Metko's grandmother. She spent a cold night in the gendarmerie and their potatoes were taken after all. But she had made her point. She had remained free, and after that, the thug-mayor was nicer to her.

Beyond the Ranger was a mosaic of forests and meadows all the way to the Birches Hotel and on to the alpine meadows. Fettahov's Broom (Metko's ancestors), Kadievi Pastures (the Clan of the Good Giant), Hawthorn, Singing Stone.

'A great-grandfather of mine had a vineyard upstream,' Metko said. 'Come harvest, he hired grape pickers from the Christian villages upstream. Entire families.'

Then came the end of Empire, the terror, the chaos, and the hired hands of yesterday came to the Ranger and took over the deserted lands and houses.

'For the next one hundred years, we would be the hired pickers in the fields that once belonged to us. Everything repeats itself.'

We went past the café tables and waved to familiar faces. Metko was known to bring researchers to The Birches.

'And over there,' Metko pointed to a house, 'lived a man who changed his name during the events of 1973, even though he wasn't a Muslim.'

'Out of solidarity?' I said.

'No, he just didn't like his name,' Metko said.

There had been people like that. One man's loss is another's opportunity.

'And across from him was a man who married a Pomak woman from another village. He didn't tell her that he was a Christian out of fear she'd reject him and she found out when she arrived. He didn't pressure her, she converted out of choice.'

But then the regime fell, her birth family started going to mosque again and taunting her. One day she drank a litre of caustic soda.

'Mixed marriages are unhappy,' Metko summarised. 'It's not the people, it's the system. Something dark in the state that seeps into people's beds.'

She killed herself in the way the regime had tried to kill her community: with poison from within.

'Mind you, there's lots of exceptions,' Metko said. A Christian woman currently married to a Pomak wore shalvars because she liked them and went to church in them. Mixed marriages were not unusual in the old days, either, but the old tolerance came to a tragic end during the Balkan Wars. In the 1890s there was a boy from a Christian village upstream who came to work for the richest man in The Birches, a *bey* formerly employed in the sultan's court in Istanbul.

'The boy's name was Petar. He and the bey's daughter fell in love as kids and he eventually asked for her hand. The parents were scandalised – not just because he was non-Muslim, but he was poor.

So, to put him off, they said: "You have to get circumcised." But Petar accepted. He was placed in a wine barrel, for modesty, and through a special hole he put out his willy which was duly circumcised. That way, everyone knew that the deed was done and the price paid. He accepted a new name too: Yusuf.

'This story doesn't end well, but it was true love,' Metko said. 'They had six children. Seven, but the last one was lost in Greece in 1912. Remind me to tell you more later.'

And now open borders changed things altogether. Younger Birchers married, divorced and re-married other nationalities abroad – Muslim, Christian and neither. Working abroad was a welcome equaliser – social, religious and sexual. Several Birchers were permanently established in Britain.

We recrossed the village square, big and empty in the daytime.

'Here lived a man who went to work in Libya.' The house front was encrusted with thousands of mirror shards like a sculpture by Gaudi. 'Some years later, he was flying back. But on the flight, his work mates took all his earnings. He came home and became deranged.'

The 'Libyan' felt that something was out to get him and wore a slate under his hat, having nailed the hat to the slate against alien radiation. He covered the front of his house with mirror shards. The 'eye' that looks back at you is a familiar custom but I'd never seen a whole house covered in it. The 'Libyan' had been the village artist.

We passed the petrol station and a sewing workshop owned by an entrepreneur. His birth family were poor.

'Once they were rich,' Metko said. 'In the nineteenth century they had an estate in Sofia, where the building of the former Communist Party HQ is.'

When the Ottomans lost the war with Russia in 1878 and large parts of Bulgaria gained independence, many Muslims left those parts, having lost their privileged status, as well as their safety overnight. A wealthy clan saddled their horses and came to the valley. The valley remained in Ottoman-administered Macedonia and Muslims were fine here, though not for long. A woman in that family rode a stallion whose leather saddle – *samar* – had a fortune in gold coins sewn inside it. They settled in The Birches.

A generation later, the First Balkan War delivered the last blows to Ottoman colonisation in the Balkans. That is, in Macedonia. But new wars were inflamed and were played out in the Second Balkan War, the First World War and the Second World War. All civilians suffered in the hands of regular armies, irregular armies, *komiti* bands, shifting borders, and finally, The Iron Curtain. But Muslim civilians were worst off because they became targets of the nationalist agenda of the new Christian Balkan states. Monoculture was the aim. The Balkan states espoused Romantic ethnic nationalism in the nineteenth- century Germanic mould rather than civic nationalism in the French and English mould. This meant that in the war on post-Ottoman diversity, Pomaks were prime targets. They had to be assimilated into the monolithic national body overnight. For a while, you had to be a Christian, or dead and gone.

'It was a reign of terror, on-and-off, for a decade,' said Metko.

The early campaigns against the Muslims of the Mesta basin had a crusade-like quality. They were organised and financed by the state and the Orthodox church, and implemented on the ground by the army with help from paramilitary groups and civilian volunteers. Entire communities were torched. Between 1912 and 1913, thousands of men were executed and thousands of women and children were left homeless and died of hunger and disease. Over 20,000 Muslim civilians across Macedonia perished in pogroms, exoduses and famine in the 1910s. Three hundred thousand people lost their way of life. Many ended up in Turkey. The Pomaks found themselves trapped between eras and agendas.

For generations, Bircher men had been *spahi*, reserve soldiers to the sultan, sometimes separated from their families for years to fight Empire's wars, or simply stationed in Istanbul.

'Complete with a song,' said Metko. 'It's called "Hey Zaim, hey spahi."'

The young spahi Zaim is engaged on a Wednesday, married on a Thursday and called up to Istanbul on Friday. He leaves his beloved who gives him a magical flower wrapped in cloth: when the flower wilts, know that I am with another. Seven years later, he is still in Istanbul when the flower finally wilts. The sultan gives him special leave and he rides home. Entering The Birches, he sees an old woman gathering thistle and when she sees him, she weeps.

'His mother. In the village square, a wedding is taking place. It's his sweetheart, marrying another. But he takes out his sword and reclaims his sweetheart.'

It is not said whether the sweetheart was pleased to see him.

Many Pomaks fought on the Ottoman side in the Russian–Turkish war. The picture was much more mixed in the First World War when some were enlisted by Istanbul as per tradition, but most fought for their nation: Bulgaria. Turkey and Bulgaria were on the same side – the side of the Central Powers – and each had their territorial wars. Some went with the Young Turk movement, which was very friendly with the infamous komiti of the Bulgarian-Macedonian freedom movement. Both were united by their mission to overthrow a rotting tyranny. After that, Pomaks fought for their nation in the Second World War and after that, in the Greek Civil War, because many Pomaks were left on the other side of the border.

'And there were even Pomaks who joined the Macedonian komiti,' said Metko. The komiti were the sub-divided armed revolutionary movement of the Internal Macedonian Revolutionary Organisation (IMRO).

'One Bircher became an executioner and did twenty years in jail for it.'

In 1912, the Birchers fled south along the Mesta corridor, following the retreating Ottoman Army for safety. Over the Drama Mountains.

'The Greek Army helped them on the other side. But things were bad in Kavalla.'

Tens of thousands of refugees from the Chech had run downstream to the land's terminus in search of passage to Turkey. They were mountain people and had never seen the sea before. The traumatised Birchers stood on the coast, only to witness the sinking of a boatful of people like them. A woman from The Birches turned to her people and yelled:

'Curses on this deep dark water! We're going back to our own water!'

The Birchers turned back for the gruelling trek home. They arrived back here several weeks later and started again in the rubble. Many had lost children, elderly relatives and their health in the exodus. Most had lost all their possessions.

'This is where the happy story of Petar-Yusuf and the bey's daughter ends,' said Metko.

The komiti had issued mass death sentences for all mixed marriages. Couples like Petar-Yusuf and the bey's daughter were sought out by the komiti and executed on the spot. So, Yusuf and his family had joined the exodus to Kavalla. When the decision was made to return, after all, the couple parted in the Drama Mountains, knowing that he would be killed by the komiti on returning. She continued north with her people, her youngest child in a *sadilka* on her back. But when marauders followed their trail, she was forced to abandon the crying baby to run unencumbered with her other children and she placed the baby under a tree.

Greek soldiers got into a skirmish with the marauders and saved the Birchers from further violence.

'And the stragglers in the refugee group saw a Greek officer on a horse, holding a baby.'

The fate of that child is unknown. The bey's daughter never saw Petar-Yusuf again.

'I remember her as an old woman in my childhood,' Metko said. 'She remarried but always said: Petar was the best, there was never one like him.'

Birchers had good memories of the Greeks from those years. During the First World War, Greece had claims over the valley because of its Greek minority and the Greek Army arrived in The Birches under orders to torch it. But a man spoke Greek and managed to charm the command into not only sparing the village, but helping a mission to a Christian village upstream that had stolen the Birchers' kurban cauldrons. Every village had its own set of these ceremonial cauldrons and they were highy prized.

'The cauldrons at least were saved.'

One way or another, Our Folk felt the earth shift beneath their feet for the whole of the twentieth century. That they managed to salvage anything is remarkable. The mountain helped them.

'Here was the old hodja's house,' Metko pointed out a large house with a garden. 'When the bandits returned to terrorise people again, this is where the forced conversions took place. They gang-raped women including the hodja's wife. This broke the hodja and he converted.'

The original houses were made by builders from The Masons across the Valley. Only five survived, which is why The Birches was not an architectural reserve. There was no one to protect it the way that Rifat Bey had protected The Masons.

Rifat Bey was the last Ottoman-era governor of the valley. A polyglot dervish politician who played nine instruments, remained celibate and lived with his mother and adopted son, and made his own herbal balms, he was the complex product of a cosmopolitan empire in its tyrannical twilight. After fighting in the Russian–Turkish war of 1877–1878 and spending seven years as a Russian prisoner of war, he earned his sabre back by applying a herbal balm against foot-and-mouth disease to the Russian imperial horses. Rifat Bey ensured the peaceful handover of the valley from Ottoman to Bulgarian rule. When he died at almost a hundred, the entire region sent him off – Christians, Muslims and Jews from the community of refugees from Russian pogroms, and who'd been welcomed to the valley by Rifat. Two of his herbal recipes survive to this day.

'I was telling you about the saddle with the fortune inside it,' said Metko. 'When the komiti raided The Birches, the woman with the saddle avoided rape, but they took her saddle. And she died of a broken heart.'

She was the great-grandmother of Metko's late wife and of the petrol station owner. He in turn married a woman from a wealthy family. Every family has a theme. Rags and riches was a theme in the family with the saddle.

'And in our family, it's tough women,' Metko said. The name Fettahov meant 'big'.

'Women have power here.' Metko smiled. 'Male power is a veneer. The Birches is a matriarchy. I don't quite know why.'

We went past the house Metko was decorating. It was in place of the old school, built during the reign of the komiti with desecrated Muslim tombstones. Today those tombstones were salvaged in the mosque courtyard. We climbed the steep streets.

'My grandfather's house.'

Across from it was a wild mound. A pagan temple had stood there, then a chapel and though the chapel fell into ruin, an old pear tree marked the holy site.

'A holy pear. My grandfather worshipped that tree. Literally. One day in the 1930s, he heard a rumour. A new church was to be built for the refugees. The pear was to be cut down.'

The new refugees had come upstream from Greece following the Treaty of Lausanne in 1923 and its 'exchange of populations'. Over the same Drama Mountains familiar to the Birchers from their own exodus ten years before. The refugees settled among the locals with whom they shared a language, if not a religion. The Birchers made space for them. They knew what it was like to run for your life.

'My grandfather got up one night, climbed the mound and cut the tree in a rage.'

Full of sorrow, he then planted a cutting from it in his own garden. But the sapling didn't thrive and the church was never built after all. It had just been a rumour.

We swung by a football match in the stadium at the end of the village. The Birches were playing Kornitsa and the running joke was that the first had quantity but the second had quality. That's because Kornitsa lost half of its people in the exodus thirty years ago.

'The kids you see here,' Metko pointed at the well-groomed teenagers, 'were all born in Turkey. But they speak Bulgarian.'

They came to their mountain villages every summer for Kurban Bairam. The old wounds were not discussed. For the new generation, it was all about opportunity and choice.

But I noticed the freakish incidence of early death in the three rhyming villages. Metko's friend, an Arabic linguist, had died at just fifty-two of cancer. Every third person I met had lost a parent when they were small, a spouse when they were still young, or an adult child.

'What is it with The Grim Reaper here?' I asked Metko.

'I've wondered the same,' he said. 'Maybe it's Chernobyl. It's the generation who were teenagers. Maybe it's the Transition that's killing us. Or some ancient darkness.'

We walked away from the football match of the exiles. Chernobyl was blamed by many for the inexplicable rate of cancers among people of mine and Metko's generations. The radioactivity levels here following the blast were 1,000 times the norm, but it was hushed up by the authorities and people found out while eating nuclear salads. Auto-immune diseases shot up among children and teenagers in the late 1980s, and I was one of them.

We climbed above the last houses, wading through a spiky plant that scratched my shins. Metko found the remains of a concrete bunker from the 1970s. It had been fitted with machine guns trained on The Birches. The army carried out drills here in the 1980s, complete with bomber planes as a form of routine terror against the insurgent Pomaks.

We climbed the former tobacco fields, sweat dripping into our eyes and ate blackberries sweet with sunshine.

'My happiest times were up here with Asiné and the boys, picking berries all day. And as a child, my mother would put us on muleback and we'd trek to Snake Creek to pick cornelian cherries.'

Snake Creek was a remote gully. The Birchers had no fear of the wild. But back then, it hadn't been wild. There were herds, people, horses, plantations.

My shins were bleeding.

'Spiny restharrow,' Metko said. 'We collected it as kids to sell to the cooperative. One kilo gave you ten pennies.'

The odd enthusiast still dug up restharrow roots in winter, just like Zaim, the spahi's elderly mother, in that song. It was sticky with oil, with small pink flowers. You got 50 cents for a kilo.

'We gathered walnuts too, by the tonne. Each autumn, we brought them to an area the size of a stadium and piled them up in pyramids. They were then loaded on trucks.'

Children had done this unpaid, sometimes during class hours. Just like the digging up of antiques. Slave labour for the ring of power.

After the fall of the regime, the walnut economy collapsed and the walnut trees were cut down and used for fire wood. It was revenge of the slaves.

A brook gurgled and we crossed a small bridge with a weeping willow.

'We had this stubborn mule. It stopped on this bridge just to annoy us.

'Every time I cross this bridge,' Metko said, 'I remember a tall guy. He was just back from military service and came with his mule to the family field. They said he had a heart attack. And his mother started coming here. She'd sit by the brook and sing, but it was a wail that froze your blood, I can still hear it.

'Have I overdone it with our stories? I don't mean to traumatise you,' Metko said. We stopped to recover our breath.

'Well, you're not big on jokes,' I said and finally, he laughed.

Everything happens twice. Once as life itself, and twice as memory – or forgetting. Metko remembered it for those who were too busy surviving. It was his act of love for his village, his mountain, his valley and his way of staying connected to his first passion: literature. And ironically, even without a university degree, what he did was more vital than many a university professor's collected tomes. Because it touched the lives of others.

We could hear the pulsing beat of a band that went around the village at Kurban Bairam, playing loud ethno-pop during the afternoon heat.

'When the ring of power wants to control the population, they start giving out free entertainment. Bread and circuses,' Metko said. 'Shiny things. To turn people into sheep and buy their votes.'

The destruction of the valley's cultural heritage was done in several phases, but all along its aim was monoculture. Sufi monasteries were wiped from the land and from the mind. The city in the valley once had twelve mosques and destroyed them all in less than a century, down to a stump of a ruin with a broken minaret and swastika graffiti that nobody washed off. It stood by the river and the market like some barbarian totem.

The commissars of twentieth-century homogenisation were as pitiless as the Latin crusaders and as systematic as the Inquisition. Into the traumatised hole left by a syncretic, home-grown Balkan Islam, two genetically engineered crops moved in: Atheist materialism with polyester mantles and fake names. And when that fell, Islamic materialism with uniform new mosques that shone with the cold glint of amnesia. Our Folk don this synthetic mantle because after all the injuries, it's all they can do to survive.

Metko possessed a valuable document – a thick book recording the crimes of the communist regime in the three rhyming villages, complete with letters by state security agents, orders of arrest and the code names of protagonists. It was incriminating for those still alive but he hadn't done anything with it. Holding it was enough.

'The world is stuck in a cycle of victims and persecutors. Victims who become persecutors. Persecutors victimised by their own crimes. And I want to challenge this by stepping out of the cycle and becoming a free human being.'

He'd been invited to join political and business cliques. But his freedom was not for sale, it was too hard-won. It went back to that essay on the pastoral story.

And that was the whole point of coming out with your lantern. Even as he cultivated the collective conscience of Our Folk, he would not join any club except that of humanity.

It was a generous day, birds everywhere. Here began people's abandoned fields and beyond them, the hills of burned grass that if you hiked for two or three hours, tapered and fell into Maiden Gorge via precipitous ridges. We surveyed the rooftops of The Birches with the jagged peaks beyond.

'Did I say that the Latin graveyard is down here!'

Inside, an overgrown patch with a brook. Nobody knew who was buried here. Perhaps straying crusaders who deserted and married locals. Upstream was a tributary called Latin River.

Time, treasure and trauma had accumulated undisturbed. Only the odd chronicler or treasure hunter noticed things, picked them up and polished them. Chroniclers were thinner on the ground than treasure hunters. The fact that those in power have been in the category of treasure hunter rather than chronicler made history rather feral. Neither justly cultivated, nor gone wild. It was down to individuals like Metko and I to wade through the remains, looking for what could be salvaged in the wake of the last barbarians.

Yet I understood the urge of the treasure hunter.

'You and I are treasure hunters too,' Metko grinned. 'But for stories.'

Where there is ruin, there is hope for treasure, said the Persian poet-wanderer Rumi.

Has there been a time without ruins? When the only ruins were geological, the earth's works rising and falling in their own time. We gave up trying to access the Latin tombs.

'On the other side of the river by St George's Church is the plague cemetery. Mostly children.'

The plague last struck in the 1830s and Valley people climbed to the mountain villages to wait it out, bringing it with them.

We passed the Libyan's abandoned allotment. Despite his paranoia, he'd leave the gate unlocked and a pair of small galoshes – for children to come and pick strawberries.

The hills were too scorched to trek, so Metko called someone in a Jeep to drive us. We bumped over clumps of burned grass. The mustard-coloured hills rolled out like an arid carpet.

'This was all tobacco fields,' Metko said. 'The whole Mesta basin smelled of tobacco.'

You get up at three in the morning, the whole family. You load up the mule and trek in the dark. The only light is the moon and a gas lamp attached to the mule. Gas lamps attached to unmanned mules: the Bulgarian highlander ruse that got the Germans over these mountains into Greece in 1941. After decades of deadly hide-and-seek games in the hills, the people and animals of this region were experts at guerrilla tricks.

Well into the 1990s, the tobacco fields were ploughed with ox carts.

'Because no machinery can climb here. That's why it fell to us highlanders to sow the small-leafed Basma,' Metko went on. At high school, he'd studied tobacco as a subject and knew its economy and agronomy, as well as the muddy practice. 'In one year, our family of six produced 800 kilos of dried tobacco. We were paid 2–3 lev per kilo. After tax, that gave us something less than subsistence.'

One year in the 1980s, The Birches produced 520 tonnes of tobacco! The state was raking it in.

'Our fields were at the far end. Two hours' walk in each direction.'

'Wow,' said the driver, who looked like he spent his time eating and drinking.

'Now, see our friend here,' Metko turned to him. 'His ancestors hail from The Good Place upstream.'

In 1912–1913, the Muslim quarters were torched. There were three children whose parents were massacred, but not before they'd packed the children off into the hills and instructed them to keep walking south. Over the jagged ridges, past the glacial cirques. Keep the sea ahead of you. The three orphans made it here, God knows how. The Birches, freshly pillaged, took them in.

'Our friend here is the great-grandson of one of those kids.'

We said goodbye to the driver who was beaming because the hunting season was starting today, which meant male parties in the forest and lots of food and booze. We continued to the ruins on foot. Sheep and goats were scattered in the distance like white stones. At dusk, I heard the call of the shepherd rounding up the animals.

'Ayeeee! Ayee yaaaa ya-ya-ya-ya ayeeeeeee!'

The call resonated in my chest as if I too was shouting. The human voice of the mountain.

'Now I see why people shout,' I said. 'It's the hills.'

I almost expected to hear the sound of the kaval flute. The instrument of the mountain shepherd.

'There *was* a guy who played the kaval,' said Metko. 'You could hear the melody like a running stream over the hills. His name was Ismail 'Atemin' Kalyor.'

Because his mother was Atemina, he was known affectionately as Atemincheto, 'little Atemin', though he was not a small guy.

'When he passed us in the fields with his flock, he always stopped to chat to my grandfather who was also Ismail. I picked up their anxiety. They could feel the gathering clouds. He was a handsome fair man with a curly moustache and an expressive face, and he wore pure tweed. He and his mother Atemina ground their own flour and refused to drink water in the village, only from the hill springs.'

Because he only trusted the hills.

'He was devoted to his animals, apolitical. Sometimes in the village they bullied him into singing. I listened to him in awe. But he preferred to sing to the hills.'

When the name-changing commissars arrived to crush the revolt in March 1973 and men with Kalashnikovs were posted in every street, it was decided that two men here would be executed in cold blood as a showcase. To show the rest what would happen if they didn't sign the register with their new names. The local party commissars of The Birches helpfully singled out two celibate men. Without families to feed. The first was not at home. The second was Atemin. He had come down from the hills and was lunching with his mother behind a locked door. When they tried to kick the door in, he leaned against it, so they fired through the door and killed him on the spot.

Then they placed an axe in his hand and photographed the body to show that he'd been a terrorist. Atemina witnessed this, just metres away. I see her collapsing, then neighbours, Christian and Muslim women, coming to help her mop her son's blood as the executioners took the body away for a needless autopsy.

Atemina and Atemin's story really got to me. In the same instant that he had lost his life, she had lost her son and they had lost their name.

'The hills remember him,' said Metko. 'Silently.'

I was conceived at the exact time the sound of flute ceased in this mountain – March 1973.

'There is one last Mohican,' said Metko. 'A reincarnation of Atemin. After him, there will be no one.'

Who was it?

'Can't remember his name. He's a marginal character. Lives in the Ranger with his mother when he's not with his horses. But I doubt your paths will cross.'

The view from the stony plateau was worth the sweat. To the south, the glow of the sea somewhere beyond. To the north, Maiden Gorge and distant blue Rila.

'Across is Ribnovo, of the weddings,' Metko pointed. Ribnovo looked like a fortress hewn into Old Woods.

Before motorised transport, people visited each other across the valley on horseback. They'd stay with friends and family for a week, bringing gifts. The women rode along with the men. Everybody had a horse.

'Ribnovo is another planet. Every village is a planet in itself. And every planet eventually grows cold and becomes extinct. We can't stop the extinction, but we can maybe delay it by making people see how precious it all is.'

There were thirty ruined forts in the valley. Romans kept an eye out for rebellious Thracians and incoming barbarians. Barbarians took over and kept an eye out for other barbarians. In the thirteenth century, the autonomous Bulgarian despot Alexius Slav ruled this region, which joined with the Crusaders' short-lived Salonica kingdom to the south, a side-effect of the Fourth Crusade. Though answerable to the Latin emperor Henry of Flanders whose daughter he married and at war with Tsar Boril up north, despot Slav answered only to himself. The forts of the valley must have been busy.

Only the bottom layer of the fort remained. We saw fresh traces of digging, discarded objects.

'Looters don't want script or story, only gold.' Metko picked up a terracotta fragment – maybe a large pot for storing oil or wine underground. Three parallel lines were drawn across the clay.

'Someone's fingers from two thousand years ago.'

We ran our fingers along the grooves. We touched the hand of the long-ago potter.

I was reminded of a mysterious tombstone in Bosnia, inscribed:
'MAY THIS HAND MAKE YOU THINK ABOUT YOURS'

A man in a belted tunic raises his right hand in the Bogomil gesture; half-wave to the unborn, half-'stop' of the Buddha. Another tombstone in that group shows a line of chain-linked men and women in tunics – a dance from the otherworld. The medieval Bogomils were probably Europe's first social and philosophical movement against feudal patriarchy.

'Let's not forget Spartacus and his movement,' said Metko.

Spartacus was born on the banks of the Struma River to the west.

'He rose against the ring of power and those bandits crucified him.

Emancipation takes a long time,' Metko said. 'It's almost a geological process.'

I picked up another fragment, with a triangular symbol drawn in the clay. The triangle turns up in Tibetan Buddhism, early Christianity and its inheritors the gnostics. The gnostic Bogomils drew the triangle and the spiral-snake, the sun, moon and stars.

'I've seen a lot of these triangles,' Metko said. 'See the far end towards Snake Gully? That was our family tobacco field.'

The far end was out of sight. The idea of walking here with just the moon and this ominous rocky plateau above you was unappealing. But this is what Metko's family and everybody else had done. They grew tobacco and engorged the pockets of tobacco barons, apparatchiks and oligarchs.

'You asked about early deaths. I remember how Soviet airplanes came to drop pesticides on the tobacco. People said some of the pilots were Russians. They got as close as 3 metres. We'd hear their buzz and we had these plastic sheets with us. We'd cover up and lie in the furrows between rows, face down, until the bombing was over.'

They were bombed with Piromor, Bi-58 and DDT, all carcinogenic. Some people passed out from the stench and vapours, others developed lung problems.

'One day, I was a kid, we'd done the morning's work. I was rooting around a cave near our field. And I found a necropolis. I moved the heavy stone lid and inside it was a complete skeleton with artefacts. Untouched. There were triangular symbols carved on the stones. I freaked out and ran to my parents.'

But his parents were freaked too – you never knew what trouble you could get into, best to say nothing. Metko returned and covered up the human remains. Later it was found and looted by others.

'I kept just one M-coin and didn't tell anyone.'

What is an M-coin?

'It stands for Millennium.'

That's why the coins had *anno* inscribed on them, vertical to the big M. The M-coins are surrounded by treasure hunter conspiracies. Metko guessed they were cut at the turn of the second millennium in the Eastern Roman Empire. The tobacco furrows threw up coins and kids picked them up: Pelasgian coins from the time of Philip and Alexander of Macedon; Byzantine coins with the robed figure of some heresy-fearing emperor; coins with the sharpbearded face of the Latin Emperor Sigismund; Dutch coins dated 1744 and inscribed CONCORDIA RES PARCRESTRA, 'in unity lies strength'. All of them were pierced and Metko guessed they had been used in decorative strings for the headdresses of local women in bridal outfits. You could still see those ensembles at a Ribnovo wedding.

'Western Christendom held an apocalyptic worldview. At the turn of every millennium there would be a catastrophe, the elders told people. This is how they stoked hysteria and recruited foot soldiers for the Crusades. Because the apocalypse was expected to come from the East. That was the theological dogma. The origin of Islamophobia is in the Crusades. Of course, the real drive was pillage.'

In the Western mind, all that is evil and exotic resides in the East. Even in the Greek states of antiquity, wandering healers and wizards supposedly came from Persia. But in reality, they were here all along. They wandered for two reasons: learning and persecution.

The Bogomils were famed in Byzantium for their wandering healers, called *vrachoo*. And these vraches had a way with plants. This is how they asked a plant whether it would agree to be diverted from its path and help the sick: they'd pick one flower and perform a quick test. They placed it in heated water with a drop of their own blood in it, then interpreted the colour of the liquid – that was the plant's answer. If it was a yes, they picked more of it. If not, they moved on and left the plant alone.

Isn't it strange that people in the tenth century, whose average lifespan was thirty-five, treated plants with reverence. And a millennium later, entire forests are wiped, together with their inhabitants, no questions asked. But we expect to live forever.

'Yes,' Metko said. 'History repeats itself. Nature will have the last word.'

I picked up a round stone with a hole in it, perfect like a pierced sun.

'Maybe for grinding grain,' Metko said. 'The treasure hunters didn't want it.'

I wanted it though. I would take it home, save it, was it wrong?

'Yes,' Metko said. 'But at least you won't sell it. So much has been wiped from the land, I too want to rescue every shard of pottery. Every memory.'

That's why the Bogomils, like the Pomaks, are a mystery – because much has been burned. Bogomil literature was burned and their history written by their enemies, but some say that a fragment of the Bogomil Bible survives. It was written on a scroll of birch bark and carried by a vrach rolled up inside a cane, and I've even heard that remains of this scripture are kept in a Pomak community in the Rhodope. Fragments of the Bogomil medicinal Green Book called *Zeleinik* were recently unearthed by a herbalist in Ukraine.

One theory about the origins of the Pomaks and the Torbesh (Macedonian Pomaks) is that some of them are descendants of the Bogomils. By the time Islam arrived, the Bogomils had endured a horrific inquisition and the survivors were scattered in remote places. Their communities were often on the move for that reason. They remained mountain people. And there is another clue: the Bogomils were mocked by their enemies for being '*torbeshi*', after the two *torbi* or bags their healers carried.

One for books, the other for plants. I liked the sound of that!

'Well, your car is full of books and herbs, and you're on the move with a healing mission,' Metko smiled. 'Like a modern-day torbesh.'

The word gnosis is a clue to the nature of all gnostic movements, including Bogomilism and Catharism. Gnosis is Greek for 'knowledge'. The aim was to gain knowledge of the self and the divine through individual experience, away from institutions and material trappings. The healer priests of the Bogomil-Cathar movement were known as *perfecti*, the immaculate ones, and lived like yogis. The church of the gnostic is everywhere and especially in nature. The gnostic carries it within. This was highly subversive stuff, a kind of inner alchemy. It undermined the top–down power of the patriarchy by freeing up the individual at the grass-roots level and putting her in direct touch with divine agency.

The Sufi mystics travelled with a bag and a staff, too. Bogomilism emerged long before Sufism but they had parallels. Both embraced an egalitarian worldview that was at loggerheads with the clerical establishment – anti-feudal, emancipatory, anti-patriarchal, and individualistic. Wandering Sufis, like wandering Bogomils, were healers and preachers in one and they travelled dressed in hooded capes. Both created a troubadour culture. Ordinary people and the elite alike were drawn to them. The establishment periodically persecuted their leaders as heretics.

Yet ironically, Sufi missionaries from Persia and east of the Caspian Sea were the main proselytising channel of Islam in the Balkans between the fourteenth and seventeenth centuries.

'Notice how from up here, it's not about East and West,' Metko said. 'It's about the river and the river runs north to south.'

Metko hummed:

'Rise up, rise up, gentle white wind/ Melt the snow and open the road to Drama/ I want to see my love.'

An old Macedonian song.

In the twelfth and thirteenth centuries, Bogomils travelled from Byzantium and Bulgaria to Bosnia, then Italy and southern France, where their teachings may have sparked off the Cathar movement. Cathar communities flowered but were eventually forced into hiding in the Pyrenean highlands. A papal campaign of terror, known as the Albigensian Crusade, was led against them for twenty years. The last of the Cathar leaders was burned in 1321 in Toulouse, and at the pyre he uttered a prediction: in 700 years, the Bogomil-Cathar flame would be rekindled in its homeland.

'What's the difference between this fort and the bunkers below?' Metko asked.

'Time,' I said.

'Correct! Otherwise, their purpose is the same. To control people. To rule top-down. But in the mountain, there are no frontlines. Only guerrilla warfare. Which always makes centralised power nervous.'

Things got trapped in the valley and you had to go high to escape.

'It goes back,' he said. 'There's something ancient about this darkness. Can you feel it?'

'I can feel it,' I said.

We rummaged for more remains of things that had served a purpose and I decided not to take the perfect stone after all. I put it back where I found it. A black raven caw-cawed overhead.

'When a single raven caws, people say someone will die,' Metko said. 'This is how screwed up we are! Always expecting the worst.'

'Maybe we're not expecting it, maybe we're remembering it,' I said and an eerie impression passed through me like a mild sunstroke. These tobacco hills, the curve of the land was utterly familiar. As Metko said Snake Gully, Latin River, I knew them already. Just as I knew the guardian of the mountain: Netikin. I knew this fort in its heyday. A rag-tag army gathered down in the valley under a tatty flag. All roads lead to Constantinople. The atmosphere was unsettling, like a gathering storm.

Then the impression passed and I was back with Metko, crouching among the pieces.

But over the next two years, I returned to these hills with someone else. And the glimpsed scene returned too, in waves of neural jolts like scrambled timelines. In some far, faraway galaxy of the soul, I stand on these hills to bid farewell to someone. I could be a man or woman. I can't see his face but he is younger, maybe a brother or son or lover. He is on horseback, wearing chainmail that is too loose because it's not his, although the horse is his. It's his favourite horse. He is a shepherd not a warrior, but he is going east. Other men are going too and he thinks they're wise because they're older. He thinks it's an adventure but it's a bloodbath. He will see and commit crimes that will destroy him. And I know this as I see him off on the tobacco hills which are not tobacco hills. There are trees and dwellings with smoke coming out and grazing horses. The fort is out of view. The wind blows sand into my mouth.

'This place is weird, can you feel it?' Metko said, as if reading my mind. 'I don't like coming here alone.'

'Why not?'

Metko went quiet and picked up another fragment.

'Have you ever found remains of dwellings here?'

'No,' he said. 'Just the fort. And shepherd's huts, like where Atemin lived with his forty or so animals.'

We stood at the edge of the plateau. There was a vertical funnel in the rock. A 'passage' with a sheer drop.

'You know I'm a cynic, but I've had flashbacks of someone who is pushed through this funnel, a sort of sacrifice,' he said.

One evening, in his teens, he was returning from the tobacco field on his own.

'I was on the path below and I looked up and saw the son of the magician who used a special cup. She's dead now. She was famous then. He stood here and threw a large ball down the funnel. An errand for his mother.'

The ball unravelled and Metko saw fabric mixed with human hair and something else. The son hid in the ruins. Metko moved on.

'That ball was so primordial. I remember it still.'

Human hair is a classic trope of black magic. A record of nineteenth- and twentieth-century valley life says: 'The black magic here is very bad indeed. It usually involves human hair. When thrown off a cliff or buried, it invariably makes the person waste away and die.'

The villages of the valley looked so sleepy you'd never guess what still went on here. Women 'took' your footprint from the road or your height if known, then cut a black thread of the same length, named it after you and made a blend with it, or tied it in knots. Com bined with spells, this sapped your life force. Atropa snips the thread. The black magic used here 'for illness and death' is thousands of years old and virtually unchanged. The British Museum has a lead tablet found in Roman London with a Latin curse identical to the curses used here.

An acquaintance upstream went to a remote ruined monastery and stumbled across a bundle. He opened it with dread and found the remains of a newborn calf that had been named after a person and slowly strangled with sisal rope with words to this effect: 'As the life expires from this calf, let it so expire from X. Alive today, dead tomorrow.'

There were still women here who 'bring the moon down'. I met a man who had seen it and the shock of it hadn't left him. Two naked women at a river crossroads in The Birches. They were not hiding, it's just that the Birchers didn't want to see what was in plain midnight view, but he was looking for a lost cow and saw them. 'They were milking the moon,' said the man, 'I'll be struck by lightning if I'm lying.' He knew that he'd seen something he was not meant to see, like Actaeon, who saw Artemis bathing in the forest and was turned into a stag and dismembered by his own hounds. Why were they milking the moon? 'I don't want to know,' said the man, 'it's women's business.'

Bringing the moon down has been practised since antiquity. You 'milk' the moon of its power and ingest it. Briefly, you become the moon. It is said that after such rituals, the moon's light is temporarily dimmed! In Aristophanes' play *The Clouds*, the formidable Thessalian magicians bring the moon down and cause an eclipse. Medea, who murdered her children in a spurned lover's revenge, was a lunar magician in the service of Hecate. And why naked? Because the naked one unhooks from the society of humans and enters primordial society.

A writer describes a Mesta village downstream, at the end of the nineteenth century. Drought was blamed on a local woman's power to 'tie up the clouds and stop the rain' and she was known for milking the moon by turning it into a cow and getting a good 50 litres at a time! The neighbour reported hearing the cowmoon low. This was a case of neighbour envy and when the rains finally came during a religious festival, the magician was absolved. She had never been in danger of stoning or banishment because this was the East and such things were normal. But the neighbour's rumour-mongering pitted the people against each other and caused a war of the babi similar to the kind I saw in Kribul; all because people believed that womankind could control nature. That womankind *is* nature.

For those interested in bringing the moon down, you need to be a lactating woman with your lactating mother or lactating daughter and you need a cauldron, a sieve, 'silent' water, the right words, the right crossroads and the right time of year. It isn't for everyone.

'Until twenty years ago, all life in our community revolved around the moon cycles,' said Metko. 'Because the moon regulates our relationship with the earth.'

The women in his youth were uncannily attuned to lunar cycles. They could forecast the weather, predict conception times, births, illnesses and the outcomes of events.

'The moon was discussed by the fire every single night.'

Here, the moon is called the monthly, *Mesechina*. It's a she, of course.

'The moon is neutral,' said Metko. 'It's us humans that are the dark side of the moon. I'm a sceptic. But the magic round here creeps me out. It's always been around and they're powerful.'

There was a whole lexicon and Metko took me through it.

Mageshnitsa was Valley dialect for healer-witch-magus and she did *mageta* or magics, plural. She was likely to be Pomak but could swing either way. *Vrachka*, from vrach or doctor was someone who could see telepathically, diagnose and heal, and this was a Christian woman. *Gledachka* or seer was similar and could be Christian or Muslim. The vrachka and gledachka were benign and had extra-sensory abilities. But the mageshnitsa was ambivalent and had tools. You never knew who she served; you or herself.

The word 'witch' was not in current use.

'Though it must have been once,' said Metko, 'because there's Witchy River across the valley.'

The root of the word for witch-warlock was *vesht* which meant 'adept'.

'Let's get out of the sun before it melts our brains,' Metko said, but there was no shade on the tobacco hills. 'Look,' he stroked an oak sapling that grew inside the funnel.

'A seed blown from somewhere,' he said. 'Before the tobacco, this was oak forest.'

The hills were remembering.

It was the third and final night of Kurban Bairam. Music blasted in the square; folk blended with the ethnic-pop called *chalga*. Under the thump of the pop beat you heard caravans laden with wine. You heard the song of the red-cheeked shepherdess, alone with a thundering avalanche or the gallop of drunken men and quickly gathering her flock to shelter in the forest of giants.

Women danced a slow *horo* circle in the square. Young and old in their pink-red, blue-green, golden yellow velvet, polyester and tinsel – stripes, florals, zoomorphic glyphs. A polyphony encoded by initiated hands but beautiful to all. Some wore jeans under their tunics. Some wore high heels, others trainers.

Organic fibres mingled with mass-produced glitter. Wool aprons dyed by grandmothers with moss pigments were overlaid with chemically dyed fabric bought in a two-dollar-shop. I recognised the faces of seamstresses among them. Women who had stitched back their stolen lives, piece by piece.

And now they stitched everybody else's clothes too, here in The Birches, so that the rest of the continent could buy them on a Saturday — a working day for the seamstress — in the fashionable streets of cities, adorned with labels that justified the price, wrapped in tissue paper and placed in gold-embossed bags that the shopper took home like a demented hunter-gatherer who has long forgotten how to hunt or gather and only knows how to consume.

Every time I see a clothes label saying 'made in the EU', I see the face of a woman from The Birches.

The men stood in clumps outside the café. I saw familiar faces. The whispering father was here, so delighted I'd been to the ruined fort he knew so well, that I suspected he was a treasure hunter. A stocky man nicknamed 'The Dog' overheard us talking about the fort and told me an old village memory. In the Middle Ages, *kolibi* people lived on the hills with their horses and flocks; pastoralists, *kolibashi*, The Dog called them. When the Ottoman Turks arrived, some of the kolibashi were slaughtered and the rest dispersed. The fort's defenders must have fled, knowing they were outnumbered they left the pastoralists to their own devices. The survivors were possibly the founders of The Birches, which began to appear as a village in Ottoman registers during the fifteenth century and over hundreds of years became fully Muslim and prospered. For a while, anyway.

The men stood: awkward, hunched, admiring the dancing women. They had not dressed up, they didn't know how to. Many exuded a silent pain, even as they laughed with poor teeth.

'Why don't the men dance?' I asked Metko, who shuffled over in his rubber slippers: 'Why don't you dance?'

We cracked sunflower seeds with our teeth and spat out the shells. 'Like at some Balkan rodeo,' he grinned.

'I don't know why we don't dance,' he said. 'We've been so often the target of assault that we've learned to disappear. Pretend you're not here. Say a name that's not your real name. Wear mocking little smiles as a defence. Remember the term "reduced"?'

Reduced, *redutsiran* – a totalitarian term for someone who resisted and was broken. Broken, disabled, insane or worse – who became a handmaiden of darkness. The Spanish conquistadors used the same term for indigenous people turned into slaves: *reducido*.

To be reduced is to be murdered while still alive. Atemin, the last flute-player of the hills was murdered, but not reduced.

'Not reduced, because we resisted,' Metko said. 'But we paid a price. All that we still take pride in comes from the women. Everywhere there's monuments to men. There should be at least one monument to the Pomak women.'

All the women, even the young girls, moved with a sombre self-possession. They were queens of the mountain, even with their bad backs and poor eyesight. When their husbands, fathers and brothers were jobless, drunk, away or dead, they kept things going – in the tobacco field, at the sewing machine, with magic if they had to. Their presence alone was monumental.

'I'm glad you're here,' Metko turned his head to me and his blue eyes smiled.

The hills encircled the village with their ruined fortresses and bunkers.

Yes, we are stuck inside some ancient planetary darkness of our own making. The stars above show us the exit. Or the entrance. And a mountain song leads the way.

I too was glad to be here, in the outer circle of this mandala, this spiral dance of the earth that weaves a spell against extinction.

Stone flower

'It's called stone breaker, yet it's such a small flower,' Metko said. 'You can't see the flowers now. It flowers in the spring, in the cracks of rocks. Look at these rosette-shaped leaves! This lichen lives in symbiosis with it. It's perennial and my mother scraped it off the stone with a spoon and used it to dye the sheep wool a light brown. I look at the stone flower and think of a line from Kafka: What you love will die, but return in another form.'

Saxifraga, a genus of perennial rock plants, literally means 'stone breaker'. Pirin has nineteen species of stone flower – about five per cent of the world's Saxifraga species – including edelweiss.

The following summer, I returned to the old tobacco fields. The stone had over-flowered again. We sat next to it on the warm rock and Metko smoked. The tobacco was gone from his mountain, but Metko held on to it.

'I often have a dream,' Metko said. 'I'm flying over these hills and they are as in my youth – a green forest of tobacco. In the distance is the ribbon of Snake Creek, red with cornelian cherries. I recognise every fold but the difference is that in the dream, I'm free and nothing can go wrong. The hills are illuminated. The closest I get to that feeling in waking life is when the stone flower blossoms. You know I'm a cynic, but the stone flower restores me. It's my remedy.'

I found a potted stone flower in a garden centre. Scotland is stony and cold enough, even at sea-level, but it languished and I wondered if it was too wild to thrive in a pot, just as some humans are.

GYULTEN AND THE POISON

Once you met her, Gyulten was hard to forget. It was her intensity, her throaty laughter and eyes like coal that burned holes in you. Small and slight, with long black hair in a pony tail, she exuded a power larger than her. Her face bore the traces of a hard life and she was a grandmother, but her wildish quality was ageless.

She stood out in The Birches. Wholesomeness was customary for married Pomak women, like with the Amish or the Mormons. Gyulten couldn't be wholesome if she tried. Metko introduced us outside her wood-clad bakery. Gyulten ran the bakery alone and worked night shifts. She served coffees, soft drinks and snacks in the evening – no alcohol – then she slept for a few hours and after midnight, she'd begin making the dough.

'Tell me what you like, I'll make you stuffed pastry,' she said – and the next morning we breakfasted on pastry filled with the leeks that we'd picked together from her allotment. She took care of it with her sisters: in addition to her large vegetable garden at home. The allotments were at the low end of the village and you needed wellies for the squelchy furrows. She didn't drive and walked everywhere.

'How do you have the energy for it all?'

'Oh, I have energy,' she laughed. 'Too much of it.'

She liked the night-time. She'd sit on a low stool outside, smoke under the stars and listen to the deep silence of the mountain.

At dawn, the trays came out of the ovens fragrant with cheese rolls. She opened the doors at six. By ten, her goods sold out and she went home to sleep. She lived at the top of the village, the last house in the last street where the forest began.

'I like it up there,' Gyulten said. 'Cos down here, you can't sneeze without someone providing a commentary. With footnotes.'

The rumour. She liked to get away from it as often as possible. And like me, she liked the area around the Birches Hotel for its air. We went for walks in the forest above and this is where Gyulten showed me a photo: an old woman in black, her eyes full of bitterness. It was her, after the death of her husband. He'd been a strong guy, then one day he sickened and wasted away, turning yellow because it was liver cancer, and died just after his fiftieth. She married him when she was fifteen.

'We made bread together for thirty years,' she said. 'It wasn't perfect but we looked out for each other. We were like one.'

If she worked a solo shift, he'd wait for her at home with a salad and chilled beer, just the way she liked it. When he died, she shut herself in their bedroom, drew the curtains, unplugged the lights and stayed there for two years. She was forty-five and her life was over.

'All I could think of was his end. I was stuck in that moment. Replaying it.'

She'd walk to the hilltop cemetery to sit at his grave and talk to him.

'The weird thing is, the more people tried to help, the deeper I sank. It's like I enjoyed being the living dead. It gave me something over them. Aren't we wicked sometimes?'

We picked a white-headed flower by the forest path. The heads were finely knitted, and the leaves too.

'Yarrow. Very good for women's problems. Anything to do with the uterus. And good for bleeding in general.'

But I don't particularly have women's problems, I said. Gyulten scoffed, her fingers moving fast. She could fill a bag in no time.

'Everybody has women's problems, sooner or later! Stock up, just in case. Here,' she handed me the full bag. 'Spread them on a newspaper. In a few days, you can make tea.'

I'd never had yarrow tea. It was bitter and mobilising. You can feel it work in your mouth, tightening things even before you swallow it.

'You mix it with fragrant herbs like thyme,' said Gyulten.

Yarrow has the distinction of being both the women's herb and the soldier's herb. In the Balkan Wars and the First World War, soldiers stemmed their wounds with yarrow poultices. When men left for The Front, their mothers and wives put bunches of yarrow in their knapsacks, with the bread and garlic – it was all they could do to hope that the yarrow would save their men. I learned to recognise yarrow and picked it in Scotland. It's hardy and grows along field hedges and in meadows. Its Latin name tells a story. *Achillea millefolium* – the thousand-leafed plant of Achilles that stemmed all his wounds, except the one that was fated to kill him.

It was a picture-still summer's day, full of butterflies and the smell of pine. I was worried about bears again. We were high up, the forest was deep and dark. The next destination was Kornitsa, over the valley, over the river where Birchers had walked that winter and a boy called Tefik was shot.

'Yep,' Gyulten said. 'There are bears. We'd have to be unlucky though.

'There's not much you can do if you meet a bear face to face,' she said. 'But the bear doesn't like to turn up in your face. That's why you keep your eyes ahead of you. Because that's where bears pop up – crossing the path, minding their own business.'

Gyulten was the child of shepherds and had spent the first fifteen years of her life roaming Pirin. Her parents were in charge of 300 sheep in a state cooperative in the Struma Valley.

'All the shepherd families on that side were from our side,' Gyulten said. 'I don't know why. Maybe cos Our Folk are hard grafters when it comes to the mountain. And the folk on the other side are more into wine and grapes.'

They spent the long alpine summers in a highland area called the Monk, in *kolibi*. The family worked hard. Gyulten still had no idea how her parents kept track of 300 sheep without losing one, except to wolves. When sheep wandered off, the kids were sent off with one of the Karakachan dogs to look for them.

'Mist was the worst,' she said. 'On misty nights the wolves came out in packs and attacked. We didn't sleep on those nights. It was like a horror film.'

There wasn't much they could do. Had they not been Muslims, they would have been issued with a gun like other shepherds at the time. One autumn when they were coming down from the Monk with the herd, the animals got crazed. Her parents knew instantly.

Her father planted himself at the front of his flock. A bear was crossing their path, 20 metres ahead. A massive black male. He saw them
and stopped.

'We froze. The dogs' hackles went up but they didn't make a
sound.'

But the bear went on his way. And so did the family, though they
felt a chill for the rest of the day.

'Look, thyme! Let's pick some.' Gyulten's fingers moved fast. The
minute flowers were purple. I crouched and inhaled. Its fragrance
lifts you up and calms you down at the same time.

'Good in tea, for flatulence and bloating,' she said. 'And for chesty
coughs and high cholesterol. You can put it in stews too, at the end.
Don't cook it or it loses its aroma. But we mustn't over pick it because
the bees love it too.'

Gyulten knew about herbs from her mother, from those years on
the mountain when she learned which plants were poisonous or
edible, which trees were good for the evening fire (pine and fir are
good fire-starters, oak is calorific), which leaves were good for vomiting children, dog wounds from wolf attacks, skin infections from
stepping on thorns, intestinal worms and sunburn.

I asked her how she pulled herself out of the black hole, how she
got from the woman in the photograph to the woman she was today.

'Herbs,' she said.

During that period of mourning, Gyulten began to have abdominal pain. It became so bad that she took herself to hospital. They did
scans and immediately sent her off to a clinic in the capital. The
oncologist gave her the diagnosis, followed by the prognosis.

'A rare, fast-growing, malignant tumour. Inoperable because of its
awkward location. The nice doctor said they could do chemo but it
might not work. It was up to me. Without chemo, I had about three
months of normal life left.'

Gyulten took the next bus home and shut herself in her bedroom
again. She didn't tell a soul. But it was like she'd been startled from a
coma. One day she climbed into the woods.

'I picked myself some roots and berries. And I made a cocktail to
wake up the dead.'

Above all, she sought Lords and Ladies. Or Cuckoo-pint. The folk name here was Snake Spindle and its Latin name is the occult-sounding *Arum maculatum*. It grows in woodlands and Snake Spindle describes it well: snake and spindle, reptile and plant in one. Its glistening red berry clusters seem poised to attack you if you get too close.

Many plant names here had 'snake' in them. Reptile and vegetal, poison and anti-poison – they go back a long way, which is why the symbol of Western medicine is the serpent; two serpents rather, coiled around a winged staff. This is the *caduceus* of Hermes, caped messenger of the gods with winged sandals, trickster, patron of travellers and mediator between realms. Like all magi, peregrines and messengers, Hermes carries a herald's staff – given to him by the god of healing arts, Apollo, or maybe by Asclepius, the patron of medicine who learned from Chiron the Centaur. Once, Hermes passed two fighting snakes and struck them with his staff. They coiled around the staff and stayed that way: in perfect balance.

The first named alchemist is Hermes Trismegistus. He was a Graeco-Egyptian magus and he was 'tris-megistus', thrice-great, in an echo of the early Egyptian god Thoth 'the great, the great, the great'. In the Middle Ages, the *Hermetica* opus attributed to him was revealed to be the work of multiple writers of post-antiquity. He was not as ancient as they thought and he was not a single person. Like Orpheus, Hermes Trismegistus is a composite figure; a faceless prophet. And what of the snakes?

When you look at painted scenes of Egyptian deities, pharaohs, priests, craftsmen and people going about their everyday business, they are crawling with snakes: snakes as crowns, snakes as earrings, snakes as hieroglyphs. Cleopatra was a latecomer to the snake story because the sacred snakes of the gods are as old as fire, and so is the wandering healer with his caduceus.

Until the era of mass urbanisation, medics of all kinds travelled great distances, Hermes-like, with a bag of cures and tools. They were no different from transhumance shepherds in the mileage they covered and the dangers they faced. And they travelled in order to learn too, because: 'The universities do not teach everything, so a doctor must seek out old wives, gipsies, sorcerers, wandering tribes, old robbers, and such outlaws and take lessons from them. A doctor must be a traveller.'

This, by Paracelsus, the Swiss physician and philosopher whose alchemical approach to the body–mind and rejection of hierarchical medical-social doctrines in favour of radical humanism puts him in the same lineage as Culpeper. Paracelsus had a courageous and colourful life, and among many other things, he pioneered the disciplines of psychosomatism and toxicology. Like Gyulten, he would have taken Arum maculatum to study its effects because his motto and message was: 'Let no man belong to another who can belong to himself.' This was the lineage of Avicenna, in whose trail modern European medicine followed.

'You dig up the root,' said Gyulten, 'and cut it into pieces the size of corn grains.'

In European folk medicine, the berries and roots of Lords and Ladies are used to purge the viscera. When taken in exactly the right amount, that is. The wrong amount can kill you. This is a highly toxic plant. Most people would have a medical herbalist advise them, but Gyulten didn't want advice.

'What was the worst that could happen?' she said. 'I had three months to find out.'

She added two other herbs of her own devices.

'I lay them all out on my table,' she said. 'Each morning I took my medicine and I said a prayer. "Allah, help me please." Suddenly, I believed in Allah!'

She laughed her smoker's laughter.

Just a week later, during her night vigil over the dough, she was overcome with pain.

'Like I was about to give birth,' she said. She went into the bathroom, expelled something bloody and passed out on the floor. Her son found her in the morning when hungry clients outside became concerned and called him.

A black mass the size of an egg had come out. Another scan in the local hospital showed no evidence of a tumour. Reeling with shock, she took the bus to the capital again and explained to the oncologist

what had happened. He didn't believe her. She hardly believed it
either. I imagine his face as he listened to her, the woman with a
regional accent on death's door, explaining that she had taken
Cuckoo-pint. He immediately put her through every scan, not quite
believing his eyes. He called colleagues as witnesses.

'Then he said: "This is unprofessional, but I'll give you a hug.
Because it's not every day that I see a miracle."'

She wept then, realising it was true. She was going to live after all.

The follow-up was easy. She had to keep to a strict diet to heal the
raw tissue left by the tumour and there were some more polyps to
purge. She kept up her diet of goat cheese, sheep yogurt, vegetables,
olives and no wheat or meat.

She continued taking her self-administered cocktail of herbs, but
in smaller doses. 'For maintenance,' she said, and the oncologist
encouraged her to stick with her herbal regime, seeing that it worked.
Though he was alarmed by her annual 'maintenance' use of Cuckoo-
pint and advised her to stop it, which she ignored. And she kept up
the smoking too.

'Coltsfoot!' She crouched in the fallen leaves under some oak trees
self seeded in the last fifty years. We were returning to the hotel.
'Not flowering anymore, but the leaves are good for chest infections
and abdominal cramps. It purges.'

'And you never know when you might need purging,' I finished
her sentence and we laughed.

We picked the broad, dark, lily-like leaf with an attractive white
underside. A plant with two sides, like Gyulten herself – the dark
side and the silver lining. I thought of Rocky and the three young
Roma with the 69 kilos of coltsfoot.

'What do you call it in English?' she asked, and laughed about the
coltsfoot.

In Scotland, it was once called son afore the father, because
unusually, the yellow flowers appear before the leaves. People used
the silky petal-threads for stuffing pillows and birds continue to use
it for their nests.

'So that's it,' Gyulten said and rose to her feet, a bagful of leaf.
'This is how I resurrected myself. I expelled the polyps too, with

smaller doses of Cuckoo-pint. And the oncologist hugged me again. And now the whole village picks elderberries come autumn!'

Elderberry had been one of the ingredients of her cocktail and Gyulten's recovery had created an elderberry frenzy among the women of The Birches. Once the tumour was gone, she started taking care of her appearance too. And reflected on her life.

She had married at fifteen to avoid a worse fate. Her parents were of the controlling variety. Everyone's parents here were of the controlling variety. Gyulten's generation had seen the last of the parental extremists. Parents tried to marry their daughters off as soon as they finished primary school to prevent them leaving for the city to study and live in the Communist Party headquarters dorms and God forbid, marry the oppressor.

All three girls in the family submitted to the parents' will, except Gyulten. Gyulten wanted to study and have a worldly life, but they'd lined up a guy for her from a relatively well-off family.

'But I didn't like him. And because I had nowhere to go, I ran to another guy who I did like and who'd already asked me out.'

They ran away from The Birches and lived in a hotel for a week. But they could go no further. Under Communism you couldn't relocate unless the state decided. You couldn't run away. They'd always find you and bring you back, kicking and screaming.

'So we returned to The Birches and got married, like good kids. I gave birth the next year. In short, I didn't have a youth at all.'

That's why she was such a young grandmother. That's why she was having a second youth now. She went to a beautician, bought fine clothes and took holidays in other parts of the country on her own to get away from the pressure cooker of the village.

But there was a further chapter to her parents' story. Gyulten had been so hurt by them for forcing her into marriage when she wanted to study that she cut off all contact with them. Soon after her marriage, her father suddenly became ill. It was terminal and he was only in his thirties. Her mother the herbalist tried everything. Gyulten agreed to visit, not realising he was on his deathbed.

'And he said to me from his bed: "Did you curse me, my child? Was it you that cursed me? I know you have the power."'

We had arrived back in the tranquil hotel grounds and drank from Fatmé's fountain.

'What did you say?'

'I said: "Yes, I cursed you. Because you took my life away from me."'

Her father seemed relieved.

'He said, "I forgive you. Please forgive me too. I need you to forgive me."'

Now Gyulten was crying, and so was I.

'I said: "I forgive you, Dad." He died the same night. I was so mad at him, I hadn't imagined that he could actually die.'

She was only a teenager. But her mother was there too, furious and accusatory in her grief and locked in a power struggle with her daughter to this day.

'It's when there's not enough love,' Gyulten said, 'that these things happen. I hope I've done it differently with my children.'

This was the shadow realm, the ancient darkness that eats its children to engorge itself with power. In his last moments, Gyulten's father had glimpsed this and freed himself of it.

'Where there is love, there is no need for power. Where power predominates, love cannot thrive,' Carl Jung wrote. It is true on a small scale in families and on a large scale everywhere.

The two men's patterns of illness were similar, and similar to her own: sudden onset, rapid decline, malignancy in the digestive organs. She could not rescue her father and her husband. But she had done the hardest thing of all: she'd rescued herself.

We ordered jars of sheep's yogurt from the hotel kitchen.

'Look, that's *funda*,' Gyulten got up and examined Shefket's marigolds.

'Not all marigolds are equal,' she said. 'A friend shrank her uterine tumour with this. Two weeks of strong tea and she avoided surgery.'

Funda was a local name for orange marigold. At Fatmé's fountain we took turns to swing in a hammock.

'Look, that's soapy flower over there! Let's wash.'

By the pond were tufted pink flowers I hadn't noticed before. Soapwort.

'When you're high up all summer without soap, you go to the soapy flower.'

Gyulten rubbed a flower head between her wet fingers. It became frothy. Delighted like children, we soaped up and washed our hands in the pond.

My friendship with Gyulten continued.

And so did another one. I saw Lords and Ladies that summer above The Birches and was startled by their scarlet berries clustered along poker stems. Forget mandrake – this was the original magical plant. Even the words 'Arum maculatum' are a spell. Cuckoo-pint is a polite version of Cuckoo-pintle: penis. And Lords and Ladies is a Victorian euphemism; the plant's male and female parts look like they're copulating. Before that, people called it Devils and Angels. The red berries are produced by the female parts and the male part has a hairy insect-trap with what botanists describe as a 'fecal odour', then the insects are released after being pollinated. The word *arum* has unclear origins and goes back to Egyptian or Hebrew when it might have meant 'reed-like'.

It's part of the lily genus and Culpeper categorises its government and virtues 'under the dominion of Mars'. It was used as an antidote for 'poison and the plague' in his time and combined with sheep's milk – sheep's milk! – it healed 'ulcers of the bowels' and brought on 'women's menses, and purges them after child-bearing'.

Two springs later, I was walking along my Scottish river past some giant reeds, when I saw a patch of inviting leaves that looked like common sorrel. I crouched under the elder tree where they lived. It wasn't sorrel. But they were friendly-looking leaves. I picked one and chewed its tip and swallowed, but something wasn't right and I tried to spit it out. Too late: my mouth began to burn and one side of my face tingled. I belatedly snapped it on my Plantsnap app. It was Arum maculatum. I hadn't recognised it so early in the season without its red berries and when the leaves were much lighter. I'd also read that it was rare in Scotland and didn't expect to see it at sea-level.

My throat constricted as I walked, then ran, home. A quick online search revealed that only the root, or a tincture extract of the dried leaves and berries was used medicinally, never fresh. All parts of the plant are poisonous. Never touch the leaves without gloves. Ingesting them raw can lead to neurological damage and death. I began to sweat. It was the weekend and we were in another lockdown. I flicked open the 'Poisonous Species' section of my forager book and sure enough: Hemlock and Lords and Ladies are Britain's top two deadly ground plants. 'Lords-and-ladies looks completely different at each stage of its growth,' the author warned, too late.

Reading that some English foragers accidentally made soup from the leaves and didn't die, and that medieval Scandinavians made flour from the dried roots in times of famine was not reassuring. I saw myself in hospital with my stomach pumped by people in masks. I dialled Rocky the Enchanter.

He laughed.

'We'll make a herbalist out of you yet!' he said. 'Like I said, you must get to know plants in the flesh. That's where the power is. Not in books. And now's the season for Snake Spindle!'

'Should I go to first aid?' I croaked.

'I'm your first aid,' he said. 'Did you swallow it, how much? That's fine. Eat something to settle your gut. Did I say it cures bowel tumours?'

'I don't have a bowel tumour,' I said, 'But my throat is closing up.'

'Relax,' Rocky said. 'Did I tell you about the time when I went picking a plant whose name is a secret and the boss from the pharma company instructed me to use gloves. Off I went, picking it with my gloves, then I sat down to have some sausage for lunch. I must have touched a branch with my bare fingers and then eaten the sausage. Well! I didn't leave the toilet for three days after that.'

He wouldn't tell me the name of the plant. It was a secret.

'May is a fine month. All sorts of plants come up. The other day I was picking black bryony. With gloves of course. And I was chewing myself some echinacea root. Well! I could have climbed a peak and made love for a year. That's how echinacea root makes you feel, my friend. Thank God I was in a forest or I might've disgraced myself. How are you getting on with mursala? I hope you're taking juniper breaks.'

I felt calmer, but still called Gyulten.

'Funny you're calling, cos I just got back from the cemetery where the best crop of it grows. I sat at my husband's grave, then my father's. And I picked myself a few roots. They're like onion bulbs, but starchy. I was cleaning them when you called.'

'Half of my face is numb,' I said.

'Take a spoon of honey,' she said. 'I put it in a bit of bread myself.'

'Aren't you gonna dry those roots first?'

'Nah. It's strongest raw and now's the time. In a couple of weeks, it'll be over.'

'But it says not to eat it raw,' I protested feebly and opened a honey jar.

Gyulten laughed her smoker's laughter. Nothing was going to stand between her and her annual maintenance course.

'And if I were you,' she added, 'I'd go to that patch and dig up a few plants, dry the bulbs and keep them in a wee jar for a rainy day.'

When the shock of it passed, I returned to the patch. I was too scared to dig anything up, but I sat beside it – as Rocky would advise. And I swear I heard the chuckle, ambiguous and smart, of the creature called Arum maculatum.

Snake-spindle cocktail

Black elderberry
Yellow gentian
Lords and Ladies (Cuckoo-pint, Arum maculatum, 'Snake Spindle')

Elderberry is for strength, Gyulten said. Gentian tones the viscera. And Lords and Ladies is for cancer.

Gyulten prepared elderberry by an extraction method: a layer of berries and a layer of sugar, which after forty days ends up as a thick fermented syrup. Some dry the berry bunches and take a few berries a day throughout the winter, for immunity. One winter I spoke to Gyulten on the phone: 'Have you made your elderberry syrup yet?' she asked. 'Good. Are you taking it? What are you waiting for, sister, get onto it!'

I was surrounded by elder whose only function until now I'd thought to be as a hayfever trigger, when it flowers. The berries blacken in September. I made a winter syrup by boiling the berries with cinnamon and adding honey at the end to avoid sugar. I also discovered that if you ingest them red, you'll throw up immediately. That's called an emetic, a useful property when you poison yourself and actually need to throw up.

Here, people call gentian 'queen of the herbs', and it is one of the main magical plants. Zmeys and intestinal tapeworms don't like gentian, the way vampires don't like garlic. That's because gentian is anti-bacterial and gently purging. Gyulten called it by its folk name: bitter root. This is a clue to its main function: bitter herbs stimulate and cleanse the digestive-hepatic ways and gentian is used in folk medicine to flush out parasites in the gut. Hildegard of Bingen recommends it as a powder taken in warm wine for purging 'fever in the stomach'.

Lords and Ladies root can be taken fresh or dried, a rice-sized piece a day with food, and for no more than two weeks. This was the key ingredient in Gyulten's cocktail. In Scotland, the root was made into pills for ringworm and constipation. The medicinal-deadly components in it are hydrogen cyanide and coniine, also contained in hemlock. But what made my throat burn was the calcium oxalate, whose purpose is to repel grazing animals. In agricultural societies, babies were put in their cradle with a dried leaf of Arum maculatum to repel demons, but also to make the babies sleepy with its sedative chemicals, just like belladonna and tobacco which release nicotine to attract certain larvae and make them sleepy. Too bad if the baby decided to nibble on the leaf! Folk medicine here recommends that women take the male (top) part of the plant and men take the female (bottom) part.

Now I knew how Gyulten had expelled her large tumour with such shocking speed: It was the 'double, double' bind of gentian and Lords and Ladies.

'Everything is poison,' said Paracelsus, 'it all depends on the dose.' Venom is the root of all things pharmaceutical. The Greek φάρμακα – farmaka – originally meant medicine, poison, spell and a set of magical objects, all in one.

The Magician and the High Priestess, the first two archetypes of the tarot arcana, are medicinal and convey this well. Tarot is a hermetic narrative in twenty-one archetypal images based on the hero's journey; from the fool to the world's soul or *anima mundi*. Tarot is a repository of ancient knowledge. It is also the easiest way to access the basics of alchemy today. The magician is the magus-pharmacologist. On his table is the full set of tools to connect heaven with Earth, the material with the spirit world: cup-vessel; pentacle-ore; wand-torch and sword-idea. They symbolise the elements of water, earth, fire and air. But older yet than the magus is the three-bodied goddess Hecate whose tools are the wheel, the fire-torch, the serpent and the dagger.

And Hecate's even older avatar is the Egyptian goddess Isis with the sun in her crown of cow horns. These proto-witches live on in the high priestess. Seated in the intra-dimensional gateway where the fabric is thin, holding the book of mysteries with pomegranates like female genitalia behind her, she is celibate like a nun or an Orphic oracle. Celibate, not sexless, she belongs to herself. One of the most enigmatic archetypes of the Hermetica, she won't show you her tools but you can see the result. The sun in her crown and the moon at her feet, where her cape becomes the ocean. She has brought down the moon.

I SEVER TO SEVER

Once the festivities ended, the Birches Hotel became quiet again. In my rooms, the herbs I picked with Gyulten were drying on newspapers. They were like flatmates who occasionally muttered as they lost moisture, shifted position and shrank.

In the morning, from Fatmé's fountain, I glimpsed a tall skinny figure with a knapsack on the forest road. He moved so fast he looked like he was gliding, and then he was gone.

'The guy with the horses, you missed him again,' said Shefket who wandered around with his watering hose and now I spied his marigolds with new eyes.

People were busy. Gyulten worked and slept, and I saw her on weekends. Metko was decorating a house. There was a construction boom in The Birches because of the money earned abroad and property was expensive. Houses competed for size and price, but often sat empty like mausoleums to success, complete with beige synthetic carpets.

At night, the restaurant's playlist was on a loop and I listened to the Greek song 'Mavro Trientafilo' (Black Rose), over and over. Then I slept at the bottom of the forest-well like a frog. One night, a voice clearly said the names of plants in my dream and I was shown their shapes. This happened again the next night, but in the morning my recall was blurry. Except for one word: *silivryak*. A voice said: look for this, it is silivryak. I forgot its shape and had no idea what it was, plus the internet was down. The hotel grounds were deserted so I drove down to the village to get provisions and ran into Kadrié K., the singer.

'Ah, I wondered what happened to you!' she said.

She was a ruddy woman with a robust voice and personality. We had only met online before and kept missing each other in the flesh.

She had an expansive quality that welcomed you into the club without making you pass any tests.

'Silivryak is immortal flower,' she said. 'We don't have it here. But if you're into plants, come on Wednesday. I'm going out for *Metya Chaush*. A friend's daughter has a bad rash on her face. Wear good shoes, there are snakes.'

I thought Metya Chaush was a person. When we met on Wednesday, which was apparently the right day of the week for this ritual, there was a second woman there; the mother of the girl with the rash. We set off for St George's Hill above the neighbourhood where Kadrié's parents lived. There were several women in The Birches who performed healing and exorcising rituals, and her mother was one of them: a *mageshnitsa*.

'We'll drop in later,' Kadrić said.

A church stood at the end of her parents' neighbourhood and next to it: the destroyed plague cemetery. A lone turbaned headstone remained in the ground.

'Saint George,' Kadrié pointed at the church. 'When I couldn't conceive, I spent a night there on St George's Day.'

It was Pomak female tradition. St George's Day, also called Ederlezi, was the best day of the year to bring blankets, light a candle, chant a prayer with the priest, sleep on the floor with other women, then take a piece of paper inscribed with a prayer from the Bible and dissolve it in water that you drink for health, a baby or the end of suffering. Just like the hodjas! Magical Islam and magical Orthodoxy have always been in conversation because they come from the same place.

'Anyway, I promised the choicest lamb kurban to Saint George,' said Kadrié.

And?

'And a little bird said "Amen," she said, an expression I'd not heard before. 'I gave birth in November 1989. I gave her a Christian name and two days later, a Muslim one.'

Her daughter was born at the exact time that the old regime died.

We climbed into a sparse grove. She and the other woman browsed the undergrowth. I realized that Metya Chaush was a plant, but also a person.

'Once upon a time, there was a woman who couldn't get pregnant,' Kadrié began. 'Then she found a herb that helped her. She found *selemet* in it.'

Selemet is salvation and also cure. When a boy was born to that woman, she named him Metya. At some point he became a *chaush*, a low-ranking Ottoman officer.

'And she gave the herb the same name. Metya Chaush. Until then, that herb had no name.'

From the hillside, The Birches lay at our feet, bathed in sun, its scorched hills the colour of dried tobacco.

And there it was – the herb with a human name. When it flowered, its blue blossoms resembled green Alkanet.

'We need three plants,' Kadrié said.

When we found a small colony, Kadrié opened up her bag and laid out her tools: little flat breads smaller than digestive biscuits, a steel knife and a pack of salt.

'The bread is made with flour, salt and water. I baked it this morning.'

There were nine of the little breads and they looked tasty. But they were not for us.

'Metya Chaush is for skin disorders, venereal diseases and eye problems,' Kadrié said.

All of these went under the folk name of 'the red one', *tsarvénoto*. It was understood to mean inflammation of the soft tissue.

The mother of the girl with the rash was briefed. She was here because two women were needed and ideally, one would be close to the afflicted. She'd taken her daughter to specialists but nothing had helped.

'My mother and I only treat people that can't be helped by conventional means,' Kadrié said. Because you didn't want to harness the spirit of plants willy-nilly.

She placed three mini breads at the base of each plant, like fairy offerings. Three times three. She then sprinkled salt on top of each bread with a spoon. To fix the intention. The two women kneeled by the plants, one on each side. Kadrié picked up the knife and circled the first plant by running the knife's point clockwise in the soil around it – three times. The two women said the spell, which was in two voices. The blade caught the morning sun. The girl's name was Dulezar.

'Bismillah Rahmani Rahim,' began Kadrié.

'What do you sever?' asked the mother.

'I sever to sever Dulezar's rash,' said Kadrié with steely intent.

'What do you sever?'

'I sever to sever Dulezar's rash.' Kadrié circled with the knife.

'What do you sever?'

'I sever to sever Dulezar's rash.'

I was glad the aim was to cure. There was something so concrete about the elfish bread, the knife, the plant, the circling, the repetition of 'sever', the two sturdy women willing the forces of the earth and the ether to come together in the service of Dulezar's face, that I felt what it meant to be under a spell. It's a biddable state. That was how the plant was meant to feel. Kadrié moved along the plants from west to east. You summoned plants west to east for good and east to west for bad.

Then Kadrié said:

> I sever to sever.
>
> I sever to sever.
>
> I sever to sever.

And with the practised move of an elf assassin, she severed each plant near the base, then placed it face down on top of the mini-breads. It had to be face down. The idea was to sever the course of Dulezar's disease by transferring it to the plant. You fed the spirit of Metya Chaush with wheat and salt and starved Dulezar's face of the rash. The plant's face took the disease from Dulezar. It was a sacrifice.

Alliteration and repetition is key in spells because a good spell is a poem, just as a good poem is a spell. It sounded like this:

> *Séka da préseka.*
>
> *Séka da préseka.*
>
> *Séka da préseka.*

There was something about human skin and Metya Chaush. Kadrié was clear that this didn't work for other ailments, even if she had forgotten why and why it had to be this plant, and on a Wednesday. It's just something the women of The Birches had always done. The plant name had changed over time but the ritual had not. Metya is an affectionate name for Mehmed and during the Ottoman era, Chaush became an occupational name, like Smith.

'That's it,' she said and we rose, brushing off our legs.

Kadrié placed her tools back in the bag and said: 'Now we walk away from it without looking back.'

That's what we did. There is something powerful about walking away without looking back, as Orpheus discovered in the underworld, too late.

I didn't find out the fate of Dulezar's rash. But after seeing the ritual, I think of skin problems differently – as a separate thing that feeds off you. Perhaps that's true of every disease; it is an entity that shares your cells and might eat you in the end. As the disease grows, you shrink. The trick was to distract it away from you, so that it vanishes. War, tyranny, illness. To paraphrase Herodotus, misfortune never does vanish, it simply moves on to another host.

Later, I identified the plant as viper's bugloss, a type of borage. It is an arid plant with strong anti-inflammatory chemicals and has had wide medicinal use in all things skin-related – from snake bites to boils, bruises, all manner of inflammatory 'redness' and was even used in facial creams for its linoleic acids. You can juice the leaves or make tea with them, and it must be a favourite with foxes because it is also called fox's grass.

It still puzzled me how *exactly* that woman had used it to conceive her child-plant named Metya Chaush. But Kadrié was at ease with puzzles. The exact was less important than the essential. And the essential was to know the plant.

That week with Gyulten and Kadrié, I realised how isolated I was by my river in Scotland, going out to meet plants face to face without a guide. My herbalist lived far away and I knew no foragers in the area. Plus, experienced foragers in Britain must be paid. Plant knowledge is a commodity, not a pastime with your friends.

In the valley, you learned from others and every village had experienced plant pickers. You went into the woods together and you smelled, chewed, spat out and collected your plants. In Scotland, I relied on the internet and books. I stayed up at night looking up plants, instead of looking up symptoms. Herbalism had happily supplanted hypochondria. But I tended to look up the plant after I tasted it – like the time I nibbled some umbrella-like white flowers of cow parsley and soon felt dizzy and nauseated. It hadn't had the usual carroty taste. I had also nibbled the leaves. It wasn't cow parsley at all. Sweet cicely or fool's parsley? Or something else? I rushed home to my books and discovered hemlock, an exact lookalike. Hemlock is called *Conium maculatum*, I read in a daze, because its flowers resemble the white cone hats of whirling dervishes, which is how you feel shortly before you die from toxic shock. You feel like Socrates after he drank the juice of the hemlock. The world spins. Your body is paralysed but you are lucid and after all the books you've read, you know that you know nothing.

The ancient Greeks said it: There are three ways to learn. Alone in the wild. With a guide. And in books. The last way is the worst. The first way can be the shortest-lived. The middle way is best.

We went to see Kadrié's parents.

We found them in a large empty room with a bed and a table. Her mother sat on the bed in a commanding way, blue-eyed, with her legs up. Her father, ninety years old, sat in a chair. He was a gaunt, haunted-looking man who didn't say a word but listened to his daughter and wife. The mother wore a gauze-like head-and-shoulders scarf, hand-painted with red flowers. Her velvet shalvars were black with red flowers and her feet were in knitted socklets embroidered with a red butterfly.

We decided that she'd do the egg ritual for me. She sat me on the bed next to her and gave me an egg to hold while Kadrié prepared a jar of clean water, a packet of sugar and a long stem of dried basil. Her mother then took the egg from me and holding it to her mouth, whispered an opening prayer in Arabic. We all kept quiet and concentrated.

'Come closer. I'll do the egg spell,' she said.

She leaned over and made circular motions over my face and chest with the egg, mumbling an incantation in Bulgarian that I could just about make out.

A pleasant sensation started in my forehead and ran through my body. I don't know if it was her rumbling voice, like a mountain spring, or the calming circles, but I felt stroked by feathers. The sensation was similar to that with baba Acivé and the melted lead. The egg that was solid now but liquid a moment later, the bullet that became molten lava, the water waiting to receive it all – it was therapeutic. Like lying under a belladonna bush on a summer's afternoon. The bush whispers. The baba whispers. You relax.

She opened with the universal *surah* 'In the name of Allah the beneficent the most merciful':

> Bismillah Rahmani Rahim.
> A little from me
> More from Allah.
> What's your name?
> Okay, Kapka.
> Here's for *uroki*,
> For fright
> For *urama*
> For deeds done to you
> For all the bad.
> Let it go like lightest feather
> Like purest silver
> Let it go
> To mountains
> To forests
> To cold waters
> To thick shadows
> To green grasses.
> Let it go.
> Gone.

She said this three times and broke the egg in the jar of water. Mother and daughter peered at it.

'Oh!' said Kadrié. 'You've got uroki. There's the eyes on top. And you've got urama.'

'She does.'

'A huge evil eye there. Yep. And there's the mist, see the mist?'

'The mist is rising,' her mother confirmed.

'Mist means urama,' said Kadrié.

The eyes were large bubbles. I knew uroki – a type of evil eye, except that evil eye can be accidental but uroki is always malicious.

Urama was new to me. It literally means that you've been 'circled', that is, you've picked up something while treading on contaminated or taboo ground. Graveyards, rubbish dumps, under bridges, borders of townships, peripheries – you had no business in such places lest you disturbed the resident spirits.

'Aye, you've picked it up somewhere.'

Urama was understood to come from *djinns* or *samodivas* – demons that are neutral when minding their own business, but turn dark when disturbed.

Just like humans.

The mother put a few grains of sugar into the jar.

'To sweeten the bad,' said Kadrié, meaning the demon.

Ritual sweetening of spirits is as old as Dionysus here.

'Aye, I sweeten the bad ones to distract them from you. Now, you're gonna lie down next door. You lie down without a word. You don't speak once you sweeten up . . . You're gonna dip your finger in the water and go like this. Like this and like this.'

The mother showed me where to 'sweeten up' with the water: on the lips, cheeks, chin, forehead, inside the palms and the tops of the hands, the soles and tops of the feet – which made me think of Christ crucified, but these are simply energy centres in the body.

'And you say the little duva I told you as you sweeten up. Remember?'

Of course I didn't. It was in Arabic.

'Kadrié, where's that basil?'

'Here,' Kadrié handed her mother the bunch and they stuck it in the jar like a long spoon. Even dried, its aroma filled the room.

'It has to be basil,' Kadrié said.

They took me next door where I lay on a large bed with the jar next to me. I stared at a plaster sunburst feature on the ceiling which was painted purple to match the curtains. Purple was fashionable in Pomak households and plaster features were all the rage. They were ugly imitations of the original ceilings from carved wood. I suddenly grasped why people had such poor taste in home decoration here, yet their gardens were lush. It wasn't just the loss of tradition and the influx of Chinese mass-manufactured ersatz. It was also that their sense of beauty was still attuned to the outdoors. That's where their lives had been lived until recently. Our lives.

Then I drifted. I daydreamed of beings with wings. They floated above me and held plants whose names I didn't know. Their intentions were ambiguous.

Then mother and daughter came in, holding plants like staffs, and sprinkled me with the basil in all the indicated places while reciting the duva. Again, the sensation of feathers.

Before I left, her mother showed me a dried flower. Orange and tufted.

Marigold!

'We call it funda,' said Kadrié.

Marigold again! It seemed to follow me. When dried, it had a pungent sweetish smell.

'If you have uterine fibroids, funda is your mother,' said Kadrié, using a folk expression. When something is your mother, it's the solution. 'A friend shrank her fibroids with an infusion of funda and iodine drops,' she added. Not the same woman as Gyulten's friend.

I took it and heard Gyulten's voice: 'Everybody has uterine fibroids, sooner or later!'

'There are two types of marigold,' said her mother. 'You want the orange one. Not the red.'

Orange marigold soothes swellings – internal, like tumours and inflamed lungs, and external – like eczema, acne and calluses, with its high amount of flavonoids, etheric oils and carotene. In pre-Hispanic Mexico, the marigold was like the European lily, the flower of the dead. But it's also used in South America as a culinary herb and a tea – a growth-shrinking tea.

When I did an online search in English, the topics were: 'Is marigold poisonous? Do cats hate marigold? Why is marigold dying? Where to buy hybrid marigolds.'

When I did a search in Bulgarian, I got: 'Learn about the long medicinal history of the marigold. Therapeutic uses of the wonder plant marigold. What *Tagetes* can do for you.'

This happened with many plants. It tells a tale: there was a fork in the vegetal-human road. The East stuck to the path of relationship, the West took the path of severance. Now that we are all ailing, East and West, South and North, we are rapidly coming to a convergence of paths.

'Why the egg, by the way?' I asked.

The egg was meant to draw out the negative from me, like a sponge. I was not convinced, but I hadn't come to be convinced. I'd come to have an experience.

'Because the egg draws things out like nothing else,' said Kadrié's mother with finality.

Later, I learned that among the current witches of The Birches, Kadrié's mother was top of the heap.

Kadrié and I walked down to the river. She carried the jar with the egg and I had the marigold and the basil. I asked about her father.

'I don't know where to begin,' Kadrié said.

In the 1960s, the state carried out its first modern assimilation assault on the Pomak communities and was met with civil resistance. They repeated it ten years later with tanks. For his refusal to tow the line that first time, Kadrié's father was deported to Belene, a notorious camp for political prisoners on a Danubian island. There, he was subjected to nine months of forced labour and torture. Then he was moved to another detention camp and the whole family were internally deported for a time, which meant that they were torn away from The Birches and forced to live with strangers in another part of the country, doing menial work. When Kadrié's mother went to visit him, she saw him on a river barge but when he tried to wave to her, a soldier bashed him with a spade. Her mother collapsed on the banks of the Danube.

We walked and Kadrié wiped her sudden tears quickly, trying not to spill the jar. That's how her childhood had been. Later, Kadrié wanted to study gynaecology, but because of her father's political record there was no chance. She had a musical gift but developing it required leaving home for the city and that was another no – this time from her parents.

'So I made it my hobby to collect stories and songs.'

Her grandfather and other survivors had walked home from the Macedonian Front west of here at the end of the First World War. Sucking lead bullets and chewing wheat from their pockets.

'Like birds, grain by grain. For forty days and forty nights, they walked over the mountains.'

They came across 'enemy' soldiers who were drinking horse urine. 'Good?' the Birchers asked. 'Good!' the poor soldiers grinned. Forty days is a symbolic period in Orthodox Christian and Balkan Islamic tradition, and in ritual magic. It's a bardo, when the soul is between realms. To lift a deed done to you, you collect forty herbs. You soak them outside at full moon and you wash your body at sunrise.

'I love gathering stories,' Kadrié said. 'Stories and plants. The crazier, the better. Cos life is crazy.'

Life is crazy and almost anything is tolerable, except saying goodbye to those you love.

'The day our daughter got married,' Kadrié said, 'her father carried her from our house to the bottom of the street where her sweetheart waited. That's the tradition.'

He put his daughter down next to her fiancé and said: 'Stay with us another day, darling.'

Kadrié's tears fell again. 'And she said: Daddy, I have to go. It's time.'

Kadrié began to sing an old song to stop herself crying:
'Don't cry, mother, don't weep, father.
My time has come to give my heart away.
My sweetheart leads the dance.'
The thing about giving away a daughter is that she will live in

another's house. Whereas, the son stays with you and you can control him for evermore. That's why the archaic *gelina* ritual in Ribnovo is celebration and mourning in one, and only women participate. Because Demeter loses control of her daughter Persephone and has to face herself for the first time.

'We have two daughters. You know from the start that you'll be left with nothing,' Kadrié said.

The liquid sloshed in the jar. Her daughter lived next door and she saw her every day, but it wasn't about that. It was about her own entrapment – she too had walked from her parents' door to her sweetheart's door in a straight line. Or worse, been carried by her father. Up and down the same village street, when she had a voice and a heart that contained the world.

Almost all the women I met in The Birches were taking tranquilisers or anti-depressants, or both. There were a lot of lonely women. And men. Healing and ailing were a major channel of self-expression because other channels were severed.

A girl from The Birches married in Kornitsa down the road and as soon as she gave birth, her mother and grandmother fell gravely ill. Driven by guilt, the girl left her husband and returned with the baby. The two women recovered at once. Stories like these were common. Illness as communication is involuntary magic. To become ill and force change on your environment is even more remarkable than making someone else ill. You don't need a ball of hair or a spell. All you need is to harness the desperate base material of your own unconscious. It is the power of the powerless.

This hobbling of the wild woman is part of the Pomak trauma. No: of all human trauma. It is our shared illness. It's just that for the Pomaks, it had gone on longer. People here had experienced total loss at the beginning of the twentieth century. Then, only a generation later, they were stripped of their land and animals and of the right to feed themselves. Then their millennial forests were cut down and they were made to work the tobacco fields and bombed with poison. Then they were stripped of their names and their clothes. No wonder they held on to their children and slowly strangled them. It's all they could do to survive.

I thought of my two grandmothers. They were very different, but they shared one thing: They were vital, wildishly creative women not suited to a life of conformity, yet that was the only life available to them. They were most alive outdoors and when writing poems, songs, plays and letters, and when being immersed in their inner ecologies. My Danubian grandmother, a German language teacher, was terrific at cards, the accordion, singing, rhyming couplets and backgammon. My Macedonian grandmother, a radio journalist, was a talented writer and a great cook. I sensed that they were gasping for air in the pressure cooker of their marriages and duties. My maternal grandmother expressed her injuries through terminal illness and early death, and my paternal one – through chronic illness relieved by two mercies: valerian and widowhood.

When I see that my house is full of drying nettles, that my spare bed is covered in rose petals, my cupboards full of dark jars with tinctures and syrups, and my garden full of garlic, I see my paternal grandmother's house. She would take an Easter egg dyed red and draw the cross over my front, for health, with it. She was an everyday herbalist, a self-soother in whose veins ran the grape juice of her ancestors and something of that was passed on to me. It could not be taken away when all else was.

Another day in The Birches, I visited an old woman known as Auntie Salé. She looked staggeringly like a witch. A charming witch with a hooked nose and wily eyes. She had a more cryptic style than Kadrié's mother.

'The water's from you. You turn it on, you turn it off,' she said, and poured water into a clay bowl.

My fate was up to me.

'Once the water's in the dish, you must be quiet,' she said.

She began to circle me with the egg, mouthing silent prayers until I felt sleepy. Her clay dish had a greenish glaze. This was the real deal. The green tinge of the bowl is a classic in nature magic.

In Ireland, green is a nod to the 'little body' fairy *leprechaun*. Here, green stood for samodiva, the wood nymph. And just as the little fairy out on the moor can suddenly turn out to be a giant, there is nothing sweet about the samodiva. She is a shapeshifter.

Ancient writers of the Mediterranean invoke 'Thrake the nymph' who could heal with one hand and injure with the other. In her chthonic guise, she holds serpent-whips and makes people go insane with love or fear. In her luminous guise, she is a healer and protector of wild animals. In Thracian votive plates she is Artemis with deer and eagles. Her name and her knowledge was passed on to those early south-eastern Europeans, the Thracians. In votive images and coins, Thracian divinities are shown holding a flowering branch. I was stunned to see a second-century coin where Rodopi the Artemisian goddess-priestess holds a sprig of immortal flower. Our friend the silivryak again.

The samodiva is invoked in healing spells as 'mother samodiva' or 'sister samodiva' and needs to be sweetened with honey and elf bread like Kadrié's. The samodivas are dormant in winter and enter the human world on spring equinox. They cover their heads with a veil called *syanka* (shadow), because they are mistresses of shadow. And mistresses of wilderness. Their solitude is sacred, it's explicit, no excuses for trespassers. Samo-diva means 'lone wild woman'.

Shepherds and luckless men like Actaeon who stumble into a samodiva circle become enchanted, then confused, then die in a freak accident. Rarely, a samodiva and a mortal man can have a relationship and even a child, but the child invariably dies.

All women magi, priestesses, witches, folk healers, mystics and hermits are heiresses of Thrake the samodiva. The first wildish woman. And just as the samodivas had their territory, so the healers of The Birches had theirs. People went to some healers and not others.

I found Auntie Salé on a bench outside her house with two other women who were knitting. Three fates spin the yarn of life . . . Auntie Salé wore loud red shalvars with bold flowers and a matching apron. She instantly knew I had come 'on business' and rose to open the gate. The other women knew it too.

'Come,' she said and led me into the twilight of her kitchen. She sat on the bed made up with a furry blanket and I sat next to her. This is where she cooked and slept, next to the iron stove, though there were other rooms. But the witch likes her kitchen best.

She broke the egg in the dish and put a thread from my scarf in it, rolled it into a small ball and mouthed mantras over the bowl without a sound.

She used a special book of 360 prayers from the Koran, published in Bulgarian by a regional foundation for Islamic enlightenment. A book that would be good to have at hand.

Afterwards, I learned that she had seen the death first of her granddaughter, then of her daughter through illness. She had nursed them both and walked with their bodies wrapped in linen up the cemetery hill, steep like a Golgotha.

'You have a nice road ahead of you,' she said. 'With small obstacles only.'

I stared at the bowl. The thread bobbed around the egg. The egg shone like a sun in the sea of life.

I found the egg in alchemical drawings. In *Hermetic Androgyne*, a famous sixteenth-century painting by an unknown artist, the winged hermaphrodite undergoing the work that will purify them holds a mirror in one hand and an egg in the other. The egg has been with us for so long, it practically hatched us. Magi saw the egg as the totem of life itself, containing all four elements: earth (shell); air (membrane); fire (yolk) and water (the white). The egg is the chalice. If you do the work, the philosopher's egg is transmuted into the philosopher's stone. Or you can just enjoy a session with Auntie Salé.

But she'll make you sip from the slimy egg water three times. From different parts of the rim.

Because they had lived embedded in nature, the people of the valley had remained close to nature's self-generating myths. Where everything is alive, the human being has no more agency than other beings. This is why illness and other problems are seen as coming from without, not within. But that is because no clear line is drawn between the two. And there is no clear line except in our heads.

The Greek-derived word esoteric means inner, something understood by the few. Exoteric is outer, something understood by all. The esoteric becomes exoteric through what we call events. Auntie

Salé took her job seriously. She knew that the esoteric is always here, while the exoteric is only briefly here. She knew that she dealt in eternity.

She dealt in the art of turning the inside out and bringing the outside in without waiting for events. Circling, the evil eye, curses, contamination – they were all caused by other people or by djinns or samodivas. In short, 'outers'. The outer is an archaic concept that goes back to the spirits known as εξωτικός, exotic ones – 'from the outside'. But there was a deeper insight here: illness and trouble was seen as environmental and this is why these women diagnosed it and treated it like that – environmentally.

Theosophists perceived demons, phantoms and spectres as 'energetic detritus' from the astral bodies of humans. According to Rudolf Steiner, we live with them on Earth because we have produced them ourselves over the millennia, through ugly speech, thought and action.

Auntie Salé poured the water carefully into a jar, and added sugar and twelve dried 'herbies' from some crates under her bed. I was to anoint myself with it for three days. What were the herbies?

She shook her head. 'No.' They were a secret, and after I threw out the liquid, I spent some time drying them to identify them. Some were picked wild, others in her garden.

I asked who came to see her.

'Everybody,' she said simply.

Or rather those who didn't go to the competition, like Kadrié's mother. People came to them for sterility, stress, family problems, love problems, illness diagnosed and undiagnosed, money and neighbour issues. In short, everything.

'But you'll not hear a squeak from me,' she added.

She had not taken the Hippocratic Oath, but her trade was older than Hippocrates. Silence had value in nature healing. You must keep silent when you 'sweeten' yourself and the demons. You must walk in silence to the plant you need. There is 'unspoken water' – water taken from one, three, seven or nine springs, placed in a vessel and anointed for your ritual, keeping silent all the way. Science is now studying how water reacts to its environment and especially how music and speech change its composition. It's astonishing to know that the same water in your glass can be in different cellular states, depending on its ambience. The natural mind has known this for some time.

Going further, there is 'undrunk water' – water from a spring that no mortal has drunk from before. Only animals and *samodivi*.

The problem with magic is not that it doesn't work. It is that power games are an integral part of it and that its belief system is biased. Medicine emerged from alchemy's noble attempt to marry the subjective and the objective, matter and mind, inner and outer, and in this way, to lift humanity out of superstition and senseless pain.

'The aim of all true Adepts is to help relieve a suffering mankind in its physical and spiritual misery,' wrote an American alchemist in the 1970s.

But like magic, the bias of modern medicine went too far in the opposite direction. Like magic, it assumes too much and has many blind spots. These blind spots come from its many uncouplings, one of which is the uncoupling of *psyche* from *soma*, the soul-spirit from the body. Another is the uncoupling of one organ system from another, and another is the uncoupling of the human being from her environment. A human being is eighty per cent water, held by the vessel of the body, but still highly mutable. After a visit to the GP, who can't afford to take meaningful note either of your mind or your body, let alone the connection between them, because she is stressed by the need to tick boxes in the allotted time, you take a pill and hope for the best until next time. In the same way, you take the jar with the egg and hope for the best. But you have no idea, you are a child sent home by the teacher and you have learned nothing.

One way or another, you gave some of your power to the witch with the greenish bowl, to the specialist in the white surgical mask.

Folk medicine and Western medicine are at extreme ends of the human-environmental spectrum. Scientific materialism has no soul and magic has no science. Both of them discourage you from taking ownership of your well-being through knowledge. Both of them keep you dumb and dependent. Western medicine does it like a squeamish patriarch with a mask on, and magic medicine does it like a manipulative matriarch, breathing down your neck. I've heard that the shamans of the Amazon are locked at all times in terrific territorial wars with one another through mind games, poisons, plants, psychic attacks, even murders. Magic pulled you into a personal power ring with side effects as unpleasant as those of antibiotics. Although, at least antibiotics are impersonal when they wipe out your stomach flora.

In his monumental study of cosmos and psyche, Carl Jung demonstrated scientifically that the symbols with which the human psyche spontaneously engages are autonomous entities. That is, they exist outside the psyche. The four-part mandala of which the cross is a product, and so is the rosette and the eight-petalled flower and the twelve zodiacs of the astro-wheel, the snake, the spiral, the egg-sphere, and the triangle. These symbols are the basic keys to what Chinese alchemy calls the holographic universe. And here we are, in Auntie Salé's kitchen, with an egg yolk floating in a bowl. The egg is a microcosm, so am I, so is her kitchen, so is this mountain, this Earth and this galaxy.

'I know people's little soul and will take it with me to the grave,' said Auntie Salé in conclusion and rose to see me off, jar in hand.

Vessel in hand, she will keep seeing off her children till there is nobody left to see.

'This is a true story about a bear and a girl,' said Kadrié just before we reached the bridge. 'Told to me by my neighbour baba Maria who remembered it clearly.'

It happened in threshing season. That's when the wheat was beaten from the chaff with the help of horses. Families climbed into the fields above the Ranger to bivouac for a few weeks. While they slept under the stars, a bear dragged a girl away. They looked for her in vain until a few months later, they found a cave whose entrance was closed with a rock. They moved the rock and inside the cave was the girl. Naked and pregnant.

'Without a single scratch on her body.'

A few months later, she gave birth.

'To a bear cub,' said Kadrié. 'Then a second one. When she looked down and saw the second one, it was too much. Her heart burst.'

'And what of the bear cubs?'

'The bear cubs ran into the woods. But the girl's heart did burst!'

'It's a great story,' I said.

'Not just a great story, a true story. Baba Maria remembered it clearly.'

This is a take on the samodiva loving a mortal man. Except here, the bear cubs survive and reclaim their forest. But the feral cannot survive. The girl is rejected by the collective because she is no longer one of them. And neither will they let her go back to the forest. So they kill her.

Like Gyulten, Kadrié was a wildish woman who had been squeezed into a doll's house, given a little shoe that didn't fit and caused constant pain, but she grinned through it all and that was part of her greatness. These women's talents had been sacrificed to the unconscious collective hunger – a beast that lived above the village and took its young people generation after generation.

Kadrié had first served the needs of her parents, then of her children and for the past twenty years, her husband had worked as a builder in France. She was like a widow but without the freedom. She cleaned her in-laws' sewing factory after hours, this woman who could have been an obstetrician or a professional singer.

Though she hadn't escaped, she'd found an outlet – in song. She was part of the revival of the female voices of The Birches. One voice led to two or three others, weaving a flying carpet of sound and story on which you could briefly escape. She started singing while stringing tobacco, which is how all folk art is born – out of threshing, sewing, harvesting, stringing, shepherding, milking and picking plants. Physical work that made people want to sing for the soul.

It is the soul that must remain wild, like those bear cubs.

We reached the bridge. There was rubbish on the river banks. If the djinns fed on refuse, they surely thrived here. Kadrié held the jar above the railing and said with steely intent, pointing a finger at the river as she spoke:

> Little water
> Little sister
> You that come

From mountains
From hilltops
Where the samodivi gather
Where the samodivi eat
And feast
You take all
You wash all
Take the evil eye
The bad spell
The envy
The catastrophe
And all the bad –
from Kapka.
Little water
Little sister
Take it now!

I thought she'd pour the liquid out. But she sent the whole jar into the river where it smashed, adding to the debris. She threw it with such force, such absolute 'I smash to smash' intent, such carelessness for the fallout that she was smashing it not just for me, not just for herself, but for all the women whose spirits are trapped in vessels that are maddeningly too small for them.

Seventy-seven-and-a-half

Tansy
Mugwort
Echinacea

Three of the 'herbies' in Auntie Salé's mix. The rest I couldn't identify for sure. In her garden on the edge of The Birches were blue irises, she watered them every day.

These three are among seventy-seven-and-a-half plants believed to straddle realms. They are used against seventy-seven 'windy ones' – or pathogens. I don't know all of them but there is also gentian, lovage, smoke tree, restharrow, oregano, bryony and primrose.

Women had gathered these seventy-seven and a half plants at summer solstice, naked and in silence. That's a lot of plants to find in one night. They wove giant wreaths with them. The wreaths were used for the rest of the year to smudge people for all manner of afflictions. The same happened in Scotland on the same night and fires were lit to ward off evil spirits, intoxicating potions were drunk and revellers danced in circles around whatever they wanted to protect. St John's wort and elderflowers hung on doorways for protection because on the solstice, the venom and the anti-venom are extra-strong, so you must know how to turn the water on and turn it off.

Tansy is a yellow-orange flower I mistook for chamomile. I saw it in the hills above Black Mesta, with an old shepherdess who told me how in her childhood they picked kilos of tansy for the wholesale buyers, but tansy has been forgotten – and maybe just as well for it. Tansy is good for warding off zmey, she added on that meadow. Zmey, tapeworms and flies in summer.

Mugwort has faithfully served for the smudging, cleansing, toning and warming of humanity's insides and outsides. Druids and Bogomils considered it sacred for its purifying power. In Scotland, mugwort leaf was placed inside shoes for tired feet. People who couldn't afford tea leaves imported from Asia drank tea made from locally picked mugwort that had the added bonus of digestive relief, and smoked it to alleviate tuberculosis and fever.

Mugwort and woodworm are in the Artemisian family. Our friend Artemis, patron of women's health. I discovered mugwort through TCM. The herb is packed and rolled into a cigar, and chunks of it are placed on top of a needle at an acu-point, and left to infuse you with warmth. This is moxibustion. The effect is body-melting relaxation and pain relief. Its best-known use in TCM is to aid childbirth and menstrual cramps, but it is also good for rheumatic pain, nervous strain, overactive minds, underactive spleens and any of what our friend Culpeper called 'cold griefs'. And it can be burned like incense or placed under the pillow to enhance dreams. The downside is that a moxa-stick smells like ganja. I was nearly thrown out of a hotel for burning it.

Echinacea was imported into Europe from North America, so its healing properties were first known to the Amerindians. Echinacea is Greek for 'spiny one', because the head of the flower is like a sea urchin. And that's what it does for you – it defends you against pathogens. Auntie Salé kept mum, but the plants spoke and echinacea confirmed what tansy and mugwort said: We will protect you against seventy-seven badnesses.

Too bad I didn't drink it.

One night in Scotland, I dreamt that a woman from The Birches came to my door. She came from the river, across the field and stood outside the back door. Not the front door. I couldn't make out her face but in her hands, she held a tray with something like a plant. Then I saw it was a tail of dark hair. Whose hair was it? She was showing me something. She waited for me to let her in but the door was half-open already.

I woke up in alarm and went downstairs. The field was empty and the river like mercury under the moon. But I couldn't shake the feeling that the women of The Birches had followed me over rivers and seas with their seventy-seven and a half cures for seventy-seven badnesses.

MAIDEN GORGE

Maiden Gorge began after Stormy River joined the Mesta on the floor of the valley. The place was marked by a village famous for its nesting storks, tasty red onions and refuge for old donkeys. Twenty years ago, a nun who had loved men lived in a hilltop monastery. They would visit her for fortune telling, and more. Righteous folk chased her away but she had become the stuff of legend. The monastery lay empty and the few remaining men looked toothless and unloved.

Soon after this, the river widened at the village of Siropol and entered Maiden Gorge. Siropol straddled the river. Old Siropol on the Rhodope side had a mosque, and new Siropol on the Pirin side had a church, both in use. Pirin was harsh, vertical and pure, but the Rhodope had a dark creeping stealth and it had spread where Pirin had height.

Maiden Gorge was where the two mountains almost touched. The canyon was in permanent shade, squeezed by metamorphic cliffs and empty of humans.

The steep rocky flanks on each side shapeshifted before your eyes into animated sculptures: The Wedding, The Saints. The Saints were a caped procession frozen in their tracks. Once, there was a libidinous monk in a nearby monastery (maybe the one with the nun?), whose lust so appalled the female icons that they walked off, turning into these flat-faced rocks – the land's judgement.

Once in the gorge, you either got stuck or fled onwards. I imagined the two mountains closing over the river one day, forcing travellers to crawl through the passage as a tax.

There were two lone dwellings in the canyon: Maiden Tower Inn and Baba Lina's. Maiden Tower Inn was in the shadow of a rockface 300-metres high. On top of it stood the ruined fortress of Maiden

Tower which followed the same timeline as other hill forts here. And
the maiden was like Mesta; her story was fed by many tributaries.

There were two sisters, Struma and Mesta, and Mesta lived in this
tower and kept watch over her gorge, while Struma kept watch over
hers. Though possessed of river kingdoms, the sisters were forever
separated by the Pirin range.

One thing was sure: a woman had kept watch over the gorge from
her tower.

Or someone had kept watch over her.

She had been a mistress of the gorge.

Or a prisoner of the gorge.

She had lived up there for many years.

Or she had died jumping in the river.

She had been a medieval 'Jewish noblewoman' who had the tower
built.

She had been Kera Tamara, the Bulgarian princess and wife of Sultan Murad I, who left his harem in Bursa and came to live here in
freedom.

She had been a girl who ran up the hill to escape 'the Turks' and as
she leapt from the edge, turned to stone.

At a push, you can see her leaping figure propping up the tower
like a siren at the hull of a petrified ship.

Locals said that the Maiden was a giant. She could stride over the
gorge. One day, she strode over to wash her linens in a lake on top of
a peak and her giant linens dried up the lake. Since then, the water
comes out of four springs instead, on four sides of that peak: east and
west, north and south. Each spring has a different taste, said the locals.
The people from the few small villages of Maiden Gorge lived half in
shadow, half in sunshine.

Maiden Tower Inn was owned by a man who had 'killed the king',
I'd heard. The king of music had the voice of a nightingale. A girl fell
for him and he seduced her. But he was already married. And her
father killed the king. After sitting out his sentence, the father built a
roadside inn and took in rescued birds and animals, planted an orchard,
a mini oasis. It became the first Pomak-owned restaurant after the fall
of the regime. The people forgave the killer of the king and his inn

was much-loved. Once every ten years, it was flooded. Such was the place – with nowhere to run between river and mountain. With local help, he and his son rebuilt after each flood and continued to feed travellers with stuffed peppers of the valley.

The river moves her bed when she feels like it, people said. They had seen her in different places, like a person. Already in the third century BC, Theophrastus mentioned the changing bed of the Nesos (Mesta). With this river, change was the one thing that stayed the same.

The road clung to the river except for a flat strip that separated the two. Here, a tributary called The Chestnuts joined in. On this precarious land stood the shack of Baba Lina.

Baba Lina was dead, but her son Pesho lived here with his Jack Russell dog. He had no running water. In winter, his chimney puffed and in summer, he chilled his watermelon in the roadside fountain. I first met him when I parked in the layby for a hike with Metko. We were going upstream along Chestnut River to a remote canyon called The Dark. The Jack Russell wagged its tail, wanting to come with us.

'The Dark? Bah, you'll never make it,' said Pesho.

Pesho had materialised by the bridge shaded by a gnarly vine as soon as I held my hands under the water spout. He was a small man in a shirt printed with incongruous snowflakes and his hair was swept back with eau-de-cologne. He had foxy eyes and there was something wrecked from within, the look of someone who had lost everything in a night of gambling.

'What, with these shoes!'

It's true that Metko wore slip-on shoes just about fit to cross the road.

But we made it. We returned at the end of the day scratched, sunstruck, with damp mobile phones, having narrowly avoided a run-in with a bear, and Pesho once again appeared by the spout. He patrolled his layby. 'Like a road siren who lures you with tall tales,' Metko said, 'and before you know it, you can't tell reality from fiction or good from evil.' He knew Pesho, everyone knew him but not well.

'Maybe you made it, maybe you didn't,' Pesho conceded. 'But you had no idea what you were looking at! The riches that place holds. If I told you what I've seen, you'd lose your marbles.'

We nearly had lost our marbles. The Dark was a vortex dug out by cascades inside the stony bed. It was reached after a hellish scramble upstream. There was no path. The most recent busy time on Chestnut River had been a hundred years ago, the time of the komiti. They slept here, held their political meetings, hid their stolen gold, kept hostages, executed 'traitors' and feasted on animals stolen from shepherds. The legends of treasure buried by the komiti populated this mountain, but they were built on previous deposits. Eras mingled like the sandy soil of Pirin and the treasure grew with time. Like a giant maiden.

We pushed past rocky banks potholed with caves scratched with neolithic drawings, we waded upstream and when the river plunged too far into the earth to be followed, we climbed the scratchy hills above, then made a reckless descent into the maw of The Dark. Something had possessed us to do this.

The river had carved itself a cathedral and it sang inside it at full throttle. Walls rose on your sides, chamber after chamber. We had to shout to hear each other. Some rooms were sunny. A cascade fell into a churning vortex: The Dark. We watched it from a stony platform of shallow water.

'Nobody knows what's inside that vortex,' said Metko. 'All my life I've had a compulsion to reach the bottom. And to be scared no more of the ancient darkness.

'Because like you, I am a demon catcher. And sometimes, you must jump in,' he added.

'Not here,' I said. 'You're not jumping here.'

We climbed out of the earth's bowels. A tree tore my T-shirt: Cornel. We chewed the acidic, still-green cherries. Cornelian cherry is one of my favourite fruits and I miss it because it doesn't grow in Scotland. Its taste is like sour cherry and cranberry in one and when I eat its bittersweet cherries, my tastebuds instantly go home. Cornel is the first tree to flower and the last to bear fruit in this climate zone, and this hasn't changed for twenty-three centuries. I discovered this from reading *Enquiry into Plants* where Theophrastus says that cornelian buds 'before the zephyr blows'. Zephyr is the southern breeze of spring time.

'Cornelian is what Circe fed to Ulysses' crew and turned them into pigs,' Metko said. 'And it's good for diarrhoea too.'

We found self-seeded hornbeam fuzzy with the green moss his mother had used as a wool dye.

'This symbiosis speaks of an ideal climate,' Metko said. 'Mild, friendly.'

We both preferred the world to be a mild, friendly place. Like the climate of the valley.

'I don't want to be mentioned on the same page as Pesho the siren,' said Metko. 'He is part of the ancient darkness.'

He was. I felt unsafe even standing by the water spout with Pesho. But we were already on the same page. We too were treasure hunters. We took a small gamble with our lives to probe this fault in the psyche of the land haunted by robbery and ransom, skeletons and artefacts, voices without bodies that echoed down time's tunnels, waterfalls that refracted the light with a thousand faces. Many things happened after that day, but a version of Metko and me continues to scramble the lizardy hills above The Dark, a bear we surprised continues to tumble into the creek, the cornelian is unripe and we have not reached our destination.

That's because Maiden Gorge was alive like plasma. Any contact with it was myth in the making.

I drank from the cold water of the layby. The siren stood between us and the car.

'There are five stone-carved chairs in a cave near The Dark and forty cauldrons of gold. It's a true story,' said the siren.

'Look up,' he invited me and Metko. We looked up. 'What do these rocks look like?'

'Animals.'

'Giant turtles, Madam, you have no idea what you are walking upon!'

He had no electricity.

'I don't need it,' he said. 'Materialism has wrecked humanity.'

'Tell us about the alleged gold,' Metko said.

'Alleged? There's lots of gold. There's lots of everything, but it's underground,' he went on. 'The other day, we rooted around Gradishta,' he said.

The ruined fort in the tobacco hills above The Birches.

'That's illegal,' said Metko. Pesho cackled with his mouth open.

The Birches had seasoned treasure hunters with nicknames like The Skeleton and The Iron One, and Pesho was part of that network. You saw the scars they left on the land, but you never saw them in action. This was because they were quick and the places they frequented were off the beaten track. The Mesta had no beaten track anyway. The hills were left to predators and their prey.

'A tunnel runs between the caves of Maiden Gorge and Nikopol,' said Pesho.

I'd heard this one. It was a persistent tale. I could almost believe it. Tunnels under the river, rope bridges over the river. I visited Pesho again in winter, on a day so cold the water running down the cliffs had formed sculptures of ice. The gaps in his shack were stuffed with plastic bags. Smoke puffed from his chimney. On his door was an anniversary death notice for his mother.

He knew he lived on borrowed land. We all do, we just don't know it. He came down the ladder in house slippers, his hair slicked back. I could smell the latrine. He didn't remember me from the summer.

His father arrived as a refugee from Greek Macedonia. He built a shack here, where an old inn already stood and was not welcomed by the inn owners. Four children later, he was murdered in the pasture over there, Pesho pointed. This was meant to chase Lina, but she stayed. She lived in the shack with her kids, goats and horses, washing in the river. The murderous neighbours ended up helping her before they left. They too had suffered a murder. In the 1920s, mass reprisals were carried out against an uprising led by the then-outlawed communists. The inn sheltered a young communist courier. The tsarist police came and hanged him together with the inn keeper, on that chestnut over there, Pesho pointed. A gravestone was built by the communist state later – for the courier, but not for the inn keeper.

Nothing was left of the inn. 'Did you flatten it in revenge for your father?'

'Nah. The One Above settles all accounts,' Pesho smiled with pleasure.

Pesho and the killer of the king were the last dwellers of Maiden Gorge. They had stayed on out of loyalty, because the gorge had always had a guardian.

A man pulled over and brought Pesho a pack of mince. The Pomaks of the valley had adopted him as one of theirs. They remembered the good baba Lina, one woman told me, who spent her life cultivating her patch borrowed from the river.

'Life is one vegetable after another,' Lina liked to say. 'That's all.'

Pesho didn't cultivate anything. The nights here were as black as entrails. He was in a real badland. Anyone could pull over, go up to his room, strangle him and drive on. There was a lock, but the key was on the outside.

'Nah, not afraid of anything except The One Above,' he said.

The Jack Russell had been run over.

'Nah, don't miss him,' he said, and pain passed over his face. 'We're all guests.'

What have humans built?

'Nothing!' he answered himself. 'Humans destroy. And they have forgotten how to be healthy! This vaccine, this virus, it's not going away. Because people are not getting the message.'

What was the message?

'To wake up and change,' he said. 'Take the bee. It understands geometry, chemistry and astronomy. And what do we do? Spray it with poison.'

'Take these trees,' he pointed at the fruit trees. 'They produce aromas, colours and healing compounds. What do we produce? Landfill!'

I asked whether he ever saw anything in the gorge at night.

'They visit,' he said, matter-of-fact. 'I see them over there,' he pointed at the cliffs opposite, where he saw a giant coin imprinted with symbols, animals, plants. Silivryak, perhaps.

'Made by the first post-Atlantean earthly race,' he said, 'who came from the cosmos. We are the fourth. The fifth is coming.'

I couldn't tell if this was good news or bad news. 'Did "they" land?'

'No. They're always moving,' he said. 'Discs or triangles of light that move at the kind of speed we don't have on this planet. Sometimes they hover.'

They never bothered him and he was pleased they were there. After a conversation under the frozen fruit trees, he'd ascend the stair and close the door with the key on the outside. His patch was fenced in from the road with wire at neck level that nearly strangled me, even in the daytime. I wondered whether the inn keeper and his fatal guest had been strangled with wire like this, and Pesho's father too.

'This is the last year,' Pesho said in 2021. 'Then the cataclysms begin. Cos we've really fucked up.'

He spent the winters by the fire reading the Bible, the Koran and the prophecies of clairvoyants who foresaw cataclysms of every kind.

After my chats with him, I'd drive across the winter valley. Past a landfill reopened by the rains where Roma men rummaged with horse carts. Past men loading bloodied horses with tree trunks. Past the riverbed quarry *inside* a bird sanctuary.

It wasn't only that we had fucked up. It was that we kept racing down the vortex on a death ride. We were not getting off. We were completely insane.

Before the river road was built in the 1940s, you climbed above the canyon on foot and horseback to access the valley. You travelled at the level of Maiden Tower. The late nineteenth- century ethnogeographer Vasil Kanchov walked this stretch of Mesta, past the abandoned Maiden Tower:

'I savoured the gorgeous panorama that lay between Pirin and the Rhodope, and wondered how it was that amidst such natural riches there could live such a wretched people.'

One hundred and twenty years later, his local insight is a global truth.

Pesho was dodgy, but from his river perch he grasped the true state of the world and lived accordingly. Pesho had been a construction worker. He had helped tar-seal the road in the 1980s. Until then, the road had been just gravel.

He was also a notorious treasure hunter then. One day, he rocked up to the pub in Siropol. He sat down at a table but the floor was uneven and to steady it, he jammed its leg with a gold coin he produced from a bag. He had just found a spectacular hoard of gold in a necropolis and wanted to celebrate, which was a mistake because Siropol bristled with secret agents. The whole valley did, because of its proximity to the Greek border. His hoard was confiscated and he was beaten to a pulp. The deadly tango between the underground locals who had knowledge and the bandit state which had power has never stopped. Afterwards, Pesho was a ruined man – having lost his gold, his health and his arrogance, he returned to live with his mother in the shack. But he never stopped looking for treasure.

'And what does that rockface remind you of?' I wasn't too sure, but he was.

If he stopped seeing codes in the cliffs, he'd fall down dead with heartbreak.

In late 2021, I heard that he had died. Dreading the sight of his collapsed shack, I squeezed through Maiden Gorge and pulled over by the fountain – and there he was, sitting with two villagers and a watermelon, like a revenant!

'Madam is back,' he croaked vitriolically.

'I heard that you were – unwell,' I said.

'Dead, you mean,' he snorted, coughing up blood.

Born of the Maiden Gorge, he had performed a symbiotic merger with it, so that by driving away from the layby after nearly strangling myself on the wire, I could leave The Dark behind. And tell myself that I was safe.

'Stay safe': the mantra of the pandemic. It was a false mantra based on a misunderstanding. It is not possible to stay safe for more than a second. Life is dangerous. Maiden Gorge was a place where this became apparent.

'I'll tell you my happiest dream,' Metko said while we were inside The Dark, perched on the vortex lip. 'It takes place here.'

He is with other children in a pool of river-polished stone. The bottom of the pool is refracted, like a mosaic of emerald tiles. In this pool are fish, and the children pick them up like glittering treasures in their hands. The fish communicate with the children through sound and vibration, and the fish tell the children the secret of life. It is something to do with light. Just — light. The children are free and out of bounds, they are one with the water and they let the fish go.

'Visit the Interior of the Earth and Rectify what you find there, and you will Discover the Hidden Stone.'

Visita interiora terrae rectificando occultum lapidem (VITRIOL). An alchemical recipe encrypted for adepts — something the alchemists enjoyed doing but also had to do, to protect their work from thieves. Vitriol stood for sulphuric acid, one of the chemical elements. And thanks to the alchemists' knack for uniting the material with the figurative, it acquired a psychological dimension too. Vitriol: virulence, violence, vortex.

Metko and I visited the interior of the earth that day. But he had already done it in his *imaginatio* and glimpsed the hidden stone.

Autumn was here. I packed my dried herbs and said goodbye to The Birches. Gyulten gave me a pair of silky trousers made in a sewing sweatshop. I heard the song 'Black Rose' one more time, drank from Fatmé's fountain and Shefket made me eat two kilos of sheep's yogurt on my last day.

'Everything repeats itself,' Metko's sceptical blue eyes crinkled in a smile. We cracked sunflower seeds in the empty square. 'You'll be back next spring, I think. Like the stone flower.'

Vortex

Pesho was the closest I'd met to a mining gnome. He lived inside the fissures of the earth and the basements of the psyche. He was part of an underground web of soil-munchers, gold-miners, pentacle exchangers, tomb raiders, skull-duggers, conspiracy-spinners and like a djinn, he guarded the edges of things and could hurt you when disturbed. He did not make the world a better place. Yet he was integral to the valley's ecology of meaning.

The gnome is the alchemical creature of the earth element. He is a trickster who moves from underground to overground. His disposition is miserly. Alchemists called the passage into matter *coagulatio*. In this earth phase, things must solidify. Or they remain volatile like fire, run away like water and dissipate like air before they have a chance to take form. In Maiden Gorge, the submerged contents of the psyche took form. Then, form once again became the starting point of the journey.

'The nature of infinity is this,' wrote William Blake in *Milton*:

> That every thing has its
> Own Vortex; and when once a traveller thro' Eternity
> Has pass'd that Vortex, he perceives it roll backward behind
> His path, into a globe itself unfolding, like a sun,
> Or like a moon, or like a universe of starry majesty. [. . .]
> Thus is the heaven a vortex pass'd already, and the earth
> A vortex not yet pass'd by the traveller thro' Eternity.

WATER

Glance at the sun. See the moon and the stars. Gaze
at the beauty of earth's greenings. Now, think.

Hildegard of Bingen

HONEY SELLERS

The honey sellers appeared suddenly at a roadside market. Alpine pastures opened up behind them in quick succession, a show the Earth had put on in an outburst of genius for its own delight.

At the market was everything that the mountain produced, including mursala. I had missed it, even if I admitted that a break in our relationship in favour of juniper had been good for me. It was late summer, the first of the pandemic. Spring had come and gone, the stone flower too.

I had landed just the day before quarantine for arrivals was lifted. In the capital, there were mass protests against the mafia state, with masks – a new sight.

On the stalls were honeys, syrups, jams, milk, yogurt, butter and cheeses – fresh and matured from cow, ewe and goat – dried and fresh berries, walnuts, hazelnuts and almonds, broad beans and dried porcini. The sellers were Pomak women, with fair skin burned by decades of summer toil without sunblock, their hands huge from planting, sowing, hoeing, digging, weeding, watering, harvesting, shelling, de-stoning, drying, stringing, milking, boiling, preserving, birthing, killing and cooking. I knew nobody in this highest part of the river, but seeing these women, I instantly felt at ease.

They extracted round cheeses from chilly bins and sliced off generous chunks as tasters, on the tip of a knife, or scooped a spoonful of honey for you to lick. Everything was grown, soured, sweetened and shaped by their hands. The cheeses were creamy with tasty grasses. Their speech stroked me with its archaic lilt – the preserve of the Mesta Pomaks. But behind this gentleness was the familiar steely note. Their power was not on display, only the fruits of their earthly work, yet behind them was the mountain. Always, the mountain.

I filled the car with jars of sheep's yogurt and blueberries. The road ran south until it converged with the first miles of Mesta. After the market, solo women with individual roadside stalls popped up, like fairies. Occasionally you saw a man at the stalls but nobody bought from the men, people only stopped for the women.

You passed places like the titles of unwritten stories: Saint Petka; Arab Peak; Yuruk Mound; The Horned One; The Treasure. The mountain kept them pressed between the pages of its hills.

Struck by the arcadian meadow behind the last seller, I pulled over. She was smiling already. I bought a jar of caramel-like pine syrup.

Her granddaughter picked berries in England. Her daughter was a nurse in Germany.

'It's better for them over there,' said the honey seller.

I asked her name.

'My name is Zaidé. I'm from The Birches.'

Ah! This was Metko's aunt. She was delighted that I knew him. Later, I learned Zaidé had been battered by a soldier with the butt of a rifle. She'd been in that march across the hills to Kornitsa.

The travellers who stopped to buy the ecologically pristine food made by Zaidé and the others didn't know what these women had been through, and didn't care. They haggled, tossed money to the sellers whose unflappable grace highlighted their customers' arrogance, then squeezed back into their cars en route to Greek beaches. But not this summer. This summer, the border was closed because of the pandemic and the road was empty.

Something came full circle that summer. Resistance to the communist mafia state had been initiated in the 1960s by the Pomaks of Mesta with great sacrifices at the time and no recognition later. Sixty years later, new resistance to the oligarchic mafia state would lead to repeated elections that would bring it down. It had taken Zaidé's entire life.

I said goodbye to Zaidé, but not before she piled the top of my yogurt jar, which I had opened to eat, with a thick mint syrup.

'Because I have a lot of everything and it's the thingiest thing on this earthly earth,' she waved me off with her big hand, 'to give a soul something to eat.'

The fortifying syrup was prepared by boiling large quantities of wild mint with mursala and sugar. I can't forget the flavour of her mint and mursala syrup, and her pine syrup which I ate every day until it was gone, even after the many other faces and tastes of the valley. The taste of pine and mint merged with Zaidé's face, with her steely blue eyes under the headscarf, like a clear note of welcome struck by the birth-mountain of the river.

Pine syrup

Young tips or cones of black pine, cedar, spruce, or dwarf pine, a
  handful
Brown sugar or honey, 500 grams
Water, 2 litres

Boil until the water is reduced to half a litre. If using honey, add at
the end. Strain, and eat yourself a spoon a day on an empty stomach,
said Zaidé, and say goodbye to gallstones, gastritis and coughs.

Pine is for bronchitis, asthma and to clear anything trapped in the
chest, like heartache. Pine is for indigestion, acid and to fortify you
against pathogens, like injustice. Pine is a nobleman in all its guises.
There are several families of pine in the three mountains of Mesta.
The only type I can spot easily is the white or Scots pine, because I
see its lonely individuals with gnarly branches every day on the shorn
hills of rural Scotland. The Scots pine is a star of Scottish lore. The
cones produce a light-brown dye and rope was made from the roots.
Their sap was used as lamp oil on sores and boils. Pine was brought to
the brink of extinction in Scotland over the last 300 years – to clear
grazing and shooting grounds, to build the boats of Empire and then
the coffins of the world wars that were sparked off in the ashes of
Empire. By 1950, ninety-nine per cent of Scotland's pine population
was gone.

The oldest pine individual in Scotland is about 500 years old. And the
oldest in Europe is the Baykusheva mura in Pirin, at 1,300 years old
and named after the forest ranger who aged it in 1897. It is a Bosnian
pine, whose last native communities are in Pirin Mountain, Slavyanka-
Orvilos Mountain and the mountains of Calabria.

BLACK MESTA, WHITE MESTA

There is something about a highland train station that feels like a theatre set. The earth is an amphitheatre and you get on and off the train, on and off, you don't really know why.

Your whole life has been like this: on and off, highs and lows, from one thing to another. The drama is yours, not the land's. You brought it with you and wherever you go, you look for somewhere to play it out. You saw your condition clearly from the scenic narrow-gauge train. Your condition was precarious, like the skinny train attached to a rail only 76 centimetres wide. It climbed the terraced mountains and plunged into precipices with joyful abandon. 'Toot-toot!'

Its inter-wagon doors flapped open and closed over plunging forests, and you could lean out with your hair wind-whipped and just a step separating you from the plunge. You squeezed through tight tunnels blasted in the rock a century ago, a feat of engineering forced by the remoteness of the Rila-Rhodope massif and lack of roads. The railway was meant to follow the Mesta all the way to the Aegean, but money and goodwill ran out and it ended just before Maiden Gorge.

At Avramovo, the Balkans' highest train station at 1,267 metres, the train stopped for a break and you got off, then on again, looking at the round station clock which looked back at you. Are we there yet? The clock hands pointed at some other moment in time.

Inside the carriage were signs: 'Wear masks at all times!' and nobody did. You breathed in the alpine air that rushed through open windows like whispers of the forest and you listened. You stopped briefly at once-handsome, now gutted little stations where the honey-sellers with sunburned faces got off with their food bundles and headed off to hidden forest settlements. They didn't drive and the narrow-gauge train was their livelihood.

One of the gutted little stations was called Black Mesta. This is where you got off. You crossed the railway on foot with your bundle and entered the miniature village.

There was something of the dark fairytale about Black Mesta. You felt it as soon as you arrived, but the full effect seeped in over time. The daily visitors with number plates from faraway places, who arrived in a cloud of dust and parked next to the street tables of the village shop, didn't take the time – they came to see Alish 'the blind healer' and quickly left. Though quick is not the word. Some of them could barely walk and were propped or half-carried by helpers. This was why I stayed for three days which turned into ten: to be close to Alish and the homeland of the river. By the end, the two had merged in my mind.

Built on six streets in a fold of the gorge like a kink in a birth canal and facing the looming hills at point-blank, the village was the nearest inhabited place to the sources of the river. Black Mesta and White Mesta made up the bulk of Upper Mesta. People said that the names came from the black stones found in one and the white stones in the other. The stones looked the same to me, but the double nature made sense. This was a place of echoes. The Rhodope threw you against Rila, like in some tossing game of Titans.

The village sat at 1,190 metres above sea level and went black at night. The hills were like Gothic ruins under the stars. A Gypsy encampment stood on the other bank of Black Mesta. They scratched a living from logging and lived here with their dogs and horses as permanently as you could live in a tent.

The river sounded closer at night, as if it grew in volume. At 5.30 a.m. I was woken by the first loud call to prayer. The *ezan* was sung with feeling by the self-appointed village hodja Alika, who was also my landlord. I rented a one-room converted barn in his garden, by his rows of green beans and next to the empty sheep pen. Alika sang with a lyrical voice that didn't match his fox eyes and weakness for the ladies. His prayer voice expressed something in him that couldn't be expressed otherwise.

'Allahu ekbeeer,' in a minor key and rather too loud for dawn,

'Eshedi en la I'llyallah'. A love call to his valley that the black hills echoed back, making it sound like two voices, and the Gypsies' dogs howled back. His genuine passion for everything he did – religious ritual, community projects, his garden – won him the respect of the villagers who were a long-suffering, faithless lot.

Alika's daughter-in-law walked a pram across the garden, cooing.

'Please pick an apple,' she'd say, rocking the pram where a newborn with an astonished face gazed at the blue sky, a face struck by a premonition of all that human life contains. He had asked for nothing, yet here he was, thrust into this world of dark vales and bright peaks.

'Yes, he is brand new,' said the mother wistfully. 'Pick some beans. We have too much. Isn't it good that you get to see different places and faces, and are changed by what you see? It's the finest thing in the world! Here, we go round and round the garden, round and round. And we look at the sky.'

She gathered her own herbs in the hills for her little family, especially elder, which for her was the most medicinal plant of Rila. 'And of the Scottish Highlands,' I said.

'You have it there too, bravo! How do people prepare it?'

She wore the nouveau-Turkish high hijab and the conservative grey overcoat.

Some Black Mestans, like elsewhere in the Mesta basin, had started describing themselves as Turks of late. It was fashionable. They didn't speak Turkish of course, but 'Turkish' stood for 'I am Muslim and don't want to feel like a second-class citizen, better to be slightly foreign.' When they went to work in the capital or abroad, including Turkey, they became Bulgarians again. A conditional identity in a conditional world.

Except for the Friday prayer when twenty or so men turned up, the mosque was empty, and Alika prayed by himself five times a day. He invited me to see it. The cube-like whitewashed mosque had a blue minaret and naïve painted scenes on its outside walls, and the calligraphic names of Allah. The water of the festive fountain in the courtyard was turned on for special occasions and at night it flashed multicoloured lights. I would not have been surprised to see a dervish

by the fountain of an evening, cross-legged in rags, playing the kaval
flute. Despite its character, the mosque was only built in the 1990s.
With the zeal of the neophyte who had once been an atheist, Alika
was proud of the mosque which he single-handedly maintained. It
was resplendent with chandeliers from Mecca, carpets from Turkey
and worry beads from everywhere. It was a monument to all that had
been denied.

Alika gave me a string of black wooden worry beads like a rosary
and told me about the happiest day of his life: when he took part in
mass prayer in Mecca. He liked how the men revolved on the outside
and the women were on the inside.

'Like sheep in a pen,' I commented.

'No, we protect them that way!' he said. 'Women need protection.'

His second wife had left him recently, like his first.

I was picking nettles around the abandoned sheep pen in his
garden.

'Pick all my nettles, if you like,' he beamed, as he brought me
something to eat every day: a half kilo of fresh butter; potatoes from
the garden; a bowl of green beans. And he immediately offered to
cook them for me himself, adding: 'And if you want to marry me,
I'm available.' And he'd glance at his watch because the prayer timetable was strict. He needed the schedule.

'5:55 is *sabah*, 13:33 is *pladnina* (from *pladne*, midday), 17:15 is *ikindi*,
20:30 is *achsham* and 21:55 is *aksi*. But it changes every day by a minute
or two. Depending on the moon.'

Every month, the country's chief mufti issued a *takwim*, an updated
lunar timetable for each geographic belt of the country. I'd had no
idea that Muslim prayer followed the moon.

These prayer-time rules came to Muslim communities in Europe
from Mecca. The word takwim reminded me of the Arabic alchemists' *takwin* – a homunculus. But I didn't say that to Alika. I couldn't
get a word in edgeways anyway.

'I can give you the train schedule too,' he beamed. 'They run as
follows –'

Alika was kept sane by the prayer schedule and the train schedule
because the world was chaotic and he was lonely, just as his

daughter-in-law was lonely and his son was lonely – a heavy guy who was born sad. It was the Pomak condition: families and communities seemed close-knit, but individuals were trapped in destinies foretold and yearned for a life unlived.

No, it was the human condition – together but disconnected, a pre-existing condition magnified by the pandemic. The virus gave a name to our shared condition: we are not what we are. We have lived under a false identity.

Alika had spent a lifetime as a signal inspector along the narrow-gauge railway and could be seen hanging off the train's loose doors, smiling bravely in the face of bitter winds. His son worked there too. Later, I heard a family tale of hardship and struggle in the post-communist freefall. He had raised the kids after their mother ran away with a gangster. What kept them from poverty was rent from ancestral land in an alpine settlement called The Horses.

People had come down from their alpine settlements in the last two generations. Until then, they had lived pre-modern lives. Pastoral lives with horses and buffalo.

Black Mesta was a communist project, built some thirty years after the railway. The line divided the upper neighbourhood from the lower and you had to cross it by foot to move between the two, careful not to be mowed down by the train – there were no barriers or signal lights, just the toot-toot.

Morning and evening, the village philosopher's voice carried up the street – a smart alcoholic with a boiled face and dirty blue eyes, fond of reciting obscene poems. He had a large repertoire. Working as a hydro engineer in a *kanton* (forest station) had driven him to the bottle. Looking at the level of the river and looking at his glass had become the same thing. His wife disappeared to a shepherd's hut high up, alone with her cows and dogs all summer. Cattle and sheep had been a major livelihood, but husbandry had all but disappeared. One hundred men, out of a population of four hundred, worked as builders in England. Inside the shop that sold sugary snacks and carbonated drinks, the poor man's foods, were notices:

'Farm hands urgently wanted in Belgium, England, Spain. No language required. Departure date – Hourly rate – Plus overtime.'

Apart from the hydro and logging, there was no human activity above the village, which some said kept the river clean enough to drink from, but others said it was polluted by plastic. It was both: rubbish-clogged downstream and pristine upstream. In the company of the locals, I began to climb to the upper realms by car, motorbike and foot. In Upstream Black Mesta and White Mesta, there was no timetable.

The interior of Rila was wild and empty of dwellings. This kept it pure. The lower slopes were dotted with near-defunct pastoral settlements, kantons, hydro-stations, dams and mountain chalets. Then there was Rila National Park and Musala 'close to God'. Under Musala sprang the springs that made the Mesta.

Black Mesta village had its timetables too. From 4 p.m., the mushroom buyers' house became busy. It stood where a riverine inn for forestry workers had stood. Today, the Gypsies were the last of those. Inns along the river and pastoralist settlements above – that's what Rila naturally allowed. All else was afterthought, with mixed results.

The mushroom pickers arrived on motorbikes or in cars so saggy that their bellies bumped the road. Here, there was a mushroomer look different to that of Old Woods and The Birches. Here, it was like a religion. The classic mushroomer was skinny and looked at the ground. They were older married couples, or pairs of friends, or solo men. They wore baggy old clothes and oilskin jackets, wellies or hiker's shoes with gaiters, clothes in which you can crawl along the forest floor. Some arrived with pine needles in their hair. They appeared on the road in the evening with bags strapped onto beat-up motorbikes. Or they popped out of the woods and walked with their rucksacks. They had a remote look I recognised – it was obsession. But it was also the musical meadows of Rila, they did that to you. The alpine chords continued to play in your head when you came down.

They said: 'I'm going out for mushroom' – always singular, as if mushroom was not a plant but a state of mind. Unlike hunting, it was not a social occasion. It was not about leisure or bonding. It was unlike any other form of foraging. Berries and herbs were done en masse – once you found the blueberry bushes or the field of St John's wort, that was it, you were there for the day. 'Mushroom' required footwork. Mushroom was spread out in mysterious ways. Mushroom liked to be near oak, pine, birch – but often it wasn't where you expected it to be. Or someone else had passed through before you. The mushroomers didn't like banter. Even the chatty ones became silent when they disappeared up the hills. They went into a kind of communion. It was between them and the mushroom. The only reason they went in couples was for safety – where there were mushrooms, there were bears.

The mushroom dealers were a couple in middle age. The corpulent man sat in a chair in the courtyard and commented on the state of mushrooms and the world, while his wife did the work of weighing deliveries, noting them down and dispatching them next door to the warehouse where drying and cutting machines were operated by two other women. Before he'd got into local politics and bitten off too much of the pie, the mushroom dealer had also been a lean mushroomer.

'I hope that in twenty years' time, there will be no more mushroom pickers,' he said, munching a pastry and watching his wife lift crates. 'I hope my children won't be picking mushrooms anyway.'

His children were scrolling on their tablets.

'But who *will* pick mushrooms then?'

'Whoever wants them, let him pick them himself.'

'Fair enough, but why the bitterness?'

'Because! Who is picking mushrooms in Germany and Italy? It's us. The Germans and the Italians have better things to do.'

'Like what – what is a better thing than spending the day in the forest?'

'They have good chanterelles in Germany,' said a skinny man. He came to deliver and have a pint. He was happy to be home after decades of work in Germany as a picker, packer, cutter. It was good to go out on mushroom in his home mountain, return before dusk and watch the sunset over the hills.

'Black Mesta is a grave pit with living people in it,' he grinned. 'But it's home.'

'We have become slaves to the West,' said the stately looking father of the mushroom buyer.

The family name Karafaiz meant 'black tax' – a perfect name for a clan living in a mountain pass. A name that told a story: generations of riverine traders, tax collectors and ransomers had weighed mushrooms, milk, logs, ore and gold, and paid the going price. Or not.

The older Karafaiz grandchildren picked fruit on a Scottish farm, pandemic or not, fourteen-hour days, rain or sunshine. This lowering of their status abroad pained them.

'Two hundred,' the wife said and handed cash to a bald young man in wellies and oilskin who sat down with a beer. He'd delivered 25 kilograms of ceps.

'Tell me the oddest thing about mushrooms,' I asked him. He was shy – visitors were rare – and didn't say anything that evening.

I went home and fried a sliced cep in Alika's butter. It was rich like a steak.

Ruined fortresses sat above the western exit of the gorge, and by the river – hot mineral springs. In a cypressy road cemetery with the best view in the world, the Christian and Muslim sections were joined by a path. The mosaic of Slavic, Arabic and Greek names told a story. Agapi, Assen, Ahmed, Aishe, Assia, Agapia rested together by the river. A silent memory of the long presence of Byzantium. The Greek language dried up in Upstream Mesta at the same time the Bulgarian language dried up in downstream Mesta – after the exchange of populations across the border.

The oldest known inhabitants of these ranges were the Bessi – a fierce Thracian tribe who practised cruel ritual sacrifices, but later produced a priestly caste that contributed to the rise of Orphism that replaced the orgiastic sacrifice with the vegetarian libation. Despite the remoteness of these ranges, foot traffic had been lively for hundreds of years. An old ore road climbed over Rila. Caravans with mined goods had used it. This is why the main town here was called Yakoruda – Great Ore.

Yakoruda was a pretty mountain town with a square full of cafés, a busy weekend market, pink sunsets, a church whose bells once sang with human voices and a mosque. Several Greek-owned sewing factories gave women jobs – in one of them lingerie was made for a

French label. To enter the town, you crossed one of several bridges. Looking at the shallow water in the concrete basin, it was hard to imagine that in the last big flood the tributaries merged and swept away the road.

'But overall, the water is decreasing,' said Feri.

Feri's café was in the square. Feri took me under his wing as a rare visitor to his town and presented me with plates of tender highland beef, mushrooms in herb butter and juicy tomatoes, and my favourite, the bean soup and potato salad.

'To show you that we still have good organic food. Even if there's no jobs and everyone has gone to pull asparagus in Germany.'

'The snow is gone. We remember snow 3 metres high,' said Ibrahim.

Ibrahim was just back from pulling asparagus in Germany. He was a hard-faced but emotional man who was blind in one eye after an industrial accident. Once an athlete, he was now looking after bedridden parents who couldn't live or die and by lunchtime he was ensconced at Feri's and had set up his drinks before him like a solitary game of chess, moving the glasses strategically as they emptied, and remaining desperately sober.

'As a boy, I fished in Black Mesta,' said Alish, the blind osteopath, who sometimes came to town for lunch to escape his stream of visitors.

'I could catch up to a hundred with my bare hands,' he said. 'Their backs glinted. It's like they were calling me. Then, I'd take two home, no more. There's fuck-all left now.'

'They've wiped out the trout, even upstream,' said Redjep. 'Overfishing.'

Redjep drove Alish between here and Black Mesta. He sat while Alish ordered pint after pint trying to get drunk. Redjep was a quiet, youngish guy with a dazzling smile, known as the best mushroomer in Upper Mesta. He had picked tonnes of mushrooms over the years, people said, literally tonnes. I never saw him at the mushroom buyers' because he went early in his beat-up old Lada – although he also had a vintage Mercedes in which he brought Alish to town – and delivered his hoard early. He spent most of the year on a German pine plantation with his wife, planting saplings and cutting branches for Christmas wreaths. She stayed on but he returned in summer because he liked to be here for the mushroom season. They had resisted going abroad for as long as they could, even trying subsidised highland cow farming to give their parents a livelihood too, but it was too much for too little. His hands were like Ibrahim's and the honey sellers': older than his face.

'That's Trendafilka the herbalist,' Erol the photographer pointed at a relaxed woman who walked past us and sat in another café.

Erol owned a grocery shop with his wife but his passion was nature photography. He was my only contact before I arrived – I'd seen his photos. It was him that introduced me to people. The hospitality was immediate.

'They say she's very good,' Erol said.

'Aye,' Alish said. 'But herbs ain't gonna fix my eyes. Is that Elijah's voice I hear?'

'Elijah works for Rila National Park. Anything you want to know, and more, he's your man,' Erol said.

A man in hiking gear bounced up to our table. He beamed, though he was in a rush. He was always in a rush and beaming. Elijah owned a mountain chalet and had two projects in life: ecology and Thracology. The first was his job, the second his hobby. He led two types of treks – ecological and esoteric. But they were in essence the same trek because the same passion fuelled them. Elijah was an ecstatic of the mountain, almost a fanatic.

'Rhodopa is where there will one day find the Temple of Solomon, inside sealed mines,' he said without preamble. He'd identified the location. 'And the main temple of Dionysus is in Rila.' He'd found that location, too.

Our lunch party looked up at him in astonishment from the table. Me especially, since the others had heard it all before and didn't dare raise any doubts because Elijah was better educated. 'Herodotus wrote: the Bessi worship at the main temple of Dionysus, which is on the highest mountain in Thrace, near Orbel.'

Orbel was the ancient name of one of the Mesta mountains but it was not clear which one. Herodotus went out of his comfort zone to meet the world (he claimed to measure Cheop's Pyramid himself!)

but he never came to Europe. So, he didn't know where Orbel was either.

'Rhodopa is Mother Earth. Rhodopa is Evropa,' Elijah leaned on the table.

He was a decoder of place names, measurer of leylines, decipherer of the mountain. His *imaginatio* ran away with itself, but he also had a kind word for everyone. Each morning, he'd rush past Feri's tables where men battered by decades of underpaid labour at home and lonely labour abroad drank coffee, and he'd wave at them:

'Good morning gentlemen! Looking good, the ladies love you.' The men couldn't help but smile.

One day, with Elijah as a guide, a small group of enthusiasts walked across vast meadows and remote glades. We found white truffles, the rare purple Rila primrose, a poisonous cep-double delightfully called Satan's bolete and a broken horseshoe. Elijah took us to stone sites that he believed to be ruined cromlechs, dolmens and stone circles, once used at Equinox and Solstice. 'Seven vestal virgins' served as priestesses and sacred sites had their own 'orpheuses' – young male initiates of the mysteries, possibly eunuchs, he said. Orpheus was not a single person, he said, there were orpheuses. It was like Hermes Trismegistus. This is how over time, a human being became an archetype; the Hermetics, the Orphics. It's an androgynous archetype – Orpheus and Hermes are male and female in one. Herodotus takes a waspish swipe at the Orphics and the Pythagorians when he writes that the Egyptians were the first to come up with the idea of the soul's immortality, that the period of a soul's full cycle of transmigrations is three thousand years and that 'certain Greek writers' have in fact stolen this from the Egyptians. 'Their names are known to me, but I refrain from mentioning them,' he quips. But he was not always right, even if he was always witty. Each ancient culture arrived at the same conclusion: the soul is peregrine.

'So, the Orpheus climbed a special stone,' Elijah showed us a stone in a meadow of late summer bliss, 'and sang and played his lyre made from a turtle shell. Animals and humans came out of the forest, lay down and became blissed out.'

In another glade, the four in our group took turns to sit and 'meditate' in a stone seat with a sweeping view over Rila. 'What did you feel?'

'I went into a vortex like dark water,' said the archaeologist. 'It was awful.'

'I was immersed in pure ether,' said his dreadlocked son, a poet.

Me, I flew into the blue abyss below, like a bird going home.

'I didn't feel a thing,' said the computer techie, 'I'm an engineer'.

'Well! This was the seat where priestesses were placed to recover,' Elijah said, delighted, though he was really making it up. 'They were drugged up to their eyeballs with wine and mandragora and other psychotropic herbs, and sometimes left for dead.'

You had to be made of strong stuff to be a mountain priestess.

Above White Mesta, I saw where he'd turned an old quarry into a lake and maintained it with his own hands by keeping it connected with a tributary. I helped him clear some stones. The idea was to introduce fish, not for fishing, but to give children a reason to leave their tablets for a day and come up here. Locals were generous with donations and money even came from abroad. 'People need to see good things happening and they gladly join in,' he said.

The old name for Mesta was Nehta, a Thracian word that lives on in an alpine area called Nehtenitsa. We walked the old caravan track towards Cobbler Peak and saw wolf and bear prints. Elijah knew the bear couple who were the kings of White Mesta, their cub and another cub from the guy's other relationship, he said.

White Mesta and Black Mesta never flooded together. From the upper realms, I saw that in every wildnerness, there is order. The closer I got to the river springs, the more distinct everything looked. On a rough map, there is just Mesta. On the body of the land, Mesta becomes a galaxy of blood vessels, each with its own sun and moon. Each with a temperament, a micro-climate, and residents with faces. It is infinite.

'This is the meaning of an ecosystem,' said Eljiah. 'This is the meaning of nature. Pri-roda.'

Priroda is literally 'with-the-clan'. To be in nature is to return to your own kind.

'This is my mission. To bring people to their own kind.'

That is why he'd appointed himself custodian of this corner of Rila. Behind the smile was Elijah's sadness at seeing forests destroyed, rewilding opportunities bulldozed by greed.

'But when I tune in with the place, it renews me. These boulders are special.'

He was exhausted at the end of the season, but had taken me climbing to a crop of boulders below Cobbler Peak that were named after the cobblers at a resting station who once provided horses with new shoes. It was a pristine place. To one side were Blacksmith Lake and Potter Lake, up towards Musala was a peak called The Healer, and below us was The Saint, both feminine.

'Healing goes back to the mineral waters,' Elijah said. 'There was once a water healer here, who treated the incurable in a cave. Free of charge. But people had to come to her.'

Healers who worked free of charge were known in the medicinal canon as *bezsrebrenitsi*, 'lucreless ones', and the most revered lucreless ones were the peripatetic Syrian doctors Cosmas and Damian. They travelled with their three other brothers as helpers. When some hilltop or chapel is called Sveti Vrach, Saint Healer, it invokes the lucreless ones and those in their lineage.

Anyway, Eljiah went on, so reknowned was this healer that people called her the Saint. It was the early Middle Ages. A Byzantine emperor summoned her to cure his leprosy-stricken daughter: but the healer wouldn't travel. Irritated, the emperor agreed to send his daughter off with an armed retinue, and for some reason, with the girl's entire dowry (a detail added retrospectively, after her tomb was raided a millennium later, because you already sense this story ends badly, as stories involving irritable emperors usually do). They travelled west from Constantinople along the Via Egnatia, dropped in at Nikopolis ad Mestum for some mineral baths, then followed the Mesta past Maiden Tower. But just before they reached the healer, the girl succumbed. She was entombed in a stone necropolis hewn by local masons. They laid her down dressed in a 'gold and silver tunic'. Four golden goblets for the four cardinal directions were placed inside the tomb with her dowry. The necropolis was then sealed with a slab and covered with soil and rocks. It became one of those mounds beloved of treasure hunters.

'I know this from an old man whose family managed the land. The story was passed down.'

And perhaps the loot too. The site was levelled in the years of collectivisation and probably looted earlier, in the nineteenth or twentieth century when most lootings took place. And what of the very detailed contents of the tomb? Elijah smiled.

'The instructions were: he who finds the tomb can take all except the tunic. Don't touch the tunic.'

Treasure hunters are a superstitious tribe and stories of malediction and nemesis make up a whole genre in oral history. There is a peak here called Anathema, curses in Greek. Afterwards, the enraged emperor ordered the armed retinue to execute the healer and declare her a traitor to the empire. Then, they headed back to Constantinople. What a miserable expedition for those men and women, but at least they got to soak in the hot springs along the way. The locals quietly buried the murdered healer above her cave.

'That hilltop is still called The Saint.'

We sunned ourselves on the boulders until the sun went in over The Healer, which had its own story.

This is where remnants of coloured truth survive the blight of official history – in the body of the land. In *The Alexiad* by the Byzantine princess and first woman historian, Anna Komnina, a fascinating and self-glorifying chronicle of the reign of her father Alexios, the Bogomils are denounced in the contemporary language of the establishment – they are the ultimate 'coalescence' of 'two very evil and worthless doctrines': the Paulicians and the Massalians. 'By this time the fame of the Bogomils had spread everywhere. For Basil, a monk, was very wily in handling the impiety of the Bogomils; he had twelve disciples he called "apostles", and also dragged about with him some female disciples, wretched women of loose habits and thoroughly bad, and he disseminated his wickedness everywhere.'

Basil was the influential Vasily Vrach, a great healer in his time. And one of the 'heretical' behaviours of Bogomil-Cathar society was that women were treated as equals, while there was even the practice of 'free love' and some of the perfecti in the elite were women. Just like Sufism which allowed a fellowship of the sexes.

Eventually, her father, Emperor Alexios had Basil burned at the stake in the hippodrome of Constantinople in IIII. A miracle was witnessed then and recorded by Anna — a column of white light appeared in his place.

Cosmas and Damian died a cruel death with their three brothers, on the orders of Emperor Diocletian. And in the fifteenth century, sultans put great Sufi dervishes to death. The patriarchy does not like lucreless healers loved by the people. Ironically, a few years later, Emperor Alexios came to Rila to seek a cure for putrid wounds on his legs from another healer. After a regimen of plants and prayer, the pus came out of his legs and he went home, probably making a large donation to the monastic community that had saved him.

Elijah had fallen asleep on the rock. Exhaustion was the cost of having this mountain as a lover, friend and life's mission, of seeing every stone as a sign and every river spring as a portal into another dimension.

'We are guests here,' said Elijah on the way down.

'What, of the spirits of our ancestors?' I anticipated.

'No, of the wild pheasant and the capercaillie.' Two capercaillies ran fast next to us, unafraid, as if for company. 'This is their kingdom. Thank God for the capercaillie. It brings us back to earth.'

Back at Feri's, Elijah had zoomed off and it was time for Redjep to drive a hiccupping Alish back to Black Mesta. Feri and his daughter were busy receiving supplies, Ibrahim reshuffled his vodka glasses and Erol and I drove to his favourite place.

It was called The Manure, a one-word story of a millennial way of life. Erol was a slim man with blue eyes and a smoker's complexion who wore a down jacket even in summer, as if suffering from a chill. The Manure was a series of playful dips among well-shaped hills dripping with greenery at this time of year. We walked along a forest road like an arboreal tunnel, which Erol called 'The Eye' because at certain times of day like now, you could look down the tunnel as if into a giant green iris with a light tunnel of a pupil.

In 1972, army lorries rolled down the river road and deadlocked Yakoruda. Men fled to the hills. The rest hid behind barricaded doors. Erol was eleven when army men kicked the door in. A soldier hung a rifle on his shoulder and held him at gunpoint as a shield: 'Boy', he said, 'let's see if we can find your father.' Civilians didn't own fire-arms, but they forced him to open cupboards so that if the father was armed with a knife, he would stab his own son.

'After that, I couldn't speak for a year,' Erol said.

He regained his speech when his mother took him to an old woman who melted a bullet 'for fright' and after seeing the shape of a gun in the melted lead, made him take three sips from the water where the lead had cooled. Erol was twenty-nine when he officially recovered his name.

'I have three birthdays,' he said. 'When I was born. When I crashed my motorbike on a blind turn of the Mesta and lived. And when I reclaimed my name.'

Later, when he was conscripted into the army, his commanding officer thought he was a Turk. 'No,' he explained, 'I'm a Pomak.' 'What sort of a name is Erol, then?' 'A worldly name,' replied Erol with pride. He was from a distinguished family and one of his ances-tors had been a hodja. There were learned people in the family and Erol was a worldly name in the sense that it wasn't a religious one, like Ali or Mehmed. It was a mark of education.

Erol's daughter was married to a Christian and their baby was named Elif, another worldly name.

We stood on the edge of Rila and looked at the Rhodope.

Yakoruda was on the Rhodope side of the river. But its lakes, le-gends and pastures ran up the Rila slopes. In The Manure gully, we were surrounded by lush forested hills dotted with ruined houses. This is where people used to live with their immense herds. Rila's meadows, colours, shapes and smells had their own tone. Erol was a Rila soul.

'I can't describe Rila,' he said. 'Because it's indescribable. I can only feel it. Because it's a part of me.'

Place names in Upper Mesta had one of three words attached to them: *koliba* (hut), *mogila* (mound) and *mahala* ('hood). Pashovi kolibi,

Avramovi kolibi, Evrovi kolibi, Pironkovi kolibi, hundreds of house clusters named after mountain clans. They spoke of the recently expired aeon when humans and mountain were one. Lots of place names were derived from Yuruk, the old nomadic pastoralists known for their woven rugs, now gone from the land, though some of the rug patterns remain. The mounds were said to contain treasure, or tombs, or both – as with the leprous Byzantine princess and her dowry.

Erol was not a fantasist. For him, communion with the mountain was a private matter. He climbed up here when he felt a tightness in his chest, walked through the Eye, from one mound to another until the chill of White Mesta reached him, though the river itself was out of sight. And when he looked at his mountain through the eye of his camera, he saw how blessed he was to live here, where the two mountains became one and it was impossible to choose between the two, you loved them both.

Another evening, I drove upstream to the White Mesta with the skinny mushroomer. From a human perspective, White Mesta was terrifying. Set in a narrow gorge with high cliffs on one side and a massive forest on the other, the river raged in its bed even now, in the driest season. If it erupted from its bed, it would flood the ribbon of the road, already full of puddles through which the car barely made it and bash you against the rock. Once the road ended, a pathless hike took you to a plateau called The Cauldron where the sources began and bears roamed. Not even mushroomers went there – it was one of the most inhospitable sites. People and animals had been bashed in The Cauldron of White Mesta.

One day, I drove above White Mesta with Redjep the star mushroomer and Ibrahim of the drinks. We walked across one rushing meadow after another, like turning the pages of a gripping book. The place called you to be alone, so we kept scattering and then calling out to each other. Ibrahim struggled with the sun and disappeared in the shade. Redjep went into his mushroomer state: deaf, mute and invisible. He found lots of ceps but hadn't brought a sack.

'Because when you bring a sack, you don't find any. They hide.'

I stood in the middle of a high meadow, vast like several stadiums

that opened up into an unfolding panorama. It was inclined like a
funnel – you ran down it and you slid into another dimension. I stood
and felt waves of orchestral sound pass through me. My whole being
vibrated with a joy so intense, I almost lifted off the grass as if I was
inside a crystal palace jubilant with harmonies. There was no floor or
ceiling. I saw that the mountain extended much higher than the eye
could see. That I was much higher too, and linked by an invisible
thread to something above. That the meadow was full of other
beings – they had no form, they were pure joy.

After these expeditions, I'd drive back to Black Mesta, past the daily
honey seller who set up her cornucopia of goods awkwardly at the
blind turn where Erol hadn't died in a crash, so that you risked a
head-on collision every time you pulled over. Yet she made up for it
with her extras – three jars of sheep's yogurt instead of two – and we
swapped recipes. Then I'd wade across Alika's green beans with
relish.

I lay on the grass and let the sounds of Black Mesta rock me into
slumber under the gold of the August sun. The voices of villagers,
the toot toot of the train every two hours, the *Allahu Ekbeeer* at five
o'clock, the shuffle of old women at dusk, Alish's coarse voice as he
walked, without a cane, up his street after a day of clients, away from
the smoking men and the foul philosopher at the table rhyming cock
with mock, and on reflection, he was doing a public service by providing an outlet for bottled-up passions, the cooing of the mother
with the pram, the disturbed woman who came down the street in
her filthy clothes, asking politely for 'a sweetie or a chocolate, or
something' to sweeten her existence.

I heard the happy hum of drying nettles on my porch. Nettle is an
optimist. Nettle is strong and never despairs, and if you eat nettle,
you'll become the same.

My back soaked up the earth's warmth and I became a worm. The
rustle of the green bean forest, the resiny smell of stacked logs, Zaidé's pine syrup in the jar, the swallows circling the hills without
sound – everything quivered in the light like a gossamer web, then
broke the moment I woke up, with my face burned and the sun gone.

At night, I sank into my iron-framed bed under a duvet. The nights were cold and the Gypsies' dogs howled. I felt the black-and-white beginnings of the river, their veins branching off under the skin of the mountain, the yin-yang whose wholeness is the Mesta. Black Mesta, White Mesta. Black pine, white pine. Black fir, white fir.

A single star above the hill looked like Venus but it was in the wrong place.

There was something constantly on the verge of manifesting here, like an unfolding bud. The mountain was saying something. I tuned in. I was inside a circle, a kind of ouroboros where the mouth and the tail meet. Discovery and sunlight filled each day, then at night, the mountain closed shut and everything felt remote, prehistoric. As if everything was yet to come.

The Arabic *al-kimia* borrowed the word from Greek and Greek had borrowed it from the Egyptian *kemi*, meaning black or black earth. That was the fertile soil of the Nile. I inhaled the fertile soil of Mesta. Underneath my bed was the great city of mycelium. Above me was the crystal palace of the mountain.

I almost knew how Zosimos of Panopolis felt when he had his alchemical visions in Egypt. He became the homunculus sacrificed in elemental processes in the divine laboratory. He'd wake up and exclaim to himself:

Is this not the composition of water?

Fire?

Earth?

Then he'd dream again. The ouroboros eats its own tail and gives birth to itself.

Zosimos was tormented because of his love for his student Theosebeia. And he transmuted his desire into discoveries that became conversations with her. She asked him tough questions in a philosophical dialogue. Like the homunculus, he had to die and be born again from the ashes of his personal passion. Sufi poets called this the search for the Beloved.

Everything you love dies but returns in another form.

One night I had a fever. Was it the virus? Would I stay forever in the grave of Black Mesta where nobody was afraid of death because they were death's familiars, just as the black cat is the familiar of the witch? Shivering under the duvet, racked with aches and loneliness, I dreamt that a disembodied voice said to me:

'Wow, there's a lot of pain here. But you'll be all right.'

I know it's Alish because there's no mistaking his rough voice. And I know he means not just my achy neck, my fever, my quest for how best to live and best to die – but everybody's.

Mycelium

'You walk past a tree and there's no mushroom. Two hours later, you walk past it again and – mushroom!' said the shy mushroomer in an oilskin jacket on the second evening, in answer to my question. 'And it's big! What the hell?'

'They pop up behind your back,' grinned the skinny man.

'Aye, they're clever.'

'Mushroom knows things that we don't know,' said the skinny man.

'When it rains in the evening, mushroom will be big.'

'The best median temperature for mushroom is 12–13 degrees Celsius.'

'You know how you identify the good one from the poisonous? By the gills.'

'Rings around the stem are bad news. Red spots means either poisonous or hallucinogenic.'

'Most people who die of mushroom poisoning are mushroomers.'

'If I don't recognise it, I treat it as poisonous.'

'The cep is heavy because it's full of wood.'

'It tastes heavy too. Like meat. I can't eat them.'

'I prefer chanterelles.'

'The cep grows till first snow. It wants to grow.'

'Just think about it. Underneath our world is another world. Mycelium.'

'We have no idea what goes on there.'

'Under the forest floor is a carpet, we don't know its true size. It's alive. From time to time it sends a messenger above ground. A mushroom. That mushroom produces millions of spores.'

'Billions,' said the shy guy who'd forgotten his shyness. 'When I'm up in the forest, even if I don't see anyone all day, it's busy like a city.'

'It's called symbiosis,' said the skinny guy.

'The roots of the trees talk to the mushrooms underground. And the mushrooms overground talk to the insects and bees.'

'Without pollinators, our forests will die.'

'Without mycelium, the whole world will die.'

'There will always be mycelium, don't you worry,' grinned the skinny guy. 'I'm not so sure about the overground cities.'

The shy guy finished his pint and got up, his empty canvas sack ready for the morning, when once again he would steal above Black Mesta and White Mesta, where the underground and the overground cities met out of view, like chords in an alpine symphony that only lovers can hear.

ALISH

Alish's sight had started rapidly declining in his early twenties. As a student at the Forestry School, he was already very short-sighted, but while studying physiotherapy in the capital, his sight failed definitively. He returned home and worked for ten years as a masseur in a resort in The Good Place. As darkness closed in, he continued to work with people's bodies.

We ate lunch at Feri's after a busy morning of patients. Alish ordered steaks, stuffed peppers, soups, salads – it was his habit to order too much food. He insisted on paying, no matter how many friends were at the table. He ate little, sipped his beer with relish and listened to you carefully. Because he was a local hero, he had a table by the bar at Feri's.

Beers and friends was how he had decompressed from the intensity of working with people in pain almost every day for the last twenty-five years.

'For those in pain there's no holiday,' he said. 'No weekends.'

He had no weekends either. Even lunch was difficult. His little old phone with buttons kept ringing – patients asking when they could come, telling him they were on their way, asking for advice, or saying: 'We're outside, where are you?'

Some had been coming to him for years – mostly with one of the many types of chronic back pain. Especially in winter, when some muscular-skeletal conditions worsen.

'Drivers, forestry workers, seamstresses, all with severely stressed spines.'

One way or another, it all came down to the back. Headaches came from the back, he said, and sometimes from an internal organ system. Whenever there's a headache, somewhere else in the body is out of balance.

'People are used to popping painkillers, but that doesn't address the root cause. That's why problems return. Because the root cause is ignored.'

He saw children with scoliosis, a twisting of the spine, often overweight. It was sometimes possible to free up the fatty tissue around the spine which freed up the nerves. He saw more and more overweight children, he said, with deformed, weak backs. Too much screen time and no exercise.

'They don't play, they don't swim, they don't walk, they don't look up from their screens. They get old before their time. It's an epidemic.'

The average age of his patients was getting dramatically younger – because of this artificial way of life and – 'And the number one reason: psychological stress. Every problem begins with some form of stress.'

For Alish, faith in your ability to heal was the single most important factor in recovery.

'The faithless ones have little hope of recovery. I don't like to talk about things I don't understand like mushrooms, but if there's one thing I can say outright it's this. Belief in your ability to heal opens the path to healing. There's no other path.'

He'd had women with large ovarian cysts who were so sure they'd be cured that the cysts dissolved. Alish didn't take credit for it, but the cysts were in turn related to some muscular-skeletal problem that he'd tackled.

'First,' he said, 'you must trust that you'll get better. Second, you must trust the person treating you. And third, trust in a higher power. They're all related.

'Lots of people are blocked. The blockage occurs in one or more places in the body. And it's linked to the mind. So I don't use oil on people's skin, cos it blocks their pores and nobody needs to be blocked any more than they already are.'

I asked him about specific cases, but he didn't discuss individuals – it was unprofessional. And one thing he couldn't stand was gossip. This town – he meant Yakoruda – is a hotbed of gossip, envy and competition about material things.

'It really gets my goat, all that stuff,' he pushed the second empty pint glass to one side and called the waitress in a denim jumpsuit, Feri's daughter. 'Give us another beverage, luv! And another potato salad for my friend.'

Overruling my protestations, he went on.

'That's why I keep myself to myself, even though I know lots of people and lots of people think they know me. But you can't truly know another. Cheers. Eat up.'

We clinked glasses. I didn't want those extra portions, I said. But Alish took pleasure in splashing out on friends and treated me as a friend from the beginning.

'Because you've got your marbles about you and your energy is good. It's a treat to mix with the healthy in body and in mind. I see people with very poor energy. Polluted energy. Energy is all about merit. You get the energy you merit. Not in a moral sense, in a literal sense.'

And then, he said, 'You leave that behind you when you're gone, like a trail.' I wasn't sure if he meant gone from the room, or gone from this life. Maybe it was the same trail.

He felt the vibrational frequency of everyone who crossed his door, he said. Sometimes, he was overwhelmed by people's emanations and got headaches and disturbed sleep.

'One time,' he leaned over the table and lowered his voice, 'I opened the door and I was face to face with vampires.'

They had been three or four, men and women, but he couldn't tell which one was the 'real' vampire. He didn't let them in, but they waited for him outside.

'I managed to get away. I fled here. They followed me. Eventually, I managed to get rid of them. After that, I couldn't sleep for a month. My sugar went up too.'

I have met vampires like these.

Those were the vagaries of operating out of his own house – he didn't know who would turn up. But he was fearless and he liked being his own boss because he was allergic to being told what to do, he said – there's always a catch when you're working for somebody. That's why he quit the resort job – because he didn't want to become dependent on his boss's whims, even when the whims were indulgences. Because of his exceptional talent, Alish had been made an offer he almost couldn't refuse: to be a private masseur to elite sportsmen and women. It was a world of beautiful bods, lucre and celebrity. But he did refuse.

'I could see where it was gonna end up, for me. It was already turning my head. I was starting to think with my dick. When you're blind, no matter how good you are at what you do, you remain an outsider. There's no two ways about it. And love is hard to find.'

Then, in the direction of Feri's daughter:

'Another beverage, luv! And chocolate cake.'

We put the uneaten food in boxes and took it back to his place. He couldn't cook for himself and there was nobody to cook for him. So he ate takeaways and the fruit and vegetables patients brought as gifts from their own gardens.

'So anyway, I somehow found it in myself to walk away from it – the girls, the money. And I returned here and set up an open-door practice.'

Since that day, his door had never stopped opening. Word spread and people came with problems beyond his expertise.

'I'm an osteopath, not a magician,' Alish said. 'I treat lots of things: coxarthrosis; shortened ligaments; neuralgia; sciatica; slipped discs. But some folks come expecting miracles. Maybe they think the blind can do magic.'

A family came all the way from Istanbul – a young woman in a wheelchair with cerebral palsy. Parents brought autistic children. Infertile women came.

'There was one who came with lower back pain, and after that she conceived. I was chuffed for her, then two of her girlfriends rocked up: "We too want to conceive." But you've come to the wrong door! I'm an osteopath, not an inseminator.'

He chuckled. His teeth were all gone. That's why he didn't eat much. It seemed unfair – he was only in his early fifties and didn't touch sugar because he was diabetic.

'You have to know the difference between what you can treat and what you can't. I too want to get my eyes back, but I can't.'

Alish lived alone in a single room reached by a flight of outdoor stairs. That was his share of the family house.

'Alone with all my problems, and those of others on top.'

Under the stairs was his bathroom. On the ground floor lived relatives, and across the street, his brother's family, who owned the little shop with sugary snacks that ruined people's teeth and where men gathered at dusk. Alish had had some chickens and rabbits in his garden, for company, but his relatives had taken them, claiming that he couldn't look after them. When you are blind, you are not only at the mercy of strangers, but of your own family. The strangers leave, but your family don't.

Inside Alish's room there was a sink, a kitchen table on which he kept a few personal items, a bottle of vegetable oil and a transistor radio. A bed for him at one end and a massage bed for his patients at the other. You lay face down with your head in the hole. There was a small pillow that was infrequently changed and I put it to one side. Alish's hands were small, warm, kind – and as strong as a vice. How many bodies had passed through this room?

'I don't know,' Alish said, 'I don't keep count.'

You had to ascend the stairs to reach his door, leave your shoes outside as if entering a temple and step into the tiny hallway filled with bottles of wine, whisky, rakia, ouzo and champagne, all gifts. But he only drank beer. The first time I went to see him, he shook my hand and said to Feri who'd brought me: 'Nice energy, very warm. Feri, give her the finest bottle of wine' – and I ended up with a vintage French red, which kind Feri kept in his restaurant and brought out glasses filled to the brim whenever I came. The ouzo was from Greeks married to Bulgarians who tried to translate. He cut them off: 'Lie down and I'll find it.'

And he did. He also remembered every detail about every returning patient and their circumstances and family relations. I sat in on his appointments one morning. A mother and daughter came. The girl was wearing silky lingerie. She was engaged and glowing.

'Excellent,' Alish gently manipulated her tailbone and lower spine. 'It's feeling so much better, eh!'

Just a year ago, she couldn't sit or lie down, or have sex, because of crippling lumbar and pelvic pain. She had spent her teens in pain. The GP had said she'd need painkillers for life. The gynaecologist had informed her that she'd be infertile. She came to Alish several times. The pain was now gone.

'Of course you'll have a baby, twins even. But there's no rush, you're young. You can get up now.'

Next was a lorry driver who could barely stand. His wife helped him up the stairs. He laughed at his own pain.

'Because if you laugh, it hurts less,' his wife said. She was a seamstress and had been cured of her own bad back by Alish.

People came as a last resort after they'd been written off by doctors, or misdiagnosed, or sent round a labyrinthine health care system until they despaired, or ran out of money.

Alish was on good terms with conventional medicine. But there are doctors out there, he said, you show them the place that hurts and they look at some other place that's fine, as if to spite you. Because they can; they have power over you. Or they're incompetent. There are also lots of charlatans that style themselves as healers and people go to them out of despair. The real healers are few and far between, he said. It was true.

His manner was brusque but never unkind. He just didn't do niceties.

'A government minister came to me once, actually lots of bigwigs come, but that one wanted to jump the queue. "Do you know who I am?" No, and I don't care. He waited his turn.'

While we lunched, Ibrahim sat down with us and ordered drinks and a salad. He asked Alish to fast-track some friends that afternoon, because 'they're special people.'

'Mate,' Alish said, 'All people are the same to me. They'll wait.'

Ibrahim raised an eyebrow at me. 'I've known him since we were kids fishing in the river. Fair to a fault.'

'Mate,' Alish said, he was getting tipsy after four pints. 'There are certain laws of nature. Do good if you can. If you can't, try not to do harm. Don't discuss others, look at yourself instead. There's a few more, but these are the basic ones.'

There really was something of the scales of justice about Alish. He had in fact wanted to study law, but realising that law was one of the elite professions reserved for Party members' children at the time, and that he was a boy from a Pomak community that only a few years previously had been targeted with army lorries, recognising that he was a second-class citizen, Alish went for physiotherapy instead. He had worldly ambitions back then and wanted to be a masseur to footballers – football was his passion. He still enjoyed matches on television and walked around in red T-shirts emblazoned with 'Manchester United'.

'And now . . . with the blindness, and then with the heart attack that made me die and come back – when that sort of thing happens, you don't care about little things like status and money.'

He'd been a large man, then, but after the heart failure and the surgery he'd melted away. I could not recognise him in earlier photos.

He was content in his one-room home and didn't go anywhere.

'I would, if I had my beloved next to me, but she is not here,' he said, not revealing more, 'because even I have the right to a private life,' he said. 'You asked me what is my medicine. Apart from Black Mesta where I go to wash when I can, wash it all away. I love this river. Like a person.'

But at the end of a busy day, he was too tired to ask someone to take him down to the river and just lay down on his bed after a quick shower, closed his eyes, and hoped the phone wouldn't ring.

'His medicine is to help people,' Ibrahim answered for his friend.

'No,' said Alish.

Alish was public property and that made people speak on his behalf, as if his sightlessness incurred other deficiencies. This annoyed him no end.

'I've known him all my life, I know everything about him,' Ibrahim said.

'No you don't,' Alish said sharply. 'You haven't a clue.'

We all went quiet. There was something utterly naked about Alish's face with its eyeless and toothless surface, always paying attention, picking up signals, refracting them back at you. His face was like a mirror. His whole being was like a mirror. You looked at him and measured your own soul's integrity. That's why it was sometimes difficult to look at him.

'You're in good nick,' he said to me on that first day, when I lay face down on his patient bed.

My neck pain came from the lower back, he said, causing the odd twinge.

'It's the tailbone, it has a slight kink,' he said. This was in fact a long-standing problem.

'Walking is recommended. You can get up now.'

Some women flirted with him and acted out their dramas. The more privileged, the more self-absorbed. A TV presenter came and said: 'Should I take off everything?'

Alish cackled. 'I said to her: You can take off anything you like. I don't care. I've seen it all before, so to speak.'

She proceeded to do just that, and when he finished with 'You can get up now,' she made a show of losing her bra. 'Alish, where is my bra?'

'I dunno, I said, "I'm blind, aren't I. You're supposed to be the seeing one." People like that drain me. And those with negative attitudes. Negativity sucks you dry.'

But he never stepped over the line with people. He waited for them to find their bra, list their complaints and saw them off at the door where they put on their shoes and drove off in a cloud of dust, re-crossing the railway and taking care not to be mowed down by the speeding train.

'Next!' he'd shout down the stairs. 'Tell them to come up!'

Payment was voluntary and there was no fixed rate. And anyway he could not see the banknotes left on his table. People were giving and never took advantage of his blindness.

With his earnings, Alish was putting his nephew through a physio-therapy degree. The boy had wanted to follow in his footsteps.

'What matters most to me is love,' Alish said at the lunch table. 'Love is the only elixir, my friend.'

Ibrahim and I were quiet.

'But there's less and less love to be had,' Alish said. 'Less love for animals. Less love for people. Less love for nature. It's all related. Cos there's only one love.'

Ibrahim had lived passionately and had many lovers and friends but, he said to me another time, 'I always end up alone.'

'Without love, nothing works,' Alish said. 'You can do nothing if you have no love in you. Love for what you do. Love for someone in this world. That's all there is.'

He squeezed my hand over the table with his vice-like fingers, then his phone went off. It was time to return to Black Mesta. Ibrahim's eyes filled with tears, the seeing brown one and the milky-blue one blinded in an industrial accident. My tears fell on my notebook, blurring words. Alish paid the large bill, overruling our protestations and we walked to my car, slowly, with Ibrahim on the other side of Alish, although it was Alish propping him up, not the other way around.

Most people seek significance through their actions and even thoughts. They want to be bigger. Alish offered all he had and asked for nothing in return.

Nothing at all. When I gave him a piece of clear quartz for his birthday, which fell on the fifteenth of August – 'the feast of the Virgin Mary, no less!' he pointed out with pleasure – he was delighted.

He had taken an oath before himself, to heal others for as long as he could and even though it drained him, he couldn't stop now. Sometimes I'd call him and he'd say:

'Ah, it's you. Nice to hear your voice. No, no, you're not disturbing me. I'm already disturbed, haha.

No, I can't do lunch in town, cos I'm waiting for some people from X.

Some people from Y said they'd come at three.

I'm waiting for the people from Z but they haven't arrived.

This morning I had two couples. Which one had problems? All of them!

No, I don't need anything. I have leftovers from lunch. That schnitzel was excellent. It's still sitting here.

People are dazed, mate. They were already dazed before, but this pandemic has really scrambled their brains.

I'm so tired. You have no idea. I want to lie down and forget. But I can't.

Ah, I hear a car. Tell them to come up!

Do you have everything you need? Good.'

In the folds of Black Mesta, in the laboratory of his being and out of prying eyes, Alish had transmuted his own pain and misfortune into something that glowed. He had produced his own philosopher's stone. And whether people understood it or not, that is what they received, on top of his bodywork. In autumn, he would contract the virus and be forced to close his room for the winter and even spend time in hospital. With his heart condition and his diabetes, he had been at high risk all along, but continued working: 'because for people in constant pain, there is no virus,' he said.

Of an evening, after the last visitors took off in a cloud of dust, Alish would shuffle past Alika's bean plantation in his rubber slippers, speaking to the neighbour in his rough voice, dressed in a Manchester United T-shirt en route to the little shop up the street that didn't sell alcohol, turn to me over the fence and say: 'They brought me too much.'

And he'd hand me a bag of tomatoes and cucumbers, and a jar of sheep's yogurt he remembered I liked, because he remembered everything about people.

If he could put the Black Mesta, where pink-scaled trout once darted downstream like reflections of a face, his boyish eyes and hands after them as if he could follow them from his penumbral highlands to the Aegean light that he would never see – if he could give that to you in a bag too, he would.

Silent weave

In Black Mesta, my duvet was woven of silence and darkness. My duvet was the mountain. That's why I stayed so long — to dream in my bed, left to myself. Like the Black Mesta.

We have lost two things that we need to be well: darkness and silence. Our nervous systems are polluted with noise and electric lights. The affluent do 'dark therapy' and silent retreats. You have to buy silence and darkness, because the civilised world doesn't provide it for free. It trains us to be afraid of silence and darkness. And in exchange for our fear, it entertains us with noise and lights. Noise and lights stand in for lost meaning and lost power. They are false idols that replace the sacred. We are prisoners of our civilisation, tortured with noise and lights, unable to rest.

Last year in The Birches, I was told about the 'silent weave'. *Nyámo plàtno*. It has been around forever, nobody knows how old it is. You don't discuss the silent weave. You don't see the silent weave. On a new moon, women sit at crossroads and weave a cloth in silence. It's finished before dawn and they disperse. She who holds the silent weave has powers, she is the silence and the night. Before she dies, she passes it on. I know the woman rumoured to possess the silent weave. Other women fight for it. They try to break it, weaken her that way. Occult wars behind locked doors. But the silent weave will not be broken. You can't unweave the silence and the night.

CONTACT

Her house was near the river, the walls inlaid with round stones shaped into sunbursts, the garden full of flowers. On the outside table was a geranium pot. Trendafilka lit a candle and set herself down.

She had always lived by the river. As a child, her grandmother would bring her to the water's edge – no concrete reinforcement yet – place her on the ground, draw a circle around her with a knife, then remove her and cut out the round patch of earth and overturn it, with a mantra.

'I was an anxious child,' said Trendafilka. 'That's how she rid me of anxiety.'

Her grandmother took her on day-long outings in the woods above Yakoruda, to pick herbs and look for interesting things.

'She'd make me pass under aerial tree roots. I didn't know it but she was preparing me to take on her mantle. I was always around her and saw how she poured a bullet and extinguished coal for fright, and did all sorts of things with herbs.'

Trendafilka didn't use other methods, she only worked with herbs. There were other women here who did other things. That same day, while I was crossing a bridge after a morning at the Yakoruda market, a tiny old woman in a headscarf and floral shalvars shuffled over to me. She had an elfish face and wanted to know who I was, why I had bought a three-pronged wooden pitchfork and a hand-crafted bell for rams at the market (good question!) and whether I needed a ritual performed for fright.

'Never mind,' she overruled me, 'take a wee sip anyway. You might not know that you have fright!'

And she produced a vial from her blue mantle and opened it. It was filled with turbid water. She'd just poured a bullet for someone and this was the leftover water. That was a no-no – sipping from another's water! She was either deranged or thought me gullible.

'I take a sip myself, from time to time.' And she did just that. Then she grinned in a rakish way that made her look just like an elf.

Trendafilka was a folk herbalist of the educated variety. She had studied anatomy, physiology and hands-on modalities like reiki. In the end, she had settled on her first love – herbs – and for the last thirty years had been a practising medical herbalist. But with a twist.

Trendafilka was a slow-moving woman with a fleshy face you felt you'd seen before and that had seen you.

'So, behind her ordinary demeanour, my grandmother was an interesting woman.'

She was like that herself. In the space of one afternoon, beyond the ordinary demeanour, I glimpsed a fathomless world.

It was thanks to her grandmother that she developed an intelligence for herbs, places and the presence of natural forces all around her. Countless people stepped through her grandmother's door, bringing their pain and their hopes. And now they stepped through hers.

'I have spent a lifetime with people and their problems.'

Trendafilka's adult life was made of two odd halves. As a young woman, she'd been a local functionary of the nationwide Communist Party organ 'Fatherland Front', which dealt with indoctrination and agit-prop, spying on citizens, and community issues large and small. Her section had been 'infrastructure'. Public spaces and sewage, domestic and neighbourhood politics. In the absence of any kind of therapy for a population half of whom was chronically traumatised – that was the Pomaks – Trendafilka had held the double role of helper and oppressor.

The second half of her life began 'with a bang' in January 1989, a watershed year in which the regime collapsed. All that she had stood for would be declared bankrupt by the end of that year. Part of her had sensed the end. And that part – her subconscious – had made a run for it.

'When it rains, it pours', she said. 'It was just after my birthday.'

It started with an urge to do automatic writing and drawing, ceaselessly. She was compelled to write outpourings of love and existential questions, stream-of-consciousness poems, and to draw cosmic-looking figures and mandalas.

'It felt like it wasn't me doing it. Rather, I was a vessel through which some other entity was trying to communicate. We entered a conversation.'

She gave me a book of poems to read and a DVD to watch. It was all there, she said, she couldn't explain it better and anyway, I might find it too much to take in. She was right.

The automatic writing and drawing had been a period of overwhelming intensity. She couldn't sleep and became detached from everyday life, from her family, some of whom (the mother-in-law!) had struggled with this radical change. From a dutiful wife, mother and busybody, she turned into a woman in the throes of a baffling passion. Not for a man though, or not for an earthling, which made it literally outlandish.

After this initial phase – a phase of initiation, she said – Trendafilka began to receive clearer telepathic messages from a collective of entities that operated together and amidst the cacophony of information, a distinct thread emerged: human health and herbs.

'Names of herbs were given to me. I didn't know them. They were not the Latin names, but folk names. I hadn't formally worked with herbs. I'd been a functionary, I was used to filling forms!'

It was the beginning of discoveries for her – of the Rila-Rhodope saddle where she lived, of people's minds and bodies, of her own unplumbed depths. She took courses. As the names were dropped telepathically into her mind, she started looking for the herb to match the name. This reconnected her to her long-gone grandmother. For instance, the grandmother had used a name for St John's wort that she didn't know – *zvanika*, 'little bell'– because its yellow flowers ring with happiness in summer. Zvanika is the folk name of the entire family of Hypericeae with its 300 members, only one of which is St John's wort.

Some of her grandmother's plant names remained a mystery to her. There was one she had called *uplanevo bilé*, or fear herb, which Trendafilka guessed was valerian. But the name was reminiscent of another herb known as *strashniché* or *frightie*, which was motherwort. Very different, though both are nerve tonics.

She shrugged. At first, she struggled with this detective work and a sense of inadequacy at her lack of knowledge. Then she realised that the names prompted by these entities were folk names because she was meant to be a folk healer. The next prompt was to use a pendulum. The pendulum gave her the names of herbs, together with diagnostic insights.

Yeah right, I thought.

'With the swing of the pendulum, the names of herbs and conditions came up as if on a screen.'

Methodical as ever, she did a course in radiesthesia – the skill of working with a tool, like a pendulum or a rod, to connect with the electromagnetic vibrations that all earthly bodies possess.

'Everything that is alive has an electromagnetic vibration – humans, plants, animals, rocks and places.'

That vibration is mutable, she explained. In people and animals, it changes according to their mental-emotional state and their physical health – and the two are inseparable. Places too hold specific geomagnetic energies according to their location, topography, natural features and the events that have taken place there.

This basic geomancy is at the core of feng shui, the Chinese art of creating a healthy home environment by harmonising the human-made with the natural. Feng shui literally means wind-water. The most familiar everyday use of radiesthesia in the Western world is dowsing for underground water.

'My journey with herbs was lonely but exhilarating. I searched in books. I searched on the mountain slopes. I experimented.'

Sitting next to the sweet-smelling geranium, I realised I had to submit myself to her diagnostic ways – otherwise it was all words. She charged a humble fee, and only for the herb preparations, not for the diagnostic test, because her clairvoyant skill was an impersonal gift and not subject to personal profit.

'Sure,' she said. 'I'll see if I can help you. With some people, I can't.'

'Because they come too late?' She shrugged.

'Some come too late, when things are too severe for herbs. Others are very passive about their health. They want me to fix a problem they've been making for themselves for twenty years. With a fifteen-day herbal course. But they're not prepared to make any changes in diet, lifestyle, or attitude.'

I'd heard the same from my herbalist in Scotland: people were prepared to drink anything out of a bottle, swallow any pills, but not prepared to change their habits.

'Anyway, first I have to ask them: can I help this body?'

By *them* she meant the entities that helped her. Who were they?

'I've asked them many times. They say: We are healers from the stars.'

'And I am just a vessel,' she went on. 'Through me, they send their knowledge of plants and other things. I am not even a healer. I just help people heal themselves, but they must do the work. And of course,' she added, 'you must look for the right healer. Again, it's individual. The herbs and the energy I put into them encourage the body to remember its tremendous healing power. It's all there in the body,' she said. 'We just have to remember.

'A great deal has been forgotten,' she continued placidly. 'About the Earth, about what health truly is. About what is available to us, every day, literally under our feet. We walk in blindness.'

Trendafilka had opened herself up to remembering.

'Because humans have forgotten who they are. And now they're forced to return. Because they're looking for remedy.'

To return.

And the entities? I didn't know how I felt about the entities. But then, I barely knew anything about my own birth planet, about my own body and mind, let alone about other galactic beings. And anyway, these healers from the stars could be seen as a metaphor for forgotten knowledge. We can cope with metaphor. We can't yet cope with the fact of being galactic denizens. We are still pretty provincial.

It was the entities that prompted the combinations of herbs for each patient.

'There were herbs that were included in all the formulas, from the beginning. St John's wort, valerian, thyme. St John's wort is a wonder plant. But since December 2019, they have stopped including it. It's not prompted anymore. Something to do with the pandemic.'

She said she didn't understand the reason behind it, but I think she just didn't want to discuss it. The entities had also told her that the virus was man-made. She neither defended nor questioned this. She just received it.

Trendafilka had worked in a phytotherapy clinic, and then for many years in a clinic in the capital that used holistic protocols: mainstream medicine, plant medicine and complementary healing modalities.

In the initial stages, when she was putting together a plant classification chart for her own use – such charts are standard in all herbal medicine – she had picked and dried all her herbs. Her circular 'herbal zodiac' contained the 100 plants that she used. Over time, they were reduced to sixty and now she mostly worked with thirty-six. They were enough, she said, because they contained the essence of all the rest.

Gradually, she switched to using a large wholesaler and the only herb she still picked herself was a type of milk thistle rich in antioxidants that grew at 2,000 metres and was used for prostate problems, immune-boosting and some cancers. My experience with milk thistle in Scotland was for chronic gall bladder issues. It was highly effective.

I asked about her favourite herbs.

'There are many,' she said affectionately, as if speaking of children. 'Many that do a lot for us. Thyme.'

Thyme was the perennial herb of choice. The genus has a staggering 350 varieties, all of them aromatic and warming.

'Mursala is a wonderful plant too, good for just about everything and safe to take. Calendula is a lovely plant. It soothes the internal organs and is a cancer-preventative. And of course, plantago for the gastrointestinal tract, for regulating blood sugar and lots of other common problems. For the gall bladder and digestion: rosemary, fennel and yellow gentian are very good. But you know, herbs are a universe.'

The infusion time was important.

'If you infuse, or if you simmer for three to five minutes, it's enough to have an effect. If you simmer for ten to fifteen minutes, however, plants become strong and highly medicinal. Which is not always needed. It depends on the individual and their condition.'

With some people, she advised 'pulsing therapy', which meant starting off with a strong brew and gradually making it weaker. She had a high success rate with internal disorders involving the gall bladder, liver and gut, the uterus, the prostate and the urinary tract. Doubters had dramatically lower healing rates, she said. Some people arrived already convinced, sometimes without even realising it, that nothing could help them. And nothing did.

There were certain well-established herbs that she didn't use, or only sparingly. Uvaursi, the bearberry, was found to be too strong. Another potent herb she didn't use was dried smoke tree leaf, widely used here. Smoke tree flowers in fluffy pink tufts like candyfloss. Rinses made from its leaves can help with even severe types of bacterial overgrowth and infection, including wounds and gynaecological infections. It tightens tissues with its powerful tannins. In traditional medicine, it tackles persistent conditions like stomach ulcers and periodontitis.

'I love smoke tree!' I said.

She nodded.

'Only externally applied. Smoke tree is very strong. It can cause vomiting.'

Trendafilka was also cautious with yarrow – the soldier's herb and women's herb, powerfully astringent and toning.

'Yarrow is good, but only for specific conditions and it must be stopped after a week.

'Everyone needs not one herb but a cocktail,' she said, 'and that cocktail is highly individual. It's about how each herb harmonises with the rest and how each herb and the final blend harmonise with the individual at a specific moment in time.' Another plant she didn't use was water pepper. I looked it up: it grows freely in Britain and is pungent like wasabi.

'There is no bad herb,' she said. 'I just work with some and not with others. It's also about where a person lives and what their body recognises. The geography is important.'

This is why, with very few exceptions, she only used herbs that grew in this part of Europe. It was something to do with the potency of a herb that grows close to you – you and the plant have to be compatible. You and the plant sense each other's vibratory nature and this determines the plant's impact on you. This has always been known to herbalists and modern biodynamic growers actively communicate with their plants.

'When you go back to Scotland,' she said, 'you should only take herbs grown there.'

But half the herbs I bought there grew here. And I didn't even know which ones because the packets didn't say.

'Then pick your own,' she said. 'That way you learn about them.' This is what she had done, too.

When we went inside for my consultation, I saw the big jars of herbs. There were other substances too: resin from pine for stomach ulcers, frankincense and myrrh resin for stress. You swallowed a grain or two at bedtime, inside a morsel of bread so as not to irritate the stomach. An age-old folk remedy. Or you could burn it on charcoal.

'It chases bad dreams and negative thoughts,' Trendafilka said. 'As kids we put grains of it on the pan and heated it. You can do the same with brown sugar. The smoke has a calming effect.'

In fact, I'd just bought some frankincense from a nuts, fruits and herbs stall at the market – without knowing what it was for. A pinch of ground frankincense was sold wrapped in a square inch of a book page from a Russian classic and sold for a couple of euros, 'to calm the nerves', the seller explained – 'just as they used to sell them in the pharmacies'. Frankincense in communist-era pharmacies – I had no memory of it but clearly, the communist cult of the industrial and the public hadn't crushed the private and the organic. In the early years of Communism, all herbal shops and practices were closed, but later, things crept back in and my mother remembers the specialist herbal pharmacy she visited to buy 'Lambrev Tea for kidneys', named after a urologist who used phytotherapy. Rocky the Enchanter and his team had been picking bearberry and cranberry and helping us all along!

Before the consultation, I asked Trendafilka: What is the key to health? She didn't think long.

'Goodness,' she said. 'To think good of ourselves and others. To do good to ourselves and others.'

Trendafilka's name means 'many-petalled rose.'

'Because thought becomes emotion and emotion materialises. It acquires a body. Your thoughts return to you in the form of energy. It's the principle of what folk call magic. But it's simply the universal law of attraction.'

Dissatisfaction and indecision, for instance, eventually affects the gall bladder, she said. Anger strikes the liver. In TCM, these mental-emotional-biological organ patterns form the meridians.

Trendafilka's prescribed mixes had between twelve and seventeen herbs. Her trademark immune-boosting tea had seventeen. I guessed that it contained thyme, mursala, pine tips, plantago and dried black elderberries.

'Correct,' she smiled, but didn't give away the rest.

Trendafilka's unorthodox method was quite orthodox. It was rooted in a well-established holistic codex that goes back to Avicenna and Hildegard of Bingen. It blends physiology, nutrition, medical herbalism, plant lore, crystal or radiesthesia diagnostics and plant-human communion of some sort.

This tradition was synthesised for the modern age by the doyen of Bulgarian phytotherapy Petar Dimkov, dubbed 'The Healer'. Trendafilka worked in the Dimkov school. Dimkov in turn worked in the Deunov school – that is the twenthieth-century mystic philosopher Petar Deunov, or Beinsa Duno, dubbed 'The Teacher'. Both believed themselves to be carriers of the Bogomil legacy with its central symbol of the light that permeates all living things. The work of Deunov and Dimkov was forced out of print during early Communism and their names were whispered. As a child in the 1950s, my grandmother took my mother to a city park to show her where Teacher Deunov and his followers had met to dance Paneurhythmy, play violins and converse among the centenarian trees. As a child thirty years later, I browsed Healer Dimkov's *Natural Living and Natural Healing* at home, when it was quietly reissued.

The Deunov-Dimkov way favoured cultivation of your inner and outer garden: plant medicine; nutrition; meditation; music therapy and 'a good relationship with truth'. They perceived that without 'a deep interpenetration' between the human being and the rest of nature, there is no lasting health. 'Nature heals at its own pace and in its own time. Its healing processes are complete and its results are lasting,' Dimkov said, and proved it. Dimkov began his career as a high-ranking army officer and, like Culpeper, he was wounded multiple times. People queued outside his house until his death. A lucreless one, he never insisted on payment. The authorities' official stance was to tolerate a doddery fool, but every other household had *Natural Living and Natural Healing* instead of a Bible or a Koran. Here's a Dimkov tea for 'anxiety, headache, and when you are plagued by unfounded fears': hawthorn, lemon balm, oregano, linden blossom, basil, juniper berries, lavender.

'Dimkov is also the father of iridology here,' Trendafilka said. 'I studied iridology but don't practise it.'

She knew, and I knew, that there was a trail from modern iridology back to eye-reading in the Middle Ages, as practised by the Bogomils. Ordinary healers used plants and animals, but the adepts called perfecti carried large emeralds. Through the refraction of the emerald, they read the state of light and soul in the patient's eye – also called aura-reading. In energy medicine, it is a marker of health. They then matched the patient's aura with the aura of a suitable plant which they could perceive at night when plants emit a particular light. Phytoexperts believe that hybridisation, monoculture, genetic engineering and pesticides in the soil have caused a dimming of the light in plant crops. Wheat is an example of a severely compromised crop, which is why gluten has become harmful to some people's gut.

Eye-gazing with a crystal was passed on by Egyptian alchemists. Theophrastus writes that the green stone called smaragdos (emerald) was good for the eyes and that temple obelisks were made from that stone. On a visit to an Egyptian temple said to be over two thousand years old at the time, Herodotus saw two pillars, 'one of pure gold, the other of emerald which gleamed in the dark with a strange radiance.'

'I don't use crystals,' Trendafilka said, 'I visit them in the hills when I feel fit.'

We were at a rustic table inside the house. Icons and textiles, all featuring the madonna-with-child motif. The symbol of the mother-goddess was everywhere and many came to her for infertility. She had a folder of photographs of women with babies: her clients. The feminine was in her early automatic drawings too, kept in an album. They were all of female figures drawn with some force in a freakish uninterrupted single line. The figures are made of convoluted spirals. Eventually, the line exits the figure like a thread on a tapestry.

'Do I have to do anything?' I asked her when we sat down.

'No,' she said. She picked up her pendulum, a simple glass cone on a little chain. 'I will ask them if I can help.' The pendulum swung. It was a yes.

I thought she would go into some kind of trance, but she simply held the pendulum, her elbow propped on the table, and began to speak, starting from my head, in her everyday voice, the voice of my favourite GP, but relaxed because she didn't have to squeeze me into a ten-minute appointment.

Here is some of what she said. All of what she said was staggeringly accurate.

'Thyroid gland. Especially the left side, it's shrinking faster.'

Overwhelming numbers of teenagers and kids in Eastern Europe developed thyroid disease after Chernobyl. I have an auto-immune condition called Hashimoto's disease. The body attacks the thyroid and destroys its tissue over time. Under attack, the gland can't produce enough of the vital hormone thyroxine, so people like me are on thyroxine supplements for life.

'Stuffiness in the sinuses. Allergy to cats, perfumes, all synthetic fragrances and dyes, gluten is out. Heart is robust, except for sudden fright. Nervous stomach. The gall bladder is irritated and forms small stones. The hepatic ways are inflamed. Damage through medication. They say it's the Pill. The right kidney periodically flushes out small stones.'

Years ago I'd had a bad infection in the right kidney and it played up a bit.

'These days it's rare to see a person with completely healthy kidneys,' she said. 'It's diets and general way of life, but also the pesticides in the food and water. They gradually damage everybody's kidneys People don't even know it.'

The pendulum swung gently.

'Groin, lefthand-side, a tendency to hernia. Don't lift heavy things. Sometimes pain in the lower back. This impacts the neck. A tendency to spurs later in life. Headaches likely from the spurs. Trauma in coccyx after a fall but no organic damage.'

I had fallen on my tailbone years ago and suffered from chronic pain for years, until an osteopath treated it.

'Low blood pressure, constitutionally. 115 over 70 just now. At times, 90 over 60. Blood sugar: normal, 5.3 at the minute. Cholesterol: 5.'

That was the exact measure of my cholesterol and I always had low blood pressure.

'I will ask them a final question.'

The pendulum swung.

'The answer is: no life-threatening conditions.'

I felt a calmness wash over me like a warm wave. Who isn't worried, from time to time, or all the time, that somewhere in your body a treacherous process is unfolding? Of course there is such a process in every body. It's called ageing towards death. But what I had lacked all my life was a belief in my own body's ability to be well, as if I was separate from it. As if our agendas were in conflict. And they were. Too often, I'd sacrificed my health to pursue some mental fixation. It is a stupid thing that clever people do. For women, it's part of our misogynistic inheritance, to make ourselves ill without even knowing it.

It was time to find out what herbs were recommended. She told me to write them down in case she forgot. And the pendulum swung again.

Elecampane

Oregano

Valerian
Speedwell
Pine tips
Thyme
Chicory
Plantago
Horsetail
Mursala
Calendula
Lavender
Nettle root
Fennel

She opened a big book and wrote down my details. I was now part of her archive.

'You are my patient number 16,978.'

She then wrote my name on a large paper bag and measured out herbs from the jars. She remembered all of them – we checked against my list.

When I returned to my room in Black Mesta, I tipped the contents of the bag on my duvet and mixed it all, feeling the different plant textures and their woody and floral fragrances, and divided it into fourteen small piles, as instructed. Each pile I wrapped inside a piece of clean linen and taped it closed. It was important to brew a fresh dose every evening, she'd said. Some people brewed the whole lot in a big pot and bottled it in the fridge, but she didn't approve. By brewing your daily herbs each night, you gave your body a signal that mending was intended. I enjoyed brewing the nightly dose in a pot outside at dusk, as the last train toot-tooted, then sipping a cup of the brew before bedtime and a cup in the morning. It was bitter, intense, buzzing with personalities, a mountain of tastes. The long simmering time made it very strong.

'And in case you need it,' she said at the end, handing me my paper bag, 'I can look up *your* plants. The plants that will accompany you like friends through your life.'

Of course I needed life-long friends! She looked up my birth date in another chart which showed which plants supported which constitutions, according to the astro-medical school of Avicenna and Hildegard of Bingen, and later Culpeper, Paracelsus, Dimkov and countless other botanists and astrologers, physicians and philosophers, stargazers and forgivers. Our friends.

Angelica archangelica
Swede
Shepherd's purse
Dandelion
Celery

I wrote them down with relish.

Shepherd's purse was unfamiliar to me. I bought it dried in a pharmacy and made some tea. Big mistake! Its pungency knocked me back – it reeks of infected urine, that's why you take it as a tasteless tincture. In a feat of sympathetic herbology, it is used to treat urinary conditions, among other things. This is called the doctrine of signatures: when a plant looks, tastes or smells like the thing it treats. Skull cap treats insomnia and looks like a skull, herbs that treat the liver (dandelion) are yellow like the jaundice you get if untreated, and on it goes.

Like many potent plants, shepherd's purse is unremarkable-looking – until you crouch by the roadside and look at it. Then you see that its small white flowers produce pods that are miniature heart-shaped purses and these purses fill with golden seeds, like elf money, hence the name. This tiny earth denizen can fix bleeding noses, bruises, heavy menstruation and even internal bleeding caused by endometriosis. No wonder the Gaelic name is *lus na fola*, 'blood herb'.

Speaking of sympathetic herbology, I'm reminded of Hildegard of Bingen's prescription for 'Ridding oneself of an inappropriate passion'. It involved betony. Betony is a brush-headed flower on a hard stalk that you walk past, because it keeps to itself. It has been used for centuries as a nerve, memory, circulation and digestion tonic – a quality known in herbalism as 'dispersant', because it disperses stagnation. In Hildegard's time, betony was a well-known aphrodisiac, but her ritual with the plant is meant to counteract desire. This is the homeopathic principle of 'like cures like', *similia similibus curantur*. *A Midsummer's Night Dream* comes to mind, although the plant squeezed on Titania's eyelids was pansy, not betony. And the plant that lifted her spell and made her see that she'd fallen in love with an ass, a common affliction among smart women? Wormwood, the purger, a cousin to mugwort.

In Hildegard's ritual, betony is an antidote after the fact.

'Find a Betony plant,' she advises those struck by inappropriate passion. 'Pick its flowers. Place one in each nostril, under the tongue, under each foot, and inside the palms. Gaze with concentration at the Betony plant. Do this every day until relief is felt. The man or woman thus treated will be cured, provided no excitable foods and drinks are ingested, and under no circumstances eat Betony.'

If you ate it, your passion would return. Everything is poison, it all depends on the dose – and the method of application.

Angelica archangelica! This poetically named and leafy plant is a kind of wild celery and I now grow it in my garden. Many grow it for its decorative round seed heads, but its leaves are edible and its roots treat anything from digestive disorders to lung afflictions to skin infections and poisoning. Culpeper reported that the candied stalks were good 'in times of infection, and at other times to warm and comfort a cold stomach'.

Culpeper was a big fan: 'On what occasion this excellent name was first given unto it, I know not; unless it was for the excellent virtues thereof, or for that God made it known to man by the ministry of an angel.'

Valerian! The first spring of the pandemic, roaming the hills above my house, I began to pick valerian, attracted by the scented white flowers. But it is the ammonia-smelling roots that are more medicinal. Valerian has been a human companion for a long time – first mentioned by Hippocrates and applied for insomnia, and used on the clothes of lovers in Central Europe to repel 'envious elves'.

The smell of valerian instantly conjures my grandmother the forager. My grandfather had a tyrannical personality and attacked everything she did, including her 'weeds'. She'd disappear to her garden at the back of their house, where she grew herbs and salads. In her *gradinka*, no one disturbed her. She sat there in a chair and consoled herself. I am sure it was thanks to valerian and her *gradinka* that she outlived her husband by thirty years. He was her enemy, but she had lifelong friends.

Chicory is a blood-cleanser related to dandelion and used for gout, joint pain, as a digestive tonic and for anaemia. Its local folk name is 'blue gall flower'. Its small flowers are a striking pale blue. I saw it everywhere and marvelled at its lavender-blue rosettes. In Belarusian folk mythology, it's called 'Mary's little dress' – because when Mary, mother of Jesus walked upon the meadows, all the plants touched by her sky-blue skirts briefly turned sky blue and a new plant blossomed, an image of her skirts. Of course, Mary was a latecomer to what sounds like an elf party in the forest. In my childhood, we made hot milky drinks with a cheap substitute for instant coffee, called 'Inka': chicory root, sugarbeet and rye. I was quite addicted to it!

Elecampane, now there's an exotic name. I had drunk it in tinctures prescribed by my herbalist.

'Ah yes! White Oman,' Trendafilka said with relish, using the Bulgarian name, 'A wonderful herb. Imported from Asia, it's almost extinct here.'

Elecampane used to be widely cultivated in Europe for medicinal purposes, including the making of absinthe. Its many names tell of a long relationship with humans. *Inula helenium* is after Helen of Troy who carried a bunch of the flowers when she was kidnapped. Elfwort or Elfshot for the Celts who considered it sacred, and called it so because it restored the strength of those stricken by invisible elf arrows. Or chronic fatigue.

Pliny the Elder writes that it helps digestion and 'causes mirth' – and it does! I bought a pack of dried elecampane root and made an infusion. The roots have a woody aroma and taste like bitter syrup. It is instantly uplifting. Within half an hour of drinking it, I was hungry, delighted and interested in everything.

It turns out that elecampane is used as an expectorant for chronic chest problems like bronchitis and was even used to treat consumption and tuberculosis with its powerful anti-bacterial component called 'helenin'. Helen of Troy would be pleased. And its taste makes it perfect sweetmeat material – for centuries, it was enjoyed in Britain as a candied snack. But wait, there's more: it's also called horse-heal because it cures skin afflictions in horses and scabwort because it fixes scabby sheep. But why had my herbalist given it to me?

I found the reason in a comment by Culpeper, who writes that elecampane syrup is excellent for warming 'a cold windy stomach and stitches to the side, caused by spleen.' That's me in the Scottish winter. Culpeper on elecampane: 'It cures putrid and pestilential fevers and even the plague,' improves eyesight, removes joint ache, convulsions, cramps, bruises, 'scabs or itch in young or old; blemishes and morphew on the face'.

Thank you, elecampane. You and the rest of the herbal kingdom had helped me silently, before I had any understanding of who you were.

Trendafilka said to give her a call in two weeks' time for a follow-up.

Before I left, I told her about my dream the previous year, with the voice saying names of plants. Like silivryak. This kind of thing was normal for her.

'Silivryak is immortal flower. We don't have it here.'

She asked where I'd had that dream. 'Above The Birches', I said.

'Ah, The Birches have a potent energy,' Trendafilka said. 'It's the mountain. That dream was a message.'

What was the meaning of the message?

'That's for you to find out,' she said.

Trendafilka's poems were not very good and she made no literary claims. But they were fuelled by a passion so great, it verged on the cosmic – literally.

In the early days of her transformation, she felt that change was coming, unstoppable like a tsunami. She was married with two children, living in the house where she still lived and which the family had built with their own hands. But a deep longing for something entirely different flowered within and she knew she would either have to break away from her current life or some inner revolution would occur. She couldn't go on being her old self.

When the automatic writing started, these poems began to emerge.

They were dictated to her by an immaterial being that called itself Dilyani and described itself as a 'being from the stars'. Over the years, Trendafilka and Dilyani had a love relationship like no other. Some of the poems are sad, others ecstatic, dripping with unfulfilled yearning and questions and it isn't clear whether the voice is hers or his, or a fusion of both. She said it was his and that he was trying to communicate with someone else via her. In that voice, I hear a being in the throes of sacred passion. It was a search for the beloved.

She wrote some of the sadder poems at a highland Rila lake where she still picks that thistle and where it often rains. It is no wonder that the Melancholy thistle grows there. Lakes, river, rain, tears and galactic yearnings.

Dilyani asked her questions too: 'What is a tear, what is indifference, what is envy, what is hate?'

'He let me know that these destructive emotions exist only on our planet.'

I pictured having a relationship with someone you can't ever see, someone who is a figment, a voice. And I could easily picture it. It was like having a muse. The only person Dilyani had shown himself to was, unfortunately, the mother-in-law. He appeared to her as a tall man in silvery robes, like a hologram. Very similar to the 'keeper' of The Passage, in fact.

He held a crystal pyramid, inside which glimmered a rose-like fire. 'She has this inside her,' the entity said. The mother-in-law was silenced forever, though Trendafilka was desolate not to have seen him herself.

The whole family lived with the quiet knowledge that 'we are not alone'.

I was unexpectedly moved when Trendafilka's husband came in. He was a short, bald man with an introverted face. Not a tall silvery creature. I told him I was stunned by the accuracy of the consultation.

'You're not the first,' he shrugged, pleased, 'and won't be the last.'

I wondered what it was like, for him, this relationship with Dilyani who had now vanished without a trace.

'There are things that humans can't grasp yet,' he said, pre-empting me. 'This doesn't mean they are not there.'

A summer storm had broken out. I stepped into a liquid garden. Trendafilka gave me a towel to wipe my sandals before I put them on.

'Illness often begins in the feet. Keep your feet warm. Soak them in hot water in winter and warm water in summer,' she said in her placid voice, the voice of a woman who had looked into the eyes and bodies of 16,978 humans including me, who had known earthly and unearthly love, and who was only the last in a long lineage.

I almost saw them behind her in the doorway, filling the room, the house, spilling down to the river and across into the flanks of the mountain: the nameless women and men of the centuries who had tuned into the whisperings of plants and planets. Yet they all looked so ordinary, so familiar, like people you'd continue to meet and they – you.

Like valerian, chicory, elecampane and thyme.

Immortal flower

Haberlea rhodopensis is a glacial relic. It is known as immortal flower, resurrection plant, silivryak and the flower of Orpheus. This small, fine-floreted plant appears in drawings and reliefs of Orpheus with lyre and animals. Animals, plants, no people. His concerts were a hymn to all of creation, humans were optional.

The only time I'd seen 'immortal flower' mentioned outside of its Rhodope homeland was on a facial cream by an upmarket cosmetics label. It used the extract of a yellow flower from Corsica, the other 'immortal flower' of Europe. The Haberlea rhodopensis has found its way into plant-based cosmetics too. A brand once used it in a cream called 'Rosa Arctica' though it has no relation to the rose genus. Here in its homeland, the flower is used in natural remedies with names like 'Everything Balm' and 'Orpheus's Tears' for skin cancer, psoriasis and acne. The profound, game-changing anti-mutagenic qualities of silivryak were better known to our ancestors than they are to us. They used it first on animals and then on themselves, internally and externally.

Silivryak is endemic to the Rhodope. It has the ability to not die, even when cut and dried for nearly three years. The technical term is extreme resistance to desiccation and this is due to silivryak's amazing antioxidant powers. The clue is in its unique gene sequencing. Orpheus's flower has survived from the Tertiary Age without pollinators.

But when Rhodopean pine forests are felled, entire populations of it disappear – even though it grows on treeless rocks up to 1,800 metres above sea-level. What was the message this flower had for me? Perhaps the message was not for me but for all humans.

Elixir exists. Immortality exists. But only in union. Not in separation. The killing of one being brings the decline of its friend. Thus spoke the immortal flower.

Silivryak still grew in two places in the Rhodope: by the abysmal cave where Orpheus is believed to have gone into Hades and in a forest reserve on the Greek side. A forest ranger there told me this, but the border was closed. I had met her on my journey for *Border*, her name was Ioanna. I couldn't see Ioanna or the flower that year.

'People know they shouldn't pick it,' Ioanna said, 'but they still do.'

Why do they do that?

'Because they're stupid. They think it grows just for them. But nothing in this mountain grows just for us, nothing.'

It was good to know that Ioanna is still there, and immortal flower too. Perhaps it was better not to see it in the flesh, not to be fooled by its beauty into thinking that, even though it is 2 million years old, it grows just for me.

IN THE LADIES' POOL

Beehives perched above the narrow-gauge railway. Then the road followed a tributary called Goodness. From Black Mesta, White Mesta – into a sun-flooded basin and the land breathed a sigh. This was not an ordinary basin. It was where the three mountains of Mesta harmonised – Rila, Pirin, Rhodope. They were all turned to the basin, each with its own chorus of faces.

The road shimmered with heat and mineral vapours. I drove through sleepy Banya (Bath) with its ruins and mineral springs, smiling for no reason. Could I accept, just now, all that was wrong with this world, could I stop being galled by the wreckage of injustice that blighted the land? My gall pain had returned with Trendafilka's herbal cocktail. The gall bladder is purging, she replied on the phone.

And the valerian is making me sleepy, I added. Then you need to relax, she replied. And so I came to The Good Place to relax in its waters.

Today, I said goodbye to everyone in Black Mesta and Yakoruda. I was on my way back to the valley at the end of time. The village of Good Place was en route. It sat in the lap of northern Pirin, like a gathering of pilgrims before its gates.

A roadside stone bore the emblems of Good Place: the mineral spring and the edelweiss. Edelweiss, 'noble white' in German, grows in Pirin and The Alps. It has always been elusive and now it's near-extinct.

At dusk, I sat on my wood-panelled balcony in a guesthouse called Macedonia Inn. The gates of Pirin turned dark and closed shut. Noiseless lightning struck the peaks with an electricity so mighty, I thought they would split – but there was no thunder. It was a film with the sound off. The storms were high up at Bezbog Peak which had two competing meanings. Crazy God or Godless, and they both made sense.

Macedonia Inn was by the old public baths. Birds performed concerts at dusk in the crowns of chestnuts and limes. The rumbling of water springs was everywhere. Hundreds of hot springs gushed from the mountain flanks that were the rims of the grand basin. The blend of fire and water reached perfection here.

Everywhere, there was the shape of Pirin – its animal flanks, its human faces. The mood changed, but the outline remained. If I were a bard, I would sing a ballad to Pirin, or maybe a single perfect note. Instead, I drew its outline in my notebook because it wasn't enough to see it, I wanted to touch it like a person.

I knew how travelling bards, soldiers, messengers, shepherds like Atemin with his flute and medicine women like Trendafilka felt when they crossed these cauldrons of the earth on their missions. They fell in rapture.

In the morning, the mountain was wrapped in white vapours, its sunny face turned to the day as if for the first time, pulling you in like a magnet. Though the days were hot, dew fell overnight. A dry towel left on my balcony became moist overnight because the basin sat at 800 metres above sea level. And here, you wandered around with a towel draped over your shoulder. From six in the morning till late, people of all ages and shapes walked across the park grounds of the baths. Past the statue of a bathing nymph and vague communist-era sculptures, past the board listing the balneo benefits of the water: rheumatoid-arthritic, stomach-bowel, skin conditions, gynaecological, neuro-motor, kidneys.

At the entrance of The Good Place, you stopped to fill up your tubs from a drinking fountain with two spouts – a cold one and a warm one. What is it good for? I asked a Gypsy man with a face pummeled with hardship. What do I know, he chuckled. Everything, they say, so I fill up and hope.

The luxurious water embraced your insides. The summer was late, life was caught in a sticky web. Something emanated from the mountain. It felt like predestination. Destiny, destination, *destino*. *Destino*, purpose, goal.

Being brimmed like an overfull cup. Being with places, with plants and with people. It was enough. Nothing more was needed.

I walked by Good River eating a peach and when I stopped to throw the stone in the undergrowth, there was a dry peach kernel by my feet. An odd impression passed over me: that the person who stood in this spot eating a peach was just another me that popped up somewhere along the timeline. I'd never been here before, yet I was retracing my own steps. And it didn't matter who I was. I was someone and no one.

These quantum flashes accompanied me daily here. Previously, I'd have described them as 'surreal'. But the surreal is simply the real out of context, discontinuous. The surreal is quantum reality. It had something to do with the pandemic – everything had fallen out of context. And all the water. It was like Oppenheimer's description of the electron:

'If we ask, for instance, whether the position of the electron remains the same, we must say no; if we ask whether the electron's position changes with time, we must say no; if we ask whether the electron is at rest, we must say no; if we ask whether it is in motion, we must say no.'

I was like the electron, outside linear time. This whole place was. But where were we, then? We were near water. *There is a river.* If you couldn't hear it or see it, its ions vibrated in the air and you inhaled water, day and night. If you walked downstream and left the village, there was a spring of colloidal water. It gushed out of a spout with some force, warm, abundant. You wanted to plunge your head in and forget your troubles. A sign said:

SILVER MINERAL WATER

EYE DISEASES

I waded in the small rock pool, where the water collected before it ran into the river, and let my feet drink from it, then splashed my eyes. The springs of The Good Place had always been about the eyes.

A man came down the steps to the silver spring with tubs to fill, thought he recognised me from somewhere I'd never been and gave me two ripe peaches from his garden. And splashed his eyes.

Further downstream, I found The Little Roman Bath – a round stone basin with carved seats inside. It overflowed with warm water. I was tempted to sit in it but felt disquiet. It was an isolated spot. Wherever there is clean running water in an isolated spot, there is a presence. I plunged my hands in and sensed the undines, the creatures of water according to our friend Paracelsus who came up with the four elemental spirits. Undines carry information from the primordial ocean to our cells, from the highland spring to the vessel of the crone that holds our fate. Our fate is in our cells. Our fate is water. I remembered Kadrié's mother, last year. She gave me a repertoire of self-healing spells. They featured three things: a mantra, a gesture, a plant. The fourth, 'magical', ingredient was intent – 'say it like you mean it,' she said, 'or it won't work.' A great spell is like a great poem: it brings change. Here is her water mantra for distress.

Pick a plant you like and go to running water. Wet the plant, pass it across your eyes left to right and say:

> Bismillah Rahmani Rahim.
> The king's court is on fire.
> No one's home to put it out.
> Sister water, you will put it out.

Do it again:

> The king's court is on fire.
> No one's home to put it out.
> Sister water, you will put it out.

And one more time:

> The king's court is on fire.
> No one's home to put it out.
> Sister water, you will put it out. Amen.

Then throw the plant away and leave.

Back on the road, a skinny old man pulled up in a battered Lada and leaned out of his window:

'Want to buy edelweiss?'

On the homemade card he proffered was written:

EDELWEISS.

TRIPS TO GODLESS AND BACK.

I got into the sagging passenger seat and went to see his edelweiss garden.

He'd worked for many years in the uranium mine, then he'd been a truck driver, then a pensioner on 150 euros a month and now he peddled his cultivated edelweiss and drove visitors to Godless. And back.

What kinds of visitors?

'All kinds, rich and poor, but especially those afraid of heights that can't take the chairlift. I take them up, then bring them down.'

What was it like, in that uranium mine?

'Days like nights underground,' he said. 'Thirty, fifty metres down, soaking in the radiation and watching your friends die in accidents. And then from cancer. I don't know why I'm still alive. It was the wife but should've been me.'

On his gate was a black-edged notice for his wife's death anniversary. His edelweiss were arranged in potted rows in the large garden which he neglected because he was obsessed with the one plant. He cultivated it from seed, slow-dried it and sold it glued to souvenir cards. They had to be in pots because they got eaten by worms and snails otherwise. Snails gobble up the leaves of edelweiss like steak, he said. He showed me where he dried them – in the pages of old books. He turned the flowers between pages, to stop them getting screwed by mould or extreme sunshine, 'cos these days it's one or the other, no middle way anymore,' he said. 'This year it's been very damp. Don't touch them for God's sake.'

As a young man building the chalet at Godless, he'd seen wild edelweiss.

'Like seeing the god of the mountain,' he said. 'But now there's hardly any left and only in the rockiest crags where people can't go. Cos they destroyed it. They pulled it out by the roots. Now, I'll give you one that'll last you a hundred years.'

He brought out pressed edelweiss cards at different prices.

'These ones are medium. And these are ideal. Which do you want, the medium or the ideal?'

The ideal of course, though they looked the same to me – they looked sublime even dry-pressed. Like many high-altitude plants, like mursala, edelweiss is unearthly – white, velvety, star-shaped. Like a visitor from another planet that took root on top of the earth.

'Here's an ideal one. Don't put it in direct sunlight or you'll fuck it up.'

He was in an ongoing argument with another gardener who said that edelweiss didn't need moisture because it was an arid flower.

'Arid, but what do you see on the ground at dawn, at 2,500 metres? Dew. Edelweiss holds moisture in its leaves.'

It was all about watering them at the right intervals, moving them into the shade and back into the sunlight, and hoping he didn't lose too many to climate extremes and 'jealous neighbours'.

The herbarised specimen were cut and you couldn't see the roots which are really something, Edelweiss Man said, all tangled together like snakes when they make love.

Edelweiss Man was a believer in karma. He had done some very bad things in his youth and didn't expect to go anywhere nice when he carked it, he said. That's why he liked to visit the 'miraculous' icon in a monastery, brought in the Middle Ages from Athos by a monk whose destination was Rila Monastery to the north, but he got lost in a storm and ended up here, taking shelter in a small abandoned forest monastery. Years later, locals saw coloured lights in the woods. And there, inside the building, were the remains of the monk and next to him – the icon, giving out unearthly light. We drove there. It was a high, dangerous forest road that climbed into the mountain, a hermit's road, a road where you won't be found for years, unless you hug an icon that shines. The icon was indeed shiny – Mary and her son were wholly made of wrought silver, only their faces were painted and nestled within the armour. The monastery was named after Panteleimon, a lucreless healer from Asia Minor who healed the blind with prayer. And mineral water. The monastery had been cared for by a brave lone nun called Domenika. She came as a young woman in the early years of Communism and must have lived a peaceful life in the forest with her hens and goats. The numerics of her lifespan bookended the twentieth century with inscrutable symmetry.

9.9.1919 and 9.9.1999

A drunk woman with a moustache was the caretaker of the monastery now, so we didn't linger.

On the way down, Edelweiss Man told me about his friend who, during the campaign against the Pomaks, had been ordered to bulldoze their graves. He didn't want to do it, but they bullied him.

'I wanted to bring him to the icon but he wouldn't come. Two years later he died.'

'Maybe it was the mine,' I said.

'It was the graves. Not the mine. A cause-and-effect thing.' Edelweiss Man didn't meet my eye and I wondered if he too had bulldozed graves.

'Make sure you go to the old baths,' Edelweiss Man said when he dropped me off. 'Before they turn them into another hotel for the rich in this land of the poor. My back is fucked from the uranium mine and the only time the pain stops is when I sit in the men's pool.'

I'd been avoiding them because of their neglect, but now I went into the old baths.

You gave 70 cents to a woman in a white overcoat and you could spend the whole morning inside. Though staying in the pool for more than thirty minutes was not recommended. You could get a headache or pass out – which I nearly did after spending two hours inside on my first day.

There was no clock inside, because time was replaced by water. Everything in the echoey building spoke of the past – of the 1930s when it was built with high glass cupolas in the main men's and ladies' pools and inlaid with those handmade mosaics that you don't see anymore, and the decades of Communism when things fell apart, and of the last decades when that which had fallen apart was not fixed. Taps dripped. The voices of water came from all sides. All was vapours, drips and rumblings and at first it was hard to see who was inside. Someone was inside. Even when empty, a presence was here: water.

You entered naked and climbed into the pool down the tiled steps in an involuntary prayer that felt as old as humanity. You climbed into the warm mouth of the earth and paid your respects.

There was just one woman in the pool, my age, with a handsome face and hard eyes. She was from here but had spent decades working in the city because there was no work here, except in hotels. Her belly bore the marks of long-ago childbirths.

'Every weekend, I come home,' she said. 'Because I'm in my place here.'

Conversation in the ladies' pool is brief. There is a code. You come naked, no towels, you don't ask questions, you don't stare, you don't take up more space than you have to and if you are asked to rub another woman's back with her hand mitt, you do it. Being asked is a show of trust.

Women descend into the pool, slow, naked. Or sit by the individual basins with milky-blue glaze that has been stripped away. They sit, plug and fill the basin with warm water – the taps are broken and water drips anyway – and pour it over their backs and heads with measured movements, using the small bowls provided. The old women bring shampoo and wash their hair, a nod to their childhood when houses didn't have baths and this was it. Soapy water runs down the blue tiles.

Throughout the day, women of different ages arrive and enter the steam. Their bodies disappear. Bodies that have given birth, endured surgeries, sat at sewing machines for decades, planted and uprooted vegetable gardens, emigrated, returned, aged, been pounded then abandoned by children and men, lain exhausted on narrow beds. Under the dirty glass dome with the drip-dripping, these rumbling memories rippled through us all, as if it was a single body in the ladies' pool.

Drip-drip. All of us are young and old.

Everybody takes a turn under the lion-headed brass spout. It is the sweet spot. A large Roma woman placed the top of her head underneath it – for headaches. A bird-like old woman held her broken hand under the spout. I bent my head and let the warm stream hit my crunchy neck, where Trendafilka saw spurs. Too much reading, too much looking down, instead of up at the stars.

You can't play a role in the ladies' pool. You just bend your head under the lion spout and have your spikes become softened by the warm water. And you accept things as they are. Dripping taps, decay and all.

The hard-eyed woman handed me a towel-mitt and asked me to rub her back. When someone bares their back to you, they are defenceless. Few things are so vulnerable-making as exposing your naked back to a stranger. The mitt felt like a gauntlet, the task was intimate and responsible because of the red streaks it leaves, no matter how gently you do it. Her back was long and thin, and I realised that I'd never seen a woman's back close up. Then she sits next to her overflowing basin and pours water over her head, her face motionless, her eyes closed, a sphynx. One bowl after another.

I look at the other women and I'm struck with awe at the female back. Later, I rub the back of the bird-like old woman with the broken hand whose face is crisscrossed with lines and whose teeth are gone. Yet her back is astonishingly smooth, untouched by the many burdens she has shouldered. It's a young woman's back. It is the same with the other women – their backs are decades younger than their fronts.

Silence. The bird-like woman thanks me, barely making eye contact. When the large Roma woman offers to scrub my back, I feel timid and decline. She smiles – she sees I am a virgin of the ladies' pool.

We sit by our chipped basins, and pour water over our heads and backs. A shard of light hits the glass dome. I pour the noble water over my head and the essence of water hits me: everything flows, everything runs away. We are the water running down heads and backs, and we are the women that never change even as we age. Our backs are like water. Our long hair, our short hair, our raven hair, our white hair, our thinning hair through which the scalp shows – our heads are vulnerable and soft under the water, yet indestructible. We have broken Berlin walls with our heads and we're not done yet.

Bowl after bowl, I pour water over my head and I cry. There's something about pouring warm mineral water on your head that dissolves you.

It's involuntary. I cry not for anything in particular. I cry because I am bewitched by these singing mountains, this talking land blighted by greed that still rises to hum a perfect note. Orpheus's head sang after being torn from his body. For these backs, these heads, these hard lives, these tributaries that crisscross the mountains like the lines on the bird-woman's face, for the builders, the gatherers, the planters, the healers, the mushroom pickers, the small-scale farmers, the labourers, the cleaners, the caretakers, the emigrants who return and those who don't.

I cry because time runs away, yet it pools in my basin long enough to see my reflection.

I cry because nothing is ours except our own backs, yet we give weight to things that are worth nothing. We carry loads that we can put down. We come to the warm mouth of the lion spout and bend our head, and we are equal.

This is how women pour water over their heads.

A fortified settlement was here in the sixth century BC above the present one. The Good Place still had a dozen old churches in place of pagan temples. And seventeen springs.

The first religion was clean water. The last will be, too.

They too sat here and poured water over their heads. Their backs were smooth and young even when old. And they cried, then laughed again. They gathered herbs and gave them to their men and horses to eat, drink and rub on – to make them strong when they rode into battle, to make them faithful, to kill them. Prostate trouble was forever the bane of riders. And when the men were away picking cotton in the Aegean south or fighting someone else's war, the women turned into men. They guarded the flocks in the giant forest, they made tar from pine in vats to sell in goatskin bags, they tilled the sloping furrows, they gave birth and buried children, they washed their linens and their wounds in springs that never changed.

What happens in the ladies' pool happens in the men's pool. The men sit by the dripping basins and pour water over their aching heads, their herniated stomachs, their lonely genitals, their sore backs, and their coughs echo in the chamber when they clear their emphysema lungs.

I cry because good things are dwindling. Snow, edelweiss, mursala, clean water, and I am meeting creatures shortly before they become extinct.

Today, a woman in the ladies' pool told me how as children, they jumped into the overflowing pool, that's how high the level was and now it didn't cover your chest. Households always had access to the mineral water, but new hotels with pools tipped the balance.

Those springs that are left alone haven't changed their output for a thousand years.

Today, I crossed the cauldron to a highland Rila village with a peculiar church. It was built in the early seventeenth century on top of the old Byzantine one, by a spring that's good for the eyes – another one. The water neither increased nor decreased, it's always the same temperature, and so is the church, its little body made of different parts like its story. Inside it were hundreds of painted figures, saints as soldiers and soldiers as saints and a large procession of female saints – Marina, Anna, Ekatherina, Varvara, Evdokia, Zlata, Nedelya. The artists had not left their names, but legend said that one of them was a woman. Faces whispered in the dark. Who lived here, who died, who washed their eyes in the spring?

The blind soldiers of Samuil, went one tale. In the wake of the eleventh-century battle between Tsar Samuil and Emperor Basil II, some of Samuil's blinded soldiers wandered here. The water relieved their eye wounds and they stayed. The singing school for the blind started by them continued for 900 years and until the twentieth century, the village was a hub for singing beggars. They busked from town to town and recruited disabled children for their bands.

The church patron was Theodore Stratilates, a Roman soldier from the Black Sea, and so *stratilati* lived here, went another tale, the multi-ethnic Balkan mercenaries who owned land and in exchange fought in Europe's endless wars. Like the crusader knights and Ottoman spahi, when called up, they mustered an army and left home under a foreign flag. The survivors returned to the mineral cauldron, hoped their wives were still there and washed their wounds in the spring that didn't increase or decrease. And maybe took up singing for their sins.

A soldier could turn bard when broke and broken. But a bard could not turn soldier. Rules and rulers came and went, soldiers lost their jobs, bards didn't.

Songs and stories were scattered like pollen across these mountains by the odd and the marginal, the deaf and the blind, the autistic with a genius for memory, who forgot to wash but memorised clan histories and long-ago battles, the outcasts and the wounded healers, mad magus magpies who carried memory with nothing but a bag of herbs and sheep lard to nibble and seal wounds, who stopped at springs to wash their matted hair, find bread and sheep's milk and move on at sunrise with the ragtag army of singing children who were born old, and in whose faces was all the pain of this world. Blind bards without borders.

The Christ is painted with a long braid, like a peasant woman, and holds the baby-soul of his mother. Then he departs in a red comet of pure ether.

The spring bubbled. Nothing goes away. I have been here before because others have been here before. Specks of them live in me like stardust. I saw it clearly, as if a veil dropped. I don't want to live behind a veil anymore. I want to sing a ballad to the mountain and walk along dusty roads in odd clothes, with my hair uncut and crazy herbs in my bag.

Today, I went to Banya (Bath), built on Roman thermae, to see a fortune-teller called Maria. Edelweiss Man took me there. When he got married, she saw his wife's head in thirty years' time. In thirty years' time, his wife died of a brain tumour. When his edelweiss was stolen, she saw the thief. Maria's father worked with Edelweiss Man in the mine and died young, and when you're down in the mine, there's no Gypsies, Edelweiss Man said, because when the vault collapses, it's the Gypsy who saves your life, and racists should work in a mine.

I saw Maria from the back. She had short spiky hair and a stocky back in a T-shirt with silver studs, like a teenaged goth. She lived in the small Gypsy slum next to the pink ruins of the Turkish baths where women wash rugs in a hot cemented spring, next to a new luxury hotel that sucks the spring, next to a row of rubbish containers rummaged by dogs.

Steam and vapours everywhere. Unemployment was ninety per

cent and the men worked abroad. In the slum's café-shop, Maria held court like a queen of the rubbish dump, drinking from eight in the morning till night, so you had to catch her early.

When she turned from the bar with a glass of vodka, I saw a face that was gnomic, toothless, dark-skinned with a boxer's nose, the face of an Indian shaman. She seemed sober as she took my measure and when our eyes met, I shuddered. The men in the café, their faces wrecked, were in awe of her, her word was law and her second sight revered. She was doctor, therapist, friend and mother of the neighbourhood. On her neck was a pendant of a bat.

This is some of what she saw in my cup, after it sat upside down and she picked it up and made a quick circle with its rim on the saucer, a gesture made a thousand times. I loved my work and 'had a lot of talent and kudos', I was at a crossroads, and a spell was cast on me by 'a woman on an island, surrounded by water.'

'My mother,' I said.

'Could be, luv, I dunno. She's done you a deed, so that wherever you go, you'd return to her out of guilt. And you turn round and round like a fly trapped in this glass,' she swirled the vodka in her glass. 'You take two steps forward, three steps back. Do you get my dialect?'

She laughed with pink gums. She could say anything to anyone.

'We can get Edelweiss Man to translate.' She winked at me, then volunteered: 'He grows a pure plant but his soul is stained.'

She'd been drinking since she was a child. 'It's my elixir,' she cackled, and the men laughed with her and raised a glass. Steam rose. Everything was ruined, plundered, alive.

Her face was slashed by a scar. When she was in hospital after a car crash, the doctors gave up trying to take the bottle from her and just lined up with their coffee cups. Her skill was blunted by the accident, however.

'Aye,' she said, 'I don't like to moan but if one bear chases you, two bears chase me.'

She offered to lift the spell cast by the woman on the island – all I had to do was write my name and date of birth on a piece of paper, leave it with her and return for instructions. She would give me an amulet. I didn't care for coffee cups and amulets, but her power was beyond doubt, even if I didn't understand where it came from and how it worked. I was afraid to give her my name and date of birth on a piece of paper. I was afraid of her fathomless eyes, her X-ray vision, her bottle-a-day sobriety, her end-of-days laughter.

She was thousands of years old. She had been here all this time, by the Thracian baths, the Roman baths, the Turkish baths, the communist baths, the plague baths – a different guise, but the same force.

When she took my money and turned to the bar for a 'wee dram', her back was once again the back of a teenager.

I could see Maria in the ladies' pool by a cracked basin, mirthful with her dark priestess eyes. The bodies melt into the steam and take their chipped coffee-cup destiny with them, yet the water sprites remain. I see her joining the sprites – whispering, cackling with dark mouths, coming and going, drip-drip-drip. The sprites dive in and out of this reality.

I hear Maria's laughter. Have a wee dram in the ruins! Laugh, laugh without teeth, because nothing is solid, because the true destination has no name, because – who said that to be empty of yourself is to be full of the world? I pour water over my head, my back is young though I am old. I am somewhere towards the end, but perhaps there is no end. Not if hot water breaks from the earth's loins, ceaselessly giving and taking nothing in return.

PIRIN

AIR

Therefore come with me
To the palace of Nowhere
Where all the many things are One.

Chuang Tzu

MEADOWS OF ASPHODEL

I squeezed through Maiden Gorge without stopping. Pesho the siren's watermelon was chilling in the roadside fountain. All was well, then. I passed the village of red onions, stork nests, refuge for old donkeys and the nun who'd loved men. Pirin loomed above. Its higher gates might just open, this time.

I passed the ruins of Nikopolis, the elephant-skinned sycamores of Thunder and Fire. The sunflower field blackened with seeds, all heads turned to the sun.

In the interregnum of sunflowers, the valley was the earth and despite it all, the earth was complete. Nothing was missing. Even as it was changing and ending lives, the virus felt peripheral here, like all events. While events succeeded each other on a flatline, spirals of another kind churned under the surface. They sped up and slowed down to their own tune.

An elderly woman in the Scottish Highlands once told me: you know, Mount Suilvan is a sphynx. Mount Suilvan is a lone hill in north-west Scotland. It's true that it looks like a sphynx, I said. No, she said, it *is* a sphynx.

The Valley does not look like a chalice. It *is* a chalice.

'Call the world if you please "The vale of Soul-making". Then you will find out the use of the world,' wrote the poet John Keats in a letter. He must have envisioned a place like this. Peaks and valleys on the surface of the planet are mirrored by peaks and vales within. In the alchemical psychology developed by James Hillman and inspired by the discoveries of Carl Jung – the vale is where the soul dwells and the peak is home to the spirit. Spirit without soul is cold and disembodied. Soul without spirit is madness of the Ophelia variety. Blending soul and spirit is a life's work.

What was it, in the valley that made even lofty concepts like this

feel natural? It was the way the valley embraced all. Humanity's sad
works were allowed to fail in their own time. Everything felt curable
in the valley. Hope never ran out.

The Empty Village café was closed because Danera's family had the
virus. I greeted my neighbours, the artist and the poet, in their garden. She gave me a pouch of a rubbed herb I didn't know – samardala,
an endemic wild onion. It is dried and mixed with salt to preserve
it as a condiment, delicious sprinkled on bread with olive oil. The
Latin name, *Nectaroscordum siculum*, does not prepare you for the
addictive taste. The gallery was closed but they were as devoted to
their projects as ever. A pandemic does not rock the world of the
devoted.

In Dogwood it was business as usual.

'Ah, it's you!' said Rocky the Enchanter, sniffing the air because he
couldn't make out my features.

He was making jars of marinated mushrooms for a client in the
capital who was 'crazy about my mushrooms, and now she wants my
jam. I can't keep up!' He looked happy about it.

'Now, I must tell you about this plant I've been picking. It's called
bray. It stings like hell. Which is why it's so good for rheumatic pain.
It sucks the fire from the body.'

What was bray?

'It's the folk name. Look it up! I'm busy now.'

But he wasn't busy, he just wanted to give me homework.

'I'll give you a clue,' he said. 'It likes to grow together with white
bryony. In shady beech forests. Remember white bryony? Its root is
heavy and weird-shaped, 3 to 4 kilos.'

Bray was black bryony. White bryony and black bryony liked to
grow together and had similar properties, including their huge
mandrake-like roots.

'Would you like to buy a little leaf of belladonna to smoke yourself into sweet dreams tonight? Okay, here's a jar of raspberry jam.
But next time, you must come and work for me.'

I dropped in to see the hodja in the city mosque. He sat in the same position behind the low table, wearing a nice shirt, but he looked tired and his back was killing him.

'People ask me: when am I going to die? I tell them: "You won't die without permission from Allah-God." And they calm down.'

'Clients, not patients, then,' I said. He laughed wearily and swung a small bottle of black seed oil.

'The Prophet said: "There is a remedy for all disease except death." That remedy is nigella oil. Look it up. Avicenna was a fan.'

He produced a sheet with the many benefits of nigella.

'Cheers.' He took a sip but didn't offer it to me in case one of us was contagious.

The Gypsy slum above Thunder smelled of burning tyres. Children and unsaddled horses played in wild flowers and rubbish. I slammed the brakes to stop for a boy who ran onto the road. Something was wrong with his eyes.

'Give me a penny,' he put out his hand and in his old face was the world's pain.

I put money in his hand.

'God give you health!' he shouted after me, like a curse.

In The Birches the men at the outdoor tables waved at me, surprised that I was back.

Gyulten and Metko both invited me to stay with them, pandemic or not, and so did the old widow with the fulling mill in the Ranger.

'I want to get infected,' she said. 'But I can't.'

At the Birches Hotel, I moved into my usual rooms, happy to be back. There were other guests: a team of Ukrainian builders who had come to laminate the mosque in fish-scales of golden aluminum mined only in Ukraine. The sponsor was the richest family in The Birches – four brothers with a halal meat business.

By the end of my stay, the mosque ended up like a film set for *A Thousand and One Nights*, so shiny it hurt to look at it on a sunny day. The vast sky-blue carpet inside it was meant to be a meadow of the virtuous mind, the chandeliers dazzled, but the most original feature was the cathedral-like stained-glass windows. In a mausoleum-like chamber to the side, was a marble slab for dead bodies to be washed and dressed before they were carried to the hilltop cemetery on a wooden platform, wrapped in white canvas. The contours of the body could be seen under the wrap. The living walked in silence behind it and the swallows circled the golden minaret.

Gyulten had just lost her cousin in Germany. He was twenty-two. Let off work because of the virus, he'd gone swimming with friends and drowned.

'I don't know. People are dying a lot,' she said, behind closed shutters in her bakery.

People here drew no line between Covid-related deaths and other deaths. Such and such died yesterday, that was all. There was no interest in the cause, since the outcome was final. And no fear, just an everyday fatalism. Many Birchers had had a lingering chest virus of late and it was accepted that it was probably Covid. Or something else.

Already in the first summer of the pandemic, the people of the Mesta Valley treated it as endemic. It was just another everyday blight to live with, and they were adepts at living with blights.

Gyulten was sad for her cousin and for having to close the café, and I missed the smell of fresh cheese buns and our drives into town to buy a 50 kilo pack of flour at the warehouses. We resumed our picnics by Fatmé's fountain. She brought tomatoes and cucumbers from her garden and we ate them with olives and goat cheese sprinkled with wild onion salt.

Each evening at the Birches Hotel, the polite Ukrainian builders sat at a long table and kept to themselves and their salads and burgers, while 'Mavro Trientafilo' played. They were a united nations of faces, from Slavic to Kazakh, no less of a Eurasian mosaic than the people of the valley. They did here what the men of the Valley did in Western Europe: they worked abroad, slept several to a room and returned home at the end of the season, put cash on the table and told tales of other places. I was alone in the hotel with them once Shefket's family went home and kept my room locked at night, but not once did I feel unsafe.

Throughout the lockdown, 'unskilled workers' like these came and went across borders. The seamstresses kept at it too. Without them, Europe's economy would collapse.

Metko's friend Ahmed, an old mountaineer, was just back from Germany. He was a master wood carver, but to supplement his income he planted pine saplings on a farm in summer, and in autumn, he cut and bound pine branches for Christmas wreaths.

'When we reached the Hungarian–Romanian border, I saw a crowd of refugees with battered bags,' Ahmed described his bus journey home. 'Then I realised they weren't refugees. They were just people like me coming home. Romanians, Bulgarians, Ukrainians. At that border, Europe ends and something else begins.'

The other Europe.

Ahmed was a warm, modest man whose children were teachers and whose wife, the dominant force in the family, had just recovered from cancer. I'd met them the previous summer when Ahmed invited me to a Kurban Bairam lunch and we'd eaten burgers from his own calf. He had one cow which was taken to pasture daily by a hired shepherd. He couldn't eat the burgers. How could he bear to have the calf killed? 'Don't ask,' he said, 'that's the downside.' His children thought him eccentric for keeping a cow, a needless expense, but for him the human animal relationship was too precious to give up.

'When my father's prized buffalo were taken in 1950, he fell ill.'

Keeping a cow was a quiet homage to his parents' loss. He also kept hives and fed the bees with syrup in spring when they were depleted, but he kept losing half of his hives of late – the bees just vanished.

Ahmed agreed to guide us on a trek from Godless Peak to The Birches. Four of us set off: Ahmed, me, Metko and Bimo who was Metko's other son. Ahmed's son, who was into off-roading, drove us in his adapted Jeep above The Good Place where we took the chairlift to Bezbog Lake. We headed south along the spine of the mountain for what turned into a ten-hour trek. Bezbog Lake was divine despite its name, and Ahmed and Metko were flooded with memories.

'We first came here as students,' said Ahmed. 'We brought beer and took turns to carry it. Except him. He was always splitting from the collective.'

'The collective is a tool of oppression,' said Metko.

'As soon as we'd stop to rest, he'd shoot off ahead,' said Ahmed.

'The right to be an individual is sacred,' said Metko.

'Yeah, but you were doing it to be difficult,' said Ahmed.

They bickered with relish, like old friends do.

'Metka, remember our old mule?' said Ahmed when we climbed an arduous slope and Metko tried to overtake him, almost collapsing with his smoker's lungs. 'He wouldn't let anyone get ahead of him.'

'I take that as a compliment,' Metko gasped. He'd just recovered from stomach trouble with the help of a spring in the village of the storks. There was something about the water of that spring that healed the gut.

Bimo and I lagged behind, talking about the apocalypse.

He reckoned it hadn't come yet, the pandemic was only a warm-up. He believed that an evil society controlled the world and I told him off for disempowering himself with such beliefs. He pulled out purple-flowering thyme by the roots, knowing I liked herbs, and Ahmed told him off. You cut thyme with a pocket knife, sparingly.

Bimo felt things so deeply that it almost incapacitated him. It's as if some defensive membrane was missing in a world that pounded you from all sides. He was ironing sleeves for Armani suits in a sewing workshop – he scoffed at himself, the absurdity of it. He'd worked in Wales as a builder, but his employer from 'the Kurdish mafia' had in the end robbed him of his earnings. And because Bimo was illegal, he didn't have the confidence to go to the police and 'the boss' threatened to break his kneecaps if he did. He returned home penniless and dispirited. His brother was picking blueberries in Essex with his wife and living in a caravan park.

'From the easternmost Roman city of Nikopolis to the westernmost Roman city of Colchester,' I said.

'The children of the east are poor,' Metko said. 'Once upon a time, the children of the west were poor and came to us. Everything repeats itself. With this pandemic, the tables might be turned again.'

I really liked Bimo and his brother, and felt with them the fact of being twenty-something in a world captured by vampiric elders who hogged the resources while you gasped for air. No wonder they saw an evil conspiracy – because there *is* one against their generation.

He'd been very close to his mother and she looked out for him now, from above, as he'd looked out for her in life, he said, and among the miraculous-shaped flowers quivering in the sun, I felt the presence of Asiné.

All of us were out of shape except Ahmed. From Godless Lake, flower-carpeted meadows alternated with deserts of granite and moraine. We passed a memorial stone to a German woman who had died here twenty-five years ago. We walked over ridges jagged like broken glass. Their names chimed with human and geological history – Iron Gate, Maiden's Court, Priest's Lake, from which we drank and our teeth hurt.

'Priest's Lake was always haunted by an evil spirit, they say,' said Ahmed. 'At night, the spirit comes out of the lake as a black ram and lures the sheep till they drown.'

We climbed a 2,668 metre granite peak called Djano, 'the vertical'. Across from it was beautifully shaped Sivrya which reminded me of silivryak. I had dreamt of it here.

'There's no immortal flower here,' said Ahmed. 'But there are a few others. Just look around you. Endangered ones like the edelweiss too.'

We didn't see Edelweiss but we saw flowers that looked too exquisite to survive. A pink-headed one made of threads, like candy floss. My knowledge of alpine flowers was zero – unless we count drinking mursala tea. But in an odd coincidence, a few weeks earlier I'd received an email from an antiquarian in Dorset.

'This is a long shot, and a long story, but it might be of interest,' he wrote. 'Fifteen years ago at a boot sale, I paid ten quid for three wooden boxes full of hundreds of magic-lantern slides.'

He'd opened a box and pulled out a slide. It showed a black-and-white alpine scene with spear-like flowers. On a label was written in ink: '*Asphodeline lutea*'. The only clue to the slides' origin was a torn piece of paper in one of the boxes: '1933–1934 Bulg . . .'

The slides were in poor condition and he had them cleaned. They revealed alpine plants, mountain villages, people with bare feet and

haunted faces, and on a few occasions – a couple who looked Western: she with a wide-brimmed hat and long skirt, he in shorts and
long socks like a schoolboy. They looked serious and formal, even
when cooking on an open fire beside a tent. The high altitude vistas,
the remote communities, the epic journey, the determined travellers –
it was compelling. There is an image of a car being pushed by men
across an avalanche of moraine stones. In another one, the couple
follow an arid path behind a buffalo-drawn cart.

The antiquarian had nothing to go on, except those dates, the clue
to the traveller's purpose, which was clearly to collect alpine plants,
and the handwriting in which Latin plant names were written on the
backs of slides. He became obsessed with decoding the story behind
the slides and hired a top researcher and a senior scholar of environmental studies who'd lived in Bulgaria. They too became obsessed,
and the result was an engaging book and a full catalogue of the slides.
It was a masterwork of detective passion.

The book is titled *The Lost Balkans* and the author Randall Baker
had just died when the antiquarian wrote to me.

'Can you help us identify some of the slides?' the antiquarian
asked, and also: 'When I die, I want the slides to be in a safe place.
Any suggestions?'

The book narrates the journey contained in the silent slides, flesh-
ing it out with its historical context and revealing its significance. It
is in fact several journeys between 1929 and 1937, across the mountains of Yugoslavia and Bulgaria. The travellers were an English trio:
a former sanitary inspector from the war; her reverend husband in
socks and shorts; and a photographer-botanist whose book *Plant
Hunting in Europe* became key to decoding the slides.

Their objective was to find alpine specimens and take them back to
England. They were members of the Alpine Garden Society and the
man in shorts had a business selling plants from the Balkans. They
had set out with military discipline, money from London's Kew Gardens and logistical support from the Royal Botanical Gardens in Sofia
whose patron was Tsar Boris III.

The woman, Maud, emerges as the most interesting of the three
and even managed to give her name, albeit her married one, to a

plant: *sempervivum* ('ever-living') *thompsonianum* (after Thompson). That plant is otherwise known as Hen and Chicks. Randall Baker notes that in all the botanical articles penned by her husband, he speaks of plants and many other people, but only ever mentions his wife Maud once – even though she is always there, a guide and speaker of Serbian and it was she who imbued this photographic journey with human interest.

The Hen and Chicks plant that Maud 'named' is similar to Metko's stone flower, though of different families.

'And the stone flower still flowers here because it's high!' Metko pointed one out for me and we crouched to admire it. Finally, I saw its star-like petals with a pink and red centre.

Some things are too beautiful to be true.

What made those hundreds of slides fascinating was that the trio passed through a traumatised landscape. Balkan borders had been redrawn after seven years of territorial wars between neighbours (1912–1919), in which colonial powers like Britain, France and Austria played a big part. All of this was very raw in the 1920s and 1930s but our protagonists were concerned with plants, not humans.

Plant hunting in Europe does not offer the thrills that can be felt in more distant countries, for almost every corner of Europe has been combed botanically, and there is a very small chance of finding anything new, writes the photographer-botanist in his own book, making it clear that the Balkans were not Europe.

As the botanists combed the Southern Balkans, they passed through villages like The Birches, recently risen from the ashes. The storm of the next world war gathered. The nature–culture blend in these lands had been unblended by war once, and would be shattered again by more armed conflict, exoduses and genocide, ethnic and social engineering, and finally – industrialisation.

'Our principals wandered through vast, timeless and silent swathes of natural drama, unaware of the terminal historical distress that would sweep away long-established human traces,' writes Randall Baker. 'Unexpectedly, and probably unintentionally, they took us toward the ragged edge of history in search of their delicate floral treasures.'

The four of us were walking that edge today. I showed the still-unidentified images to Metko.

He and Ahmed identified several of them. An early chalet in place of a modern one. The photo where the couple walked with a buffalo cart.

But it was the plant portraits that haunted me, like people's faces. The grainy black-and-white close-ups of alpine flowers touched me unexpectedly. I understood how the nurse, the reverend and the photographer had become obsessed with high places and their human- and plant-people.

And I understood how the antiquarian, the researcher and the academic had become obsessed with the images they left behind them.

And now the wood carver, the writer, the builder-intellectual and his son had the joy of seeing these places in full colour. Without even trying, we found some of the plants they'd hunted for. And some that they hadn't.

Here was blue gentian, its bells ringing with sunshine!

'Looks like Pirin bluebells,' said Ahmed.

Maybe it was the same thing? We were clueless but delighted.

Elecampane – my first glance of it in the wild! Its long, thin petals, its yolk-yellow that makes you smile. It looks like a small-headed sunflower and sure enough, it's in the sunflower family.

To Metko's delight – yet more stone flowers that bloomed white and yellow, tough and velvet-coated like edelweiss, like mursala.

Thistles, soft ones and prickly ones, milk ones and melancholy ones, and one of them was from the mystery blend that Auntie Salé had put in my water. There *is* a thrill in identifying a plant, recognising its facial features, its essential nature. Even when it's been picked, dried, soaked and dried again under another sky, it is still itself. We were walking in the original alpine garden and I was grateful there were still more natives here than the four of us could name.

Was that asphodel?

A yellow cluster-flowered plant that was wide in leaf and tall in stem.

'No, that's chemerika,' Metko said. I looked it up – false hellebore. Searches in English gave: highly poisonous; pest for farmers; all parts of the plant to be avoided. Chemerika was once used as arrow poison and in Scotland it was cooked with venison to tenderise it.

'A psychotropic plant,' said Metko. 'When you dry the roots and grind them into powder, it makes people lose control and sneeze like crazy. They used to do this at village gatherings to some poor bugger and amuse themselves that way.'

In America it is ingested by shamans to induce psychic journeying. The ancient method of uprooting false hellebore was Kadrié's method: you drew a circle around it with a knife and turned east to greet the spirit of the plant.

'There's a place called Meadows of Chemerika,' said Metko. 'In Eagle Reserve.'

'And mursala still grows wild on Eagle Peak. Or did, when I was last there twenty years ago,' said Ahmed.

We saw bog cotton flowers, their heads white and fluffy just like their cousins' on the west coast of Scotland. And another sharp, yellow-flowering plant I mistook for asphodel.

'Mullein,' said Ahmed.

'The seeds of mullein are thrown in rivers by fishermen to stun fish and make them inert,' Metko said. 'I guess they're toxic.'

Mullein is used in traditional medicine, though not the seeds. The mullein of Pirin is one of eighteen endemic plants unique to this mountain. The Pirin thyme is another, and there's also the Pirin yellow poppy.

And who was hiding in the undergrowth? The Enchanter! A tough little red flower with an attitude mingled with the chemerika. Its Latin name, *Geum coccineum*, doesn't do it justice, because it really *is* an enchanter. Among its English names are blessed herb, wild rye and goldy star of the earth. It was worn as an amulet against poisonous animals and people. Shepherds hung bunches of it on their sheep's necks against eye disease.

Plant Hunting in Europe by Hugh Roger-Smith, to whom we owe the valuable slides, is a revealing read. Despite the interesting geo-botany of its narrative, driven by an obsession that made him and the Thompsons cross and re-cross the high places of Europe from the Swiss Alps to Mount Athos, the clinical tone is strangely wounding.

The plants are dehumanised. They are there to be cut out, classified and preserved. Like an edelweiss on a gift card.

Ah, and here was a five-petalled white flower with a yellow centre along a red stem that made you want to sit down beside it and forget your troubles. It looked like pasque flower, *Anemone narcissiflora*, but the stems were different.

'It'll take more than a flower to forget my troubles,' said Bimo, sneering at himself, not me. 'But it's true, you feel like you're in *Avatar* here.'

'It is hopeless to try and collect deep rooting plants such as *Anemone alpine* and *sulphurea*,' writes Hugh Roger-Smith, something he discovered when some of his collected specimens did not survive, especially the rock plants with long roots which 'resent very much' being pulled from their homeland. He admits that of the 'considerable number' of *Adonis pyrenaica* (Pyrenean pheasant's eye) he plucked, none survived.

Already in 1930, plant collectors were depleting alpine habitats in Switzerland, Australia, Italy and Britain. He writes: 'The difficulty is to find the point of distribution of a "rare" plant, if one happens to be in a district outside the centre, the plants are necessarily scanty in numbers and here they should be let alone. This applies pretty generally to the British Isles, where our Alpines are merely vestiges of a possible former abundance. I know of no district at home that could be called a centre of distribution of any of them and they should be therefore duly respected; there is no excuse for anyone to collect such things as *Gentiana verna*.'

This depletion at home provided the excuse to deplete other lands.

Hunting and collecting really meant uprooting and transplanting. This forced exodus of plants across borders was aided by the Linnaeus System.

In the eighteenth century, Linnaeus, 'the father of taxonomy', established the use of Latin and Greek names for all organisms except humans. This made plants sound like something already dead and ready for the museum. The Latin name severed the human–plant relationship – first mentally, then physically. Because 'to understand plants and Earth's ecosystems, they have to be viewed as *living systems,*' writes Stephen Buhner in *The Lost Language of Plants*, 'not isolated collections of unrelated mechanical bits – an illusion embedded within the language of Western taxonomy. Naming plants instead by their function, by their relationship to their habitat, connected people to that habitat . . . Such naming carries within itself the implicit knowledge of what will happen if a plant is driven to extinction or declines in population. Many older folk taxonomies – often more complex than Western systems – have long recognized that plants play unique and important functions in ecosystems.'

Like elder, a tree of extraordinary longevity that looks like white bones in winter. Elder, from 'eldo' in Old English which means old age, was called this because of its ability to instruct plant communities in matters of growth, propagation and interspecies relationships. Elder is understood as the relational key of an ecosystem and if elders are destroyed, the rest of the vegetal community become confused.

Who cares if the *Sambucus* or the *Geum conccineum* disappear off the face of the Earth?

We would, if we knew their real names: elder and Enchanter.

'On the other hand,' said Ahmed, 'an expert can do crucial work for preservation. Otherwise, people might not appreciate what's under their feet.'

The first classification of the plants of Pirin was undertaken in the 1830s by the Austrian botanist August Grisebach. He is credited as the first scientist who recorded for the outside world the existence of the majestic Balkan pine, also called the Macedonian pine.

'It's like with human communities,' said Metko, 'plant communities have histories that need telling in a fair way. We can enjoy it but if we don't know what we're looking at, in twenty years' time, the purple flowers of thyme will be gone from these hills.'

'I've learned my lesson,' said Bimo. But it seems that the lesson is learned the hard way – only when the purple colour begins to disappear from the hills.

The leading herb grower in the Scottish Highlands told me that wild harvesting is unsustainable. Only small amounts should be picked. The ethical way to use herbs is to grow them.

We passed Iron Gate – a saddle in the stony flanks through which shepherds and refugees had travelled with their horses and where armed men had attacked them, and each other.

'A wine merchant was fleeing on horseback through Iron Gate during the bands' reign,' said Metko. 'They caught up with him and asked where his fortune was buried. He told them, but they still broke his neck and left him for dead. One of them returned to shoot him, out of guilt. Having shared the wine merchant's money, he settled in The Birches with the loot. Years later, while stepping with his horse through another saddle like this, he fell and broke his neck in exactly the same way as his victim.'

But there was no one to finish him off.

The orphaned children from The Good Place, great-grandparents of the driver-hunter, had passed through Iron Gate.

This too was the scene of territorial shepherd wars between villagers on The Birches side and those on The Godless side. Because here overlapped grazing lands.

'There was this shepherd in The Birches,' said Ahmed. 'Feared far and wide for beating up other shepherds and stealing their stock. A reiver. This was his turf.'

It was up here that he stole thirty black long-haired goats from a passing Karakachan shepherd, and took them home, where a massive goat blanket was made from the sheared wool that a cousin of Ahmed's had at home. Or rather, his wife did. A blanket stolen from the back of the mountain a hundred years ago.

'There's a shepherd called Pasko who used to bring his flock here during Communism,' said Ahmed. 'One time some armed men from a village over the way saw him and when they heard he was from The Birches, promised to shoot him if he didn't clear off and he knew they meant it. It was evening. So he walked with three hundred sheep and goats, and turned up at dawn in The Birches. Without a single one missing.'

'Another time, stoking the evening fire, Pasko got a surprise visit from two East German hikers,' said Metko. 'Lost. He shared his food with them and they pitched a tent. Pasko hadn't seen a woman all summer. Or a man. He tried to get into their tent in the middle of the night, since they were so friendly. But he was drunk and couldn't find the zipper. He spent a long time looking for it before he gave up. In the morning, they were gone.'

'Poor Pasko,' I said.

'Serves him right,' said Bimo.

Then our banter was silenced by a change in weather. After hours of sun dazzle, a fog crept from the north.

'The fog is grazing,' said Ahmed. A shepherding expression. It passed through Iron Gate like a ghostly flock.

But the only thing to graze on was glacial rock. We were inside a stone palace. We scaled down a massive corrie, the iron peak across loomed like a magnet and every time I looked at it, I felt a vertigo.

'I feel it too,' Metko said, 'It draws me and repels me.'

The fog grazed until it ate us. We lost the track which was unmarked beyond Djano Peak anyway – that's why you needed a guide. After Metko and Ahmed argued about which way to go, Bimo and I decided to follow Ahmed. An hour of descent down a funnel of scree where we fell often and two lakes appeared that shouldn't be there. We were heading in the wrong direction – west instead of south. We re-climbed the funnel, the jagged scree bruising us in the same places. The cold was biting and we gritted our teeth.

'Are you pleased you chose to follow Ahmed?', Metko said.

'I can't apologise enough,' Ahmed said. 'This is the lowest point in my whole mountaineering life.'

But we got a glimpse into what it must have been like for shepherds like Pasko who spent months doing this with his sheep. No one to argue with.

'One of the lakes we saw that we shouldn't have seen,' Metko said. 'Is called Mitrovo. After the Persian Mitra who killed the bull. Iran is a long way but everything is connected. Like in those English slides.'

Cattle bells rang, dogs barked. The fog lifted like curtains and in the theatre of the valley we saw highland cows guarded by two Karakachan dogs with bared teeth, and picked up big stones to throw at them.

'I don't feel like getting mawled right now,' said Bimo.

The highest of the Breznitsa Lakes at 2,579 metres was within sight below us, almost immaterial in its funnel. I could see why another

lake group here was called Samodivski, after the nymphs. Everything
was nymph-like. We were truly in the element of air.

The final stage in the alchemical process is *sublimatio* – where matter is etherised and the personal ego is sublimated. Its element is air
and its expression is the sylph. And in this place, there was only one
way to feel. Sublime.

In the lower world, things weigh a tonne. Here, only the essence
remains. I have wasted precious time on things that don't matter.

'You're right. We are not what we are,' I said to Metko, who
looked exhausted but happy.

'And I wouldn't be surprised if the Netikin made an appearance
now,' he said. 'This is his stomping ground.'

We stopped at the middle lake, the most vivid of the three with
floating lilies, mosses and darting fish.

'When I was young,' Ahmed said, 'I wanted to draw something on
that rockface. To let the people of the future know that someone
lived here.'

A massive vertical rockface looked down on the lake. And beyond
it, as if carved by a human hand into the wall of the looming ridge – a
stony pass like a doorstep: Kornitsa Gate.

This was the Pirin portal along the 'wine road' between Mesta and
Struma, the sister valleys. Merchants and marauders stepped through
it for centuries, hoof by careful hoof.

'Once two merchants met here. One a wine merchant from Struma
and the other a sausage merchant from Mesta,' began Ahmed. 'Let's
try some of your wine,' said deli man and gave a coin. 'And I'll try
some of your sausage, here's your coin back,' said wine man. And
on it went, the coin changed hands. In the end, they ate and drank
all, and went back empty handed. It is not said where the coin
ended up.'

Maybe in this icy lake.

'But in the end, all I did was engrave on a small stone: 1978,'
Ahmed said.

While we rested, he walked the rim to look for the stone but
couldn't find it. Ahmed had been a talented artist, but for the usual
political reasons hadn't had the chance to study fine arts and became

a wood carver. He and his brother were athletes from an early age and led the football team.

'And now we can't agree on ecological matters,' Ahmed said. 'I can't even agree with my own son.'

His son brought off-roaders in their vehicles to the lowest lake. It wrecked the forest road and filled the pristine meadows with fumes.

'Our grandparents and parents were poor,' Ahmed said, 'but they left us the mountain intact. And in a generation or two, we've managed to wreck entire ecosystems. There is no production. Just consumption.'

Bimo lit up a cigarette with a guilty face.

'We must care for things. Not just consume them,' Ahmed said with rare intensity. 'Maybe it's time for eco terrorism!'

'But we need an outsider to lead, or we'll bicker,' said Metko.

'Why don't you buy yourself a place here?' said Bimo.

'We can get a group going and take over a forest. Organise brigades to pick up the rubbish dumped by the sewing factories. Have you seen the river? It's an emergency,' said Ahmed.

This part of Pirin was off the beaten track and largely preserved as as side effect. The potential for ecological, educational, cultural and all manner of specialised tourism here was phenomenal, we all knew it, but what was lacking was vision. Local business owners and politicians were products of the kleptocracy. They outbid each other on houses, land and party votes in a cycle of extraction and exploitation that was part of the broken old system.

Lower down, Stormy River was an open-air dump, full of refuse from households and sewing sweatshops. The local eco-police was inert and the three rhyming villages didn't care.

'I've heard that the last wild or at least semi-wild rivers left in Europe are in the Balkans,' Ahmed said.

'Ours is not among them anymore,' said Mehmed. 'There is a large dam downstream in Greece and lots of smaller ones on our side.'

100 per cent of major Western European rivers are impounded – that means heavily dammed and diverted, their natural features destroyed. The last uncaptured rivers are in the Balkans. Mesta has

multiple smaller hydrostations and only one large dam – Platanovrisi – which makes it relatively well preserved for its size. The trouble is that a dozen new schemes have been funded for the next decade and some seem to be under construction. Corrupt Balkan officials and careless European subsidies may be the death of Mesta. Helped by ignorance and inertia on the ground. I was seeing this river already clogged with rubbish wherever humans came into contact with it. But it was still running free in its upper parts. Free enough to move its bed when it felt like it.

Curtains of rain fell down and we walked in single file, drenched. After the middle lake, we crossed rain-struck meadows full of St John's wort that glowed with a yellow I'd never seen. A yellow that was liquid like plasma.

I'd hoped to see meadows of asphodel – because of that first black-and-white slide the antiquarian had drawn from the box. It was a strangely poignant portrait of a lone asphodel. It has stayed with me.

Asphodel has been the preferred food of the dead. It was planted on graves. In Homer's *Odyssey* there is a place 'past the gates of the Sun and the land of dreams', and that place is 'the meadow of asphodel, where the ghosts dwell, phantoms of men who have done with toils.' In the pre-Raphaelite artist John Millais' painting of Ophelia drowned, she clutches white asphodel mixed with other flowers. European necromancers used asphodel to call the spirits of the dead. And in Corsica, home of the other immortal flower, the shamanic dream hunters known as *mazzeri* went to remote highland places where they ritually whipped themselves with dried asphodel – their power flower.

We didn't see meadows of asphodel and I don't know why asphodel is such a sad flower for humans.

But I will never forget this happy meadow of St John's wort.

Water dripping off me and the plants, I stopped to pick a few, and in the rain-and-sunshine all was blurred. When my hand reached for the flower, I didn't know if the flower was coming to me, or I was going to it.

As we approached Dry Lochen, feet squelching in boots, I heard a continuous ringing of little bells, like giggles. At first I thought it was women laughing somewhere ahead of us, or behind. But there was no one on the path. The last hikers we'd seen were on Djano Peak, before the fog.

'Can you hear that?' I asked Bimo.

'Yep. Like samodivi laughing,' he said. 'Creepy.'

'Raindrops hitting the needles of dwarf pine and juniper,' Metko said.

The rain eased and we stopped at Dry Lochen, the lowest of the lakes at just under 2,000 metres, where Ahmed and his brother had built a four-spout fountain and connected it to a spring by digging a kilometre of earth by hand. In memory of his brother's wife.

TO AVA

1965–2015

I love these lonely fountains that speak of the brevity of our personal lives, of asphodel meadows and meadows of St John's wort.

A small shepherdess in red shalvars and blue mantle appeared out of the dwarf pine wood. She held a plastic raincoat over her head. I saw her scattered herd.

'Hey,' she smiled, recognising us. 'Where have you wet chooks been?'

'To Godless and back,' we said, hoping to impress her.

'A fine thing too,' she said, unimpressed. 'Back in the day, Metya took milk on horseback from here to Bezbog.'

'Wow,' Bimo said. 'My dream job is to be a shepherd. So I don't have to deal with people and rumour.'

'How would you like to sleep with the wolves?' I said.

He laughed. But it was my fantasy too.

On the shepherdess's back was a sadilka, for herbs and other things. 'Cos you never know what you'll find when you're out on pasture,' she said.

Fatma and Metya had 300 sheep and milked them manually. He'd bought a brand-new Jeep, but continued to ride up here on horseback. He was seventy.

Just before dark, we reached the private chalet built by Ahmed and his brother. It was the only house in this highland area called The Meadow – a series of wild pastures and pine forests. The rain stopped and everything looked laundered. I went outside after changing my clothes. I ached everywhere. We could stay the night in the two-room chalet with a big fireplace and a kitchen, but Ahmed had to milk his cow.

At the other end of the meadow, a tall skinny man suddenly appeared out of the woods and walked to a mare and her foal, and lay down near them. He lay on his side – the age-old posture of the shepherd at rest. He was barefoot. The mare sniffed his face. Then a rush among the pines – sheep, goats, Karakachan dogs. Fatma walked past the chalet, smiling – and knitting – as she walked. Later I learned that Fatma's father was killed during the changing of the names, when she was a young woman.

'Tired?' she said. 'You'll sleep well.'

'Aaaya! Eeeeeey-ya, eeeeey-ya, ya ya ya ya!' shouted the man with the mare, now standing, a voice like a megaphone, and the forest cantoed with him. The sheep ran. They were gathering the flock in a pen for the night, one meadow down. Then they were gone and only the horses remained.

Ahmed's son came to pick us up and I was grateful for his off-road vehicle. Back in the Birches Hotel, I slept at the bottom of my forest-well, this time without dreams.

In the morning, I was spreading oregano on the table by Fatmé's fountain when the tall skinny man materialised from the forest, moving past me so fast I almost didn't see him, just as I hadn't heard him.

'Is there enough oregano?' he smiled, not meeting my eye.

He was dirt-streaked with sweat and walked on without missing a beat. He wore patched-up trousers from tweed and a filthy sleeveless top. He moved like he was wired to a higher voltage. The atmosphere became static as after a storm. A nutter, or maybe the last sane one. I recognised him from last night on the Meadow. He'd helped Fatma round up the sheep and slept up there.

A rope was wound around his shoulder and arm, and he carried a small axe, the head in his palm, handle down. He looked like an animal tamer. This could only be the horseman.

All afternoon, his voice rumbled like a river while he worked on the house roof with Shefket. He didn't shut up once. In the evening, Shefket told me that Emin had gone home but could meet me here tomorrow. I was busy with Gyulten tomorrow.

'Emin is the last of the Mohicans,' said Shefket. 'Uneducated, but no one knows this mountain like him.'

Shefket gave me a handful of pods. *Tagetes* is a label given by Linnaeus and doesn't say much about marigold, but Mary's gold does.

'Plant them in Scotland so you don't forget us. Have you met the puppies?'

I walked in the woods with four small Karakachan dogs that would come up to my thigh in a couple of years. They were elated. They sniffed every flower and chewed things, they ran ahead fast, then ran back, they tumbled in the grooves made by off-road vehicles, climbed out again, and each had a different expression on its little face.

We are not what we are. Our tragedy is that we don't even know it. The world is not what we think it is. It is fathomlessly alive. None of us is a single entity, we are many-formed, polytropos. Everywhere, all the time.

There is a scene in *Plant Hunting in Europe* that moved me unexpectedly:

'I had a curious experience in Cyprus,' writes the photographer. 'I had discovered the plant for the first time, and was anxious to get a specimen and began to dig round it with my trowel; soon quite a crowd of little boys collected watching the proceedings. When I thought I had sufficiently loosened the roots, I began to pull on the plant, immediately there was an uproar, I had no notion what they were saying for they spoke in Greek, but the eldest of the boys forcibly pushed me from the plant and by signs indicated that he was fetching something and ran off to a cottage near by to return with a mattock; he then proceeded to hack the plant out and presented it to me. Although unable to understand what the children said, I am sure their behaviour was the result of belief in the medieval legend, which has been handed down all these years.'

I saw him struggling on that bright mountain where oregano

grows, and mandrake, and children, and I knew how he felt. Who doesn't? Our entire human drama is summed up in that scene.

In that scene, we have a monomaniac, a man like an island, split from his own *imaginatio*, unable to speak with children or plants, surrounded by wonder he desires enough to climb peaks and vales, cross meadows of asphodel and meadows of St John's wort, trowel in hand and Latin dictionary in pocket, roaming the Earth's valley in search of a rare flower, and once he has found it, he kills it on the spot.

Anima mundi

European alchemists called it the *quinta essentia,* the fifth element. Plato called it the soul and intelligence of the world. The soul of the world is an animating force that runs through all living things in a web of interconnection. The world-as-a-machine does not have a soul. To reconnect with the fifth element, you must perceive the world-as-garden. This is the invitation of the Gaia paradigm – to step out of our mechanical isolation and step into a world of wonder.

When the ecopsychologists of the 1960s realised that 'the core of the mind is the ecological unconscious' they described in modern language the ensouled universe in which Gaia is mysteriously but undeniably a player.

'There is a certain truth in natural things which is not seen with the outward eye, but is perceived by the mind alone, and of this the philosophers have had experience, and have ascertained that its virtue is such that it performs miracles,' wrote a fifteenth-century Belgian alchemist. I found this in Carl Jung's *Aion*, an enquiry into the phenomenology of the whole self. Sometimes, the world's soul is winged like a bird. Sometimes, it is spherical, like the metaphysical fish first mentioned in an alchemical text: 'There is in the sea a round fish.' Jung calls it the alchemical fish. This spherical creature from the primordial ocean stands for the dragon's *lapis,* or philosopher's stone, or *al-iksir.* It is both inside and outside of the self.

It is supposed that the outward eye cannot see any of this. But there are places where the eye becomes inward and the soul of the world becomes outward. Places where something is collectively alchemised. The bottom of the ocean and the desert exist at the same time in the same place. There, the soul of the world roams free.

PILGRIMS

Gyulten had been telling me about a place called Gold Leaf, with its millennial sycamore that grants wishes, and its resident spirit of one Stoyna who still appears in local people's dreams when they are in need. Stoyna had granted Gyulten's previous wish and she wanted to ask again.

Stoyna was connected to another seer nearby: Vanga. The two women had died fifty years apart, but their similarities were striking. Both drifted here along tributaries of the Struma River. One from the south, the other from the west. Both were born into poverty and war and suffered misfortune in childhood that left them blind. Their blindness led to an acceleration of their psychic gift.

'We can visit both, kill two birds with one stone,' said Gyulten.

Vanga died in the 1990s, but Rupité where she lived was still visited by pilgrims, fans and the curious. I'd heard that Gold Leaf and Rupité had quite the atmosphere.

'It's not far,' Gyulten said. 'It's on the other side of Pirin.'

There was just one road that linked the sister valleys of Mesta and Struma. To Gyulten it was not far, but to me it looked like a pretty long way over the saddle and it was my first time too.

Gyulten's friend Sanusha joined us. Sanusha owned a grocery shop in The Birches and did well with it. Sanusha had a guileless face ready to welcome you as you were.

'It's being in the shop,' she said. 'You get to know people. Everybody has some pain.'

'We get on because she's not a gossip,' Gyulten said.

'When you walked in the other day,' Sanusha said, 'I knew you were one of the good ones. And now you're driving us all the way to Stoyna!'

'And Vanga,' Gyulten clarified.

Like me, Sanusha hadn't been to Gold Leaf or Rupité. She had brought water for everyone and snacks from her shop. Then she handed me a bag full of gifts. Inside the bag was a pair of velvet shalvars made from fabric imported from India, with midnight flowers against a golden-yellow field like the sunflowers of the valley. And a round apron with silver-thread embroidery on a violet background, a white cardigan knitted with one needle and patterned hand-knitted socks. She and her mother had crafted it all, many years ago, for her dowry. Women here had large dowries, entire households of stuff. Outfits, blankets, kilims, furniture throws, cushions, towels, enough to fit out an entire life and more. Out of their treasure chests, they gave choice gifts to other women. The Pomaks are some of the last to uphold the homemade dowry and its sharing with the sisterhood.

Gyulten had gifted me a pair of loose, flower-printed trousers in Arabian blue with a threaded belt, cowboy style. They were from the rhyming sister village of Laznitsa. The shalvars of Mesta are like yoga slacks, but encoded with meaning. You could tell a woman's birthplace from the patterning of her shalvars. Even the three rhyming villages had different colour codes and Ribnovo of the weddings was known as 'pink pants'. Wearing shalvars was like wearing an atlas. I wore these today – even if Gyulten and Sanusha chose to wear jeans and smart shirts. The Pomak trousers signalled difference in places without Muslims and today, we were going to such places.

We drove through the city in the valley and began the climb to the saddle of Papaz Chair. Along the high road, signs pointed to forest chapels. The stereo played a yoga mix and Sanusha dozed off in the back. It was a still September day dripping with birdsong. The road was empty. The whole world felt empty. We could hear the bells of sheep and goats. A Karakachan dog lay in the shade of a tree. One of its ears was missing.

'They cut them off when they're puppies,' Gyulten said and laughed at my shock. 'To make them mean.'

She grew up with this. This was her old stomping ground. Shepherding dogs were there to protect the flock from wolves and thieves.

'It was a very basic life, but free,' Gyulten said. 'Always an open horizon. Like this, like what you see now. The nights were so full of stars, you can't imagine. The stars keep you company and you're never alone.'

We passed over the saddle of Papaz Chair. Majestic panoramas unfolded fast, snatching my breath. Western Pirin and the Struma Valley opened up. The peaks and valleys ahead were so blue and still they brought tears to your eyes. It was like driving into infinity.

Papaz Chair was also called Popovi Livadi and both meant The Priest's Meadows. Papaz was a Greek word, reflecting the long-standing presence of Karakachans. The Karakachans were nomadic shepherds, Greek- and Bulgarian-speaking, who travelled seasonally with their flocks between Pirin and Rhodope, and the Aegean Plains. Just as Gyulten's parents had travelled between these highlands and the warm basin of Struma.

Before this road blasted its way in the last century, there were entire highland populations: shepherds; monastic communities; forest workers.

The Monk, Priest's Meadows, Karakachan Church, the place names said it all. A Bektashi monastery and a church had stood on Papaz Chair, but the twentieth century had wrecked them all, even at the top of the mountain, even without a proper road.

'Way over there is Eagle Reserve. And Chemerika Meadows,' said Gyulten. 'Chemerika makes your hair strong. If you come across it, get yourself some roots just in case.'

False hellebore again! After she told me this, I bought some roots of false hellebore and boiled it with burdock root, because my hair was in fact falling out — it happens to people with thyroid problems. The results were instant. After two rinses, the problem stopped. But before I made my rinse, I recalled Rocky's sniffing ways and put my face in the bag of dried roots. To get to know the plant. I only recalled what Metko said about it when I was seized by uncontrollable sneezing. It didn't stop all day and drove me mad.

Respect to false hellebore, a plant that has the last laugh!

'I love the shadiness of this road,' Gyulten beamed.

After the mountain pass, we entered the climate zone of the Struma basin. It was warm, lush. Mixed forests formed tunnels over the road. We stopped to pick sour cherries and plums. The odd broken village – overgrown handsome houses, gutted streets, as after an exodus. Men and women sat with dogs outside ruined municipal buildings.

'They cultivated peanuts here,' Gyulten's voice choked, though she was not one for wistfulness. 'Grapes, hazelnuts, peaches, lemon trees, olives, and figs. And afiyon. You could walk along this road and fill your belly all year round.'

Afiyon: poppy seeds. The names of villages bore their fruitful past. And potential future: Cherry Village; Village of the Peppers; The Onions; The Vineyard; Vinograd (Wine Town). There was no Opium Village, but it was a safe guess that the communist state had operated a neat opium economy, for export.

Gyulten liked to return here.

'I love this side of Pirin,' she said, 'I feel free here. Look!'

I pulled over. It was the cooperative farm where her family had spent many winters. The small house was gutted. A curtain hung over a broken window, the kitchen of her childhood. The pen where the animals had lived was disused, though in the hills above was a flock of goats.

Sanusha woke up and spotted a fig tree, and we picked a bagful of leaves.

'You dry them and they make delicious tea,' said Gyulten.

'Regulates the blood sugar,' Sanusha gave me the whole bag.

'See that bridge,' Gyulten pointed to an Ottoman bridge over a tributary, 'it's where I slept with my passport in my pocket the night I ran away from home. My folks were thrashing us so much, I couldn't take it and made a runner for the border!'

She'd been ten years old. She ran to the Village of Peppers, which still has the best red peppers and was the last before the border, but it was perched on a canyon and bristling with border soldiers. She turned back. Border soldiers found her under the bridge and brought her home, in time for the next thrashing.

'I was a wild one even then!' Gyulten laughed her hoarse laugh.

Sanusha, who'd never been a wild one, shook her head in awe. What impressed me was that Gyulten chose to love her childhood.

When I sip the infusion of fig leaf, her bitter-sweet memories of the Struma Valley mix with my own, seep into my blood and perhaps even lower its sugar.

To get to Gold Leaf, we came off the main road and followed a sandy dirt-road. The landscape changed, like a stage curtain lifting. From a shady forest to an open semi-desert.

Gold Leaf (population: 7) had emptied after the demise of the tobacco industry that had been its raison d'être. It lay in a plateau overlooked by a ridge of sandstone pyramids called *mels*. Rain and wind sculpted them without cease.

The valley of the mels was bleached and deeply strange, an unexpected piece of biblical desert. In the shimmering heat ahead, we wouldn't have been surprised to see cloaked pilgrims with bare feet or ghostly horsemen riding towards us like a desert storm.

Beyond the white mels rose more blue peaks. I felt far from anything familiar.

'I've never been to a place like this,' Sanusha said, awakening from her nap again.

'This is my heaven,' Gyulten said. 'See those mels? We used to climb them and look for wild partridge eggs. You could get twenty in a nest!'

They were 100 metres high, with crumbly ridges. I would have never been allowed to climb them and didn't see any kids climbing them now. We passed the derelict houses of Gold Leaf. The afternoon heat flattened all with its 44 degrees. Birdsong stopped and sound was muffled as on the bottom of a sandy ocean. I was behind the wheel with my foot on the accelerator, but time stood still. There was nowhere further to go.

A whitewashed church materialised, modest in size. This is where Stoyna had lived for twenty years, from her arrival until her death in 1933. She was buried in the courtyard, near the oriental sycamore. The crown of the sycamore was as big as the church.

Stoyna was one of hundreds of thousands of Bulgarian refugees who had poured across the border from Greece, while local Greeks were expelled south. This church was Greek. We were further west in the geographical region of Macedonia.

Stoyna and Vanga had arrived in the Struma Valley at the age of thirty, at different points in time.

Vanga looked like a blind peasant woman in a headscarf, but there was something fateful about Stoyna, in the paintings and drawings of her, since there were no photographs. She looked just like we imagine a prophet should look, with her sewn-up eyes, her long bony face abruptly closed by a long mouth and her head in a black shawl.

'I told you it's freaky!' Gyulten said. 'They're like the same woman.'

We stroked the warm hide of the oriental sycamore and sat in the 'wish' swing hanging from its thickest branch. A faded sign said that the tree had been planted 1,100 years ago. Who and why planted you in the tenth century in the valley of mels? A bearded ascetic with dreadlocks, a beggar bard, a woman in rough-cut sandals who came to draw water from the well and load it on her mule for the long trek back, past the edible trees that could fill your belly and who had wanted us, the people of the future, to know there had been someone here? Or was it self-seeded, blown in from the mountain?

Holy trees like this dotted the epic routes of mystics. All old trees were seen as holy trees here, and called chinar. Sufi and Christian missionaries stopped to rest by this chinar or that chinar. The oldest known holy tree, planted by human hand, is the fig tree Jaya Sri Maha Bodhi in Sri Lanka, believed to be the sapling from the original tree under which a privileged young man called Siddhartha Gautama starved for seven years, attained enlightenment and became the Buddha.

Gyulten and her childhood friends had often made wishes by the chinar. At the time, the church was padlocked and ruined, bats flying in and out. People came to touch the tree, although Stoyna was wiped from official history. When the regime collapsed, spiritual yearnings rushed over the collapsed dam of Marxist–Leninist repression and Stoyna was rehabilitated. Once spontaneously called Stoyna the Nun, she was now decorated with the pretentious 'Venerable'.

The few elderly people who remembered Stoyna were taken aback by this sudden interest in their local saint and watched with bewilderment as their valley of the mels darkened with cars. This new cult was part of the post-communist, neo-Christian revival – except that the Orthodox Church was always ambivalent about Stoyna. A church statement explains why she is 'as discreditable as any yogi or Buddhist mystic'. But Stoyna was supported and revered by local clergy in her time. Local clergy were often humble individuals serving and healing the community. But Stoyna's ways were just too weird for words.

'I feel it,' Sanusha said, holding on to the chinar. 'It's strong. I will make my wish now.'

Her wish was to be cured of diabetes. I too was drawn to its smooth body. The vibrational frequency of the chinar has been recorded by people who research the music of plants. You can hear it online: 'Music of the Plants – *Platanus Orientalis* in the garden of Prepodobna Stoyna.'

The valley of the mels was like the bottom of an ocean. The mels held time in a harness, suspended above the material world.

At the stalls selling natural products, Sanusha bought herbal balms for varicose veins. I bought pine tar, because you never know when you might need it. Gyulten bought a silver pendant in the shape of a bat.

'Bats attract love,' she said. The hodja we'd visited in the mosque last week had told her to surround herself with bats. I thought it was batty, but she did it.

When she'd first come, years ago, with a group of fellow holidaymakers from a spa hotel nearby, they dragged her into the church – the once-locked church of her childhood. She had an aversion to crucifixes. The gunpoint christenings had been too many, too recent and for some Pomaks, Christian symbols were tinged with trauma. But she'd gone inside that time.

'And my wish was granted.'

'That's because Jesus loves everyone,' Sanusha said. 'That's the whole point.'

But the power of this place was in its location. That's why a great tree had grown and a temple was built.

'There is an energy triangle,' the caretaker told us. 'Its three points are Gold Leaf, Rupité and Rozhen Monastery.'

People liked energy triangles. And why not – the triangle-pyramid has always been with us. Like the mandala and the sphere, it enjoys geometric autonomy. Rozhen Monastery a few miles down the sandy road was a late medieval monastery set among remote mountain meadows, with the mels beyond like a memory of arrival. Two monks live in silence and silence is required from visitors. On an earlier visit to that monastery, I'd met a Frenchman travelling across Europe in a campervan. He had sold his house after a personal tragedy and now went around holy places. Though he was an atheist, he felt the merciful nature of these places and he needed mercy, he said.

Everybody needs mercy, I said.

It's just that we don't realise it until – he said. We hugged in the silence of the white pyramids.

Now we entered the sepulchral church. Skylights on the roof let in bunches of light. The place swirled with golden dust particles. People creaked around in silence. The frescoes were weird, wild. Everything had a twist. A naked woman possessed by demons is bent at an unnatural angle. The saints, sinners and regular folk are so naïvely expressive, they look three-dimensional, as if coming out of the smoke-blackened walls. The patron of traveller-pilgrims, St Christoper, has a dog's head, like the Egyptian Anubis. Saint Haralampius tramples a grey-faced creature with a scythe – the plague. Haralampius was a healer, a vrach from Asia Minor venerated as patron of beekeepers to this day, because he 'sweetened' the plague with honey to draw it away from humans.

A scene showed Folks Going to the Vrachka (Seer) for Healing.

These frescoes preceded the arrival of Stoyna. The church was built in the mid-nineteenth century by a wealthy local who, after spending 'the good part of a century as brigand and robber', in the words of a travel writer, decided to redeem himself. Twenty years later, two artist brothers painted the frescoes. The Minovs were from the Mesta basin and the youngest was just eleven years old! They had given free rein to their youthful imagination and the result is a pagan, quasi-erotic playfulness. I see them travelling over the mountain between the two river valleys just as we had today, on horseback, with their brushes and paints and their bread and wine in saddle bags, stopping by the edible trees to fill their bellies. The nights they spent en route under the stars of Pirin, like Gyulten, their awe at the valley of the mels, like mine now, their evenings under the chinar at the end of a day's work inside the dark church, the rest of their lives as travelling church painters unfolding before them like a dangerous road, full of rapture.

Who said that the purpose of life is rapture? I agree, I agree.

Stoyna had lived with these eerie paintings without seeing them. She had spent twenty years in a whitewashed cell on the mezzanine traditionally reserved for women. The mezzanine was an open space with a railing made from lattice-carved wood, like lace. Creaky stairs led to it. It was homely. Over the doorway of Stoyna's cell hung a fresh wreath of leaves from the sycamore, changed weekly by the caretaker. Here was Stoyna's narrow bunk with a blanket and a goat-skin rug. People queued up to enter, one at a time, removing their shoes. As they had queued up during her life. Inside the roomlet was a tangible presence. As if a hand was placed on your shoulder to let you know that all would be fine, or at least okay, or if it isn't okay, there is still some kind of peace available to you. Now or later. Now and later were the same thing here. The low ceiling of her cell was plastered with photographs of people, an unsettling sight. It was believed that leaving an image with Stoyna would cure the person in the photograph.

The whole mezzanine floor was covered in paintings, icons and tapestries crafted by fans – Stoyna and Mary, Stoyna as Mary. She often appeared with a bunch of red flowers in her joined hands that looked like rose geranium. Those to whom she appeared said that she asked them to bring her 'live red flowers'. Not cut, but planted.

On two small tables with a chair each, were thick log books. People took turns to sit and write their wishes and woes. They were heart-rending to read. They all began:

'Dear Venerable Stoyna, please'

'Dear Holy Stoyna, please'

'Mother Stoyna, please'

'Stoyna, I beg you'

'Venerable' was clearly hard to spell.

The book couldn't be lifted. It was heavy with pain and hope.

Downstairs, people took turns to stand on the stone before the iconostasis. I stepped on it and almost immediately experienced a surge from beneath. I felt alone, as if on an island, yet connected with all around me. A risen sea of suffering, the world upheaving with an anguish that was not separate but one, like water. I felt hope flowing through everything, an underground river of mercy that would carry us to the final destination which was not final. Christopher who crossed the desert, then the river, with his dog head and walking stick, and child on his shoulders, knew it.

I don't know if it was the spirit of Stoyna or the spirit of *misericordia* that I felt, but this place was infused with it. The three of us regrouped outside. The bleached outdoors was a shock after the dark church. The Birches and our own valley felt a long way away. The women from the nearby villages who sold embroideries and socks, herbs and teas, saw my Mesta Valley trousers and were delighted that 'we' were Muslims, because Stoyna welcomes everyone, they said.

They found the energy calming, that's why they came every day. One woman said her migraine disappeared when she was here. Another woman had high blood pressure before she started coming, but no longer. This place takes your stress and dissolves it, said another woman, like a bath.

Even Vanga came here, to spend the night in Stoyna's room, said another woman who was knitting. Vanga had said that this place was like a washing machine for the soul.

It was like this before Stoyna, and will stay like this after we're gone, added another woman.

'Inshallah,' said Sanusha, who felt best under the tree.

What was it about this place? The sycamore, the stone in the church where everyone stood or the whole valley? It was like a benign vortex. The original all important stone in the church had been stolen and replaced with the current one with the crowned double eagle of the Byzantine patriarchy. Behind the fascistic double eagle is the original one – Mesopotamian or Assyrian, which links it with Zoroastrianism whence Gnosticism evolved. It's a long trail across the deserts and the direction of travel was east to west. The

two heads are good and evil, sun and shadow and the psyche split into
conscious and unconscious parts. They are joined, but look in different directions.

Yet in this place, dualism dissolved. The stone was simply a piece
of the valley. You could stand anywhere in the valley of mels and feel
your divided self dissolve. You were the grain of sand *and* the
desert.

There were legends about how the Holy Grail was buried in the
valley of the mels by returning Crusaders and rumours about how
the Russians surveyed the area during the Cold War from above.
Which sounds like pilots spraying the tobacco with pesticides.

Until the mid-twentieth century, Gold Leaf was called Drought,
and Drought had been a centre of iron-ore mining. Locals made a
living from making iron rings for wine barrels – big business then,
because this wine-exporting area traded with the rest of the Ottoman Empire. Wine fortunes were made and unmade as empire
collapsed. The wealthiest person in the once-thriving nearby medieval town of Melnik had been a Greek wine merchant, killed with his
family during the Balkan Wars by Turkish bands.

And Stoyna? The girl who looked after her until her death was a
hundred years old and not one for spiritual matters. She remembers
practical stuff – bringing water from the spring, getting logs for
Stoyna's fire and her last days when she came back from the dead –
true to style.

Stoyna Dimitrova was born in 1883 in Ottoman Macedonia, in the
village of Haznatar (now Chrysohorafa in Greece). Her family
were poor. One night, when she was around seven years old, she saw
little lights hovering outside her window. She opened the window.
The lights spoke to her. They told her the exact date of her death: 22
December 1933. An unfriendly thing to tell a child, but there you are.
Terrified, the girl went to her mother who didn't believe her. Stoyna
ran a fever and was struck with chickenpox. The virus got into her
eyes and due to lack of treatment, she began to lose her sight. She
spent the next ten years in her room – a hermit by the age of ten. This
is when she started having visitations from 'Saint George'. Among

other things, he instructed her to go to a place called Drought. She
had no idea where that was.

The entity called Saint George told her to dig in a disused spot
nearby. She begged the villagers to dig there and they duly found an
icon of a horseman. The paleo-Balkan figure known as the Thracian
Horseman is a recurring motif in Thrace and Macedonia, the proto-
parent of Saint George and other protagonists on horses. A chapel
was built in that spot by the villagers and Stoyna lived there from
then on, praying day and night and receiving people in distress. She
was also learning about herbalism and picking her own plants. She
was completely blind.

When the Second Balkan War came to town in 1913, her people
fled upstream of the Struma River. She stayed in her chapel. For
months, she lived in the gutted village, alone with the left-behind
cattle, horses and dogs which must have run wild over all those rav-
aged parts of Macedonia that would change hands four times between
1912 and 1919: Turkish-Bulgarian-Greek-Bulgarian-Greek. It is not
known how she survived. Eventually, her uncle fetched her and took
her to his new home, unpromisingly called Drought. But she knew
she'd ended up in the right place. Stoyna was thirty years old and her
parents were dead, though she had a surviving sister here

Drought would be renamed Gold Leaf half a century later when
the communist regime turned it into a tobacco colony. For another
half-century, the toil of these refugees' children would fill the pockets of the nationalised Bulgartabac.

When Stoyna arrived, she was drawn to the chinar and demanded
to live in the church, not with her family. It was decided that some
young women would do the work of cleaning, bringing water and
food, and lighting the fire. Local men built the roomlet on the mezzanine for her.

Stoyna was low-maintenance. Her centenarian carer recalled how
she lived for twenty years on olives, grapes, apples, water and herbs
that she picked herself in the vicinity. No bread, no meat, nothing
cooked. She was a raw vegan, an ascetic and there is 'Stoyna's cave' in
the bowels of the white pyramids. There, she would disappear on
long fasting retreats.

In the dead of night, when families walked to the tobacco fields past the graveyard, they would see Stoyna in her black cape, wandering among the graves.

'And singing,' recalled one woman. 'Singing her own songs that nobody else knew. And that sent shivers up your spine.'

Everybody came to her for health advice and solace. With her herbal knowledge, she directed them to the right plants and foods. She seems to have been able to connect with the energy field of her visitors, because she 'read' their problems as they arrived. She put this down to her companion Saint George. Other than herbs, her main method of healing seems to have been prayer. Incessant prayer. She was said to have raised a child from a coma through prayer.

She breathed hope into people and revived them this way, said one local man who remembered her from early childhood. She would spend days and nights in a state of transcendental meditation, motionless, senseless, dead to the world like a sadhu, and leave her body. When she came back, she would tell of her travels to faraway places with interdimensional beings. Astral travel and omnipresence seemed to be among her abilities: being in more than one place at the same time, bending time–space.

The dreams reported by locals are curious, there is a whole compendium of them. They feature sand pyramids, intense lights and Stoyna herself, who sometimes speaks but mostly heals the dreamer with her mere presence. A woman who broke her arm and was put under anaesthetic found herself in the desert. There, a camel appeared and she rode that camel – all the way to the sycamore. There was no church. When she stepped down from the camel, it vanished and was replaced by a horseman made of light. She saw Stoyna rise from her grave, still horizontal, flanked by the horseman who had a most merciful expression, the woman reported. Stoyna placed a hand on the woman's broken arm.

Stoyna admitted that 'God has granted me two steep ladders. To rise above the ground when I pray. And to leave my body on wondrous wanderings. There is a third too, but I'm afraid of saying it, for fear that the villagers will stone me. What is not understood, frightens.'

I wonder what her third ladder was.

A man who came to the church regularly saw her praying on the stone (the original one or the replacement that I'd stood on, we don't know). Except, she was levitating some 5 to 10 centimetres off the floor. She begged him not to tell anyone until after her death. In Buddhist, Daoist and Yogic cosmology, Stoyna would be seen as dwelling in the sixth and seventh dimensions, where the soul passes through a space–time tunnel called stargate. In the fourth dimension, humans can travel to other planets but rely on technology. From the fifth dimension up, travel is meant to be ethereal and body and spirit can be separated and reunited at will.

This is how she lived until she contracted pneumonia in an incident with a cat that fell into the church well. Trying to save the cat, Stoyna became drenched, caught a chill and died the same winter. Of course it was no ordinary death. She warned the women close to her that she would be 'like dead' for several days, nothing unusual, then she'd come back briefly and not to bury her until she was properly dead on the date she gave them – 22 December. This is exactly what happened.

Her wish to be buried in the church courtyard was fulfilled and her warning had been: Don't ever dig me up! She had moved once already and that was enough. Two locals, ignoring the warning, started digging up her bones, hoping to find that they were 'holy' – that is, oozing ambrosia – and thus have her canonised and get rewarded for it, but before they finished, one went insane and the other was killed.

Stoyna's curses were as potent as her prayers. One night, drunken shepherds tried to break into the church and rape her. The head shepherd was a wealthy Karakachan with 12,000 sheep. They were bivouacking in the valley of the mels, en route from the Aegean to the Pirin meadow called The Monk, of Gyulten's childhood.

'Stop bothering me,' Stoyna yelled from her cell, 'or you'll regret it.'

They didn't let up and even tried to upsail to her room on a rope. So she cursed the leader: You will lose your favourite lamb. They stumbled off into the night, laughing at the feeble threat. He had 12,000, it hardly mattered. A few days later, while overseeing his flock on the high plateau, he had his young son with him. Chasing a sheep, the boy got too close to the ridge of a mel and fell to his death.

In a later incident, Stoyna was being harassed by some youths who had come to the church. They mocked her for being blind and weird. She warned them to leave her alone, or they would go rabid like dogs. These youths all went to early graves, through madness or opium or tobacco. Don't fuck with Venerable Stoyna.

Stoyna was acquainted with darkness because she was on intimate terms with suffering, first her own, then that of her people, of the very land. Yet her voice had been like her presence – a channel of mercy. This is what kept people coming here. The place held mercy. It was palpable.

While she was alive, a young abbot tried to write down her recollections of the subtler spiritual transformations, ordeals, visions and visitations, but he had been semi-literate and the results were poor. In the days before her death, when she must have been ill with fever, she dictated a few statements to a young woman close to her.

We will never know her mentally and she would be fine with that. But we may know her through her landscape – the room, the sycamore, the valley of the mels. Thus spoke Stoyna:

'Since I was wee, I sensed that the human soul was akin to water. It walks upon the earth for a time, then rises up and comes back as rain or snow, or wrathful hailstones. That's why I liked looking at the rain, as a girl. Why, here's the earth's soul returning to itself!

Nourish your souls with faith, and they will grow strong and resilient.

Love, love is what folks need. Without love, this wondrous land will empty of its people.

A white bird was born in these lands. It was borne out of pain. I don't know what kind of bird it is. But in times to come, those who see it and touch it will be blessed.

Mercy is the part in us which is divine.'

The white church vanished in the shimmering heat behind us. We drove west in silence, through rolling, sun-drenched vineyard country.

We passed through a panoramic village once known for its delicious produce and during Communism, for its lunatic asylum, Gyulten said, but she didn't know if it was still going. I pulled over to ask a young man in a winter jacket with the collar pulled up. But when he turned to me, avoiding my eyes, I saw the face of madness. He shook his head in an all-encompassing 'No' and walked on fast.

'Yep,' Gyulten said, 'the asylum is still going.'

There was nobody else about. A time will come, Stoyna said, when bad politics will empty this beautiful land of its people, but a few will stay to keep the home fires burning until the land fills again.

'Here we are girls,' Gyulten said. 'In the valley of Spartacus.'

We were perched on the high doorstep of the Struma Valley. Settlements here dated from antiquity because of the mineral waters and for over a millennium, the main town's name was Saint Healer, Sveti Vrach.

Like Mesta-Nestos, Struma-Strymonas is a confluence. Already in the twelfth century, the Sicilian Arab geographer Al-Idrissi described its intensely cultivated hills. This strategic geography and perfect climate is a blessing in peacetime. But strategic geographies and perfect climates attract armies and border-makers. The Struma Valley changed hands between Byzantium and Bulgaria more times than historians could count and in the twentieth century, the sister valleys of Struma and Mesta bore the brunt of three big wars. Today this valley, like its sister Mesta, is divided by the Bulgarian–Greek border. In the 1970s my grandparents brought me here for winter holidays because the air is good for bronchitis. Gyulten and Sanusha hadn't had childhood holidays. Or bronchitis. They'd worked instead, Gyulten in the animal hills, Sanusha in the tobacco hills.

The September light turned ripe like Sauvignon grapes. Soon, the storks would head south along the Via Aristotelis. Everything had already happened here, and still the air was full of balmy promise.

The first thing that struck me about Rupité was its theatrical setting. Rupité sits on the west bank of Struma, in a flat basin that was once part of the riverbed.

It is surrounded by cultivated fields and orchards, and overlooked

by the tree-furred hills of an extinct volcano named Fur Coat. The
basin was the bottom of a crater formed by Fur Coat's last eruption
thousands of years ago and the plain is criss-crossed by mineral brooks
that reach 75 degrees Celsius. Sulphurous vapours rise from the coloured clay. If you fall in, you will be boiled. But in winter, when
snow covers Fur Coat and you soak in the medium-hot spring with a
glass of red from the local Mavrud grape, you feel strong like a gladi-
ator. Or so I imagined. Here, you could imagine anything. You were
inside the laboratory of a mysterious planet.

'Wow!' Sanusha said. 'This is like heaven.'

'Or hell,' Gyulten said.

We walked the gauntlet of stalls that lined the walkway from the
car park to the complex. Locals sold the produce of the Strymonian
country: raspberry wine, plum and grape rakia, honey, jam, pumpkin seed butter and peanut butter, tahini from sesame seeds, peaches,
cherries, figs, olive oil from Greece in large tubs, and of course –
bunches of herbs.

Sanusha and Gyulten were interested in everything, because it was
slightly different from our valley. Even the names.

'Look, that's *babini zabi*,' Sanusha picked up a spiky bunch. Grandma's Teeth. 'I've been looking for it for ages.'

Caltrop. It had small yellow flowers.

'Good for undoing spells,' Sanusha said and bought a bunch. 'For
when someone has thinked you a thought, done you a deed. You
hang it on your doorway.'

'And good for menopause,' the seller added. 'A cup a day keeps
flushes away.'

'Not to mention men's problems,' a male seller threw in, and
flushed.

I remembered Rocky, caltrop and the spare trousers.

'Do you have merciful herb?' Sanusha wanted to know. The question was passed down the lane.

Merciful herb was hard to find and it was even harder to agree on
what it was. It made sense to talk herbs here, where Vanga had listened to tens of thousands of people and their symptoms, sorrows
and secrets – and sent them off with recipes, hard-hitting home

truths, warnings and messages from the otherworld. Or other worlds. To her, there were many.

We entered the park. It was busy, but noise was muffled and movement slowed down.

Here by the river, Vanga said, had been a city, buried with its people in the last volcanic eruption. Vanga perceived their souls roaming the valley. Souls move just above the ground, she said: the good ones are a translucent white and the not-so-good ones are slimy. Her compassion for the thousands of souls roaming the valley led her to fund the construction of 'a temple' in their memory. She funded it with her earnings from the united nations of souls who queued outside her door every day of her life, for fifty-five years, until her death.

Each year, on 15 October, the name day of Saint Petka Paraskeva in the Eastern Orthodox canon, she hosted a large open feast by the springs. Because on that day, she said, the volcano had erupted and put an end to a way of life. For her, the waters that gush from beneath the earth are full of the transmogrified souls of those people. And anyway, Vanga liked a good party. She was very social, everybody's confidante, enmeshed in the dramas of her family and community, but also fed up with it all. Her life was a blend of the banal and the extraordinary. The banal has faded, the extraordinary remains.

Rupité is a peculiar place, Vanga said, it's like an engine and I get energy from it. And it was, all three of us felt it. A legend claimed that a human-sized horseman made from gold was buried here. Vanga was not interested in literal treasure but she was apparently accompanied by a cosmic horseman made from light and only perceptible to her.

And here was Vanga's temple. It was one of the first new churches to be built after the fall of the regime and the personal and cultural politics surrounding its construction brought her more pain than joy at the end of her life. Vanga named it Saint Petka, but in the popular imagination, Petka of Rupité is simply Vanga. The church, ugly and full of martyr-faced modernist frescoes painted by a celebrated artist and friend of Vanga, featured Vanga herself as a holy woman, her head covered like a desert pilgrim. Vanga was sensible enough to reject any idea of saintliness projected onto her by people, though she did feel like a martyr at times, she said. Patriarchal monotheism mixed with atheistic materialism – this was her environment and it provided her with a vocabulary to express the inexpressible. The Orthodox Church did not consecrate this building, so it remains just what she had intended it to be: a temple where all faiths gather.

A larger-than-life bronze statue of her sitting in a chair stands by a small bridge over a brook. These monuments were the work of those who took ownership of her legacy when she was too frail to resist. In the same way, false prophecies are ascribed to her, pseudo-biographical debris and conspiracy theories orbit her name, and random dates are attached to her predictions. Though she did see numbers, she did not deal in years and decades. But people's need to define reality by their own calendar has debased her cosmic visions into 'predictions', the way that horoscope pages in magazines debase astrology. In life as in the afterlife, everybody wanted a piece of her and she attracted imitators, users, parasites and a whole industry of Vanga kitsch. Those close to her bickered among themselves and competed for her attention even posthumously.

But the rest of the place was still hers. Everything here was water, plants, rock and light. And everything whispered with life. Underfoot and overhead. Flocks darkened our sky momentarily. Vanga often mentioned the birds – she knew that a big migratory route passed overhead, she just didn't know its name.

Vanga's relationship with authority and humanity itself was torturous. She was vulnerable to abuse and seduction. But it is her complexity that makes Vanga such an interesting character, as well as a clairvoyant whose inner reality could not be fully expressed. That is of course the nature of inner reality, just more so for mystics.

Her humble wooden cottage was here, almost a fairy tale house-in-the-woods with chicken legs, and her grave was here. This was the true temple. The rest of the park was a lawn with trees, magnolia bushes and a hot spring where Japanese tourists were boiling eggs. People moved around silently, trying to take in something of the place. It was very different in the 1980s and 1990s before it became a tourist destination. Local women brought sheep's wool to wash in the springs before selling it. Villagers came in horse-drawn carts and everything was free. Now you had to pay to sit in the springs.

'It's so calm,' Sanusha said. 'Makes me want to sleep.'

Gyulten was distracted, still in the land of her childhood.

'Just leave me here,' Sanusha said, and lay under a weeping willow near the hot spring. 'And come for me later.'

Gyulten and I walked around the grounds, grazing on plums.

'When my father got sick,' she said, 'my mother came to see Vanga. She arrived at night to get a place in the queue, cos Vanga saw people from five in the morning. When she walked into the room, Vanga shot out at her: "Stop wasting your gold coins on doctors. Your husband's a goner, you can't bring him back. Keep your gold for your kids."'

Vanga was not polite in delivering the truth. Gyulten's mother had run out of money for treatments and had started paying doctors with antique coins found while ploughing the furrows. Vanga simply confirmed what Gyulten's mother knew.

Before she ailed, Vanga saw up to three hundred people a day. This in itself was an assault. The literature tells us that psychics should only see a few people a day, to leave them time to recover.

The querent had to bring a lump of sugar on which they had slept overnight. The sugar crystals picked up auric data from the person. When Vanga held the sugar in her hand, she found all she needed in its field of information – from ancestors to scenes that unfolded like a film.

'I wish I could ask Vanga about my problem,' Gyulten said.

'But you already know what you have to do,' I said.

'Guess so,' Gyulten said, 'but I still need someone to say it. Like Vanga.'

But Vanga did spare people the entire truth and only gave them some of it, because 'if I told them everything I see, they'd want to quit this life at once.'

Vanga's own husband died at forty-two, after a long illness brought on by malaria contracted during the war. He had returned diminished in body and spirit, but kept his promise of building a house for Vanga's growing practice. His family house, to which he had brought his bride and her sister at the end of the war (on a hay-filled horse-drawn cart covered by rugs to make it festive), was a hovel where the two sisters found a tubercular, war-widowed household. This was in the green regional town of Petrich near Rupité. Vanga and her sister put the house in order, planted flowers, introduced a routine with fixed meal times and soon enough, Vanga was queen of the proceedings. A long line of people – sometimes a stampede – appeared in the humble courtyard that was soon to become a medicinal garden. Today, her Petrich house is a museum, just like the little house here with Vanga's possessions and gifts from visitors.

Vanga plunged back into her practice the day after her husband's death. She admitted that she had seen the exact day of his death, but had refused to believe it until the end.

The souls of the dead don't like it when we grieve for them excessively, she said, because the grief pulls them down with its low vibrations. And they want to be released.

Next to the shop full of multilingual books about Vanga, a video on a loop showed footage of Vanga throughout her life. Always surrounded by people wanting something from her, small but immovable, Vanga cut a lone figure. She always looked placid, carefully listening – to people, to voices only she could hear, to the music of the spheres.

There were visitor signs for the nearby site of Heraclea Sintica. The existence of an ancient city, provisionally dubbed Petra, had been known to historians for decades but not its exact location. Some years ago, an archaeologist discovered a lapidary inscription in Latin, confirming that Petra was the city of Heraclea Strymonos (or Heraclea Sintica). Excavations revealed a *polis* a few kilometres west of Rupité. It was built by Philip II of Macedon and the inscribed stone was a missive from a Roman emperor to the Strymonians, restituting their lapsed civil rights after a crisis. The polis cut its own coins in Greek: 'Herakleans of Strymon'.

That hill contains a secret, Vanga had said, before anyone suspected the city's presence.

'A great woman,' Gyulten said when we entered Vanga's little house, the narrow corridor where people had waited, the room with a table and rug-covered bench where she had sat, listening. And sometimes cutting people short, impatient, tired, annoyed at their vanities and self-deceits. She had heard it all before.

Leave me alone, stop pestering me, what do you want from me, for heaven's pity, I have nothing left for you, she'd shout, exasperated by the human and non-human voices.

Her favourite were the voices of plants. Plants spoke to her. 'There goes the rose geranium,' she said. 'I'm nerve medicine, tell people about me, it says.'

'She and Stoyna are still with us,' Gyulten said.

Vanga was driven to Gold Leaf, and everywhere else, by a state-appointed chauffeur, a retired bodyguard who became a friend. She was shadowed by state security agents, put on a payroll by the state, who persecuted her in the early years but could not stop her popularity, and ended up using her services themselves. Sometimes, a Soviet-produced Volga sedan with tinted windows, the kind associated with the Communist Party Politburo and the sight of which struck fear into the rest of us, would come and whisk her off to the capital – not asking her, just bundling her inside the car – because someone in the Politburo wanted access to her.

The dictator's daughter was a protector – and Vanga needed protection. In the end though, she got too much protection and became the property of the communist elite, increasingly removed from ordinary people. The elite of the country, from Olympic medalwinners to pop singers, ministers, official guests from abroad, state-approved film-makers, writers and scientists – all came to court, record, consult or just gawk at Vanga. She received them. She had her vanities and enjoyed being important. Like any high-profile individual, to survive she had to swim in a toxic political soup. I am surrounded by morally unclean people, they're all after money, they don't get it that money has no value whatsoever, she complained to her family.

Stoyna the ascetic had never been confronted with power in this way. Her life had been pure and obscure, a true mystic.

Though Vanga was conservative, patriarchal and judgemental, she kept the measure of things, rarely lost her equanimity and sent cynical visitors packing. Because what she could see inside people gave her the last word. There were cases of visitors losing the ground beneath their feet and fainting from the shock of what she had seen inside them — their innermost secrets. The slimy soul inside, as Vanga would put it. Powerful men and vain artists from all over the Soviet bloc seemed especially prone to passing out.

When asked what kind of people she liked best, she said: 'All humans are equal to me. There are no exceptions.'

The Vanga case histories, recorded by her sister, niece and others, make for gripping reading.

Don't think you can hide, she said. Everything remains. Everything is here all of the time. And everything catches up with you, as she told the man who'd lost twelve babies, and reminded him of how he had beaten to death his own mother and her unborn baby out of shame when she'd fallen pregnant in older age. Vanga did not use the word karma and had not heard about the concept of rebirth, but saw it in action as she watched 'the film' of people's lives. And she saw what she described as the trajectory of 'the higher soul'.

She spoke of death as a woman whose presence she sometimes felt — like one time when she and her sister were making plum preserve in the garden and Vanga felt death pass through the trees with her long, loose hair.

'Sometimes it was like listening to a poet, not a peasant woman,' her niece writes. A famous film-maker once visited her and told her of his plan to make a film about Orpheus. 'Your film won't be any good,' she cut him off, because your view of him is wrong. 'Orpheus's gift is of the earth. He puts his ear to the ground and sings. The wild animals listen. He plays on a willow leaf and on a young willow branch, on elm bark and on bark of beech and oak. He lies on the ground and the earth sounds her song to him. He sings with her. That's how I see him. Wherever he goes, he sings with the trees and the birds sing back to him, and the sky tells him something so he writes it on the ground and when he passes again, he is reminded of it and sings it. There he goes, a boy in rags, wretched, filthy. Then a man, unshaven, with long hair and nails. All his voices come from the earth.'

Vanga and Stoyna never met in the flesh, because Vanga arrived in the valley after Stoyna's death. But they must have met energetically, in that roomlet full of Stoyna's presence. Vanga maintained that Stoyna was 'at least three times more powerful' than her and that the valley of the mels had protection from the spirit realm. She spoke of Stoyna in the present tense.

A whole literature exists on Vanga: memoirs by family and friends; studies by physicists; neurologists; psychologists and parapsychologists. She was semi-literate and never wrote a thing. Her brash, crude voice in her Macedonian dialect has been well recorded. Like Stoyna, Vanga was born in a land convulsed with mass suffering, navigated through a world of personal pain and political treachery, and in this miasma, she cultivated her gifts and remained attuned to the light. Though with time and overuse, and with the growing crowd of hangers-on, researchers and self-aggrandisers wanting to record her and squeeze every last bit of insight from her for their own purposes, the light dimmed. In the last years, she became drained and unhappy.

Vanga died by the hot springs of breast cancer. By then she was a national treasure. Her family received word from five Pomak villages in the Rhodope that they were holding a continuous vigil for her in the mosques, led by the local hodjas.

Vangelia Gushterova, née Surcheva, was born premature and with her fingers and toes joined in a web on 31 January 1911 in the town of Strumitsa, Ottoman Macedonia (now Strumitsa in North Macedonia). She was wrapped in a raw hide by the fire to keep her alive. Her home town was named after a tributary of the Struma River. Her parents can't have known how self-fulfilling her name would become: Evangelia means 'messenger' in Greek.

Her mother died when she was small. When Vanga was two, in the winter of 1912–1913, the Balkan War erupted and Vanga's father joined either the Bulgarian army or the komiti, of which he was already a veteran. Strumitsa had a large Muslim population. In the winter of 1912, up to 4,000 Pomak men were slaughtered in the town's slaughterhouse by the occupying Serbian army. Their families fled to Turkey via refugee camps in Thessaloniki.

One of Vanga's visions of death is this: 'Death is a man, a man in military dress, with carp scales on his head instead of hair.'

In 1915, Vanga's father enlisted again and the orphaned Vanga was taken in by kindly neighbours: the hodja and his wife, one of a handful of Muslim families who'd stayed after the pogroms. Vanga's father returned from the war to find his daughter thriving. Her favourite game was to instruct her friends to lie down in the garden and be patients. She would then administer herbal remedies. A more disturbing game was when she placed a bowl somewhere outside the house, returned to the doorway, closed her eyes and pretending to be blind, looked for the bowl.

When Vanga was twelve, a freakish event occurred. She and two cousins were returning from the sheep pens with pails of milk when a hurricane suddenly descended on them. It swirled like a column from the sky. The cousins sheltered inside the stone basin of a drinking fountain, but Vanga was lifted up and swept into the field. They found her some time later covered in clumps of soil and branches, her eyes full of dust. Her eyes became infected and a cataract formed. A series of operations in Belgrade bankrupted the impoverished family but were unsuccessful and she lost her sight completely. She did not like to recall this accident later in life. Some things were too painful even for her who channelled the world's pain every day.

At the age of fifteen, Vanga was sent to a school for the blind where she learned to read Braille and do everything a woman was expected to do: cooking; housekeeping; sewing. She made friends, plans and had a sweetheart, also blind – she was eighteen – but just then a message arrived from home. Her stepmother had died in childbirth. Vanga returned from the city glamour of the home for the blind to find her siblings sunk in filth. Her sister was two and her brothers were four and six years old. Even blind, she was expected to manage the household while her father worked in other people's fields. Then, an earthquake destroyed their house and overnight, they were forced to move into a windy shack where they remained for years. Fate was out to get them. As soon as the two boys were able, they too wandered off in search of menial work. Vanga and her sister coped alone.

It was during those harsh years – her twenties – that Vanga

developed her herbal knowledge and started to advise the community. She began to see with her third eye. Peasants came to ask about
lost horses, objects, relatives and lovers, and Vanga was always right.
She learned to stoically minister to her own suffering. One day she
walked into a rusty cauldron in the backyard. The wound on her shin
wouldn't heal and became gangrenous. Vanga asked her sister to
bring her some copper sulphate, used as a pesticide, and heaped it on
her open wound. The women in the neighbourhood were horrified,
but after the wound suppurated overnight, it began to heal. Vanga
didn't utter a sound, despite her agony. Around that time, she also
contracted pleurisy and was bedridden. She wasted away and was not
expected to survive, but her sister cared for her and would carry
Vanga outside into the sun in a small wooden tub until Vanga could
treat herself with herbs.

'Everything begins with herbs and will end with herbs,' Vanga was
fond of saying.

And also: 'For every *bolka* there is *bilka*.' Bolka (pain) and bilka
(herb) are separated by just one vowel – a feat of sympathetic
linguistics.

Years later in Rupité, she would apply another painful self-remedy
to her legs when they seized up with arthritis. She asked her sister to
take her to the nearest beehives and sat among the bees all day, until
her legs were covered in hundreds of stings. Her arthritis was cured
and she regained her mobility. My grandmother did this with sting-
ing nettles.

But Vanga was a big fan of mainstream medicine and had a knack
for referring people to the right doctors and specialists.

Those early years in Strumitsa, when the four kids were so poor
that they walked barefoot in winter, marked Vanga and her sister forever. Vanga's only 'spiritual training' was bottomless privation and
loss. She was a star student of the Stoic school of life. At night, her
sister recalled, Vanga would sit by the fireplace and tears would flow
from her sightless eyes. But come dawn, she'd get her siblings off
their sleeping mats and start the day's chores. The kids were often
sick with malaria and Vanga made them drink a whole egg soaked in
wine vinegar until the shell dissolved. Around that time of illness and

despair, the two sisters were fetching water from a well one day, when Vanga went into a trance. She told her terrified sister that she'd been talking with a horseman who came to water his horse at the well: 'I told him not to mind you, it's just that you can't see him.'

The horseman had shown Vanga a plant by the well. 'See this,' he'd said, this is star herb, it cures a lot of illnesses on Earth. Then he'd left. Her sister saw the plant: it had small, star-shaped white flowers. What was that plant?

Dimkov the Healer had a special area for white flowers in his garden, because in astro-herbalism white flowers are connected to the moon and emit a special cool light.

Vanga's first big visions started as dreams and continued as waking dreams. A year before war arrived in her town, Vanga told people that it was coming, to stock up, prepare and pray. People dismissed her warning – its magnitude was too great – though they came to her with their small problems. Stoyna had said it: 'what is not understood frightens.' Early in 1941, Vanga started having full-on visitations of the horseman, according to her sister. The horseman, made from light and filling the dingy little house with light, and whom she later called Saint George, told her: 'Soon the world will turn itself upside down. A great many people will be lost. You're to stay here and help the living and the dead. I'll help you.' When German tanks rolled into Strumitsa, villagers fled into the hills but Vanga and her sister stayed. A soldier kicked down their door. In the dark room stood two young women, frozen with fright. But there was no food, not a single chicken. The tanks moved on. When people came down from the hills and checked on the sisters, they saw something odd.

Vanga spent all her time in a corner, radiating light. She had melted away and her dress hung on her, but she was full of passion. Her voice had changed too, it had become strong, firm and sometimes, not hers at all. From her dark corner, she saw the war unfolding, she saw the faces of the local men who would be killed and the dates. And she saw those who would return, and when, and how they would look when they walked back to the village (next month – in his underclothes, or carrying a suitcase, or without a leg). She saw everything at once and it unhinged her. Her sister later said that Vanga 'didn't sleep for a year' which is hardly possible. She must have been in an altered brainwave state, between waking and dreaming, flooded with images and voices. A portal had opened and the information was flooding in.

One of those whose death she saw was her little brother, who joined the Yugoslav resistance. I beg you, don't go, or you'll be killed at twenty-three, she said to him. He was executed by the Germans on the day of his twenty-third birthday.

One day, in spring 1942, neighbours ran in to say that an important guest was coming to see Vanga. A cavalcade stopped by the little house and a bald man with a moustache in a tweed jacket and jodhpurs walked in. Before he'd said anything, Vanga stood in her corner and pronounced:

'You have grown muchly. You've spread yourself. But be ready to shrink back into a walnut shell. Remember 28 August.'

Disturbed, the man walked out after giving her his card and saying: 'when you come to the capital, ask for Boris.'

Bulgaria had occupied and annexed much of geographical Macedonia. Tsar Boris III died on 28 August the following year. His country lost the annexed territories when the war tide turned. Strumitsa was part of those territories.

Another day, some Bulgarian soldiers arrived to see Vanga. She came out and called for 'the one named Dimitar'. He was a thin twenty-three-year-old from the Struma Valley. 'I know why you've come,' she said to him without preamble. 'I know who killed your brother, but I'm not gonna tell you. Because you must never take revenge. They'll come to sticky ends anyway and you'll live to see it.' Dimitar Gushterov stumbled out in a daze. His brother had just been killed in a skirmish unrelated to the war. Dimitar returned to see Vanga and eventually proposed. He was almost ten years younger. This is how Vanga ended up in the Struma Valley, across the traumatic Macedonian-Bulgarian border: brought by a tributary in the river, a kink in a history foreseen.

It is not because of the statue, the church, the temple, or even the sycamore, that Vanga and Stoyna are infused in the land.

It is because in Rupité and Gold Leaf, the psyche of the land and the human psyche are in constant conversation. That conversation goes on everywhere, all the time, but in these places it becomes audible. Both women were friends of humanity at times when all governance, all institutions, all aspects of life, even the air itself, became poisonous. Sound familiar?

They were small, blind, poor, virtually illiterate, yet the power of their healing intent touched countless lives: and continued to do it from beyond the grave. They embody Chiron the centaur, the wounded healer and teacher who could not heal himself, only others.

All human communities had clairvoyants. But the loss of affinity with the more-than-human world has led to a loss of extrasensory ability. The fact that Sweene MacDonald, who died in the 1990s, is known as 'the last seer of Scotland' and that people are on the look-out for Vanga's reincarnation, tells of that loss. Vanga said that the spirit of her mother from a past life talked to her. In that life, they lived in Egypt and her mother was a pharaoh who had two daughters. One of them drowned in the Nile. That was Vanga. The spirit instructed Vanga to go and meet her in Notre Dame of Paris, and that was Vanga's dream – to see Notre Dame. She didn't otherwise like to leave her Struma Valley. But once again she was let down by the regime. They wouldn't grant permission for her to travel abroad under her own name and she refused to travel on a false passport. 'Like a spy!', she said indignantly. 'No way.' And she would have been expected to spy – psychically – on the French. Vanga allegedly said that she would next incarnate as a girl in rural France.

Cosmos and psyche are one and Vanga spoke of the 'immutable laws of the cosmos'.

'You all sleep at night,' she said. 'What do I do? I turn the pages of humanity's book and it is a tragic read, I can tell you that.'

The evidence suggests that Vanga could tap into synchronic time–space – where phenomena are at once latent, current and past. She was able to see the energetic imprint of processes, before and after they had taken place: physical processes (flourishing and illness, birth and death); psycho-emotional processes (people's state of mind and the circumstances created by it); karmic or re-balancing processes (inheritance and ancestral dynamics) and the likely outcomes. Then she took that to a collective, impersonal level and saw broader pictures that were likely to become events. Among them are the ruination of Syria, which she saw in the 1980s when it didn't make as much sense (though in 1980 there was localised civil conflict in Syria). Then there were the environmental cataclysms of our time ('a time will come when all the water and soil will be poisoned by humans, and the bees will start to die off, and that's when you should really worry about your human race, when the bees start to die off').

Many of her impressionistic insights into man's impact on earthly health were scientifically narrated around the same time by Rachel Carson in *Silent Spring*. Carson wrote about the separation effect, whose most dramatic expression is the splitting of the atom and the resulting 'uncoupling' of cells caused by nuclear radiation. This led to cancer and the death of organisms. Splitting – on the physical, mental, political and metaphysical level – results in decline and extinction. War splits, evil splits. To reduce an ecosystem to a single crop – it begins with splitting. Vanga wouldn't know what 'synergistic interplay between planetary and personal well-being' meant, but she was a pioneer of ecopsychology – in the way she lived, in the way she mediated between humans and non-humans and in the way she gruffly educated people about themselves and their world.

Despite the universal sorrow she felt, Vanga's messages to humanity were always of love and unity. Thus spoke Vanga:

'There is complete harmony in nature and we are a part of that. There is no dead nature. All nature is alive, and subject to a higher consciousness and a higher order that you can't see. Get that into your heads.

'There is good and evil in each human. It's the way humans are made. What's the key to human happiness? Patience. Temperance.

'When I leave this earth, you must change your ways. Stop spying on each other. Stop bickering. Love each other because you're all my children.'

I see Stoyna and Vanga as messengers. They are like the mineral vapours that the earth sends out, a message without words.

Sanusha had fallen asleep under the weeping willow.

'Ah! I could stay here forever,' she said and arose with difficulty. 'I know why Vanga chose this place.'

Tired, happy and provisioned with herbs, nut butters and tacky souvenirs, we re-crossed the golden vineyard country, the mels in the distance, the crumbling villages with delicious names, the tunnel of trees where you could still fill your belly. We climbed again and watched the unfolding of the hills like a silent film about our lives, our *life* – because as I drove, our three lives converged into one.

'A mountain is a sort of music, theme after counter-theme displaced in air', wrote the poet Norman MacCaig. The mountain played its variations for us. Pirin was a virtuoso storyteller, with its rivers, springs, green shades, ruins, paths and phantoms.

Although we were moving too fast to hear the full story, we had experienced the essence of what it is to be a pilgrim. It is to travel through a changing landscape in a state of wonder.

A pilgrim needs a nominal destination, but it is the road that makes the journey. Pilgrims travel out of the sheer yearning to discover something missing, a previously unexcavated layer that, once revealed under the grime, shines like gold. The pilgrim desires knowledge through experience. She desires the fullness of the big picture. Zen pilgrims like the poet Basho lived on the road, with a bag and a question that they carried with them in search of a master who could answer it. The exquisite melancholy of Zen being that, even when you found the master in that remote hilltop monastery, his answer was yet another question, the sound of one hand clapping.

The pilgrim's road is a climb to the next level of koan, where the air thins and mysteries accumulate.

'This world is a stage or market-place passed by pilgrims on their way to the next,' wrote al-Ghazali in his *Alchemy of Happiness*.

We stopped on the saddle to pick a tree with trembling, silvery leaves that a robust old woman in patched clothes and a black headscarf, walking along the road looking for crab apples, told us was

poplar. She was the last resident of her village and delighted to have
a bit of company. Although she was poor and lonely, she had the
forest on her doorstep. She had the nearby spring, and a vegetable
garden. All of that was in her stride, in the way she was at home in
the edible mountain, on the high road that still smelled of pilgrims,
brigands and drovers. Not afraid of wolves, men, memories or the
future.

Perhaps that's what it means to be at home, in this life.

We began our descent into the valley at the end of time. The sun
was out of view. We pulled over. A shower of sun-struck rain fell
over the city white like a polis. Then the shower head moved across
and watered Old Woods.

When you look at Nikopolis ad Mestum and Heraclea Sintica, you
can't help but feel that the fate of all human cities is to be reclaimed
by the non-human. It is only a matter of time.

But those who ever lived in the sister valleys of Struma and Mesta
had access to something that was not a matter of time: wonder. Wonder never runs out.

'Sisters,' Sanusha said, elated. But Gyulten had gone off into the
bushes.

'Isn't it nice to see other parts of the world,' Sanusha turned to me.
'Then come home and fall in love with it, as if for the first time.'

Merciful herb

Vanga was in conversation with the plants in her garden. When people who'd lost a loved one came to her, she asked them to bring a potted plant with them so that the plant would absorb some of the distress they felt and it wouldn't all fall onto her. The plant was her merciful friend. 'Don't bring me cut flowers,' she said, 'they're like children with their hands cut off, bring me a living plant.' She then ended up with thousands of potted plants outside her house. She'd take them out of the pots, feel their roots and some of them were planted in the ground and given a better life.

I still don't know what merciful herb is.

'A local name,' said Trendafilka on the phone. 'I probably know it but under another name.'

'Merciful herb? Not for me. Get me the Enchanter, that's the one I need,' said Gyulten who had love troubles. Everyone has love troubles, sooner or later.

'We'll make a herbalist out of you yet,' said Rocky the Enchanter. 'Never heard of it, but then again, every herb is merciful herb. You just have to get to know it.'

'Merciful herb, how can I describe it to you?' said Sanusha. 'It doesn't look anything special. It doesn't taste anything special. I can't even remember why I'm looking for it. Some things are like that.'

THE HORSE WHISPERER

Emin met me by the marigold beds of the Birches Hotel.

'I was looking for you yesterday,' he was talking and walking across the meadow with his large strides and flicked his fringe with a toss of the head. His hair was otherwise shorn. 'Shefket said you wanted to meet me.'

'And your horses.'

'They're up. It's a trek.'

He stank of long-unwashed clothes. His T shirt was threadbare. His feet were slender. We sat down and I ordered two salads which I ate alone. He only drank water. At one point, he brought out a lurid white lump and nibbled on it: sheep lard. He avoided eye contact and talked to the space before him in a stream of consciousness, like someone with a neurological disorder.

'When I drink water from this plastic bottle, I can taste the plastic. I have a glass bottle in my rucksack. I'm not competent, I had low grades at school, but plastic is killing the river. There's a drinking fountain at the end of The Birches where the road to here begins. When I wake up at night, I go there. The water runs warm in winter and cold in summer. That water's clean. No plastic.'

His energy was high-wired, torrential like a river in spring. He lived in the Ranger with his mother who had beautiful cheekbones and was bent at a 90 degree angle, and his blind brother.

'They've been through a lot,' said Gyulten when I told her I was meeting him. 'But I don't know him. He's always up in the hills.'

'Nobody does what he does anymore, because like I said, living with herd animals is for old-fashioned lovers only. You lose money,' said Metko.

'He keeps the horses out of stubbornness,' said an old shepherd. 'Some call him crazy.'

'He should get cows with subsidies and get rid of the horses. The Gypsies will buy them off him for meat or logging,' said a pragmatic young shepherd. 'But he's a fanatic.'

Emin unzipped his bumbag, spat on his hand and took out a wad of banknotes and started counting them.

'They say I look like a beggar but I have money, don't think I don't.'

He placed the banknotes on the table and the breeze picked them up. I caught them and put them down on the pile again. He was airing them like linen in a cupboard. Often, he wouldn't bother to collect his pay for the day and it was given to his mother later. 'It's too little,' he'd shout, 'it won't fix my problems!' Then he'd complain about not being paid and rant at people without looking at them. He couldn't be stopped. Then he'd walk away fast with his unhinged gait, spitting on the ground with contempt for those who knew the price of everything and the value of nothing. He did general labour – unloading lorries for the local shop owners, splitting and stacking logs, pouring cement. He did this because his trade had ended. He was the end of an era and the horses were its legacy.

For twenty-five years, he and his father had been log transporters on horseback, on the hand-made *samar* saddles which were not crafted anymore. With their herd of wild-grazing horses, they'd ply this ancient trade across the valleys, carrying logs from remote parts of the forests over snowy passes, often sleeping in the open.

Some jobs required them to walk with the horses for two days, crossing from one mountain range to another along paths that nobody else remembered. This is the single most dangerous outdoor work since the time of the gladiators. You could be crushed by a tree, fall into a precipice with your horses, have a horse break a leg and get hernias from lifting the raw logs. That's without counting the large predators.

'A raw log a metre long is heavy like iron,' Emin said.

It had to be lifted high enough to be loaded onto the saddle. That meant first, hip-level, then shoulder-level, like a weightlifter. It took two. A Karakachan horse could carry 200 kilograms on a saddle.

'It's the Wild West,' Emin said. 'You've got to be a bit tough.

Like the horses. Or you drop dead. Like the horses. Sometimes when I walk those paths, my tears fall on the ground. I remember everything.'

His father died and Emin couldn't carry on alone. But he also knew that the era of the beast of burden was over. He was glad to free his horses of it, let them roam free and breed them naturally. But even wild, they were still his horses and he had to make sure they didn't graze on someone's meadow and get poisoned or shot, or stolen. Or attacked by wolves in spring–summer.

'I sleep with them up to five months of the year, till the wee ones toughen up. Cos they're like children. The Haflinger lost two foals. A male the other year and a female last year. I found two legs. She's pregnant again.'

A horse pregnancy lasts eleven months.

'Then there was this orphan, her mother died but she survived the winter in the snow. Then a wolf got her in spring. But didn't eat her. I found her with her throat ripped open, still alive. She died in my arms. You take it in your arms, like a child. You feel its pain. Horses cry. Wolves are wicked animals.'

He started counting banknotes again on the table.

'Are you going to buy me?' I laughed. He put the banknotes back inside.

'I like to carry cash when I go places and meet people. In case I see a nice horse or something else catches my eye.'

For me, this meeting was one of many. For him, it was a date. He had ceremonially come with money, his way of showing me that he was a contender.

'Once the father and I sold a stallion for 500. Cos his leg was broken. We knew he was going for meat. He was family. But we had no choice.'

The choice was to shoot the horse. A few men in the region still transported logs on horseback, mostly Gypsies from the slum. The profession had been much degraded. I saw the odd bloodied saddled horse along Maiden Gorge, being overloaded with logs by men as wretched as the horse, a painful sight.

'There's no market for my savages,' Emin started making small piles of coins on the table. 'If I sell a horse, I have to make sure it's not for meat. They buy it by the kilo.'

There seemed to be a market with Italy where Balkan horse meat was sold. But locally too. There were horse thieves and healthy horses that would be prized elsewhere were carted off to a meat plant somewhere in the country. I didn't want to imagine the rest.

'That's like meat taken off my own body. Cos they're useless buggers, but they're my family. My father and I, we gave away 170 horses in our time.' He meant sold.

'Too cheaply. They have no price. Each one I knew personally. Cos they're like people. There was this black foal. His mother was The Grey and his father was Arap. Then his mother died, she just disappeared up above the middle lake and I couldn't find her. I slept up there three summers to keep an eye on the orphan. One summer, a wolf bit through his leg, I treated it with pig lard and it healed. Then someone wanted to buy him but cut me down on the price, down to 250. That's three summers of work, I'd be damned if I give it away. "Three hundred or nothing," I said! He didn't budge. Then on St George's Day, I go up and find the colt sitting on his back legs. His back legs broken. Up above Snake Gully, no way to get transport, it's all rock. I had to call a guy with a rifle to shoot him, I almost said to shoot me.'

The colt was shot and Emin had rolled on the ground howling.

When he described a horse, I could see it – the Haflinger with her white mane, the black stallion Arap, the orphan with its throat ripped open. He became the horse, shook his head, his teeth were horse teeth, his fine-boned face was equine, his body was all muscle and sinew just like a horse. He went on. It was relentless – the births and deaths, the emotion, the vast distances, the impossible terrain. I began to get vertigo, like I was sucked into an air vortex and lifted off the ground.

'Have I tired you out?' he said. 'I talk too much. What's the time?' He looked at his little old mobile, with buttons. 'It's early. If you wanna come up to The Meadow, I'll wait till you're rested. If I said anything wrong, I'm sorry.'

He went off to work on the new house with Shefket again, and I went up to my rooms and fell into the well. When I woke up, it was dark. Emin had waited till dusk then gone up to The Meadow. Instead of a torch, he used a cigarette lighter that didn't work except for its dim electric nightlight.

We went two days later. We cut through the forest some of the way, to avoid the dug-out forest road and look for ceps which he collected in a dirty canvas bag. The forest floor was too inclined for human feet, you had to get on all fours. The flank of the mountain was unrelentingly steep and we didn't meet a soul, except two mushroomers on a motorbike the following morning who almost fell off their bike when they saw Emin with a woman.

'Watch out, these furrows are bad. Not even the horses can pass here anymore. Go through there, it's easier. Mind your legs, that's spiky. Here's a stick. If you're tired, we'll stop.'

We could hear the river below, then we climbed higher and couldn't. The evening light hummed through the green crowns of the forest like a choir. He touched a branch here and there, like introducing me to a friend.

'This is sycamore maple. That's wild willow, goats like it. This is aspen, meet aspen. And you know the Balkan pine already. The heart of the tree is used for lighting fires because of its resin.' We saw a tree that had been hacked and was bleeding resin.

'When I see this, it's like a piece of my flesh. But it burns well.'

There was evidence of logging.

'They pick trees where they feel like it now.' That was the term here to pick a tree, the way you pick a herb. 'The easiest is by the side of the road. Cos they're fat and lazy with their trucks. But they should be using logs from inside the forest, to thin it out in the right places. Not cut healthy trees at random.'

The horseback log-transporting had been the most environmentally sound way to gather burning wood. Small-scale, labour-intensive, ecologically smart. You leave no mark on the forest.

Emin was quiet much of the two to three hours it took to reach The Meadow because when he walked fast, he stopped talking. As soon as he stopped walking, the talk returned, unrelenting. It was intimate on the path, it was just us and the forest. I could almost see faces among the trees. With his tatty clothes, sprite-like step and walking stick, Emin looked like Pan. Or Peter Pan.

'My horses like grazing in that wood. In winter they'll eat anything, even broom.'

The green perennial broom shrub used to make domestic sweeping brooms with handles. I made my own: I picked a bunch, tied it at one end and swept my floor. It grew brown as it slowly wilted.

'Here, I found remains of that foal. The bear had buried it for later.'

'Ferns. Like with reeds, when they start shedding you know autumn's coming.'

I was concentrating on not falling into a hole in the forest floor.

'Fox,' he pointed his stick at a fresh print. Further on: 'Wolf. A big one.'

'Aren't you scared to walk here at night?' I asked.

I was a bit jumpy even now, in daylight and with the best guide. This was a deep dark wood – even if not the original deep dark wood – and it went on. At the end of it were glacial lakes, ridges and stony portals to the western chapters of the mountain. Between here and the highest visible peak, Yanuzov Ridge, were just two houses: the brothers' hut and a mountain chalet.

'Nothing can touch me,' he said. 'Nobody can do anything to me. I've walked these paths a million times. In transit, like this. Do you know what'll kill me? I almost said killed me.'

'Too much walking?'

'No. Loneliness,' he said. 'It's made me feral and demented. Don't think I don't know it. It creeps up on you.'

By the time we reached The Meadow, it was dusk. The peaks were indigo and the sky was a colour I can't describe. The horses appeared suddenly in a clearing like the chords of a nocturne. They were blue like the mountain and they grazed in the same position, like rhythmic gymnasts. The Meadow was a cathedral. The clearing was its altar.

I kneeled in the high grasses and took in the scene.

Emin went up to them, one after the other, walking-talking in a low rumble, hugging their necks, pulling their tails which they didn't mind. They rubbed his face with their noses, sniffed his hands.

'See, see?' he was like a bulb switched on. 'See why I do it now! I do it for these bandits. What do you say, is it worth it or am I crazy?'

'Yeah,' I said, not knowing what I was saying or where I was.

'Hey, Grey! Grey!'

They were all stunning, but the Grey was a queen. She came over slowly and sniffed his hand. There were seventeen of them.

'My savages are Karakachans,' he said. 'The Balkan mountain breed. See how they're small and lean. That's because of the terrain. That way they can climb even with a load on. The big heavy ones wouldn't make it here. Like people.'

'Hey, Arap!' A shiny black stallion lifted his head. 'Even he doesn't kick. Look.' He grabbed his tail. 'None of them kick! If they kick me, they can kill me on the spot.'

The adults were all young mares, apart from Arap and another stallion that had never been caught. Actually, most of them hadn't been caught, they followed the Chocolate One who had a commanding aura, a natural leader. The rest were 'children'.

'The Chocolate One lets me put a bell on her but she's not been caught. This one is hers, born in the spring.'

The foal had pretty white and grey markings across his whole body. Two weeks later, he would be dragged away by wolves, on a night that Emin wasn't there.

He hugged a reddish mare by the neck and climbed onto her, to show me that they were tame, though wild. She had knowing eyes and there was something wrong with her legs.

'This is Marta the Red. The eldest here, born May 2000. She's been birthing foals without fail and they all survive. She's amazing. We wrecked her legs with the logs but we wrecked ourselves too. Do you want to ride her? You can climb on the water basin first.'

He helped me up. I'd never been on a horse before. It was surprisingly high. Her reddish foal, fuzzy with youth, shadowed her every move.

There was no saddle and none of them were cobbled. That was the highland tradition. After an hour with the herd, the thought of any one of them being butchered caused me distress.

'They move together, they're social animals,' Emin said. 'Like people. The Chocolate One leads the others. The guys come and go. The problem is when someone else's stallion lures them away and breaks up the herd. Then I run my feet off. I run my feet off anyway. I'm always in transit.'

'This is the Haflinger. The only breed that's not indigenous. She's a savage.'

She was stunning, with a white mane, and she didn't let him get close.

At the far end of The Meadow was the shepherd's shelter where he slept. A pine wood stood between it and the brothers' house. The Meadow area was a mosaic of alpine meadows and glades, the last habitat before the glacial belt.

The shelter was once used by Fatma and Metya, but they'd got themselves a static caravan in the meadow next door. It was a primitive structure made from wood, with a plastic sheet for roof and walls. But it was a small compound nevertheless. Inside the fence made from branches was a space for a fire where you ate, and under the plastic roof was a raised wooden plank wide enough for two, with a dirty sheepskin on it and a rolled-up mat. This is how Gyulten had spent her childhood.

'Welcome to hotel Under-the-Stars. It's a bit basic and you're used to luxury.'

'Are we both going to sleep on that?' I asked.

'Unless you want to sleep on the ground,' he said rudely. 'I can sleep anywhere. It's still light. Wanna stretch our legs? We can go up to Dry Lochen, there's a view.'

Dry Lochen was an hour uphill.

'I've stretched my legs enough,' I said and sat on a stump.

'You're the boss,' he said. 'Let's get the fire going then.'

He quickly stoked a fire with a few pine branches and went to fetch water from the stone fountain with a barrel. It was far. This main meadow of The Meadow was about 600 metres long and had two water fountains, the stone one I'd used to climb on Marta and another one further on, made by Ahmed the mountaineer, where families from The Birches came to picnic in pick-up trucks. While he was gone, the stillness of the scene struck me, chord after chord. I saw The Meadow and I heard it at the same time.

It was different now. It wasn't raining like it had been with the Godless party, but it was also that with Emin, everything looked different. It was a scene framed by dark woods and I was small and remote inside it, like a memory.

The thought of sleeping here alone, eating alone, lighting the fire alone and returning to its cold ashes alone, listening to the black mountain alone and the sunny mountain alone, year after year – it was crushing. I couldn't do it, I would go insane. It was too big, too awesome to bear.

I watched him stride back casually with the heavy barrel of water, talking continuously. Talking to himself and talking to me was the same thing. He was bringing the barrel as others bring a glass of wine in a living room. He moved across The Meadow the way others move through their house. This *was* his house. The meadows and glades were the rooms and different music played in each.

'We'll heat the water if you want to wash,' he said. 'Cos the spring water is cold.'

Darkness crept from all sides. It closed in around our little hut, then the only light left was the smoky fire which made my eyes sting all night. The horses became outlines on the edges of The Meadow, then nothing.

'Aren't you gonna gather them now?' I said.

'It's early yet. After we've eaten.'

'How will you find them? They're scattered.'

'They're here. Can you hear them? Can you see the Chocolate One?'

I couldn't see or hear a thing.

'Yala yalaaaaa!' he yelled.

A bell chime answered him. The Chocolate One.

'Look.' He switched on a head torch with a strong beam. 'I bought it the other day in case you wanted to come up and have proper light. I've been walking like a vampire with this old lighter. Giving the wolves a fright.'

We ate the burgers and potato salad I'd packed, and some sheep's cheese, bread and rakia from his rucksack, though he drank even less than me. Alcohol, coffee, cigarettes, any strong substance made him sick. He kept the lard lump out of view this time. A few things were left in a box inside the pen – sugar, shrivelled cucumbers, old socks and a spray for horse wounds.

'I use it too when I cut my foot or get a thorn in my hand.'

No table salt. He'd given it to the horses.

The Meadow was strewn with yarrow. As the moon rose and the forest became black, the yarrow turned a colour I'd never seen – a fluorescent white that glowed. They glowed so that you could walk without a torch. I saw how a single yarrow plant had 128 chemical components. I saw how this kind of white had staunched the blood of soldiers and women for thousands of years. The yarrow glowed like the stars above which suddenly appeared in their millions. The yarrow was stardust. The Meadow was the cosmos. We were spinning upside down. The earth was a suspended garden.

'Yeah, it's beautiful,' Emin chewed. He had missing teeth. 'But when you've got nobody to see it with, it grows ugly.'

Emin rose and picked up a horse-hair harness. It was woven by his father in the Karakachan tradition he'd learned as a boy in the 1950s. You used your knees and elbows in the process, your whole body. Emin hadn't had the patience for it. With his father was gone the art of the horse-hair harness. It was called *yular*. Another one for the museum. The harness was light like lace.

'Stay by the fire. Don't go wandering.'

I had no intention of going wandering. He melted into the darkness.

Clouds obscured the moon. The primal flooded in. The absence of sound was like the bottom of a sea. His axe lay on the ground and he hadn't taken the torch. No phone signal. There was not another human being between here and the Birches Hotel. I laughed when I remembered my first night there the previous summer, when I thought I'd reached the end. In this mountain, the end cannot be reached.

A thump in the woods. I stood up and threw another pine branch on the flames. But my dread was not really of the bear. It was of my own self. Of what I would become overnight if Emin didn't return. Of shrivelling inside, of forgetting, of feeling that never being touched was worse than being attacked by a bear. This is what he talked about when he talked about loneliness.

A whistle in the distance, drawn-out like a spell, like something played through a reed flute. He was gathering the horses. We are dream weavers of our lives and others' lives, and we don't even know it.

'Your life is like a film,' I said to him later. 'Or a dream.'

'A nightmare, more like it,' he said.

Emin was returning with the horses, silent except the chime of the Chocolate One's bell and the ground that thumped under the hooves, because even when they walked, the horses were running. I can't explain it but that's how it is. Man and horses looked like one.

He removed the yular from Marta and loosely tied her to the fence. She was the only properly tame one. The others gathered for the night, snuffling, breathing, warm – like a fire themselves.

'The foals will lie down,' he said. 'When I'm up by the lakes without shelter, I curl up on the ground and they lie down next to me. That's how I survived cold nights, I almost said didn't survive cold nights.'

He stepped through the opening in the twig fence and smiled nervously, finally making eye contact, and in his face was all the broken beauty of this world. The full moon made a sudden appearance from behind cloud – corn-yellow. It was September. A scream in the forest made me freeze.

'A fox,' Emin said.

We were inside a pulsing grid. Everything felt multiple. Three entities were stepping through the fence, three Emins.

One, a boy born of a mare who, for thousands of years had roamed this mountain with foxes and wolves, bears and birds, singing with elm bark, wading across spring torrents, dressed in rags, walking-talking and playing reed flutes. His history has not been written, the film of his life has not been made, but it has been transmitted through the cells of the living mountain, like seeds from the original giant forest.

Two, an eccentric horseman whose path nearly didn't cross mine.

I was about to share a plank with him for the night, wrapped in raw-wool cardigans, under a torn blanket he kept tucking around me.

'Here, take my cardigan. Do you want a toffee?'

He chewed toffee like a horse and talked ceaselessly, not letting me sleep.

And thirdly, someone who was my own creation. In him I saw reflected the electrical mountain with its yarrow-starred meadows, its crystal peaks and its vales of fathomless feeling, its layers of mood and weather, its saplings rising from the ashes. In him I saw a lost part of myself, an uncoupled half that might just restore the lost ecosystem.

I could thankfully smell geranium – Fatma the shepherdess had planted it, to make her nights here more pleasant. The horses were quiet all night. Just the occasional hoof, a sneeze, or a jet of urine hitting the ground.

'There are horses with human heads on them. I had one, dark grey, he pulled the cart. Nothing scared him. We always took him with us to the city market. He carried logs and tobacco and ploughed the field for thirty years. When he grew old, he went white. Like a person. When I was wee, I rode him. There was never one like him again. Horses have personalities.'

'Like dogs,' I said.

'Like humans,' he said. His voice was strangely old.

'That's because I'm a hundred years old,' he said. 'I was born old.'

'Or maybe because you talk too much,' I said.

'Too much or not at all,' he said. 'That's how things are for me. Sideways is too wide, below is too deep and above is too high. I can't get things right. That's why I'm here.'

'Horses have the same feelings like us. I found him dead one day. Horses don't make a fuss when they die. I grew old with that horse.'

'Are you cold? Two o'clock. I'll put a log on. Can you see the moon? She's looking at us. I wonder what she sees. I'm talking too much. I'm starved for conversation. For love.'

'Three o'clock. Want a toffee? Okay, you get some sleep. I don't sleep much in summer. I close one eye and open the other. I don't want to fall asleep because I'll snore and wake you up.'

'But you're not letting me fall asleep in the first place!' I protested.

'Yes, yes,' he said to the darkness. 'I'll let you sleep now. Should I toss another log on the fire? I'm repulsive. I've let myself go, I know it.'

'Yes, you really need a bath,' I said. 'You smell like a rubbish bin.'

'Aye, it's a true story. But I don't have time to bathe. I'm flying all the time, up the hill then down the hill.'

A howl nearby, then another. I sat up.

'Dogs, not wolves,' he said. 'That's Fatma and Metya's sheepdogs. When I sleep by Dry Lochen on the ground, sometimes I don't light a fire. I just gather the horses by the fountain and I keep one eye open. And I can hear the wolf in the bush. But they don't dare come out when they know there's a human. There's no animal in this forest that wants to meet a human.'

'Three thirty. What sort of book are you writing?'

'It's called *Elixir*,' I said.

'Elixir.'

'How people look for it and can't find it.'

'Tell me about it,' he said. 'Four fifteen. I'll feed the fire. Can you hear the owl? Loneliness kills. You walk around and they think you're alive but you're dead inside.'

'Five o'clock. The empty years. I've no words for it. Thank you for coming, for showing interest. I'll never forget you.'

'Five-thirty. I'll untie Marta and let them off. Mornings are the coldest. Pirin is a mountain of four seasons. You stay here and keep warm.'

'Six o'clock. There's no coffee but I'll put some water on the fire. No tea either. You like coffee and tea, I saw you drinking it. I've no brain, but I have eyes in my head at least.'

The Meadow had tea. I went to pick some. The horses scattered, finding good patches for the day. The moon had crossed the sky, white like a ghost. The sun hadn't risen over The Meadow yet. Everything had a tentative outline, making up its mind between night and day. I walked through cold dew and flowers still closed shut for the night. It was like the first day of creation. The world unfurled. I was somewhere inside it. The meadows of flowers with us two human flowers. The mixed forest, the pine forest, the darker dwarf pine and juniper, the glacial lakes and beyond them – the blue peaks.

The dandelions were folding back into the earth. The yellow was long gone, the seed heads long scattered. In the last week, the birches had turned golden and my right temple had gone silver, but not the left. I hear it grow already, the bone of dandelion that I will be.

Everything was mellowing, rounding up for autumn. Everything was spherical, like a dandelion head.

I greeted Marta and her foal and they greeted me back. Why do horses have that look of knowing? They just know.

Wild horses are a big part of a mountain ecosystem, like here, called a mosaic biosphere, where every piece fits with the rest. Their movable feast makes it easier for other wild animals and plants to partake. Emin and his herd were the last of their kind in Europe. ·

At the stone fountain, he had taken off his T-shirt and was washing under the spouts. His back was a galaxy of sun damage. He reached for his T-shirt. Under his rib was a huge purple bruise.

'I tried to get Arap off a mare. It was black but it's fading.'

We have a rich canon of nature literature in English, but nature and wilderness have parted ways. Nature and culture meet on culture's terms only. Their creatures don't mingle, not as equals. The last wild places and their few denizens have become a reservation to visit while wearing expensive gear, then return to one's own kind to report. At literary festivals, academic conferences and climate conventions, people who rarely venture beyond Starbucks wear designer cowboy boots that Emin the last cowboy can't afford, sip vegan lattes and discuss wilderness.

People like Emin almost don't exist anymore because wilderness almost doesn't exist anymore. But we used to be everywhere. The wreath of seventy-seven and a half herbs was woven from the Beauly River to the Mesta to the Nile and beyond. Until the herbs became weeds, the women became witches and the child of nature became a madman.

The early ecopsychologists of the 1960s could not be more explicit about their discoveries of how the health of the human mind and the health of the earth are inseparable, and how the ecological ego's 'maturation moves towards ethical responsibility with the planet'. Emin embodied this symbiosis and it made him an outcast. An outcast of a corrupt and demented civilisation. The price we have paid to be collusive members of this corrupt civilisation is the bankrupting of the organic world. And with it – the core of our collective mind. Emin was borderline insane because he carried the collective insanity, alone.

'Why do you do it?' I asked Emin when we sat by the rekindled fire, me with meadow tea and him eating the remains of dinner.

'Because when I look at the horses, I see my father. He could've done easier and better-paid jobs but he was crazy about horses. This whole way of life in the forest. Even in his early days horses were on the way out. It was never good business. He got the bug from the old Karakachans. They're the last of the animal people. Once, an old Karakachan logger we knew crossed us with his horses. "Mate", he said, "we are condemned to death." "Aye," my father said, "us and the horses both."'

Emin means loyal.

'And I see other things when I look at the horses.'

Tomorrow when I'm gone, he'd walk up here again. And the day after. In winter, he waded through snow. It was not just the mileage, the scale, the loneliness, the privation, the predators, the quixotic devotion, the sneer of those in the lower world. There was something else.

'I didn't choose this,' he said. 'It's an inherited condition. Some inherit diseases. I inherited horses.'

There was a bitter pride. 'I look for no one and no one looks for me. They're all fucking imitators,' he spat on the ground. His heart was full of sorrow, it was in his eyes.

I began to frantically think of solutions. Something had to be done.

'Wanna stretch our legs to Yanuzov Ridge? That peak there.'

I looked up at it – 2,600 metres, a two-hour hike from Dry Lochen and Dry Lochen was an hour from here. My phone battery was flat and there was no signal anyway. Maybe the only thing that had to be done was to walk?

'I'll show you the source of Stormy River. The area's called

Crooked Burns. There's a view. We don't have food but there's blueberries and mushrooms. We can stay in luxury in the shelter. Or walk
down to The Birches before dark. I'll drop you off at the hotel and
come back up for the night. I don't mind. Or we can return now.
You're the boss.'

At Dry Lochen where Emin had slept countless nights by Ava's
fountain, I heard the laughing bell voices again, this time in plain
sunshine. Emin was too busy battling his own demons to be bothered
by it. One autumn he'd looked for a lost mare and found her dismembered remains in the meadow of St John's wort above Dry Lochen,
where the rain made the world a liquid yellow.

'That mare was special and her foal was now an orphan. Orphaned
foals are easy prey.' He'd raged and cursed his luck. Hungry and not
wanting to return to The Birches, he'd gone all the way up to the
alpine shelter to raid the cupboard for food and found a jar of pesto.
It was dark by then but he didn't stay the night, he was too deranged
and headed down in the blackness. Here at Dry Lochen he opened
the jar which broke into his hand. A fountain of blood erupted.

'I thought about opening a vein too,' he said. 'Guys like me hang
themselves when they've had enough.'

He'd bandaged it with his T-shirt in the end and walked down to
The Meadow, then The Birches, leaving a trail of blood in the
woods.

The alpine shelter was a new chalet with bunk beds and a wood stove,
luxury after the plank. There were cans, bread and sugar left behind.
Sometimes, blueberry and juniper pickers from the three rhyming
villages spent the night here.

On the vertical cone of the top ridge we saw horned alpine goats
that seemed to fly and a smaller herd of wild horses who ran downhill, shaking the ground, and crowded around Emin in a circle. They
pulled the grass around him with their teeth while he chopped dwarf
pine for the stove with his left hand, then with his right – the first
ambidextrous person I'd met. The horses took no notice of me and
when Emin went inside to light the stove for the evening, they
dispersed.

'Have you been to the sea?' I asked him.

'Once. On a day trip delivering tiles in Kavalla with a friend.'

But they hadn't stayed the night.

'This is my sea,' he pointed his axe handle at the gigantic waves of land. Peaks and vales in slow motion. 'This is where I've been drowning for forty five years.'

Crooked Burns was literally on top of the world. The air was rarefied and I felt light-headed, transparent, like a hologram. The scree, the tussock, the icy springs of Stormy River from which we drank without hands, faces in the water – peaks really are the home of the spirit. That's why you can't stay on them for long, unless you are an aerial spirit.

But Emin did.

'Eeh-eeeeh! Aydeeeee!' he boomed at the peak with a voice like a megaphone and the whole cirque rang like a singing bowl. I've heard that the ideal Tibetan singing bowl is made from a blend and each ore is linked to a heavenly body: gold, silver, mercury, tin, lead and copper. Just like this electrical mountain.

Always, there is a lashing of poison in the blend.

'Aydeeeee!'

The white stones were in fact dozens of wild goats who bounded up and out of view.

At Crooked Burns, I saw my first salamander. It really did look like a remnant of a fallen angel. It is not supposed to live this high up, but there it was, under a stone, then over a stone. Its little legs carried its black and yellow body like a miniature fire dragon. It spends the first half of its life as an amphibian and the second as a terrestrial.

'A stubborn relic of a bastard, like me,' said Emin.

I saw the places where I'd been – moments in time. I saw the corridor to the Aegean full of light. And I saw why this place was such a magnet. It had ideal wind and water proportions – it was a dragon topography where the vital chi of the earth was perfectly balanced. The valley was backed by a 'black turtle' – a round mountain to the north. To the west and the east were mountains of a different character, one yin ('the white tiger') and one yang ('azure dragon'), with waterfalls, pines and lakes. To the south was the 'red phoenix' – sea,

space and sunshine. The movement of air was constant down the
Mesta corridor, a self-cleaning mechanism. And if a geomàncer came
to work out the 'head of the dragon'– the perfect place for habitation
in this dragon valley – she would point at the ribbon of villages in
Old Woods: Fire and Thunder, Empty Village and Dogwood. Where
I was almost struck by a lightning a few seasons ago.

On the porch of the shelter, we watched the sun rise over distant
Old Woods and flood the Earth with new-born light. We are born
into an ensouled universe. Time opens and closes like the dandelion –
not in a flat line, but in circles of expansion and contraction. Seasons
of experience. When we touch another's, they overlap and this produces a note in the empty universe that isn't empty.

The dragon breathed. Our whole species tumbled into a new
cycle. We had no name for it yet, but it was inexorable – perceptions,
relationships, purpose, everything was changing. The experience of
being here was so complete that whatever came after would not
increase it or decrease it. The task ahead was to hold on to the view
from the peak as we descended into the vale, gorging on blueberries
which covered the side of the mountain like a rug.

The previous summer, I had driven into Greece, all the way to the
delta. A preliminary journey that I planned to revisit. The road had
taken me from the shady depths of the Rhodope ranges, past the
most spectacular canyon of the Mesta where it meandered with reptilian ease and you could only follow it by foot along an ancient
cobbled high road. After that, the smell of the sea quickened the pulse
and you became like the river – running faster into the sun-drenched
Aegean Plain. The white, open flats dazzled with their southern light.
This is the northern edge of the Levant. The mountains released you
from their grip and you rushed into the magnetic pull of the Aegean,
drunk on happiness as if in your first summer ever, or your last. The
Nestos Delta was thick with birds and so labyrinthine in its blind
sandy alleys with wall-high reeds and kiwi plantations that I got lost
and dehydrated in the 45 degree heat, and nearly had a panic attack.

The delta was on a mellow sand strip where salt water and fresh
water mingled and the island of Thasos loomed at a swimmable

distance with its dark green glades, its marble face hacked by multi-national quarries. I swam in the sweet spot where the river becomes the sea and departs for Africa. I wanted to stay another day but my schedule was busy. I'd return another time.

Then the border closed. There was no other time.

Still on The Meadow, we gathered our things and put our rubbish in the ashes. Marta lifted her head from grazing and so did her foal. On The Meadow, time had stopped yet something shifted. Something pushed me to seek out the outer realms, join Emin on his Sisyphean path.

I can't tell you what elixir is. You have to search for it yourself. All I know is that our Earth makes it in her cauldron, ceaselessly, every-where and you are a part of the crazy recipe. You can't buy it or sell it. It begins when money and words run out and you become what you are, something worth scaling peaks and vales for.

And if you are engulfed by flames in an experiment gone too far, you must suffer the loss and become a salamander all over again.

'Are we going up or not?' Emin asked on The Meadow.

'We are,' I said. 'Take me to the Crooked Burns, then.'

Iris

The phone rang. It was Rocky the Enchanter.

'Is that you?' He shouted down the line.

He had dialled my number, but without the smell in the room, you could never be sure.

'Have you written your book?' he said. 'I forgot to tell you that there are four medicinal types of wild iris. Remember iris? Now there's an interesting plant. It was born in the Mediterranean. The main ones are the blue and the white. Otherwise there are nine types. One is protected. They should all be protected. Iris is the flower of women.'

The goddess of the rainbow Iris touched heaven and Earth with her many-coloured wings. Her message was: as above, so below. In her chalice, she carried water from the Styx to the realm of thunder. In turn, the thunder gods brought water back to the Earth.

Iris is the original alchemist mixing interdimensional essences. Iris is depicted as the archetype of Temperance: a winged figure with two cups, tempering her liquid. It's a process without beginning and with no end. Time is literally of the essence. Iris embodies the sacred triangle. Maiden, mother, crone. The father, the son, the holy ghost. You, me, our place. The lover, the beloved and the act of loving. Biology, spirit, ecology. Iris makes whole again what has been uncoupled, split, reduced.

Iris is the sister of Hermes the messenger. Rocky used the folk name Perunika, and Perunika is the twin sister of Perun on his chariot of fire.

In the Hermetic Arcana, Iris the temperer is neither male nor female, but both. On their forehead is the sun, on their chest – the triangle. In William Blake's poem, *Milton*, the eponymous character merges with the Virgin of Providence, Ololon, and becomes a complete being – 'beyond the outline of Identity'.

'Perunika root is for pain,' Rocky went on.

What kind of pain?

'All pain,' he said. 'Do you know why the petals of perunika are lined? To guide pollinators to the nectar within. But it's no use describing it. You have to see it in the flesh. Do you have it in Scotland?'

I've never seen it in the wild, I said.

'You haven't looked for it. What altitude are you? Too low. You have to go higher. What's the climate?'

'You have to see a wild iris,' he said, 'or your life won't be complete.'

'Where are you? I can hear birds,' he said.

Migratory birds, I said. I'm back in Scotland.

'Do you know what birds eat to keep them strong when they fly to Africa? Elderberries.'

We have them here, I said.

'What are you doing anyway? I hear a noise.'

I'm picking hawthorn by the river, I said. And the quarry is crushing gravel.

'Pick it when it's in bloom. It doesn't like its leaves picked before it flowers. And anyway, you want both flowers and leaves.'

Hawthorn hadn't flowered yet. It was a cold May.

'Hawthorn is a calm tree. It calms the heart. What else is there right now?'

Scurvy flower, I said. It's white.

'How does it taste?'

Salty.

'I thought you were on a river bank.'

Yeah, but it's where the river meets the sea.

'Ah, you're in a sweet spot! Now, I want you to know a secret. Because in a hundred years' time, I won't be around and you won't be around. Are you writing it down?'

Yes, I said and leaned on the hawthorn.

'It isn't just the iris and the enchanter. And the hawthorn. Each one of them is a love plant. But you have to learn their language. That's all for now. I hope I'm not too late.'

No, Rocky, you're not too late. There is time yet.

ACKNOWLEDGEMENTS AND REFERENCES

I have translated or cross-referenced some localities to capture their meaning for non-local readers. The city in the valley is Gotse Delchev and its old name is Nevrokop. Ancient Rock Sanctuary Goat Stone is Kozi Kamak, Old Woods is Dabrash, Eagle Reserve is Orelyak. Thunder is Garmen, Fire is Ognyanovo, Empty Village is Leshten, Dogwood is Gorno Dryanovo, Stormy River is Tufcha, Witchy River is Vishteritsa, Clear Water is Bistritsa, The Birches is Breznitsa, the Ranger is Padarka, The Dark is Tevnoto, Siropol is Gospodintsi, Black Mesta is Cherna Mesta, White Mesta is Bela Mesta, The Saint is Svetitsata, Healer Peak is Zavrachitsa, the Good Place is Dobrinishte, the Good River is Dobrinishka Reka, Bath is Banya, Drought is Sushitsa, Gold Leaf is Zlatolist, Fur Coat Mountain is Kojuh.

The Mesta River appears throughout history as Mestum, Nestum, Nesos, Nestos and Mesta.

For more on the last wild rivers of Europe, go to www.balkanrivers.net

The writing of this book partly overlapped with my time as non resident Fellow at the Institute for the Humanities in Vienna (IMW). I acknowledge their support of my related research into the livelihoods of the people of the Mesta basin.

Thanks to Mehmet Buyukli, Darina and Boris Hristov, Erol Hodjov, Fatme Myuhtar-May, Ilian Buchkov at Treshtenik Chalet and Nick Nasev for being an early reader. I thank the healers in my daily life: Emma Roe in Edinburgh and Jenny Ren in Inverness, and also Bisong Guo during her time in Nairn. Most of all, T.D. green-fingers, gold-heart, for all the nourishment of leaf and love. Deepest thanks to Alba Ziegler-Bailey, Sarah Chalfant and to my editor Bea Hemming at Cape for travelling this road with me.

This book blends complex areas of expertise: ethno-botany and folk medicine, ethnography, medical herbalism, psychology, the history of religion and magic, spirituality, consciousness and eco-psychology. My only claim to absolute accuracy is in the realm of personal and transpersonal experience.

The poems and incantations cited are from: *Evening Trumpet* by Boris Hristov (my translation of the poem fragment 'Dandelion Bone'), *The Way of Chuang Tzu* by Thomas Merton, *Thracian Magic: Past and Present* by Georgi Mishev, *Scots Herbal* by Tess Darwin, *Carmina Gaedelica* by Alexander Carmichael, *Alchemical Psychology* by Thom F. Cavalli (in the chapter 'Maiden Gorge'), *Mirabilia: Miraculous and Magical/* 'Magical Rituals for Gathering Plants' by Georgi Mishev. The itinerant bileri are described by Tsani Ginchev in *Something on Bulgarian Folk Medicine*. The banishment of plant medicine by pharmaceuticals is described in detail by Stephen Buhner in *The Lost Language of Plants*. The following books have helped my understanding of various complex areas of knowledge.

Aion: Researches into the Phenomenology of the Self by Carl Jung

Alchemical Psychology by James Hillman

Alchemical Psychology by Thom Cavalli

Alchemist's Handbook by Frater Albertus

Alchemy and Psychology by Carl Jung

Between Heaven and Earth: A Guide to Chinese Medicine by Harriet Beinfield and Efrem Korngold

Български народни баяния,врачувания, гледания и лекувания 1 и 2 (*Bulgarian Folk Mantras, Spells, Rituals and Healings 1 & 2*)

Вечерен тромпет (*Evening Trumpet*) by Boris Hristov

Carmina Gadelica by Alexander Carmichael

Cosmos and Psyche by Richard Tarnas

Culpeper's Complete Herbal by Nicholas Culpeper

Дарбата на Ванга (*Vanga's Gift*) by Jeni Kostadinova

Enquiry into Plants (Books 1–5) by Theophrastus

Фолклорът в контекста на социалната промяна (*Folklore Amidst Social Change*) by Haralan Alexandrov

Herbs of the Highlands and Islands by Duncan Ross

Hildegard von Bingen's Physica by Hildegard von Bingen

Identity, Nationalism and Cultural Heritage under Siege by Fatme Myuhtar-May

Internal Alchemy: A New Perspective by Bisong Guo

Les remèdes de santé d'Hildegarde de Bingen (*The Health Remedies of Hildegarde of Bingen*) by Paul Ferris

Mirabilia: Чудесно и магическо ('Mirabilia: Miraculous and Magical', *Studia Balcanica* 33) ed. Vanya Lozanova-Stancheva and Valeria Fol

Mountain Republic (27 min, dir. by Janet Barrie and Velislav Radev) https://www.mycentury.tv/bg/bulgaria-bg/281-planinska-republika.html

Нещо по българската народна медицина (*On Bulgarian Folk Medicine*) by Tsani Ginchev

Природолечение и природосъобразен живот (*Natural Healing and Natural Living*) by Petar Dimkov

Plant Hunting in Europe by Hugh Roger-Smith

Plant Magic by Gregory J. Kenicer

Поливки: ритуални измивания (*Water Rituals*) by Georgi Mishev

Принос към българската народна ботаническа медицина (*Field Writings on Bulgarian Botanical Folk Medicine*) by Ananie Yavashov

Пътуване по долините на Струма, Места и Брегалница (*Travels along the Struma, Mesta and Bregalnitsa Rivers*) by Vassil Kanchov

'*Сакрална топонимия и култови обекти около селищата по поречието на Горна Места*' ('Pagan Cult Names and Places in Upper Mesta') by Angel Yankov

Съвършената: преподобна Стойна (*The Immaculate: Venerable Stoyna*) by Neda Antonova

'*Стари якорудски истории*' ('Old Tales from Yakoruda') by Ilian Buchkov

Silent Spring by Rachel Carson

Tarot: History, Symbolism and Divination by Robert M. Place

'*The Agony of a Traumatised Pair of Archaeological Sites*' by Meryl Marshall, North of Scotland Archaeological Society (NOSAS)

The Alchemy of Happiness by Abu Hamid Al-Ghazali

'The Ancient Thracian Endemic Plant *Haberlea rhodopensis* Friv. and Related Species' by Yordan Georgiev et al., *Journal of Ethnopharmacology*

The Asian Journals by Thomas Merton

The Complete Herbal by Maude Grieve

The Golden Bough by Sir James Frazer

The Lost Balkans by Randall Baker

The Lost Language of Plants by Stephen Buhmer

The Scots Herbal: The Plant Lore of Scotland by Tessa Darwin

The Tao of Physics by Frifjof Capra

The Way of Chuang Tzu by Thomas Merton

Thracian Magic: Past and Present by Georgi Mishev

Торбешка декларација (*A Torbesh Declaration*) by Sherif Ajradinoski

Ванга ясновидката (*Vanga the Clairvoyant*) by Krassimira Stoyanova

Women who Run With the Wolves by Clarissa Pinkola Estés

KAPKA KASSABOVA is a multigenre writer and most recently the author of *Border* (2017) and *To the Lake* (2020). *Border* won a British Academy Prize, the Scottish Book of the Year, Stanford-Dolman Travel Book of the Year, and the Highland Book Prize. It was also a finalist for the National Book Critics Circle Award. The French edition of *To the Lake* won the Prix du Meilleur Livre Étranger (nonfiction category) in 2021 and the Polish edition was shortlisted for the Angelus Central European Literature Award. Kassabova grew up in Sofia, Bulgaria, and studied in New Zealand. Today she lives by a river in the Scottish Highlands. *Elixir* is the third book in her ongoing Balkan quartet exploring the relationship between humans and their environment, following *Border* and *To the Lake*.

Typeset in Bembo Book MT Pro by Jouve (UK).
Manufactured by McNaughton & Gunn on acid-free,
100 percent postconsumer wastepaper.